# DEFINING MAGIC

# CRITICAL CATEGORIES IN THE STUDY OF RELIGION

Series Editor: Russell T. McCutcheon,
Department of Religious Studies, University of Alabama

*Critical Categories in the Study of Religion* aims to present the pivotal articles that best represent the most important trends in how scholars have gone about the task of describing, interpreting, and explaining the place of religion in human life. The series focuses on the development of categories and the terminology of scholarship that make possible knowledge about human beliefs, behaviours, and institutions. Each volume in the series is intended as both an introductory survey of the issues that surround the use of various key terms as well as an opportunity for a thorough retooling of the concept under study, making clear to readers that the cognitive categories of scholarship are themselves historical artefacts that change over time.

## Published

*Syncretism in Religion: A Reader*
Edited by Anita M. Leopold and Jeppe Sinding Jensen

*Ritual and Religious Belief: A Reader*
Edited by Graham Harvey

*Defining Hinduism: A Reader*
Edited by J.E. Llewellyn

*Religion and Cognition: A Reader*
Edited by D. Jason Slone

*Mircea Eliade: A Critical Reader*
Edited by Bryan Rennie

*Defining Buddhism(s): A Reader*
Edited by Karen Derris and Natalie Gummer

*Defining Islam: A Reader*
Edited by Andrew Rippin

*Myths and Mythologies: A Reader*
Edited by Jeppe Sinding Jensen

*Defining Judaism: A Reader*
Edited by Aaron W. Hughes

*Religious Experience: A Reader*
Edited by Craig Martin and Russell T. McCutcheon, with Leslie Dorrough Smith

*Defining Magic: A Reader*
Edited by Bernd-Christian Otto and Michael Stausberg

*Readings in the Theory of Religion: Map, Text, Body*
Edited by Scott S. Elliott and Matthew Waggoner

# DEFINING MAGIC

## A READER

Edited by
Bernd-Christian Otto and Michael Stausberg

LONDON AND NEW YORK

First published 2013 by Equinox Publishing Ltd, an imprint of Acumen

Published 2014 by Routledge
2 Park Square, Milton Park, Abingdon, Oxon OX14 4RN
711 Third Avenue, New York, NY 10017, USA

*Routledge is an imprint of the Taylor & Francis Group, an informa business*

Editorial selection and matter © Bernd-Christian Otto and Michael Stausberg, 2013. Essays © individual authors and publishers.

All rights reserved. No part of this book may be reprinted or reproduced or utilised in any form or by any electronic, mechanical, or other means, now known or hereafter invented, including photocopying and recording, or in any information storage or retrieval system, without permission in writing from the publishers.

Notices
Practitioners and researchers must always rely on their own experience and knowledge in evaluating and using any information, methods, compounds, or experiments described herein. In using such information or methods they should be mindful of their own safety and the safety of others, including parties for whom they have a professional responsibility.

To the fullest extent of the law, neither the Publisher nor the authors, contributors, or editors, assume any liability for any injury and/or damage to persons or property as a matter of products liability, negligence or otherwise, or from any use or operation of any methods, products, instructions, or ideas contained in the material herein.

ISBN: 978-1-908049-79-7 (hardback)
ISBN: 978-1-908049-80-3 (paperback)

**British Library Cataloguing-in-Publication Data**
A catalogue record for this book is available from the British Library.

**Library of Congress Cataloging-in-Publication Data**
Defining magic : a reader / edited by Bernd-Christian Otto and Michael Stausberg.
     p. cm. — (Critical categories in the study of religion)
  Includes bibliographical references and index.
  ISBN 978-1-908049-79-7 — ISBN 978-1-908049-80-3 (pbk.)
 1. Magic—History   Sources. I. Otto, Bernd-Christian. II. Stausberg, Michael.
  BF1589.D48 2012
  133.4'3—dc23
                            2012018503

Typeset by JS Typesetting Ltd, Porthcawl, Mid Glamorgan

# CONTENTS

*Preface* ix
*Sources* xi

General Introduction 1

**Part I: Historical Sources**

Introduction 16

1. Plato 19
   *Alcibiades* I and *Laws*

2. Pliny the Elder 23
   *Historia Naturalis*

3. Plotinus 28
   *Enneads*

4. Augustine of Hippo 33
   *City of God* and *On Christian Doctrine*

5. Isidore of Seville 41
   *Etymologiae*

6. Anonymous 46
   *Suda*

7. Thomas Aquinas 48
   *Summa Theologica*

8. Agrippa of Nettesheim 54
   *Three Books of Occult Philosophy*

| | | |
|---|---|---|
| 9. | Denis Diderot<br>*Encyclopédie* | 59 |
| 10. | Helena Petrovna Blavatsky<br>*Theosophical Glossary* | 64 |

**Part II: Foundational Works of the Academic Debate**

| | | |
|---|---|---|
| | Introduction | 68 |
| 11. | Edward B. Tylor<br>*Primitive Culture* | 71 |
| 12. | James George Frazer<br>*The Golden Bough* | 81 |
| 13. | Marcel Mauss and Henri Hubert<br>"A General Theory of Magic" | 97 |
| 14. | Émile Durkheim<br>*The Elementary Forms of Religious Life* | 111 |

**Part III: Mid-Twentieth-Century Approaches to Magic**

| | | |
|---|---|---|
| | Introduction | 126 |
| 15. | Gerardus van der Leeuw<br>*Religion in Essence and Manifestation* | 129 |
| 16. | Edward E. Evans-Pritchard<br>*Witchcraft, Oracles and Magic among the Azande* | 141 |
| 17. | Bronislaw Malinowski<br>"Magic, Science and Religion" | 156 |
| 18. | Robin Horton<br>"African Traditional Thought and Western Science" | 172 |
| 19. | Stanley J. Tambiah<br>"Form and Meaning of Magical Acts: A Point of View" | 178 |
| 20. | Edmund R. Leach<br>*Culture and Communication* | 187 |

**Part IV: Contemporary Voices**

| | | |
|---|---|---|
| | Introduction | 194 |
| 21. | Susan Greenwood<br>"Magical Consciousness: A Legitimate Form of Knowledge" | 197 |

| 22. | Christopher I. Lehrich<br>"Magic in Theoretical Practice" | 211 |
| 23. | Jesper Sørensen<br>"Magic Reconsidered: Towards a Scientifically Valid Concept of Magic" | 229 |
| 24. | Kimberly B. Stratton<br>"Magic Discourse in the Ancient World" | 243 |
| 25. | Randall Styers<br>"Magic and the Play of Power" | 255 |
|  | *Bibliography* | 263 |
|  | *Index* | 277 |

# PREFACE

In the summer of 2000 I held a seminar on the myth–ritual theory at Heidelberg University where I used Robert Segal's excellent reader *The Myth–Ritual Theory*. Later that year I gave a seminar on critical terms in the study of religions. Bernd-Christian Otto attended both classes. Now, twelve years later, these two courses have jointly come full circle: as we argue in the Introduction, "magic" is a key critical term in the study of religions and when discussing the shape of the present volume, Robert Segal's reader was an inspiration (even if not serving as a template). In the years following these classes, when I had moved to Norway and Bernd to Spain, we occasionally remained in touch. In 2009, following the defence of his massive doctoral thesis (a revised version is now published by de Gruyter), where I was one of the examiners, we started to discuss a future collaboration that would fuse Bernd's expertise on the conceptual history of magic with my interests in theories (of ritual and religion) and in the history of the study of religions. The Equinox Critical Categories in the Study of Religion seemed like the right venue and we wish to thank Janet Joyce for her enthusiasm for this project. In 2011, sponsored by a Yggdrasil Mobility Grant awarded by the Norwegian Research Council, Bernd spent six months at my department at the University of Bergen. During this period we read through an enormous amount of literature on "magic" in order to fine-tune our selection of texts to be included in that volume. We discussed and eventually agreed on the criteria for inclusion. Unfortunately, many of the texts selected fell prey to various sorts of constraints so that the final product is a rather reduced form of how we envisioned the volume.

We would like to thank the Norwegian Research Council for sponsoring Bernd's stay in Bergen and the Department of Archaeology, History, Cultural Studies and Religion for hosting him and providing us with excellent working conditions.

Special thanks are due to the five colleagues who have generously agreed to contribute original chapters to this volume (and actually also delivered their pieces!) so that this book goes beyond the framework of a reader, turning it halfway into an edited volume. Our gratitude also goes to Marios Skempis for providing a new translation of a key passage from Plato. We also wish to thank Brian Smith, Jörg Rüpke, Marios Skempis and Richard

# PREFACE

Gordon for comments on various parts of the editorial material and Ngoc An Phan Tran for her help with finalizing the bibliography.

Bernd patiently scanned and edited all the sources and he took care of all the tiresome paperwork necessary to obtain permissions. He also wrote the first drafts of the introductions to the historical sources (in Part I); from me commenting on and editing his drafts, the texts eventually grew into shared products until we, in the final phase, wrote some editorial material together.

"Magic" continues to conjure creative mental energies of various sorts and we hope to provide novices with a convenient and solid entry-point into this crucial interdisciplinary field of study. Despite the many attempts at defining "magic" documented in this volume, the last and final definition to put the case at rest has so far not been pronounced – and if it ever were, this would be a truly magical formula.

Michael Stausberg
Bergen

# SOURCES

## PART I: HISTORICAL SOURCES

**Plato, *Alcibiades* I 120e–122c**  W. R. M. Lamb (Ed./Transl.), *Charmides; Alcibiades* I and II; *Hipparchus; The Lovers; Theages; Minos; Epinomis/by W. R. Lamb* [The Loeb Classical Library; 2018], London: Heinemann, 1955 (reprint 1927), 165–9. Reprinted by permission of the publishers and the trustees of the Loeb Classical Library. © The President and Fellows of Harvard College, 1927. Loeb Classical Library® is a registered trademark of the President and Fellows of Harvard College.

**Plato, *Laws* 933c–e**  New translation © Marios Skempis (University of Erfurt).

**Pliny the Elder, *Historia Naturalis* 30.1–6**  W. H. S. Jones (Ed./Transl.), *Natural History: In Ten Volumes. Volume VIII: Libri XXVIII–XXXII; with an English translation by H. Rackham, W. H. S. Jones, D. E. Eichholz* [The Loeb Classical Library, 418], Cambridge: Harvard University Press, 1963, 279–91. Reprinted by permission of the publishers and the trustees of the Loeb Classical Library. © The President and Fellows of Harvard College, 1963. Loeb Classical Library® is a registered trademark of the President and Fellows of Harvard College.

**Plotinus, *Enneads* 4.4.40–44**  A. H. Armstrong (Ed./Transl.), *Plotinus. With an English translation by A. H. Armstrong. Enneads IV, 1–9* [The Loeb Classical Library, 443], London: Heinemann, 1984, 261–75. Reprinted by permission of the publishers and the trustees of the Loeb Classical Library. © The President and Fellows of Harvard College, 1984. Loeb Classical Library® is a registered trademark of the President and Fellows of Harvard College.

**Augustine of Hippo, *City of God* 21.6**  William Benton (Ed.), *The Confessions. City of God. On Christian Doctrine. By Saint Augustine* [Great Books of the Western World; 18. Augustine], *Encyclopaedia Britannica*: London, 1988 (13th reprint, original publication 1952), 564–65. Text translated by Marcus Dods.

**Augustine of Hippo, *On Christian Doctrine* 2.20.30.74f**  William Benton (Ed./Transl.), *The Confessions. City of God. On Christian Doctrine. By Saint Augustine* [Great Books of the Western World; 18. Augustine], *Encyclopaedia Britannica*: London 1988 (13th reprint, original publication 1952), 646–49. Text translated by William Benton.

**Isidore of Seville, "De magis", *Etymologiae***  Stephen A. Barney et al. (Ed./Transl.), *The Etymologies of Isidore of Seville/[translated by] Stephen A. Barney, W. J. Lewis, J. A. Beach, Oliver Berghof; with the collaboration of Muriel Hall*, Cambridge: Cambridge University Press, 181–83. © Stephen A. Barney, W. J. Lewis, J. A. Beach, Oliver Berghof, 2006. Published by Cambridge University Press, reproduced with permission.

# SOURCES

**Anonymous, "μαγεία", "γοητεία", *Suda*** *Suda* online. © Catherine Roth, 2002. Reproduced with permission of Catherine Roth.

"μαγεα", 9 October 2012: <http://www.stoa.org/sol-bin/search.pl?db=REAL&search_method=QUERY&login=guest&enlogin=guest&user_list=LIST&page_num=1&searchstr=mu,9&field=adlerhw_gr&num_per_page=1>

"γοητεία", 9 October 2012: <http://www.stoa.org/sol-bin/search.pl?db=REAL&search_method=QUERY&login=guest&enlogin=guest&user_list=LIST&page_num=1&searchstr=gamma,365&field=adlerhw_gr&num_per_page=1>

**Thomas Aquinas, *Summa Theologica* 2.2.92.1–4** T. F. O'Meara, M. J. Duffy (ed./transl.), *St Thomas Aquinas. Summa Theologica. Latin text and English translation, introductions, notes, appendices and glossaries. Volume 40 (2a2ae. 92–100): Superstition and Irreverence*, Cambridge University Press: New York, 1968 (reprint 2006), 71–85. © The Dominican Council as Trustee for the English Province of the Order of Preachers, 1968. Published by Cambridge University Press, reproduced with permission.

**Agrippa of Nettesheim, *De Occulta Philosophia* 1.1–2** Donald Tyson (ed.), *Three Books of Occult Philosophy Written by Henry Cornelius Agrippa of Nettesheim, Completely Annotated with Modern Commentary; translated by James Freake; edited and annotated by Donald Tyson*, Llewellyn Publications: St Paul, 1997 (third printing, original publication 1993), 3–6. © Donald Tyson. Llewellyn Worldwide, Ltd. 2143 Wooddale Drive, Woodbury, MN 55125-2989. All rights reserved, used by permission of the publisher.

**Dennis Diderot, "Magie", *Encyclopédie, ou dictionnaire raisonné des sciences, des arts et des métiers*** *The Encyclopedia of Diderot and d'Alembert Collaborative Translation Project. Translated by Steve Harris*. Ann Arbor: Scholarly Publishing Office of the University of Michigan Library, 2010. http://hdl.handle.net/2027/spo.did2222.0000.730 (accessed 5 April 2011). Originally published as "Magie" in *Encyclopédie, ou dictionnaire raisonné des sciences, des arts et des métiers*, Vol. 9: 852 (Paris, 1765). Reproduced with permission of Steve Harris.

**Helena Petrovna Blavatsky, "Magic", *Theosophical Glossary*** Helena P. Blavatsky, "Magic", *Theosophical Glossary*, New Delhi: Asian Publication Services, 1986 (original publication 1892), 197–8.

## PART II: FOUNDATIONAL WORKS OF THE ACADEMIC DEBATE

**Edward B. Tylor, *Primitive Culture*** Edward B. Tylor, *Primitive Culture: Researches into the Development of Mythology, Philosophy, Religion, Art, and Custom*, London: Murray, 1903 (revised 4th edition), Vol. 1: 112–21, 133–6, 158–9.

**James George Frazer, *The Golden Bough*** James George Frazer, *The Golden Bough: A Study in Magic and Religion. 1 Volume, abridged edition*, New York: The MacMillan Company, 1940 (original publication 1922), 11–12, 48–60, 711–14.

**Marcel Mauss and Henri Hubert, "A General Theory of Magic"** Marcel Mauss and Henri Hubert, "A General Theory of Magic". Translated from the French by Robert Brain, London: Routledge and Kegan Paul, 1972, 18–24, 86–90, 137–44. © The publisher, 1972. Reproduced by permission of Taylor & Francis Books UK.

**Émile Durkheim, *The Elementary Forms of Religious Life*** Émile Durkheim, *The Elementary Forms of Religious Life. Émile Durkheim. Translated and with an Introduction by Karen E. Fields*, New York: The Free Press, 1995, 38–44, 304–05, 360–67. Reprinted with the permission of Free Press, a division of Simon & Schuster, Inc. © Karen E. Fields, 1995. All rights reserved.

# PART III: MID-TWENTIETH-CENTURY APPROACHES TO MAGIC

**Gerardus van der Leeuw, *Religion in Essence and Manifestation*** Gerardus van der Leeuw, *Religion in Essence and Manifestation*. Translated by J. E. Turner with appendices incorporating the additions to the second German edition by Hans H. Penner. With a new Foreword by Ninian Smart, Princeton, NJ: Princeton University Press, 1986, 543–55. © Princeton University Press, 1986. Reprinted by permission of Princeton University Press.

**Edward E. Evans-Pritchard, *Witchcraft, Oracles and Magic among the Azande*** Edward E. Evans-Pritchard, *Witchcraft, Oracles and Magic among the Azande. By E. E. Evans-Pritchard. With a Foreword by Professor C. G. Seligman FRS*, Oxford: Clarendon Press, 1958 (original publication 1937), 11–12, 63–74, 79–83, 475–8. Reprinted by permission of Oxford University Press.

**Bronislaw Malinowski, "Magic, Science and Religion"** Bronislaw Malinowski, "Magic, Science and Religion", 50–71, in Idem, *Magic, Science and Religion and other Essays by Bronislaw Malinowski. With an Introduction by Robert Redfield*, New York: Doubleday Anchor Books, 1948, 1–71.

**Robin Horton, "African Traditional Thought and Western Science. Part II"** Robin Horton, "African Traditional Thought and Western Science. Part II", 155–61, in *Africa* 37, 2 (April 1967), 155–87. © International African Institute. Published by Cambridge University Press, reproduced with permission.

**Stanley J. Tambiah, "Form and Meaning of Magical Acts: A Point of View"** Stanley J. Tambiah, "Form and Meaning of Magical Acts: A Point of View", 218–29, in Robin Horton and Ruth Finnegan (eds), *Modes of Thought: Essays on Thinking in Western and Non-Western Societies*, London: Faber and Faber 1973, 199–229. Reprinted by permission of Faber and Faber Ltd.

**Edmund R. Leach, *Culture and Communication*** Edmund R. Leach, *Culture and Communication: The Logic by which Symbols Are Connected. An Introduction to the Use of Structuralist Analysis in Social Anthropology by Edmund Leach*, Cambridge: Cambridge University Press, 1991, 29–32. © Cambridge University Press, 1976. Reproduced with permission. Thanks to the Esperanza Trust for Anthropological Research.

# PART IV: CONTEMPORARY VOICES

All of the contributions in Part IV comprise original essays.

# GENERAL INTRODUCTION

## "MAGIC": A CRITICAL CATEGORY IN THE STUDY OF RELIGIONS

If there are critical categories in the study of religion\s,[1] as the title of this series suggests, "magic" certainly qualifies as one. "Magic" is critical in several senses of the word. To begin with, "magic" is a category that for far too long has been used to negatively determine the nature of "religion". As we will see, "religion" and "magic" are traditionally defined in mutually exclusive terms: "religion" is purified from "magic", and "magic" is what does not qualify as "religion". "Magic" is therefore also a critical category in the sense of providing an implicit critique: "magic" is illegitimate religion, unless it is given a positive twist and serves as the positive other to traditional religion – for example, in the case of modern or contemporary "Magick". Accordingly, "magic" is critical by being a category of distinction: it distinguishes things, practices or ways of thinking from others, including religion, rationality and science. Last but not least, "magic" is a critical category because it has been variously criticized and remains a matter of intense dispute: despite its being a common term in all modern western European languages, there is no unanimously agreed academic definition of "magic", nor any shared theory or theoretical language – and apparently not even any agreement on the range or type of actions, events, thoughts or objects covered by the category. Accordingly, during recent decades the scholarly validity of the category as such has been vigorously criticized by several scholars, but also emphatically defended by others. In the following, we can only outline some main parameters in the intellectual struggles involved in "defining magic". Our constant use of the quotation marks when speaking of "magic" is meant to alert the reader to the need to hold one's breath before joining the chorus of voices who have made pronouncements on the nature and work of "magic".[2]

---

1. The "idiosyncratic use of the backslash is meant to index a series of theoretical and metatheoretical questions regarding the referents and framing 'religion' and 'religions'" (Engler and Stausberg 2011: 127).
2. This is not meant to imply that "magic" is in any way more problematic than several other concepts used in this book: recall similar debates about concepts such as "rationality", "religion" and "science".

# PRESENTING THE FAMILY

For most people, "magic" seems to pose no problem at all. After all, "magic" seems like a cross-cultural given. When looking at encyclopaedias or the research literature, the label "magic" is used to refer to a wide range of phenomena. Here is a partial list of phenomena typically addressed under this heading in the literature:

- ablutions;
- alchemy;
- amulets;
- apotropaic substances and words;
- arousal of love/driving couples apart;
- astrology;
- causing harm onto others (including death);
- charms;
- conjuration of spirits;
- curses (including binding);
- divination;
- dolls;
- evocation of agents;
- expelling malevolent forces;
- exorcism;
- exploitation of powers;
- formulae;
- fumigations;
- (amuletic) gems;
- *grimoires*;
- healing;
- herbs;
- incantations;
- invocations;
- lapidaries;
- manipulations/transformations;
- miracles/marvels;
- necromancy;
- opening locked doors;
- (spirit) possession;
- potions;
- prestidigitation;
- protection against a variety of ills by various means;
- sacrifices;
- signs;
- sorcery;

- spells;
- talismans;
- witchcraft.

Note that there are numerous varieties and specifications of all these phenomena. If we are to understand why such a perplexing range of phenomena has been associated with "magic", we need to take a brief look at the emergence and semantic shadings of the concept.

## TERMS AND CONCEPT(S)

"Magic" belongs to the conceptual legacy of fifth-century Greece (BCE). Etymologically, the term is apparently derived from contact with the main political enemy of that period, the Persians, and "magic" has ever since served as a marker of alterity, of dangerous, foreign, illicit, suspicious but potentially powerful things done by others (and/or done differently). From referring to concrete objects and practices, "magic" eventually turned into a rather abstract category. Part I of this reader ("Historical Sources") documents the main stages of the conceptual history and some opposing interpretations of the term in European history from Plato (d. 347 BCE) to Madame Blavatsky (b. 1831; d. 1891). As it turns out (see the Introduction to Part I for further details), "magic" has been a term with an extremely versatile and ambivalent semantics: it is the art of the devil or a path to the gods, it is of natural or supernatural origin, a testimony to human folly or the crowning achievement of scientific audacity, a sin or a virtue, harmful or beneficent, overpowering or empowering, an act of othering or of self-assertion.

Furthermore, in the course of its conceptual history, "magic" was associated with a variety of related terms, whether in ancient Greek (consider *pharmakeía*, *goēteía*, *katadesmos* or *epaoidē*), Latin (consider *veneficium*, *maleficium*, *defixio* or *carmen*) or modern European languages, resulting in a polyfocal semantic field that continues to shape the meanings of "magic". If we therefore regard, rather tentatively, "witchcraft" (including German *Hexerei*, French *sorcellerie*, Spanish *brujería* or Italian *stregoneria*) and "sorcery" (including German *Zauberei*, again French *sorcellerie*, Spanish *hechicería* or Italian *magia/stregoneria*) as partial synonyms of "magic", the task of "defining magic" becomes ever more complex. Consider also modern scholarly creations such as fetishism, occultism, mana or shamanism. All of these terms are recognizably distinct from "magic", yet they were applied and are still understood to be instances of "magic" (e.g., "sorcery" as "[black] magic") or the other way round (e.g., "magic" as a feature of "occultism").

The complexity of this semantic field is reflected in the fuzziness of scholarly discourses: given the semantic overlap, scholarly work on "sorcery" and "witchcraft" should have immediate repercussions on our understanding of "magic" (and vice versa); yet scholarship on "witchcraft" and "magic" often follows distinct paths, the one, for example, being pursued by anthropologists and social historians, and the other by intellectual historians and scholars of Western Esotericism. Even within these sub-discourses, scholars tend to selectively assign specific shades of meanings to their preferred terms, partly derived from their empirical materials, from selected (and often selective) reading of the literature, or simply from preconceptions derived from everyday language. Evans-Pritchard referred to the Zande belief of attributing misfortune to "*mangu*" as "witchcraft" (see Chapter 16); but later anthropologists, particularly during the so-called "rationality debate" of the 1960s and 1970s, would subsume it under "magic", or use "sorcery" as the main category for interpreting ethnographic data (see, e.g., Kapferer 1997) or engage in amphibologies or pleonasms such as "the magic of witchcraft" (Stroeken 2010).

## AN UNHOLY CONSTELLATION: "MAGIC", "SCIENCE" AND "RELIGION"

In modern academic research, "magic" is caught in another conceptual-semantic constellation: the magic–science–religion triangle. Scholars have often defined each of these terms in relation to the other two. "Magic" has been conceived as being similar to and/or different from "science", on the one hand, and "religion", on the other, both terms being themselves at the centre of intense debates. The modern academic discussion has to a large extent been devoted to sorting out these structural relationships with regard to functions, levels, modes and origins.

"Science" has served as the main foil of "magic" among the founding fathers of academic anthropology, Edward B. Tylor (see Chapter 11) and James George Frazer (see Chapter 12), and the magic–science dyad has tended to preoccupy anthropological theorizing ever since. Claiming that "magic" derives from the (unsuccessful) desire to understand and control the natural environment, both Tylor and Frazer regarded "magic" as a "pseudo-science", or the "bastard sister of science" (see Chapters 11 and 12). Whereas these early anthropological definitions aligned "magic" with "science", while postulating a fundamental difference between "magical" and "scientific" thinking, the twentieth-century debate came to stress the emotional roots of "magic" (e.g., Malinowski: see Chapter 17), or focused on its cultural embeddedness and emic "rationality" (e.g., Evans-Pritchard: see Chapter 16). It was, above all, Edward E. Evans-Pritchard's *Witchcraft, Oracles and Magic among the Azande* with its emphasis on the logical and empirical basis of "witchcraft" belief among the Azande (of what is now south Sudan) that set, some thirty years later, the stage for an emphatic debate on the theoretical implications of the magic–science relation (see Wilson 1970; Horton and Finnegan 1973; Kippenberg and Luchesi 1987 [1978]). The so-called "rationality debate" not only addressed epistemological issues (such as the alleged immunity to falsification of "magic" or the general difficulties of understanding non-Western cultures) but also questioned the validity of the opposition of "magic" and "science" by pointing out the ethnocentrism of this Western "mode of thought". While Robin Horton maintained the comparison but changed the parameters, resulting in a different evaluation (see Chapter 18), Stanley J. Tambiah shifted attention from the supposed causal effects of speech/ritual acts to their performativity (see Chapter 19). More radically, Michael Winkelman argued in 1982 that the generally shared assumption of the causal inefficacy of "magic" in academic discourse would need to be revised in the light of new perspectives and findings in parapsychological research (Winkelman 1982; see also his various later publications on ethnomedicine). In line with these attempts to rehabilitate the causality of "magic", Susan Greenwood advocates its conceptualization as a "legitimate form of knowledge within a synthetic view of science" in this volume (see Chapter 21). Likewise in this volume, Christopher Lehrich insists that "science" and "magic" can be usefully distinguished, but also questions the notions of "science" invoked in earlier debates on the grounds that they were based on often problematic and simplifying models of the natural sciences (see Chapter 22).

From the perspective of the study of religion\s, the main conceptual tension of "magic" is with "religion". The idea that there is a realm of "magic" in addition to or distinct from religion is part of a long conceptual history inherited by modern academic scholarship, and the question of the distinctiveness and compatibility of these two domains has been a matter of on-going dispute. Interestingly, the early theorists not only attempted various (and not always consistent) explanations of "magic", but by doing so they inherited the depreciatory, dismissive or even hostile attitude of earlier Christian and Enlightenment thinkers. Tylor, for example, refers to "magic" as a "monstrous farrago" (see Chapter 11); for him, "magic" is all bad and fundamentally so "because when any of it becomes good it ceases to be magic" (Tylor 1883: 206). This, of course, can hardly qualify as a result of academic scholarship, but rather as an instance of ideologically impregnated tautology. Durkheim's distinction between "magic" and "religion" (see Chapter 14) has also been characterized as an instance of "circular reasoning of a surprisingly elementary kind" (Hanegraaff 1999: 342) and as offering "little more than a reformulation of Christian heresiological categories" (344). "Magic" and "religion" are here clearly distinct but incompatible domains. That approach was about to change as the twentieth century progressed. Malinowski (see Chapter 17), for example, continued to substantially oppose "magic" to "religion", but at the same time held that they were functionally compatible as they both addressed existential human needs (which in modern society, however, would be made partly irrelevant by "science").

In 1949, while noting that several prominent scholars such as Lowie, Radin, Marett, Goldweiser, Herskowitz and Benedict had found varying degrees of overlap between "magic" and "religion", the sociologist William J. Goode, nevertheless, tried to save the distinction by proposing a continuum of "magic" and "religion", understood as ideal types. In 1963, the anthropologist/sociologist pair Murray and Rosalie Wax reviewed the situation as follows: "while few scholars have advocated discarding the differentiations and dichotomies between magic and religion or magic and science, most have continued to employ them as they derive from Frazer, Durkheim and Malinowski. Yet, these conceptualizations have been subjected to severe criticism: the critics have been eminent; their data have been excellent; and their critique has never been refuted" (Wax and Wax 1963: 500). Nevertheless, even the Waxes could not bring themselves to abandon the term and fell back on the notion of a "magical worldview". And so it went on, even though further theoretical and empirical evidence continued to be adduced against the usefulness of the distinction. The category was unmasked as an example of uncritical ethnocentrism (see Otto 2011: 87–104) that played its part in colonialist schemes of subjugation of other peoples' mind sets and legitimizing a "civilizing" mission or efforts at conversion to Christianity (see also Styers 2004: 69ff). Despite these fundamental critiques and although an overwhelming overlap between "magic" and "religion" is constantly addressed (e.g., Thomassen 1999; Benavides 2006), "magic" still seems to function as a self-evident category and analytical tool for many scholars in the study of religion\s.

## "MAGIC" AS AN ETHNOCENTRISM

The magic–science–religion triangle points to a number of problems that has also been discussed under the heading of ethnocentrism. To begin with, the magic–science–religion triangle is a genuine product of modern Western history. Therefore, the application of the concept of "magic" to other cultures (or pre-modern periods of Western history) may not always be a promising strategy: while it may at first sight appear to yield a meaningful interpretation of data from these cultures, on closer inspection it may, in fact, be nothing but the projection of deeply entrenched modern Western "modes of thought" and colonialist fantasies. Imposing "magic" as an analytic tool on other cultures may direct attention away from local contexts and suppress difference resulting in distorted findings, interpretations and narratives. In the belief that one is discovering "magic" "out there", one may, in fact, end up with just universalizing one's own Western categories and background assumptions.

Innumerable examples from the past but also from contemporary scholarship lend themselves to this kind of criticism. The vast corpus of cross-disciplinary scholarship on "magic" may create the impression that it can be found literally everywhere, whether in prehistoric cave drawings, in ancient Egypt, Mesopotamia, Greece or Rome, in ancient India or China, from the European Middle Ages until modern times, among Jews, Christians, Muslims, "tantric" Buddhists, Indian "*saddhus*", New Age "shamans" or Bavarian peasants, in contemporary Africa, South America, Sri Lanka, or on North American baseball fields. The overwhelming quantity and often taken-for-granted validity of these narratives point to a sometimes dramatic unawareness (or even deliberate ignorance) of the ethnocentricity of the concept of "magic" in scholarly discourse and indicates that a more thorough, interdisciplinary reflection on this topic would probably contest or entirely dismantle a major part of these "findings".

Those (few) scholars who address the problem of ethnocentrism and nevertheless defend the category of "magic" and continue to use it in their works rightly emphasize that all scientific concepts are necessarily ethnocentric (particularly in the study of religion\s), that the problem of Western preconceptions in scholarly research cannot be avoided on principle, and that these concepts are necessary to do comparative work (note the similar debates in defining "religion", "culture", "ritual", etc.). Yet, this acknowledgement should not be misused to side-step the problems that must be addressed rather than silenced, especially with an ideologically loaded concept such as "magic".

## DEVIANCE, IDENTITY AND PRACTITIONER DEFINITIONS

A different conceptualization of "magic" referred to as the "deviance theory" (Otto 2011: 25) takes a relational approach. Some historians of religion\s have noted that the concept of "magic" was often applied in situations of inner- or inter-religious conflicts and thereby operated as a polemical weapon to devaluate their respective "theological opposition" (Phillips 1986: 2711) or the "religion" of the other (even if not all processes of distinction and othering involved talk of "magic"). Given that "magic" here functions mainly as a relational category, this approach emphasizes its fuzziness and wide-ranging applicability. The academic debate on "magic" could, at least in large part, be interpreted in the light of this perspective as it mainly followed in the footsteps of former marginalizing discourses and inherited most of their polemical arguments (see Parts I and II for more detail). Scholars have usually spoken of "magicians" from an external, often haughty perspective, with the result that "magic" has largely operated as a tool of scholarly othering. Randall Styers in this volume points to some of the underlying motives of this procedure (see Chapter 25).

However, the "deviance theory" falls short in at least one respect, in that it fails to account for the fact that some people also apply the concept of "magic" to refer to themselves and their own practices and beliefs. This is not solely a modern phenomenon as manifested in contemporary esotericism, paganism or fantasy literature, but goes as far back as late antiquity, where some anonymous Egyptian ritual specialists designated their activities as "*mageía*" (see *Papyri Graecae Magicae*, e.g. I.126/127, IV.2318/19, IV.2446–49). In fact, self-referential uses of the term can be found throughout the conceptual history of "magic" (see Part I and, in more detail, Otto 2011). Today, people referring to themselves as "magicians" form part of various new religious movements and, not least through the new communicative possibilities offered by the internet, also take part in a public endeavour to "define magic".

Yet, practitioners of "magic" themselves are not immune to the troubles of defining "magic" and they actually face similar problems as the scholarly community, such as the fuzziness of the concept, its overlap with other concepts, or its multiplicity of potential meanings (see the various practitioner definitions and discussions described in Luhrman 1989 and Berger 1999 & 2005). In this regard, comparing the practices and beliefs of contemporary (e.g., "Chaos" or "Wiccan") "magicians" with those of Eliphas Lévi, Agrippa of Nettesheim or the authors of the *Papyri Graecae Magicae* reveals that there is no common or shared feature in various self-identification accounts of "magic" over longer periods of Western history. When today some scholars adopt both roles (such as Susan Greenwood; see Chapter 21) or when the various new periodicals devoted to "magic" (such as the journals *Magic, Ritual and Witchcraft* or *Preternature: Critical and Historical Studies on the Preternatural*) are also used by practitioners of "magic" – both as readers and contributors

– the task of "defining magic" becomes even more confusing: it is now equally involved in the proclamation and legitimization of (new) religious identities.

## SPLITTING THE FAMILY

Once the various problems surrounding the category of "magic" are put on the table, there are basically four partly interrelated strategies to defend its use as a legitimate part of our scholarly vocabulary. One finds various combinations of these strategies in the literature:

1. The study of religion\s can or should not disaffiliate from first-order concepts so that as long as people (including other scholars) speak of "magic" or claim to observe or perform acts classified by someone as "magic", this constitutes a legitimate discursive reality and subject of study.
2. The study of religion\s is in need of terms that allow its practitioners to do comparative research; "magic", despite its problems (which it shares with many other such terms), can be expected to do such work with appropriate reflexive caveats and qualifications.
3. One needs to strip the concept from several of its secondary encrustations and rehabilitate the elementary forms of "magic" that could then be explained as such; the purified concept could then be used as a theoretical or analytical tool to analyse empirical materials (data).
4. Like many other concepts, "magic" refers to a range of phenomena sharing a family resemblance; accordingly, the concept cannot be defined in terms of a closed list of specific traits but needs to be thought of in the light of generally accepted prototypical examples from which an open list of typical features could be generated.

Given that they potentially apply to terminological matters in general, this is not the place to discuss the value of these strategies as such; we limit ourselves to the issue of defining "magic". For the first strategy, any definition of "magic" is purely lexical or descriptive (i.e., these definitions seek to reflect the way in which the term, or its presumed equivalents in other languages, is actually used or attested in the sources). For strategy two, one would need to identify the appropriate caveats and qualifications (e.g., that "magic", as a scholarly concept, should not be used in such a manner as to imply value judgements – i.e., to stigmatize something as "magic"), but the content of the definition remains to be specified. For the third strategy one needs to know the essential features (either as taken for granted or as the result of a theoretical investigation). For this and the fourth strategy, one would need an inventory of traits and examples to start with. The question will then be, for strategy three, whether any features are more essential than others – ultimately a theoretical question – or, for strategy four, whether the features can be meaningfully joined to a kind of family or whether we are dealing with illusory kinfolk. Let us start by giving a brief catalogue of features as provided by the academic literature. The focus of selection is on the denotations, definers or indicators of "magic", the signals that trigger a recognition of X as an instance of M ("magic"/"magical"), rather than on the overarching theoretical interpretations (e.g., the psychological or social functions ascribed to "magic"). While most of these can be found in the theoretical definitions reprinted in this volume, others have been extracted from implicit definitions of "magic" encountered in the empirical literature (e.g., on "magic" in antiquity).

"Magic" is said to be:

- coercive;
- manipulative;
- seeking to exercise control of others or change the state of things or other human beings;
- interventionist;
- purely mechanical;
- powerful, self-efficacious ritual action;
- analogical/symbolic/sympathetic;
- typically operative in the form of contagion or similarity;
- imitative and/or mimetic;
- instrumental ritual action with limited aims and scope;
- a practice of obtaining ordinarily unavailable this-worldly benefits;
- a ritual counter-measure against "witchcraft" attacks;
- performed on "critical" occasions;
- based on associative thinking;
- immune to falsification;
- compulsive, hallucinatory behaviour;
- based on a non-ordinary "participatory" worldview or consciousness;
- derived from strong emotions such as anger or fear, related to desires;
- related to (supernatural, invisible) agents or agency typically distinct from gods;
- non-legitimate dealing with the supernatural;
- private and/or secret;
- egocentric and/or autistic;
- antisocial or related to societal sub-groups;
- performed by self-employed non-institutionalized specialists (the "magicians") serving their "clients";
- lacking institutional (infra)structures;
- a specific kind of technique, art or craft requiring special knowledge and/or training;
- associated with "others" such as marginalized groups or outsiders;
- a category and discursive practice of denunciation of "others";
- immoral or lacking moral considerations;
- characterized by strange or exotic behaviours;
- characterized by the use of strange or exotic objects;
- characterized by a distinctive use of language and words;
- an illocutionary or performative (speech) act;

- producing miraculous events;
- an art of creating illusions, also employed in entertainment.

Are there ways to put some order in this perplexing catalogue of features? One is to distinguish between different types of magic such as homeopathic versus contagious (see Frazer in Chapter 12), transformative versus manipulative (see Sørensen in Chapter 23), prospective versus retrospective (see Sørensen in Chapter 23), or "white" and "black" magic (see Blavatsky in Chapter 10). While such distinctions can be helpful, they are far from achieving a necessary degree of overall coherence to sort out the heterogeneity of our catalogue. Another potential approach is to assign these features to a model of action comprising the actors (including clients and specialists), their qualifications, roles and mental conditions, their intentions and goals, linguistic and extra-linguistic means and forms of the action, its social and societal context, and a patient at whom the action is directed. While this may, indeed, enable one to assign many of the elements to a shared structure, this strategy faces the problem that there are few cases where all these elements converge and that there are many other cases where only some of the features or elements from this action structure occur in combination with other features not listed in the above catalogue. The classification therefore necessarily remains fuzzy (which holds true for many acts of classification). The main problem, however, is that so far no sound reasons have been presented why one should actually lump all of these features together into one category in the first place. In other words, while all these single features do exist *per se*, or in some limited combinations, to identify something as "magic" or "magical" based on the observation of one or a few of these characteristics is problematic because this inference automatically triggers a set of further descriptive and theoretical assumptions that in most cases are not warranted by the available evidence. This bears the risk of creating misunderstandings. Instead of instinctively interpreting the occurrence of a limited number of features from our catalogue as evidence for the existence of a family-like concept, we suggest splitting the extended tribal family into a number of nuclear families. Instead of instances of "magic", we suggest speaking of patterns of magicity.

## PATTERNS OF MAGICITY

To summarize the argument so far, as a second-order scholarly category, "magic" poses a number of apparently insurmountable problems: the broad range of disparate phenomena usually covered by the concept; its semantic diversity; conceptual heterogeneity; ethnocentric bias; and undesirable ideological implications. All of this would seem to militate against retaining the concept. Yet, it refuses to disappear; Randall Styers (2004 and Chapter 25 in this volume) has read the academic preoccupation, if not obsession, with the problem of "magic" as a way of dealing with the self-representations of modernity. However, the persistence of scholarly discourse on "magic" also reflects the recurrent observation of "facts" signalled by the kinds of examples and features listed above. One might argue that abandoning the term "magic" only risks silencing us by depriving scholars of ways of addressing these persistent observations; after all, amulets, curses, healing procedures and other such things exist and it is easy enough to find practices that can be characterized as manipulative or that are typically performed on critical occasions, to pick out only some examples and features. In other words, should we stop speaking of "magic" even when we cannot help observing perceived evidence for it?

Our point is that even if such phenomena impose themselves on observers (scholars and non-scholars alike, from their respective perspectives and with their respective interpretations), as scholars we should, indeed, stop treating these observations as evidence for "MAGIC". Instead, we should either just speak of amulets, curses, etc., or of private rites (rather than intuitively and unreflectingly allocate them to a single overarching macro-category). In addition, we should try to arrive at a more differentiated and less fragile and ethnocentric conceptual apparatus. Nothing would be gained by treating one ideological disease by another one of the same type, in this case by flatly denying the occurrence of some cross-culturally identifiable "patterns of magicity". In physics, "magicity" refers to "The condition of a heavy isotope of having a *magic* number of protons and neutrons, and therefore of having particular stability" (http://en.wiktionary.org/wiki/magicity). We have no ambition of emulating that model here in a quasi-scientific manner; but the point is the idea of some forms and conditions of structural stability. "Patterns of magicity" do not automatically involve "MAGIC" (as the supreme meta-category), nor are they "magic" (as referring to ontological features), but they are a way of dealing with cross-culturally attested observations. "Magicity" acknowledges the fact that they were traditionally assigned to the overall category "MAGIC" in which we have stopped believing. As we see it, based on a meta-analysis of definitions and theories of "magic", and the catalogue of objects to which that category is applied, future work should seek to model such patterns. These will then reflect and effectively re-describe different items from the lists of phenomena and features we have drawn up above, without aiming to provide the single key to the whole of "MAGIC" in all of its amorphous multiplicity.

One such pattern, for example, involves the ritual use of words and their perceived direct efficacy; we might call it the pattern of "word efficacy" (and index it as "$M_{WOR}$", standing for "Magicity [words]"). Note that this pattern can be found both within and outside religion. Since the "patterns of magicity" proposed here step back from the larger category of "MAGIC", they also render irrelevant the – historical but also scholarly – disputes over whether a specific rite using efficacious words is actually "religious" or "magical". Instead, "$M_{WOR}$" is derived from the recurrent observation that humans tend to ascribe efficacy to the utterance of specific words in ritual sequences and that this pattern of ascription is attested cross-culturally in a multiplicity of sources. The same approach could be applied to other potential "patterns of magicity", such as the supposed efficacy of certain kinds of signs ($M_{SIG}$), objects ($M_{OBJ}$) or places ($M_{PLA}$), the idea that it is actually possible to control other people's desires ($M_{DES}$) or harm them ($M_{HAR}$) by ritual means, or the ascription of miraculous capabilities ($M_{MIR}$) to particular individuals. Yet another pattern would concern modes of evaluation of ritual activities conducted by specific actors and the views on, and social position of, such actors ($M_{EVA}$). There can be, but need not be, cross-references or correlations between patterns. These and other patterns of magicity would need to be identified, analysed and explained in their own right (lack of space prevents us from attempting that task here).

## THE SELECTION OF THE TEXTS AND THE ORGANIZATION OF THE VOLUME

"Magic" is not only a diffuse subject but also an extremely popular one, both outside and within academia. While certain religious groups and discourses continue campaigning against "magic", in popular culture and other religious discourses "magic" is nowadays mostly regarded as a positive thing. There are many practising "magicians" who have presented a huge number of definitions of "magic". At least for the twentieth and twenty-first centuries, however, this reader focuses on definitions and interpretations proposed by academic writers.

Given that influential scholarly conceptualizations of "magic" seem to continue pre- or non-academic understandings of that concept, Part I presents a selection of twelve texts (by ten authors) comprising several of the most influential or representative definitions of "magic" throughout Western history. Our first source – an excerpt from (pseudo-)Plato – is very close to the formative period of the concept in ancient Greece, while our last source, taken from the writings of one of the inventors of modern Western Esotericism (Madame Blavatsky) is in close historical proximity to the early academic sources. Of course, ours is only a minimal selection of relevant sources, and whereas we have included one Byzantine source (see Chapter 6), for practical reasons we were unable to include Islamic (Arabic) and Jewish (Hebrew) sources, even though we would be the first to acknowledge both their relevance (in their own right) and their impact (upon subsequent developments).[3]

Parts II to IV of the volume take the reader through the main periods of the scholarly debate.[4] Part II presents some of the foundational texts for the academic study of "magic" in Britain (Tylor and Frazer) and France (Durkheim and Mauss/Hubert), expressing ideas that have remained benchmarks and signposts for the subsequent literature. Part III takes the reader into the middle of the twentieth century. Apart from the inclusion of one scholar of religion, van der Leeuw, who has been selected to illustrate a different line of thought – namely, the phenomenology of religion (which was the main approach to the study of religion\s of that period) – Part III focuses upon a sequence of prominent (British

---

3. Note that the footnotes in the historical chapters are reprinted from the original editions.
4. Other scholars sometimes map the debate by assigning approaches to categories such as rationalist, symbolist, pragmatic, performative and emotionalist (Sørensen 2007a: 1–28), or intellectualist, emotionalist, phenomenological, structural-functionalist, symbolic, structuralist, cognitive and feminist (Cunningham 1999) approaches. Cunningham reviews "the study of the sacred" (1999: vii) in general and the book contains short portraits of the views of some thirty-seven scholars on religion, ritual and "magic". Although "magic" is not covered in all the sections (it is not discussed, for example, under cognitive and feminist approaches), Cunningham's book can be used with profit alongside the present volume.

or British-trained) anthropologists who debated "magic" mainly in its relationship to rationality and science (Malinowski, Evans-Pritchard, Horton, Tambiah and Leach); that debate also brought the issues of ethnocentrism/Eurocentrism (see above) to the fore. The debate on "magic" is by no means a closed chapter in the history of anthropology and the study of religion\s, and Part IV of this reader presents original contributions by some of the leading voices in the contemporary debate on "magic" (Greenwood, Lehrich, Sørensen, Stratton and Styers).

It goes without saying that the present volume only presents one possible selection of texts. Any reader, especially one dealing with critical categories, presents severe constraints of space; as a result, we had to curtail sharply the number of reprinted sources. In addition, in several cases there was an unfortunate mismatch between the royalties requested by some publishers and the budget put at our disposal, so that we were unable to reprint some texts we would otherwise have wished to include. These and other practical constraints aside, we have selected sources with a very explicit focus – namely, on defining "magic" (i.e., attempts to determine its nature, delimit its boundaries, set forth its most relevant features, and to explain its working). Moreover, we have, in general, given preference to texts that have constituted points of reference for later authors (i.e., texts that have significantly shaped the subsequent discussion).

In addition to this general introduction, the volume offers two further levels of editorial materials. On the one hand, each reprinted text is prefaced by a very brief introduction, which provides some information on the respective author and summarizes the main points of the argument. On the other hand, the four main sections of the reader are each introduced by a short essay. In the cases of Parts II to IV, this device has allowed us to acknowledge some other important contributions that, mainly because of the constraints already mentioned, we were unable to reprint. The introductory essays thus seek to compensate for the lacunae and create a somewhat richer texture for the debate as a whole.

# PART I

## HISTORICAL SOURCES

PART I: HISTORICAL SOURCES

# INTRODUCTION

The conceptual history of "magic" spans around 2500 years and pervades a huge number of texts and different cultural-religious epochs (see Otto 2011). In order to understand the degree to which the academic debate inherited ideas and valuation patterns from former pre-academic discourses, in this part we present twelve key texts that illustrate main features of the conceptual history of "magic". These texts have been selected because of their historical impact, their mainly theoretical and often encyclopaedic approach, and the variety of semantic patterns and connotations they exemplify. As we shall see, the pre-academic conceptual legacy of "magic" is characterized by some haziness and polyvalence that has not least contributed to the academic problem of "defining magic".

Etymologically, the concept of "magic" goes back to the ancient Iranian appellative *maguš*, but the etymology of this word is unclear. Greek sources ascribe a variety of functions to the Iranian *mágoi*. According to Herodotus, who also refers to them as one of seven Median tribes, besides being in charge of religious rites such as sacrifices and the interpretation of dreams, the *mágoi* served as functionaries at the Persian (Achaemenian) court and advisers to the king (*Histories*, e.g., 1.101f; 3.30f; 7.19f, 37f, 113f, 191f).

During the late sixth and early fifth centuries BCE, the term *maguš* was picked up and Graecicized (into μάγος, μαγεία) by ancient Greek authors and thereby developed a life of its own. The Greek adaptation of the concept implied some fundamental semantic transformations, which may be particularly due to the fact that the Greek city states faced serious military conflicts with the Persian Empire at that time. To the Greeks, the *mágos* represented the religious specialist of a threatening foreign – "barbaric" – culture so that the concept quickly assimilated a variety of negative stereotypes. The *mágos* was regarded as a charlatan and "magic" (i.e., the ritual art of the *mágos*) a mere fraud (see, e.g., Sophocles, *Oedipus Rex* 387f; Hippocrates, *De morbo sacro* 1.10f). "Magical" rites were perceived as strange, unconventional and dangerous (see Hippocrates, *De morbo sacro* 1.39f; Gorgias, *Encomium of Helen* 9–10). The extraordinary, miraculous abilities allegedly possessed by *mágoi* were regarded as sacrilegious and suspicious (see Hippocrates, *De morbo sacro* 1.28f; Euripides, *Orestes* 1493f). In line with these notions, the Greek concept of "magic" came to signify all sorts of unsanctioned rites performed by private ritual entrepreneurs outside the institutionalized cults. The texts from Plato hosted here reflect this development in a twofold manner: in his *Laws* (see Chapter 1), Plato proposes harsh punishments for specialists of "magic" (he uses the synonym *pharmakeía*), which he classifies as a form of *asebeía* ("blasphemy", "impiety", "false religion"). On the other hand, in his *Alcibiades* I (see Chapter 1), (Pseudo-)Plato, reflecting the historical and etymological background of the term, claims that *mageía* refers to the "worship of the Gods" (i.e., "religion") among the Persians. Some later authors would use this argument to elevate the concept of "magic" and question the negative stereotypes predominant in Western discourse.

In the first century BCE, the Greek concept was picked up and Latinized (into *magus*, *magia*) by Roman authors. The Roman reception of the term continued main features of the Greek usage, but with a greater emphasis on its judicial application, semantic scope and theoretical explanation. At least since the mid-first century CE, court cases were carried out against "magicians" or "magical rites" (see Tacitus, *Annales*, e.g., 2.27, 12.59; 16.31, etc.); the late ancient *Codex Theodosianus* points, in fact, to the increased elaboration of statues against "magic" in the Roman Empire (see *Codex Theodosianus* 9.16.3f). The trial against the philosopher Apuleius of Madaura is the most famous example of the ancient prosecution of "magic" (see his extant defence speech *Apologia sive pro se de magia*). To the Romans, "magic" signified a fraudulent ritual art that pervades a multiplicity of (foreign) cultures and goes back to a distant past. Our third text – an excerpt of Book 30 of Pliny's *Historia Naturalis* – is a fine example of this already ancient pattern of generalization and historicization of "magic". Eventually, ancient authors proposed theories of the possible mechanisms underlying the rites and thoughts associated with "magic". Chapter 3 shows how the philosopher Plotinus accomplished this task by embedding the concept within his "Neoplatonic" philosophical framework.

In the first centuries CE, the concept of "magic" was picked up by Christian authors who incorporated it within Christian theology and also adopted former Jewish conceptual patterns (in particular, the opposition of "magic" and "miracle"). As a result, the negative stereotypes already implied in the Greek and Roman understanding of "magic" were enhanced: the texts in Chapter 4 by Augustine of Hippo show that, for Christian authors, "magic" not only refers to some fraudulent, superstitious, unsanctioned ritual practice, but to the very opposite of "religion", as "magic" now exclusively relies on the working of demons, the henchmen of Satan. This radicalization – the idea of the "demon pact" – turned the "magician" into an enemy of God and, as a polemical weapon, made it possible to devaluate inner and outer enemies of Christendom (such as pagan religions), a pattern that was continuously applied throughout Christian history. The idea of the "demon pact" was handed on by Christian authors throughout the Middle Ages (see, e.g., Chapters 5 and 7), early modern and modern times, and can still be found in modern Christian polemics against *Harry Potter* (see, e.g., Arms 2000, 83).

Despite the predominantly derogatory usage of "magic" in Christian discourse, more affirmative conceptualizations were likewise pronounced in the course of Western history. While the conceptual background of the – surprisingly ambivalent – definition of "magic" in the Byzantine *Suda* (see Chapter 6) remains to be investigated, the early modern conception of *magia naturalis* is a striking example of affirmative interpretations of "magic" in pre-academic discourses. That concept was introduced in the late fifteenth century by two Italian humanists – Marsilio Ficino (b. 1433; d. 1499) and Giovanni Pico della Mirandola (b. 1453; d. 1494) – who, inspired by the rediscovery of the works of Plato and Plotinus (see Chapters 1 and 3), regarded "magic" as an elementary force pervading all sorts of natural processes. Accordingly, they promoted *magia naturalis* to the rank of a new philosophical discipline that ought to systematically investigate this natural force. With this novel concept, Ficino and Pico influenced fifteenth- and sixteenth-century scholars such as Johannes Reuchlin, Johannes Trithemius, Agrippa of Nettesheim, Theophrastus of Hohenheim (also known as Paracelsus), Giordano Bruno and others. We reprint one important example of this first scholarly discourse of "magic" in Western history – namely, an excerpt from Agrippa of Nettesheim's extensive work *De occulta philosophia* (see Chapter 8).

The concept of "natural magic" remained influential in some scholarly milieus but could not fundamentally alter the negative perception of "magic" predominant in Western discourse. The increasing success of natural sciences and, in particular, the philosophical movement of Enlightenment contested the notion of *magia naturalis*, mostly by criticizing its alleged fallaciousness and charlatanry. We reprint one representative anti-magical text of the Enlightenment discourse in eighteenth-century France – namely, Diderot's article "Magie" in his *Encyclopédie, ou Dictionnaire raisonné des sciences, des arts et des métiers* (see Chapter 9).

While the Enlightenment movement adopted traditional anti-magical rhetoric as part of its agenda of human rationality, there also existed anti-Enlightenment movements that retained a positive view of "magic". The last text in this part, written by the Russian occultist Helena Petrovna Blavatsky during the late nineteenth century (see Chapter 10), illustrates this continuous stream of positive interpretations of "magic" in Western history. While the precise semantic meaning of "magic" in Blavatsky's work remains fuzzy, our text brings home the point that the late nineteenth century founding fathers of the academic discourse could, in fact, have chosen very different contemporary models of defining "magic". Yet, they adopted, for the most part, traditional Western stereotypes – in particular, the notions of irrationality ("magic" as false "science") and of a-religiosity ("magic" as false "religion"). The texts presented in Part I show that these polemical notions are deeply rooted in the conceptual history of "magic". Their "survival" in academic discourse has made the concept particularly vulnerable to criticism and been one of the main reasons why, in recent decades, some scholars have opted for abandoning the category.

# 1

# PLATO

*Alcibiades* I 120e–122c, translation W. R. M. Lamb
*Laws* 933c–e, translation Marios Skempis

Although he neither wrote systematically nor extensively on the topic, Plato (b. 428/427 BCE; d. 348/47 BCE) played a formative role in shaping Western discourses of "magic". The two statements presented here – *Alcibiades* I 120e–122c and *Laws* 933c–e – albeit contradictory, exerted a major influence on later writers.

The *Alcibiades* I, a work dubiously ascribed to Plato, discusses the traits and skills that a potential political leader such as the young aristocrat Alcibiades, Socrates' interlocutor in the dialogue, ought to possess. In our passage, Socrates refers to the Persian kings and their manners of educating their sons; we learn that at the age of fourteen the Persian princes learn "magic" (Greek "μαγεία", translated by Bury as "magian Lore") from the "wisest" teacher in the Persian Empire. "Magic" is here defined as "worship of the gods" (θεῶν θεραπεία) – an apparently positive statement often quoted by later authors who intended to valorize the concept (see, e.g., Chapter 10 in this volume). Furthermore, the *Alcibiades* I is one of the first extant texts that links Zoroaster to the concept of "magic", another idea that had substantial impact upon later authors who advanced Zoroaster to the rank of one of the founding fathers of "magic" (see Chapters 2 and 5; see in more detail Stausberg 1998 I: 503–69). However, Plato's definition in the *Alcibiades* I hardly had any influence on modern academic definitions of "magic", the more so since "worship of the gods" is typically subsumed under the concept of "religion".

In the eleventh book of his *Laws*, Plato, on the other hand, puts forth a law against *pharmakeía*. In ancient texts, the term *pharmakeía* can be used as a rough synonym of *mageía*, but it has different etymological roots (*pharmakon* can mean "poison", "medicine", "herb", "drug", or "charm") and thereby refers to different things. In our excerpt, *pharmakeía* refers to methods of harming someone by means of substances ("drinks, foods and unguents") or verbal practices ("binding spells or conjurations or incantations") – that is, by methods whose *modus operandi* is not perceptible (contrary to, for instance, injuring someone with a knife). Plato's law against *pharmakeía* derives from his law against *asebeía* ("blasphemy", "impiety"), which is described shortly before our passage, in the end of the tenth book (*Laws* 907d–910d). Accordingly, Plato claims that people offering *pharmakeía* to upright citizens of Athens act blasphemously as they believe that "the gods are easy to win over when bribed by offerings and prayers" (*Laws* 885b, trans. Bury 1926: 299). Plato systematically questions this belief (*Laws* 905d–907d), inasmuch as he regards these persons as "ravening beasts" that despise men and "try thus to wreck utterly not only individuals, but whole families and States for the sake of money" (*Laws* 909a–c; Bury 1926: 383). Hence, in the end of our text, Plato proposes harsh punishments for specialists of *pharmakeía*, while suggesting more moderate adjudgements for laymen. Note that Greek *asebeía* is the antonym to Greek *eusebeía*, a term often associated with the modern concept of "religion". Thus, Plato provides us with the first opposition, at least in Classical Greece, between *eusebeía* and *pharmakeía*, an opposition equivalent, in some modern translations, to "religion" and "magic".

Plato's contribution to Western discourses of "magic" appears, therefore, as ambivalent. On the one hand, the *Alcibiades* I offered later authors the possibility to claim that "magic" is nothing else than "religion" – by arguing that this classification purely depends upon one's perspective. The Roman philosopher Apuleius of Madaurus (b. ca. 125 CE; d. ca. 180 CE), who was accused of being a "magician" in a public court case around 158 CE, takes up this argument when he asks the court "what a magician really is. For, if what I read in most authors is correct, that 'magician' is the Persian word for our 'priest', what crime is involved in it? Can it be wrong to be a priest, to have the proper knowledge, competence, and experience of ceremonial rules, sacred rituals, and religious laws? This, at least, is how Plato interprets 'magic', when he examines the branches of study in which, among the Persians, a young heir to the throne is educated" (Apuleius, *Apol.* 25.9f, transl. Harrison and Hunink 2001: 50). On the other hand, Plato's idea of "religion" (*eusebeía*), as sketched out in the tenth and eleventh books of the *Laws*, which is based on a devout, selfless belief in morally irreprehensible gods, prompted later polemics against "magic" that centred around the coercion and blasphemy argument. Plato's desire to put forth a law against *pharmakeía* seems to anticipate various Roman statutes addressing "magic" (*Lex Cornelia de sicariis et veneficis*; *Codex Theodosianus* 9.16.3f), which also influenced mediaeval and early modern European juridical discussions of the *crimen magiae*. Turning to modern academic discourse, Plato's opposition of *eusebeía* and *pharmakeía* could be held to anticipate James G. Frazer's distinction of coercion ("magic") and submission ("religion") (see Chapter 12).

# *ALCIBIADES* I 120e–122c

SOC. Then let us consider, by comparing our lot with theirs, whether the Spartan and Persian kings appear to be of inferior birth. Do we not know that the former are descendants of Hercules and the latter of Achaemenes, and that the line of Hercules and the line of Achaemenes go back to Perseus, son of Zeus?
ALC. Yes, and mine, Socrates, to Eurysaces, and that of Eurysaces to Zeus!
SOC. Yes, and mine, noble Alcibiades, to Daedalus, and Daedalus to Hephaestus, son of Zeus! But take the lines of those people,[1] going back from them: you have a succession

---

1. The kings of Sparta and Persia.

of kings reaching to Zeus – on the one hand, kings of Argos and Sparta; on the other, of Persia, which they have always ruled, and frequently Asia also, as at present; whereas we are private persons ourselves, and so were our fathers. And then, suppose that you had to make what show you could of your ancestors, and of Salamis as the native land of Eurysaces, or of Aegina as the home of the yet earlier Aeacus, to impress Artaxerxes, son of Xerxes, how you must expect to be laughed at! Why, I am afraid we are quite outdone by those persons in pride of birth and upbringing altogether. Or have you not observed how great are the advantages of the Spartan kings, and how their wives are kept under statutory ward of the ephors, in order that every possible precaution may be taken against the king being born of any but the Heracleidae? And the Persian king is so pre-eminent that no one has a suspicion that an heir could have been born of anybody but the king; and hence the king's wife has nothing to guard her except fear. When the eldest son, the heir to the throne, is born, first of all the king's subjects who are in his palace have a feast, and then for ever after on that date the whole of Asia celebrates the king's birthday with sacrifice and feasting: but when we are born, as the comic poet[2] says, "even the neighbours barely notice it", Alcibiades. After that comes the nurture of the child, not at the hands of a woman-nurse of little worth, but of the most highly approved eunuchs in the king's service, who are charged with the whole tendance of the new-born child, and especially with the business of making him as handsome as possible by moulding his limbs into a correct shape; and while doing this they are in high honour. When the boys are seven years old they are given horses and have riding lessons, and they begin to follow the chase. And when the boy reaches fourteen years he is taken over by the royal tutors, as they call them there: these are four men chosen as the most highly esteemed among the Persians of mature age, namely, the wisest one, the justest one, the most temperate one, and the bravest one. The first of these teaches him the magian lore of Zoroaster, son of Horomazes; and that is the worship of the gods: he teaches him also what pertains to a king. The justest teaches him to be truthful all his life long; the most temperate, not to be mastered by even a single pleasure, in order that he may be accustomed to be a free man and a veritable king, who is the master first of all that is in him, not the slave; while the bravest trains him to be fearless and undaunted, telling him that to be daunted is to be enslaved. But you, Alcibiades, had a tutor set over you by Pericles from amongst his servants, who was so old as to be the most useless of them, Zopyrus the Thracian. I might describe to you at length the nurture and education of your competitors, were it not too much of a task; and besides, what I have said suffices to show the rest that follows thereon. But about your birth, Alcibiades, or nurture or education, or about those of any other Athenian, one may say that nobody cares, unless it be some lover whom you chance to have. And again, if you chose to glance at the wealth, the luxury, the robes with sweeping trains, the anointings with myrrh, the attendant troops of menials, and all the other refinements of the Persians, you would be ashamed at your own case, on perceiving its inferiority to theirs.

---

2. The saying, which became proverbial, is thought to have occurred in one of the (now lost) plays of Plato, the Athenian comic poet, who lived c. 460–369 BC.

## *LAWS* 933C–E

The fatal incidents in which someone causes injury to another person by means of *pharmaka* have been discussed in length. But those incidents in which one causes harm on purpose and beforehand by means of drinks, foods and unguents have not been dealt with as yet. And since there are two kinds of *pharmakeia*, one has to treat them separately. The one we have thoroughly dealt with just now inflicts damage on bodies by bodies according to the law of nature. Yet the other one, which, drawing on trickeries, incantations and the so-called binding spells, convinces those who dare to cause harm that they can do so, and others that they have been harmed by whoever is empowered to practice *goēteía*. Precisely how these things and their cognates stand, it is difficult to know, and even if one knows, it is difficult to convince others. It is no use trying to convince the souls of those who are distrustful to one another with respect to this sort of things and urge them to take no heed of such signs, should they come across moulded images of wax at doorways, at crossroads or at the tombs of their parents, since we are ourselves still to shape a clear view of them. Given the need for a twofold distinction concerning the law about *pharmakeia* according to which way one makes an attempt at poisoning, first we have to encourage and advise them that they should not proceed to such an act nor scare the majority of people who are frightened in a childlike manner nor compel the lawgiver and the judge to liberate people from such fears, since the person who makes an attempt at poisoning in the first place cannot be in full control of his actions either as far as the bodies are concerned, unless he is a doctor, or with regard to trickeries, unless he is a seer or a diviner. So let us formulate the following law about *pharmakeia*. Whoever resorts to poisoning with the intent to injure someone not in an harmful way either for himself or his relatives or with the intent to harm his herds or his hives, he should be sentenced to death, if he is a doctor or he is found guilty of poisoning; or it should be left to the court to decide what he should suffer or pay, if he is a layman. In case he appears to be one who causes harm by means of binding spells or conjurations or incantations or anything of this sort of *pharmakeia*, he should be sentenced to death, if he is a seer or a diviner. But in case he is unaware of the *pharmakeia* pertinent to a diviner, he should suffer the same sentence as the layman guilty of poisoning. For in his case, too, the court is to decide what he should suffer or pay.

# 2

# PLINY THE ELDER

*Historia Naturalis* 30.1–6, translation W. H. S. Jones

The *Historia Naturalis* (HN) of Gaius Plinius Secundus (b. 23 CE; d. 79 CE) is the oldest extant encyclopaedic work in Latin comprising 37 volumes and 2493 chapters on all aspects of (ancient) knowledge. Its wide scope, consistent reference to sources and comprehensive list of contents in the beginning of the HN made it a model for many later encyclopaedias. The passage presented here stems from the beginning of Book 30, which forms part of a set of twelve books treating botany, pharmacology and medicine (Books 20 to 32) and, in particular, of five books on remedies made from animals (Books 28 to 32).

The excerpt represents the first attested attempt to historicize "magic". Pliny's historical synopsis suggests, however, that there must have been in circulation more Greek and Latin works about "magic" during the first century CE. Due to the variety of these sources, the text is complex; therefore, we limit ourselves to a few general observations. Pliny claims that "magic" originated from medicine and additionally adopted the powers of "religion" and "astrology" in order to hold "men's emotions in a three-fold bond" (HN 30.1). Taking a closer look at the various "magicians" mentioned in our text, one wonders, however, whether there is a semantic bond that holds them together – he classifies, among others, Zoroaster, mythological figures from Homer (the Sirens, Circe, Teiresias), the Thessalians, Orpheus, Osthanes, Greek philosophers (Pythagoras, Empedocles, Democritus, Plato), Moses and the Jews, and even the Gallic druids as experts in the field. Given the very diverse origins of these figures, Pliny's concept of "magic" does not seem to imply clear semantic criteria, but rather operates as an umbrella term for a vast variety of alien, uncertain or deviant beliefs and practices perceived as being "fundamentally antithetical and external to Roman Culture" (Ogden 2002: 44). Pliny even claims that the Romans, in 97 BCE, finally managed to forbid human sacrifice: "It is beyond calculation how great is the debt owed to the Romans, who swept away the monstrous rites, in which to kill a man was the highest religious duty and for him to be eaten a passport to health" (HN 30.4).

Given the polemical intent of these remarks, our text counts as an example of the "deviance theory" (see the General Introduction in this volume). Whenever Pliny speaks of "magicians" in the HN, he drops remarks about the inefficacy of their practices, the fallaciousness of their knowledge and their "fraudulent lies" (HN 30.1; see also HN 22.20; 28.12; 30.18; 32.34; 37.155, etc.). In Pliny's view, "magic is detestable, vain, and idle; and though it has what I might call shadows of truth, their power comes from the art of the poisoner" (HN 30.6). Despite these negative evaluations, however, Pliny believes in the immense cultural influence, historical persistence and worldwide reputation of "magic" as "the most fraudulent of arts has held complete sway throughout the world for many ages" (HN 30.1). His strategy of subsuming a large amount of apparently heterogeneous phenomena under the concept of "magic" is echoed by modern scholars who were themselves, to use the words of Randall Styers, "culling diverse forms of behaviour, modes of knowledge, social practices, and habits from an indiscriminate range of cultural systems and historical epochs and transmogrifying them into a unified phenomenon" (Styers 2004: 223).

## *HISTORIA NATURALIS* 30.1–6

I. IN the previous part of my work I have often indeed refuted the fraudulent lies of the Magi, whenever the subject and the occasion required it, and I shall continue to expose them. In a few respects, however, the theme deserves[1] to be enlarged upon, were it only because the most fraudulent of arts has held complete sway throughout the world for many ages. Nobody should be surprised at the greatness of its influence, since alone of the arts it has embraced three others that hold supreme dominion over the human mind, and made them subject to itself alone. Nobody will doubt that it first arose from medicine, and that professing to promote health it insidiously advanced under the disguise of a higher and holier system; that to the most seductive and welcome promises it added the powers of religion, about which even today the human race is quite in the dark; that again meeting with success it made a further addition of astrology, because there is nobody who is not eager to learn his destiny, or who does not believe that the truest account of it is that gained by watching the skies. Accordingly, holding men's emotions in a three-fold bond, magic rose to such a height that even today it has sway over a great part of mankind, and in the East commands the Kings of Kings.

II. Without doubt magic arose in Persia with Zoroaster. On this our authorities are agreed, but whether he was the only one of that name, or whether there was also another afterwards, is not clear. Eudoxus, who wished magic to be acknowledged as the noblest and most useful of the schools of philosophy, declared that this Zoroaster lived six thousand years before Plato's death, and Aristotle agrees with him. Hermippus, a most studious writer about every aspect of magic, and an exponent of two million verses composed by Zoroaster, added summaries[2] to his rolls, and gave Agonaces as the teacher by whom he[3] said that he had been instructed, assigning to the man himself a date five thousand years before the Trojan War. What especially is surprising is the survival, through so long a period, of the craft and its tradition; treatises are wanting, and besides there is no line of

---

1. Or "Few themes deserve more to receive fuller treatment."
2. An *index* might be a mere title or a brief list of contents (or both).
3. The omission of the pronouns makes the subject of *diceret* uncertain – Zoroaster or Hermippus.

distinguished or continuous successors to keep alive their memory. For how few know anything, even by hearsay, of those who alone have left their names but without other memorial – Apusorus and Zaratus of Media, Marmarus and Arabantiphocus of Babylon, or Tarmoendas of Assyria? The most surprising thing, however, is the complete silence of Homer about magic in his poem on the Trojan War, and yet so much of his work in the wanderings of Ulysses is so occupied with it that it alone forms the backbone of the whole work, if indeed they put a magical interpretation upon the Proteus episode in Homer and the songs of the Sirens, and especially upon the episode of Circe and of the calling up of the dead from Hades, of which magic is the sole theme. And in later times nobody has explained how ever it reached Telmesus, a city given up to superstition, or when it passed over to the Thessalian matrons, whose surname[4] was long proverbial in our part of the world, although magic was a craft repugnant to the Thessalian people, who were content, at any rate in the Trojan period, with the medicines of Chiron, and with the War God as the only wielder of the thunderbolt.[5] I am indeed surprised that the people over whom Achilles once ruled had a reputation for magic so lasting that actually Menander, a man with an unrivalled gift for sound literary taste, gave the name "Thessala" to his comedy, which deals fully with the tricks of the women for calling down the moon. I would believe that Orpheus was the first to carry the craft to his near neighbours, and that his superstition grew from medicine, if the whole of Thrace, the home of Orpheus, had not been untainted by magic. The first man, so far as I can discover, to write a still-extant treatise on magic was Osthanes, who accompanied the Persian King Xerxes in his invasion of Greece, and sowed what I may call the seeds of this monstrous craft, infecting the whole world by the way at every stage of their travels. A little before Osthanes, the more careful inquirers place another Zoroaster, a native of Proconnesus. One thing is certain; it was this Osthanes who chiefly roused among the Greek peoples not so much an eager appetite for his science as a sheer mania. And yet I notice that of old, in fact almost always, the highest literary distinction and renown have been sought from that science. Certainly Pythagoras, Empedocles, Democritus and Plato went overseas to learn it, going into exile rather than on a journey, taught it openly on their return, and considered it one of their most treasured secrets. Democritus expounded Apollobex the Copt and Dardanus the Phoenician, entering the latter's tomb to obtain his works and basing his own on their doctrines. That these were accepted by any human beings and transmitted by memory is the most extraordinary phenomenon in history; so utterly are they lacking in credibility and decency that those who like the other works of Democritus deny that the magical books are his. But it is all to no purpose, for it is certain that Democritus especially instilled into men's minds the sweets of magic. Another extraordinary thing is that both these arts, medicine I mean and magic, flourished together, Democritus expounding magic in the same age as Hippocrates expounded medicine, about the time of the Peloponnesian War, which was waged in Greece from the three-hundredth year of our city. There is yet another branch

---

4. That is, "Thessalian". The word suggested witchcraft.
5. With the reading *fulminanti*: "whose only thunder was that of their War God".

of magic, derived from Moses, Jannes, Lotapes,[6] and the Jews, but living many thousand years after Zoroaster. So much more recent is the branch in Cyprus. In the time too of Alexander the Great, no slight addition was made to the influence of the profession by a second Osthanes, who, honoured by his attendance on Alexander, travelled certainly without the slightest doubt all over the world.

III. Among Italian tribes also there still certainly exist traces of magic in the Twelve Tables, as is proved by my own and the other evidence set forth in an earlier Book.[7] It was not until the 657th year of the City[8] that in the consulship of Gnaeus Cornelius Lentulus and Publius Licinius Crassus there was passed a resolution of the Senate forbidding human sacrifice; so that down to that date it is manifest that such abominable rites were practised.

IV. Magic certainly found a home in the two Gallic provinces, and that down to living memory. For the principate of Tiberius Caesar did away with their Druids and this tribe of seers and medicine men. But why should I speak of these things when the craft has even crossed the Ocean and reached the empty voids of Nature? Even today Britain practises magic in awe, with such grand ritual that it might seem that she gave it to the universal is the cult of magic[9] throughout the world, although its nations disagree or are unknown to each other. It is beyond calculation how great is the debt owed to the Romans, who swept away the monstrous rites, in which to kill a man was the highest religious duty and for him to be eaten a passport to health.

V. As Osthanes said, there are several forms of magic; he professes to divine from water, globes, air, stars, lamps, basins and axes, and by many other methods, and besides to converse with ghosts and those in the underworld. All of these in our generation the Emperor Nero discovered to be lies and frauds. In fact his passion for the lyre and tragic song was no greater than his passion for magic; his elevation to the greatest height of human fortune aroused desire in the vicious depths of his mind; his greatest wish was to issue commands to the gods, and he could rise to no nobler ambition. No other of the arts ever had a more enthusiastic patron. Every means were his to gratify his desire – wealth, strength, aptitude for learning – and what else did the world not allow! That the craft is a fraud there could be no greater or more indisputable proof than that Nero abandoned it; but would that he had consulted about his suspicions the powers of Hell and any other gods whatsoever, instead of entrusting these researches to pimps and harlots. Of a surety no ceremony, outlandish and savage though the rites may be, would not have been gentler than Nero's thoughts; more cruelly behaving than any did Nero thus fill our Rome with ghosts.

VI. The Magi have certain means of evasion; for example that the gods neither obey those with freckles nor are seen by them. Was this perhaps their objection to Nero? But his body was without blemish; he was free to choose the fixed days, could easily obtain

---

6. See Torrey, *The Magic of Lotapes* (Journal of Biblical Literature, 1949, 325–27). Pliny should have written Iotape = ἰῶτα πῆ = Yahweh. Jannes was not a Hebrew but an Egyptian magician who competed with Moses. See *Epistle to Timothy*, II. 3, 8.
7. XXVIII. § 17.
8. 97 BC.
9. Or "agreement in that subject of magic".

perfectly black sheep, and as for human sacrifice, he took the greatest delight in it. Tiridates the Magus had come to him bringing a retinue for the Armenian triumph over himself, thereby laying a heavy burden on the provinces. He had refused to travel by sea, for the Magi hold it sin to spit into the sea or wrong that element by other necessary functions of mortal creatures. He had brought Magi with him, had initiated Nero into their banquets; yet the man giving him a kingdom was unable to acquire from him the magic art. Therefore let us be convinced by this that magic is detestable, vain, and idle; and though it has what I might call shadows of truth, their power comes from the art of the poisoner, not of the Magi. One might well ask what were the lies of the old Magi, when as a youth I saw Apion the grammarian, who told me that the herb cynocephalia, called in Egypt osiritis, was an instrument of divination and a protection from all kinds of sorcery, but if it were uprooted altogether the digger would die at once, and that he had called up ghosts to inquire from Homer his native country and the name of his parents, but did not dare to repeat the answers which he said were given.

# 3

# PLOTINUS

*Enneads* 4.4.40–43, translation A. H. Armstrong

In his *Enneads*, Plotinus (b. 205 CE; d. 270 CE) developed one of the first extant theories of "magic". Plotinus is generally regarded as the founder of Neoplatonism, a late antique philosophical school that represents a new phase in the history of interpretation of the Platonic tradition. The *Enneads* consist of fifty-four treatises, edited and arranged into six groups of nine texts by Porphyry, his most famous pupil (Greek *ennea*: "nine"). The passage presented here is part of the fourth treatise of the fourth *Ennead* (modern scholars number the *Enneads* in their chronological order, classifying our treatise as number twenty-eight); it is the second of three treatises bearing the title "On difficulties about the soul".

Compared to other ancient sources, Plotinus' theory of "magic" (most often he uses the Greek term *goēteía* as a synonym of *mageía*) has some unique features. First, instead of referring to transcendent beings, Plotinus claims that cosmic "sympathy" (*sympatheía*) underlies the works of "magic" (*mageía/goēteía*). For Plotinus, *sympatheía* signifies an all-pervading force that ties all existing things together. Accordingly, "magic" works by ritually activating or controlling *sympatheía*; to give one example, Plotinus points to the widely attested practice of ancient love charms. Second, Plotinus claims that there is no general difference between the effects of "magic" and those of "prayer" as he assumes a "natural drawing power in spells" (*Enneads* 4.4.40); here, Plotinus seems to parallel "magic" with established religious ritual. Third, his perception of "magic" is not altogether negative: Plotinus even holds that "magic" – now he uses the Greek term *mageía* – is responsible for all cosmic processes of attraction and repulsion: "the true magic is the 'Love' and also the 'Strife' in the All" (*Enneads* 4.4.40). This idea influenced the early modern concept of *magia naturalis* (see Chapter 8), which was, in fact, inspired by the rediscovery of the *Enneads*.

Nevertheless, Plotinus ultimately dismisses "magic" because the final objective of his philosophy implies the ascension of the individual soul to God, a process that involves the overcoming of bodily desires and lower emotions. Plotinus regards "magic" as an obstacle for the soul's ascension because the motives usually associated with the practice of "magic" in antiquity (gaining love or wealth, harming others, foreseeing the future, etc.) correspond to these lower emotions and bind the soul to human affairs. He asserts that only the mind is capable of resisting the many allurements of human existence, including the influence of *sympatheía*: "Contemplation alone remains incapable of enchantment because no one who is self-directed is subject to enchantment" (*Enneads* 4.4.44).

One cannot overestimate Plotinus' impact upon Western discourses of "magic". However, his reception by modern theorists of "magic" remains unclear. Did Plotinus' concept of *sympatheía* influence James George Frazer's theory of "sympathetic magic" (see Chapter 12)? Frazer gives no clear answer to that – he may have adopted the term from Tylor's *Primitive Culture* (see Chapter 11), who, in turn, could have taken it from the nineteenth-century mesmerist William Gregory (see Otto 2011: 627f). Even if there has been an indirect influence, the shift in meaning is striking: *sympatheía*, for Plotinus an aspect of the world soul and, therefore, itself a godly force, appears in Frazer's work as a primitive, illusionary principle of thought based on a false association of ideas.

## *ENNEADS* 4.4.40F

40. But how do magic spells work? By sympathy and by the fact that there is a natural concord of things that are alike and opposition of things that are different, and by the rich variety of the many powers which go to make up the life of the one living creature. For many things are drawn and enchanted without anyone else's magical contrivance: and the true magic is the "Love" and also the "Strife" in the All.[1] And this is the primary wizard and enchanter, from observing whom men came to use his philtres and spells on each other. For, because love is natural to men and the things that cause love have a force of attraction to each other, there has come into existence the helpful power of a magical art of love, used by those who apply by contact to different people different magical substances designed to draw them together and with a love-force implanted in them; they join one soul to another, as if they were training together plants set at intervals. They use as well figures with power in them, and by putting themselves into the right postures they quietly bring powers upon themselves, since they are within one universe and work upon one universe. For if anyone put a magician outside the All, he could not draw or bring down by attractive or binding spells. But now, because he does not operate as if he were somewhere else, he can work on his subjects knowing by what way one thing is drawn to another in the living being. And there is a natural drawing power in spells wrought by the tune and the particular intonation and posture of the magician – for these things attract, as pitiable figures and voices attract; for it is the irrational soul – not the power of choice or the reason – which is charmed by music, and this kind of magic causes no surprise: people even like being enchanted, even if this is not exactly what they demand from the musicians. And we must not think that other kinds of prayers either are freely

---

1. The reference is to Empedocles: cp. e.g. fr. B 17, 19–20. This and the following chapters make clear that magic was for Plotinus a manipulation of natural forces, attractions and sympathies resulting from the living organic unity of the physical universe. His interest in it was philosophical rather than practical. An idea of the sort of magic of which Plotinus is thinking can be obtained from the spells published in the *Papyri Graecae Magicae*, ed. and trans. K. Preisendanz (2 volumes, Berlin and Leipzig, 1928, 1931).

PART I: HISTORICAL SOURCES

and deliberately answered: for people charmed by spells do not act with free deliberation, nor, when a snake fascinates men, does the one who is fascinated understand or perceive what is happening, but he knows only afterwards that he has had the experience; his ruling intellect, however, remains unaffected. But, when a man prays to a heavenly body, some influence comes from it upon him or upon another person.

41. But the sun, or another heavenly body, does not hear his prayers. And that which he prays for comes about because one part is in sympathetic connection with another, just as in one tense string; for if the string is plucked at the lower end, it has a vibration at the upper. But often, too, when one string is plucked another has a kind of sense of this by its concord and the fact that it is tuned to the same scale. But if the vibration can even pass from one lyre to another in so far as a sympathy exists, then there is also one single harmony in the All, even if it is composed of opposites; and it is in fact composed of parts which are alike and all akin, even when they are opposites. And all the things which harm men do not come with the intention of harming, but as when the passionate spirit is drawn down with the bile and enters the nature of the liver; just as if someone, taking a light from a fire, hurts someone else – either the person who has made arrangements to go or that one who took it does the damage by having given some fire to someone who, in a way, moves it about from one place to another; and the fire which has come hurts if the person to whom it was transferred was unable to take hold of it.[2]

42. So there will be no need for the heavenly bodies to have memory, either, for this purpose [of answering prayers] – this was the reason why this investigation was undertaken – or sense-perceptions arising from the lower world; nor, if we look at it in this way, do they deliberately choose to attend to prayers, but we must admit that some influence comes from them both with and without prayer in so far as they are parts, and parts of one whole; and that there are many powers which work even without deliberate choice, both without contrivance and with [magic] art, as in a single living being; and one thing is benefited and harmed by another because it is naturally so disposed, and by the arts of physicians and magicians one thing is compelled to give something of its power to another. And in the same way the All gives to its parts, both spontaneously and if someone else magically attracts [its power] to a part of it; for it lies at the disposal of its parts by its own natural disposition, and so the one who makes the prayer is no alien. But if the man who prays is evil, there is no need to be surprised; for the wicked draw water from the streams and that which gives does not know itself to what it gives, but only gives; but all the same that which is given is also co-ordinated with the nature of the All; so that if someone takes what he ought not from what lies at the disposal of all, justice pursues him by an inevitable law. We must not therefore assume that the All can be affected; or we must grant that its ruling principle is altogether impassable, and when the parts come to be affected, the affection penetrates to them, but since there is nothing there which is contrary to the nature of the All, it is unaffected, directed as it is towards itself. For the heavenly bodies,

---

2. The text here is very uncertain. H.-S.'s critical note, printed under the Greek text, gives the principal suggestions for improvement. I, very hesitantly, follow Cilento's suggestion (see his commentary *ad loc*) in my translation, as it gives some sort of sense without too violent alteration.

too, in so far as they are parts, are subject to affections; they are however impassable in themselves, because their powers of choice, as well [as that of the All], cannot be affected and their bodies and natures remain unharmed, and if they give something by means of their soul, their soul is not diminished and their bodies remain the same, and if anything flows from them, it goes imperceptibly, and if anything is added to them, it is unnoticed.

43. But how is the good man affected by magic and drugs? He is incapable of being affected in his soul by enchantment, and his rational part would not be affected, nor would he change his mind; but he would be affected in whatever part of the irrational in the All there is in him, or rather this part would be affected; but he will feel no passionate loves provoked by drugs, if falling in love happens when one soul assents to the affection of the other. But, just as the irrational part of him is affected by incantations, so he himself by counter-chants and counter-incantations will dissolve the powers on the other side.[3] But he might suffer death or illnesses or anything bodily from such incantations; for the part of the All [in him] would be affected by another part or by the All, but he himself would be unharmed. (That the effects of magic do not follow immediately, but later, is not out of line with nature.) But spirits themselves, also, are not incapable of being affected in their irrational part; it is not out of place to ascribe memory and sense-perceptions to them and to grant that they are charmed by attractions appropriate to their nature and that those of them who are nearer to the things here below hear the prayers of those who call upon them according to the degree of their concern with things here below. For everything which is directed to something else is enchanted by something else; for that to which it is directed enchants and draws it; but only that which is self-directed is free from enchantment. For this reason all practical action is under enchantment, and the whole life of the practical man: for he is moved to that which charms him. This is the reason for saying "The citizen body of great-hearted Erectheus looks attractive".[4] For why does a man direct himself to something else? He is drawn not by the arts of wizards but of nature, which brings illusion and links one thing to another not spatially but by the magic draughts which it gives.

44. Contemplation alone remains incapable of enchantment because no one who is self-directed is subject to enchantment: for he is one, and that which he contemplates is himself, and his reason is not deluded, but he makes what he ought and makes his own life and work. But in practical life there is no self-possession, and the reason does not produce

---

3. I still think it probable that, although ἐπῳδαῖς in this sentence means ordinary magic spells, when Plotinus speaks of the σπουδαῖος as ἀντᾴδων καὶ ἀντεπᾴδων, he is thinking of Plato's metaphorical use of ἐπῳδή for salutary philosophical exhortation in *Charmides* 156-7. He uses the word himself in this way, of the highest sort of philosophy, in V. 3. 17. 18–20. For a further discussion of this passage and, in general, of the attitude of Plotinus to magic, see my contribution to Armstrong, Arthur Hilary (ed.). 1967. *Cambridge History of Later Greek and Early Medieval Philosophy*, Cambridge, pp207–8, and the literature there referred to.

4. This is a reference to Plato *Alcibiades* I 132A5, where Plato is adapting *Iliad* 2.547 to his own purposes. Plato adds "but you ought to see it undressed", and the context is the attempt by Socrates to prevent Alcibiades from being corrupted by falling in love with the Athenian *demos*. This serves Plotinus as a good Platonic illustration of the charms of the lower world, which are always illusory, whether political or sexual.

the impulse, but the irrational also has an origin in the premises derived from the affection. For the care of children and concern for marriage have a manifest drawing power, and so do all the things caused by our carnal desires; political activity and the pursuit of office have the desire of power in us provoking them. And the activities which are undertaken to avoid suffering have fear as their origin, and those for the sake of getting more, carnal desire. Those undertaken because of necessary requirements, since they seek to satisfy a need of nature, obviously have the force of nature behind them making survival our own essential concern. But if someone says that noble practical activities are free from enchantment, or, if they are not, contemplation also, which is of noble objects, is under enchantment, [the answer is] that if one carries out the so-called noble activities as necessary ones, and grasps that what is really noble is something else, one has not been enchanted – for one knows the necessity, and does not look to this world, and one's life is not directed to other things – but one has been enchanted in this way by the force of human nature and by the essential concern for the survival of others, or indeed of oneself – for it seems, perhaps, reasonable not to take oneself out of this world on account of this essential concern. But if one is content with the nobility in practical activities, and chooses activity because one is deluded by its vestiges of nobility, one has been enchanted in one's pursuit of the nobility in the lower world; for, in general, to be actively occupied with the semblance of truth and drawn towards it in any way is characteristic of someone who has been deluded by the forces which draw one to the lower world: this is what the magic of nature does; for to pursue what is not good as if it was good, drawn by the appearance of good by irrational impulses, belongs to one who is being ignorantly led where he does not want to go. And what would anyone call this other than magical enchantment? The man, then, is alone free from enchantment who when his other parts are trying to draw him says that none of the things are good which they declare to be so, but only that which he knows himself, not deluded or pursuing, but possessing it. So he would not be drawn in any direction.

# 4

# AUGUSTINE OF HIPPO

*City of God* 21.6, translation Marcus Dods
*On Christian Doctrine* 2.20.30–2.24.37, translation William Benton

Augustine of Hippo (b. 354 CE; d. 430 CE) was the first Christian author to develop a comprehensive theory of "magic". Due to Augustine's impact upon Christian theology, this theory has had a lasting imprint on the Christian concept of "magic" up to the present day. The first excerpt is taken from his work *City of God* (*De civitate dei*) that was written in the aftermath of the pillage of Rome by the Visigoths in 410 CE. To explain this event, Augustine suggests a distinction between the "earthly" and the "divine" state. While the latter (the "City of God") could be experienced only by those who believe in the eternal truths of Christianity, the earthly state could be ruled also by unholy satanic forces, among them "magic".

In the excerpt (*City of God* 21.6), Augustine claims that "magic" (Latin *magia*) relies on a pact with demons, the henchmen of Satan who have taught "magic" to humankind in the first place. Accordingly, the material artefacts used in "magical" rites operate as "signs" that provide specific instructions to demons. Augustine develops a complex demonology in order to demonstrate that demons are responsible for the miraculous effects associated with "magic". Due to their aerial bodies, acute senses and infinite lives, they can, at least to some extent, foresee the future (and they also put this "foreseen" future into effect: *City of God* 9.22). By pointing to its dependence upon demons, Augustine seeks to invalidate the ancient practice of divination, a practice lying at the heart of Graeco-Roman religion. Furthermore, demons can deceive the sensory perceptions of humans by generating illusions such as inextinguishable lamps (as in our passage) or humans morphing into animals (see *City of God* 18.18). However, to Augustine, the miraculous effects produced by demons are limited by the framework of God's creation and hence inferior to the "miracles" worked by Judaeo-Christian thaumaturgists. In line with this argument, Augustine asserts that the Egyptian priests mentioned in *Exodus* 7.9f lost against Moses because the superior powers of God and his angels were under his command (*City of God* 10.8). Given the polemical intent of these remarks, Augustine's demonological theory of "magic" served to gloss the inferiority of paganism and, at the same time, the superiority of Christian religion.

But as our second passage (*On Christian Doctrine* 2.20.30–2.24.37) indicates, the semantics of Augustinian "magic" appears to have a wider scope. In his *On Christian Doctrine* (*De doctrina christiana*), Augustine describes how to interpret and teach the holy scriptures properly; in the second book (published in 397) he reflects, among other things, on the value of Graeco-Roman sciences for understanding Christian doctrine. In our excerpt, Augustine discusses "magic" as one of these pagan sciences, subsuming it under the superordinate concept of *"superstitio"*. "Magic" is thus equated not only with idolatry and nature worship, but also with the ritual performance of songs and dances, with amulets, "signs" ("characters") and other material objects. Furthermore, Augustine adds unusual forms of behaviour (such as "to go back to bed if anyone should sneeze when you are putting on your slippers"), divination and astrology to his catalogue of *"superstitio"*. In his view, all these practices ultimately rely on forms of communication with demons. Again, "magic" serves as an umbrella term covering a vast variety of beliefs and practices that are tagged as fallacious and irreligious and are therefore excluded from (Christian) "religion".

Augustine inherited these polemical patterns from former Christian and Graeco-Roman authors (such as Pliny; see Chapter 2); but he was the first to systematically anchor the concept of "magic" in Christian doctrine, a manoeuvre that radicalized the negative impetus of "magic". For Augustine, "magic" is a "demon pact" and thereby implies not only idolatry, but, what is more, blasphemy, an act against God. This classification of "magic" as fallacious, immoral and blasphemous passed on to Christian authors up to the present age. Repercussions (if not "survivals") of these evaluative statements pervade modern theories of "magic", again recalling the impact that the Christian doctrine and terminology had on the academic study of religion\s.

# CITY OF GOD 21.6

## Chap. 6. *That all marvels are not of nature's production, but that some are due to human ingenuity and others to diabolic contrivance*

At this point they will perhaps reply, "These things have no existence; we don't believe one of them; they are travellers' tales and fictitious romances"; and they may add what has the appearance of argument, and say, "If you believe such things as these, believe what is recorded in the same books, that there was or is a temple of Venus in which a candelabrum set in the open air holds a lamp, which burns so strongly that no storm or rain extinguishes it, and which is therefore called, like the stone mentioned, above, the asbestos or inextinguishable lamp." They may say this with the intention of putting us into a dilemma: for if we say this is incredible, then we shall impugn the truth of the other recorded marvels; if, on the other hand, we admit that this is credible, we shall avouch the pagan deities. But, as I have already said in the eighteenth book of this work, we do not hold it necessary to believe all that profane history contains, since, as Varro says, even historians themselves disagree on so many points that one would think they intended and were at pains to do so; but we believe, if we are disposed, those things which are not contradicted by these books, which we do not hesitate to say we are bound to believe. But as to those permanent miracles of nature, whereby we wish to persuade the sceptical of the miracles of the world to come, those are quite sufficient for our purpose which we ourselves can observe, or of which it is not difficult to find trustworthy witnesses. Moreover, that temple of Venus, with its inextinguishable lamp, so far from hemming us into a corner, opens an advantageous field to our argument. For to this inextinguishable lamp we add a host of marvels wrought by men, or by magic – that is, by men under the influence of devils, or by the devils directly – for such marvels we cannot deny without impugning the truth of the sacred Scriptures we believe. That lamp, therefore, was either by some mechanical and human device fitted with asbestos, or it was arranged by magical art in order that the worshippers might be astonished, or some devil under the name of Venus so signally manifested himself that this prodigy both began and became permanent. Now devils are attracted to dwell in certain temples by means of the creatures (God's creatures, not theirs), who present to them what suits their various tastes. They are attracted not by food like animals, but, like spirits, by such symbols as suit their taste, various kinds of stones, woods, plants, animals, songs, rites. And that men may provide these attractions, the devils first of all cunningly seduce them, either by imbuing their hearts with a secret poison, or by revealing themselves under a friendly guise, and thus make a few of them their disciples, who become the instructors of the multitude. For unless they first instructed men, it were impossible to know what each of them desires, what they shrink from, by what name they should be invoked or constrained to be present. Hence the origin of magic and magicians. But, above all, they possess the hearts of men, and are chiefly proud of this possession when they transform themselves into angels of light. Very many things that occur, therefore, are their doing; and these deeds of theirs we ought all the more carefully to shun as we acknowledge them to be very surprising. And yet these very deeds forward my present arguments. For if such marvels are wrought by unclean devils, how much mightier are the holy angels! And what can not that God do Who made the angels themselves capable of working miracles!

If, then, very many effects can be contrived by human art, of so surprising a kind that the uninitiated think them divine, as when, e.g., in a certain temple two magnets have been adjusted, one in the roof, another in the floor, so that an iron image is suspended in mid-air between them, one would suppose by the power of the divinity, were he ignorant of the magnets above and beneath; or, as in the case of that lamp of Venus which we already mentioned as being a skilful adaptation of asbestos; if, again, by the help of magicians, whom Scripture calls sorcerers and enchanters, the devils could gain such power that the noble poet Virgil should consider himself justified in describing a very powerful magician in these lines:

> *Her charms can cure what souls she Please,*
> *Rob other hearts of healthful ease,*
> *Turn rivers backward to their source,*
> *And make the stars forget their course,*
> *And call up ghosts from night:*
> *The ground shall bellow 'neath your feet:*
> *The mountain-ash shall quit its seat,*
> *And travel down the height;*[1]

---

1. Aeneid, BK. IV. 487–491.

If this be so, how much more able is God to do those things which to sceptics are incredible, but to His power easy, since it is He Who has given to stones and all other things their virtue, and to men their skill to use them in wonderful ways; He Who has given to the angels a nature more mighty than that of all that lives on earth; He Whose power surpasses all marvels, and Whose wisdom in working, ordaining, and permitting is no less marvellous in its governance of all things than in its creation of all!

# ON CHRISTIAN DOCTRINE 2.20.30 74F

## Chap. 20. *The superstitious nature of human institutions*

30. All the arrangements made by men for the making and worshipping of idols are superstitious, pertaining as they do either to the worship of what is created or of some part of it as God, or to consultations and arrangements about signs and leagues with devils, such, for example, as are employed in the magical arts, and which the poets are accustomed not so much to teach as to celebrate. And to this class belong, but with a bolder reach of deception, the books of the haruspices and augurs. In this class we must place also all amulets and cures which the medical art condemns, whether these consist in incantations, or in marks which they call *characters*, or in hanging or tying on or even dancing in a fashion certain articles, not with reference to the condition of the body, but to certain signs hidden or manifest; and these remedies they call by the less offensive name of *physica*, so as to appear not to he engaged in superstitious observances, but to be taking advantage of the forces of nature. Examples of these are the ear-rings on the top of each ear, or the rings of ostrich bone on the fingers, or telling you when you hiccup to hold your left thumb in your right hand.

31. To these we may add thousands of the most frivolous practices, that are to be observed if any part of the body should jump, or if, when friends are walking arm-in-arm, a stone, or a dog, or a boy, should come between them. And the kicking of a stone, as if it were a divider of friends, does less harm than to cuff an innocent boy if he happens to run between men who are walking side by side. But it is delightful that the boys are sometimes avenged by the dogs; for frequently men are so superstitious as to venture upon striking a dog who has run between them – not with impunity however, for instead of a superstitious remedy, the dog sometimes makes his assailant run in hot haste for a real surgeon. To this class, too, belong the following rules; To tread upon the threshold when you go out in front of the house; to go back to bed if anyone should sneeze when you are putting on your slippers; to return home if you stumble when going to a place; when your clothes are eaten by mice, to be more frightened at the prospect of coming misfortune than grieved by your present loss. Whence that witty saying of Cato, who, when consulted by a man who told him that the mice had eaten his boots, replied: "That is not strange, but it would have been very strange indeed if the boots had eaten the mice."

### Chap. 21. *Superstition of astrologers*

32. Nor can we exclude from this kind of superstition those who were called *genethliaci*, on account of their attention to birthdays, but are now commonly called *mathernatici*. For these, too, although they may seek with pains for the true position of the stars at the time of our birth, and may sometimes even find it out, yet in so far as they attempt thence to predict our actions, or the consequences of our actions, grievously err, and sell inexperienced men into a miserable bondage. For when any freeman goes to an astrologer of this kind, he gives money that he may come away the slave either of Mars or of Venus, or rather, perhaps, of all the stars to which those who first fell into this error, and handed it on to posterity, have given the names either of beasts on account of their likeness to beasts, or of men with a view to confer honour on those men. And this is not to be wondered at, when we consider that even in times more recent and nearer our own, the Romans made an attempt to dedicate the star which we call Lucifer to the name and honour of Caesar. And this would, perhaps, have been done, and the name handed down to distant ages, only that his ancestress Venus had given her name to this star before him, and could not by any law transfer to her heirs what she had never possessed, nor sought to possess, in life. For where a place was vacant, or not held in honour of any of the dead of former times, the usual proceeding in such cases was carried out. For example, we have changed the names of the months Quintilis and Sextilis to July and August, naming them in honour of the men Julius Caesar and Augustus Caesar; and from this instance anyone who cares can easily see that the stars spoken of above formerly wandered in the heavens without the names they now bear. But as the men were dead whose memory people were either compelled by royal power or impelled by human folly to honour, they seemed to think that in putting their names upon the stars they were raising the dead men themselves to heaven. But whatever they may be called by men, still there are stars which God has made and set in order after His own pleasure, and they have a fixed movement, by which the seasons are distinguished and varied. And when any one is born, it is easy to observe the point at which this movement has arrived, by use of the rules discovered and laid down by those who are rebuked by Holy Writ in these terms: "For if they were able to know so much that they could weigh the world, how did they not more easily find out the Lord thereof?"[2]

### Chap. 22. *The folly of observing the stars in order to predict the events of a life*

33. But to desire to predict the characters, the acts, and the fate of those who are born from such an observation, is a great delusion and great madness. And among those at least who have any sort of acquaintance with matters of this kind (which, indeed, are only fit to be unlearnt again), this superstition is refuted beyond the reach of doubt. For the observation is of the position of the stars, which they call constellations, at the time when the person was born about whom these wretched men are consulted by their still more wretched dupes. Now it may happen that, in the case of twins, one follows the

---

2. Wisd. 13. 9.

other out of the womb so closely that there is no interval of time between them that can be apprehended and marked in the position of the constellations. Whence it necessarily follows that twins are in many cases born under the same stars, while they do not meet with equal fortune either in what they do or what they suffer, but often meet with fates so different that one of them has a most fortunate life, the other a most unfortunate. As, for example, we are told that Esau and Jacob were born twins, and in such close succession, that Jacob, who was born last, was found to have laid hold with his hand upon the heel of his brother, who preceded him?[3] Now, assuredly, the day and hour of the birth of these two could not be marked in any way that would not give both the same constellation. But what a difference there was between the characters, the actions, the labours, and the fortunes of these two, the Scriptures bear witness, which are now so widely spread as to be in the mouth of all nations.

34. Nor is it to the point to say that the very smallest and briefest moment of time that separates the birth of twins produces great effects in nature and in the extremely rapid motion of the heavenly bodies, for, although I may grant that it does produce the greatest effects, yet the astrologer cannot discover this in the constellations, and it is by looking into these that be professes to read the fates. If, then, he does not discover the difference when he examines the constellations, which must, of course, be the same whether he is consulted about Jacob or his brother, what does it profit him that there is a difference in the heavens, which he rashly and carelessly brings into disrepute, when there is no difference in his chart, which he looks into anxiously but in vain? And so these notions also, which have their origin in certain signs of things being arbitrarily fixed upon by the presumption of men, are to be referred to the same class as if they were leagues and covenants with devils.

## Chap. 23. *Why we repudiate arts of divination*

35. For in this way it comes to pass that men who lust after evil things are, by a secret judgment of God, delivered over to be mocked and deceived, as the just reward of their evil desires. For they are deluded and imposed on by the false angels, to whom the lowest part of the world has been put in subjection by the law of God's providence, and in accordance with His most admirable arrangement of things. And the result of these delusions and deceptions is, that through these superstitious and baneful modes of divination, many things in the past and future are made known, and turn out just as they are foretold; and in the case of those who practise superstitious observances, many things turn out agreeably to their observances, and ensnared by these successes, they become more eagerly inquisitive, and involve themselves further and further in a labyrinth of most pernicious error. And to our advantage, the Word of God is not silent about this species of fornication of the soul; and it does not warn the soul against following such practices on the ground that those who profess them speak lies, but it says, "Even if what they tell you should come to pass, hearken not unto them".[4] For though the ghost of the dead Samuel foretold the truth to

---

3. Gen. 25. 24.
4. Cf. Deut. 13. 1–3.

King Saul,[5] that does not make such sacrilegious observances as those by which his ghost was brought up the less detestable; and though the ventriloquist woman[6] in the Acts of the Apostles bore true testimony to the apostles of the Lord, the Apostle Paul did not spare the evil spirit on that account, but rebuked and cast it out, and so made the woman clean.[7]

36. All arts of this sort, therefore, are either nullities, or are part of a guilty superstition, springing out of a baleful fellowship between men and devils, and are to be utterly repudiated and avoided by the Christian as the covenants of a false and treacherous friendship. "Not as if the idol were anything", says the apostle; "but because the things which they sacrifice they sacrifice to devils and not to God; and I would not that ye should have fellowship with devils."[8] Now, what the apostle has said about idols and the sacrifices offered in their honour, that we ought to feel in regard to all fancied signs which lead either to the worship of idols, or to worshipping creation or its parts instead of God, or which are connected with attention to medicinal charms and other observances; for these are not appointed by God as the public means of promoting love towards God and our neighbour, but they waste the hearts of wretched men in private and selfish strivings after temporal things. Accordingly, in regard to all these branches of knowledge, we must fear and shun the fellowship of demons, who, with the Devil their prince, strive only to shut and bar the door against our return. As, then, from the stars which God created and ordained, men have drawn lying omens of their own fancy, so also from things that are born, or in any other way come into existence under the government of God's providence, if there chance only to be something unusual in the occurrence – as when a mule brings forth young, or an object is struck by lightning – men have frequently drawn omens by conjectures of their own, and have committed them to writing, as if they had drawn them by rule.

### Chap. 24. *The intercourse and agreement with demons which superstitious observances maintain*

37. And all these omens are of force just so far as has been arranged with the devils by that previous understanding in the mind which is, as it were, the common language, but they are all full of hurtful curiosity, torturing anxiety, and deadly slavery. For it was not because they had meaning that they were attended to, but it was by attending to and marking them that they came to have meaning. And so they are made different for different people, according to their several notions and prejudices. For those spirits which are bent upon deceiving, take care to provide for each person the same sort of omens as they see his own conjectures and preconceptions have already entangled him in. For, to take an illustration, the same figure of the letter X, which is made in the shape of a cross, means one thing among the Greeks and another among the Latins, not by nature, but by agreement and pre-arrangement as to its signification; and so, anyone who knows both

---

5. 1 Sam. 28; cf. Ecclus. 46. 20.
6. See 1 Sam. 28. 7.
7. Acts, 16. 16–18.
8. 1 Cor. 10. 19, 20.

languages uses this letter in a different sense when writing to a Greek from that in which he uses it when writing to a Latin. And the same sound, *beta*, which is the name of a letter among the Greeks, is the name of a vegetable among the Latins; and when I say, *lege*, these two syllables mean one thing to a Greek and another to a Latin. Now, just as all these signs affect the mind according to the arrangements of the community in which each man lives, and affect different men's minds differently, because these arrangements are different; and as, further, men did not agree upon them as signs because they were already significant, but on the contrary they are now significant because men have agreed upon them; in the same way also, those signs by which the ruinous intercourse with devils is maintained have meaning just in proportion to each man's observations. And this appears quite plainly in the rites of the augurs; for they, both before they observe the omens and after they have completed their observations, take pains not to see the flight or hear the cries of birds, because these omens are of no significance apart from the previous arrangement in the mind of the observer.

# 5

# ISIDORE OF SEVILLE

"De Magis", *Etymologiae*, translation Steven A. Barney

Isidore of Seville (b. ca. 560; d. 636 CE) composed, around 630 CE, the most influential encyclopaedic work of the Middle Ages, the *Etymologiae* or *Etymologiarum sive originum libri XX*. The *Etymologiae* consist of 448 chapters in 20 books and represent the first systematic attempt to compile and summarize all aspects of ancient learning considered relevant by a mediaeval Christian author. The structure of the work adopts the ancient curriculum of the seven liberal arts; our passage, entitled "De magis" ("Of the magicians"), is located in Book 8 on "De ecclesia et sectis" ("Of the church and sects").

Isidore collates a variety of former statements on "magic". Like Plato (see Chapter 1) and Pliny (Chapter 2), he associates Zoroaster with "magic"; like Augustine (see Chapter 4), he regards demons as being responsible for all kinds of "magic". His phrase "this foolery of the magic arts held sway over the entire world for many centuries through the instruction of evil angels" (*Etymologiae* 8.9.3) appears, in fact, like an amalgamation of Pliny's and Augustine's words. He picks up several familiar topics of preceding works on "magic" such as Moses' contest with the Egyptian priests (*Exodus* 7.9f), or Circe's transformation of Ulysses' companions into pigs (Homer, *Odyssey* 10.233f). Furthermore, Isidore quotes Virgil on the miraculous powers of "magic" and goes into some detail with "necromancers" – that is, "those by whose incantations the dead, brought back to life, seem to prophesy, and to answer what is asked" (*Etymologiae* 8.9.11). To give an example, he points to the "witch of Endor" (1. *Samuel* 28). In the last part, he provides an elaborate overview of divination techniques, including astrology, and adds amulets with incantations or figures ("characters") to his catalogue of "magic". Isidore stresses that "the craft of demons has issued from a certain pestilential alliance of humans and evil angels". Accordingly, "all these things are to be avoided by a Christian, and entirely repudiated and condemned with every curse" (*Etymologiae* 8.9.31).

Isidore's *Etymologiae* are another intriguing example of the polemical use of the concept of "magic" in Western history. Again, "magic" is used to separate Christian and non-Christian beliefs and rites. Isidore even includes technical terminology from a Roman handbook of divination that, most likely, had treated "augury" as a legitimate ritual practice. However, these former contexts of beliefs and practices associated with "magic" are of no more interest to Isidore, deliberately following the Christian strategy to take from ancient knowledge what is useful, but to reinterpret, omit or reject what is not in line with Christian doctrine. The *Etymologiae* were regarded as an authoritative text at least until early modern times – only then (some) scholars transcended the negative stereotypes of "magic" predominant in Christian discourse (see Chapter 8).

## "DE MAGIS", *ETYMOLOGIAE*

### IX. MAGICIANS (DE MAGIS)

1. The first of the magicians was Zoroaster (*Zoroastres*), king of the Bactrians, whom Ninus, king of the Assyrians, killed in battle. About him Aristotle writes that the two million verses composed by him are made evident by the catalogues of his volumes.

2. Democritus expanded this art after many centuries, when Hippocrates also flourished with the discipline of medicine. Among the Assyrians the magic arts are abundant, as Lucan bears witness (cf. *Civil War* 6.427):

> Who could know of deeds by means of entrails, who interpret the birds, who might observe the lightning of the sky, and examine the constellations with Assyrian skill?

3. Consequently, this foolery of the magic arts held sway over the entire world for many centuries through the instruction of the evil angels. By a certain knowledge of things to come and of things below, and by invoking them, divinations (*aruspicium*) were invented, and auguries (*auguratio*), and those things that are called oracles (*oraculum*) and necromancy (*necromantium*).

4. There is nothing surprising about the trickery of the magicians, since their skills in magic advanced to such a point that they even countered Moses with very similar signs, turning staffs into serpents and water into blood.

5. A certain sorceress (*maga*) is also reported, the very famous Circe, who turned the companions of Ulysses into beasts.

We also read about the sacrifice that the Arcadians burnt in offering to their god Lycaeus; whoever consumed this was turned into the shape of a beast. 6. This does not appear to have been completely doubtful, because the noble poet writes of a certain woman who excelled in the magic arts (Vergil, *Aen.* 4.487):

> She promises with her spells to soothe whichever minds she wishes, but to bring hard cares to others; to make the water of rivers stand still, to turn the stars back, and to raise night ghosts; you will see the earth groan underfoot, and wild mountain-ashes descend from the hills.

7. Further, if one may credit it, what of the Pythoness (I Kings 28:7–19 Vulgate), when she called up the spirit of the prophet Samuel from the recesses of the lower region and presented him to the view of the living – if, however, we believe that this was the spirit of the prophet and not some fantastic illusion created by the deception of Satan? 8. Prudentius also spoke thus about Mercury (*Against the Oration of Symmachus* 1.90):

> It is told that he recalled perished souls to the light by the power of a wand that he held, but condemned others to death.

And a little later he adds:

> For with a magic murmur you know how to summon faint shapes and enchant sepulchral ashes. In the same way the malicious art knows how to despoil others of life.

9. There are magicians who are commonly called "evildoers" (*maleficus*) by the crowd because of the magnitude of their crimes. They agitate the elements, disturb the minds of people, and slay without any drinking of poison, using the violence of spells alone. 10. Hence also Lucan (*Civil War* 6.457):

> The mind, polluted by no poison of swallowed venom, yet perishes under a spell.

With their summoning of demons, they dare to flaunt how one may slay his enemies with evil arts. They make use of blood and victims, and often handle the bodies of the dead. 11. Necromancers (*necromantius*) are those by whose incantations the dead, brought back to life, seem to prophesy, and to answer what is asked, for νεκρός means "dead" in Greek, and divination is called μαντεία. The blood of a corpse is applied for the cross-questioning, for demons are said to love blood. And for this reason, whenever necromancy is practiced, gore is mixed with water, so that they are called more easily by the gore of the blood. 12. Hydromancers (*hydromantius*) are so called from water, for hydromancy is calling up the shades of demons by gazing into water, and watching their images or illusions, and hearing something from them, when they are said to consult the lower beings by use of blood. 13. This type of divination is said to have been brought from Persia.

Varro says that there are four kinds of divination: earth, water, air, and fire. Hence are named geomancy (*geomantia*), hydromancy (*hydromantia*), aeromancy (*aeromantia*), and pyromancy (*pyromantia*). 14. Diviners (*divinus*) are so named, as if the term were "filled with god" (*deo plenus*), for they pretend to be filled with divine inspiration, and with a certain deceitful cunning they forecast what is to come for people. There are two kinds of divination: craft and madness. 15. Those who accomplish their craft with words are called enchanters (incantator). 16. Arioli are so called because they utter abominable prayers around the "altars of idols" (*ara idolorum*), and offer pernicious sacrifices, and in these rites receive the answers of demons. 17. Haruspices are so named as if the expression were "observers (*inspector*) of the hours (*hora*)"; they watch over the days and hours for doing business and other works, and they attend to what a person ought to watch out for at any particular time. They also examine the entrails of animals and predict the future from them. 18. Augurs (*augur*) are those who give attention to the flight and calls of birds (*avis*), and to other signs of things or unforeseen observations that impinge on people. These are the same as "observers of auspices" (*auspex*). 19. For auspicious signs are what those who are making a journey take heed of. They are called "auspicious signs" (*auspicium*) as if it were "observations of birds" (*avium aspicium*), and "auguries" (*augurium*), as if it were "bird calls" (*avium garria*), that is, the sounds and languages of birds. Again, *augurium* as if the word were *avigerium*, that is, how "birds behave" (*avis gerit*). 20. There are two types of auspicious signs, one pertaining to the eyes and the other to the ears. To the eyes, as the flight of birds; to the ears as the voice of birds.

21. Pythonesses (*Pythonissae*) are named from Pythian Apollo, because he was the inventor of divination. 22. Astrologers (*astrologus*) are so called, because they perform augury from the stars. 23. *Genethliaci* are so called on account of their examinations of nativities, for they describe the nativities (*genesis*) of people according to the twelve signs of the heavens, and attempt to predict the characters, actions, and circumstances of people by the course of the stars at their birth, that is, who was born under what star, or what outcome of life the person who is born would have. 24. These are commonly called astrologers (*mathematicus*); the Romans call this kind of superstition "constellations" (*constellatio*), that is, observation of the stars – how they relate to each other when each person is born. 25. The first interpreters of the stars were called Magi (*magus*), as we read of those who made known the birth of Christ in the Gospels; afterwards they only had the name *mathematicus*. 26. Knowledge of this skill was permitted only up until the time of the Gospel, so that once Christ was born no one thereafter would interpret the birth of anyone from the heavens. 27. "Drawers of horoscopes" (*horoscopus*) are so called because they examine (*speculari*) the times (*hora*) of people's nativities with regard to their dissimilar and varied destiny.

28. "Interpreters of lots" (*sortilegus*) are those who profess the knowledge of divination under the name of a false religion, using what they call "lots (*sors*, gen. *sortis*) of the saints", or those who foretell the future by examining one passage of scripture or another.[1] 29. The *salisatores* are so called because whenever any part of their limbs leaps (*satire*), they proclaim that this means something fortunate or something unfortunate for them thereafter. 30. Associated with all these arts are amulets consisting of curse-charms. The art of physicians condemns these, whether used with incantations, or magical characters, or whatever is hung on or bound to a person. 31. In all these the craft of demons has issued from a certain pestilential alliance of humans and evil angels. Hence all these things are to be avoided by a Christian, and entirely repudiated and condemned with every curse. 32. The Phrygians were the first to discover the auguries of birds, but Mercury is said to have first invented illusions. 33. They are called illusions (*praestigium*) because they dull

---

1. A *sortilegus* would predict the future by examining a randomly selected verse of the Bible or another authoritative text.

(*praestringere*) the sharpness of one's eyes. 34. A certain Tages is said to have first given the art of *aruspicina* (i.e. divination by inspection of entrails; see 17 above) to the Etruscans. He pronounced divinations orally, and after that did not show himself. 35. It is said in fable that when a certain rustic was plowing, he suddenly leapt up from the clods and pronounced a divination, and on that day he died. The Romans translated these books from the Etruscan language into their own.

# 6

# ANONYMOUS

"μαγεία", "γοητεία", *Suda*, translation Catherine Roth

The *Suda* is the most important and comprehensive encyclopaedic work surviving from mediaeval Byzantium. It consists of over 31,000 entries written in Greek and arranged in alphabetical order. The *Suda* was composed around 970 CE and, until the twentieth century, (falsely) ascribed to an author called Suidas – its real authors remain unknown. The work contains two short but interesting statements on "magic".

Our first excerpt, the entry for the Greek term *mageía*, distinguishes between three terms. First, *mageía* is defined as "the invocation of beneficent spirits for the production of something good". By way of example, the author points to the oracles of the Pythagorean philosopher Apollonius of Tyana (b. around 40 CE?; d. around 120 CE?; note that his biographer Flavius Philostratus claimed that Apollonius was not a "magician": Philostratus, *Vita Apollonii*, e.g., 1.2, 5.12). Second, Greek *goēteía* (the term predominantly used in Plotinus' *Enneads*; see Chapter 3) is defined as "the invocation of maleficent spirits" and associated with "graves" (i.e., presumably, with dead people or spirits). Finally, Greek *pharmakeía* (the term predominantly used in Plato's *Laws*; see Chapter 1) is defined as harming a person by means of concoctions or potions; the article ends with a short note on haruspicy. This distinction is repeated in our second text, the entry for Greek *goēteía*, which further adds etymological speculations on *goēteía* – the author claims that it stems from the Greek verb *goáw* ("to wail") – and *mageía* – here, the author posits a Persian origin of the art.

Our two entries from the *Suda* seem to indicate that the Byzantine history of these terms followed different trajectories compared to their reception in Western Christianity. The historical implications of this differentiation remain to be investigated: was the term *mageía* generally used in a positive sense in medieval Constantinople? Does this also imply a more liberal exposure to "the invocation of beneficent spirits for the production of something good"? In any case, the *Suda* again points to the ambivalence of the historical concept of "magic".

# "ΜΑΓΕΙΑ", "ΓΟΗΤΕΙΑ", *SUDA*

μαγεία: It is an invocation of beneficent spirits for the production of something good; like the oracles of Apollonius of Tyana. [By contrast] sorcery [γοητεία] is an invocation of maleficent spirits which takes place around the graves. But [the term] witchcraft [φαρμακεία] [is used] when some death-dealing concoction is given as a potion or otherwise by mouth to someone. But haruspicy is the dissection of the entrails [of sacrificed animals], by which they used to foretell coming events. For when dissecting they observed certain signs in the livers. See also under γοητεία. Concerning μαγεία, see under Persians.

γοητεία: Sorcery [γοητεία] and magic [μαγεία] and witchcraft [φαρμακεία] differ; Medes and Persians discovered them. So magic [μαγεία] is of course the invocation of beneficent spirits for the production of something good, like the oracles of Apollonius of Tyana. But sorcery [γοητεία] [refers] to raising a dead person by invocation, whence [the word] is derived from the wailing [γόων] and lamentations which are made at burials. But [the word] witchcraft [φαρμακεία] [is used] when some death-dealing concoction is given as a potion by mouth to someone. Magic [μαγεία] and astrology began with Magousaeans, for the Persians are called Magog by their countrymen. Also Magouseans, the same people. [There is] also [the verb] Γοητεύω ["I bewitch"], with the accusative.

# 7

# THOMAS AQUINAS

*Summa Theologica* 2.2.96.1–4, translation T. F. O'Meara and M. J. Duffy

The *Summa Theologica* (ST) of the Italian Dominican priest Thomas Aquinas (b. ca. 1225; d. ca. 1274), intended as a manual for students of theology, is one of the most important theological and philosophical texts from the Middle Ages. Often considered as the masterpiece of Scholasticism, the *Summa* is divided into *quaestiones* ("questions") that are disputed by measuring arguments and counter-arguments in order to arrive at a conclusion that is in accordance with Christian doctrine. This dialectical structure also underlies the passage presented here – namely, Articles 2 to 4 of *quaestio* 96 on "superstition in various practices" (we omit Article 1 on a specific mediaeval text called *Ars notoria*); it belongs to the "Second part of the second part" (*Secunda secundae*) of the *Summa Theologica* dealing, in general, with morality and, in particular, from *quaestio* 57 to 122, with "justice"; *quaestiones* 80 to 100 specifically deal with (Christian) "religion" and its various aberrations.

In the excerpt, Thomas frequently refers to Augustine's *City of God* and *On Christian Doctrine* (see Chapter 4). Like Augustine, Thomas assigns "magic" to the superordinate concept of *superstitio* and ascribes it to the workings of demons. By way of example, Thomas discusses fortune-telling (ST 2.2.96.3), amulets (ST 2.2.96.4) and "astrological images" (ST 2.2.96.2); with the latter term, Thomas refers to talismans, most likely inspired by Latinized Arabic works on the topic. Interestingly, the criteria underlying his evaluation of these practices appear quite similar to some modern discussions of "magic": he regards it lawful to use "things […] in order to produce an effect" when this effect is "produced naturally" (i.e., when there are "natural causes for their proper effects"). In regard to healing, therefore, the use of herbs is legitimate. However, if in addition to herbs "cyphers, words or other vain observances" are applied, the healing rite becomes "superstitious" since these practices do not produce any "natural" effects. In a similar vein, for talismans, Thomas assumes that there is no "natural" cause for the effects ascribed to them – hence, they can only operate as "signs" for demons.

Thomas goes beyond Augustine's theory of "magic" in his emphasis on unconscious or inadvertent pacts with demons (*pactum tacitum*). As a result, the span width of the Christian idea of the "demon pact" is widened: actions that do not rely on natural causes or that are not explicitly addressed to God inevitably imply the danger of evoking demonic forces, independent of the practitioner's view or his intentions. However, in the last part of the excerpt (ST 2.2.96.4)

Thomas argues that amulets and incantations for healing and other purposes are lawful as long as words and symbols from the Holy Scriptures are used. Forbidden are signs other than the cross, unknown words – both imply the danger of the *pactum tacitum* – and "vain" practices. Here, Thomas adds a third cause for effects that relies on God solemnly, respectively, on "divine power". This distinction between "natural", "demonic" and "divine" causes seems to anticipate modern distinctions between "science", "magic" and "religion" and points to the long history of this conceptual pattern.

## *SUMMA THEOLOGICA* 2.2.96.1–4

Question 96. Superstition in various practices.

NEXT TO BE considered are superstitious observances, and here there are four points of inquiry:

1. concerning practices for acquiring knowledge through the art of magic [*arte notoria*];
2. and common practices for effecting certain bodily changes;
3. and fortune-telling;
4. and the wearing of charms.

[…]

### Article 2. Are practices for effecting bodily changes unlawful?

THE SECOND POINT:[1] 1. It would seem that practices for effecting bodily changes for the purpose of health or the like are lawful. It is legitimate to make use of the natural forces of bodies in order to produce their proper effects. Yet these have hidden powers which man is not yet capable of explaining, for instance, why a magnet attracts iron: Augustine cites many other examples.[2] Therefore, it seems that to employ them for the transmutation of bodies is not unlawful.

2. Moreover, as natural bodies are subject to the heavenly bodies, so are artificial bodies. Natural bodies are invested with occult powers, corresponding to what kind of thing they are, through the influence of heavenly bodies. Therefore artificial bodies, images for instance, can also be so invested with occult forces for the production of certain effects. And therefore to make use of them is not wrong.

3. Moreover, demons are able to transmute bodies in many ways, as Augustine admits.[3] Their power is from God. So then it is lawful to make use of their power for this purpose.

---

1. *CG* III, 105. *De Potentia* VI, 10. *Quodl.* XII 9, 2.
2. *De civitate Dei* XXI, 5, 7. PL 41, 715, 718.
3. *De Trinitate* III, 8, 9. PL 42, 875, 878.

ON THE OTHER HAND Augustine says that to superstition *belong the experiments of magic arts, amulets, and nostrums condemned by the medical faculty; they include incantations and cyphers and brooches, or any kind of charm which is worn.*[4]

REPLY: When things are used in order to produce an effect, we have to ask whether this is produced naturally. If the answer is yes, then to use them so will not be unlawful, since we may rightly employ natural causes for their proper effects. But if they seem unable to produce the effects in question naturally, it follows that they are being used for the purpose of producing them, not as causes but only as signs, so that they come under the head of a compact entered into with the demonic. Augustine says, *demons are lured by means of creatures, which were made, not by them, but by God. They are enticed by various objects, differing according to the various things in which they delight. Not by means of various kinds of stones, herbs, trees, animals, songs, and rites.*[5]

Hence: 1. There is nothing superstitious or wrong in using natural things for the purpose of causing effects which are thought natural to them. But if in addition there be employed certain cyphers, words or other vain observances, which clearly have no efficacy by nature, then this is superstitious and wrong.

2. The natural forces of things result from their substantial forms which come to them under the action of the heavens, and so through the same influence, they have certain active forces. On the other hand, the forms of artifacts result from the conception of the artist, and since they are nothing else but things of composition, order and shape, as stated in the *Physics*,[6] theirs is not one single natural active force.[7] Consequently, because they are artificial wholes, they get no power from the heavenly bodies, for that is impressed only on their natural matter. And so what Porphyry held is false, according to Augustine: *by herbs, stones, animals, by certain particular sounds, words, shapes, devices, or again, by certain motions observed in the course of the heavens, it is possible for men to fashion on earth forces capable of carrying into effect the various dispositions of the planets and stars.* This is as though the results of magic were to be ascribed to the power of the heavenly bodies. In fact, as Augustine adds, *all these things are to be ascribed to the demons who delude souls swayed by them.*[8]

Therefore, those images which are called astrological derive their efficacy from the actions of the demonic. A sign of this is that it is requisite to inscribe certain characters on them, which are not conducive to any natural effect, since artificial shape is not a principle of natural action. Astrological images differ from necromantic images in that the latter include certain explicit invocations and trickeries, and so are a kind of express agreement made with the demonic, yet they do imply a tacit agreement through the tokens they use.

---

4. *De doctrina Christiana* II, 20. PL 34, 50.
5. *De civitate Dei* XXI, 6. PL 41, 717.
6. *Physics* I, 5. 188b15–21.
7. The unity of an artificial thing lies in its shape or in the coordination or composition of several things; its singleness is of "accident" (e.g., of figure or of relation, not of substance). Only a natural whole has a single natural action.
8. *De civitate Dei* X, II. PL 41, 290.

3. It belongs to the domain of the divine majesty, of which the demonic powers are subjects, that God should employ them to whatever purpose he wills. But man has not been given power over the demonic, to use it for his own purposes. On the contrary, he is required to wage war against it. And so in no way is it lawful for him to make use of the demonic by compacts, either tacit or express.

## Article 3. Is fortune-telling wrong?

THE THIRD POINT: 1. It seems that the common observations for telling whether the future will bring good or bad fortune are not wrong. Sickness is one of man's misfortunes. Now sickness is preceded by certain symptoms, which medical men observe. Therefore, it does not seem wrong to pay attention to like signs.

2. Moreover, it is unreasonable to deny what nearly everyone experiences. Now nearly everyone has experienced that certain times or places, the hearing of certain words, chance encounters with men or animals, or odd or uncanny actions have presaged good or evil to come. So then, it does not seem wrong to take note of these things.

3. Moreover, human actions and events are disposed by divine Providence in a certain order, which seems to require that preceding events be signs of subsequent events. And so, the Apostle writes, what happened to the fathers of old are signs of things that take place in our time.[9] Now it is not unlawful to observe the order proceeding from divine Providence. Nor, therefore, does it seem to be wrong to observe the presages it provides.

ON THE OTHER HAND Augustine says, *A thousand vain observances are comprised under the head of compacts entered into with the demons, the twitching of a limb, a stone, a dog or a boy coming between friends walking together, a passer-by kicking your doorpost, going back to bed if you happened to sneeze while putting on your shoes, returning home if you trip when beginning a journey, rats gnawing a hole in your clothes – superstitiously fearing a future evil rather than regretting the present hurt.*[10]

REPLY: Men pay attention to all these presages, not as causes, but rather as signs of future events, whether good or evil. They do not observe them as signs given by God, for he does not seem their author; they arise rather from human silliness with the co-operation of demonic malice, which strives to entangle them in these vanities. And so it should be clear that these observances are superstitious and illicit. Apparently they are the remains of idolatry, which authorizes the recognition of portents, of lucky and unlucky days, which is allied to divination by the stars, which sees one day as being more propitious than another. As devoid of reason and art, they are the more futile and superstitious.

Hence: 1. The causes of illness are seated in us; and they produce certain signs of approaching sickness which doctors rightly observe. It is not wrong to consider the presage of a future event as proceeding from its cause, as when a slave fears punishment when he

---

9. 1 *Corinthians* 10, 6, 11.
10. *De doctrina Christiana* 2, 20. PL 34, 50–51.

sees his master's anger. Possibly the same might be if one were to fear for a child lest it be harmed by the "evil eye", on which we touched in the Prima Pars.[11] But this does not apply to the observances we are discussing here.

2. That there is some degree of truth in these experiences is due to chance. But afterwards, when a man begins to tie himself up with repeated observances of this kind, many events do occur by the trickery of the demonic, so that, as Augustine says, *men entangled in these observations become more and more curious, more and more caught up in the manifold snares of a deadly error.*[12]

3. Among the Jewish people from whom Christ was to be born, not only words, but also deeds were prophetic, as Augustine notes.[13] Therefore, it is lawful to apply these deeds to our instruction, as signs given by God. But not all things which occur through divine Providence are ordered so as to be signs of the future. The argument, consequently, is not sound.

### Article 4. Is it wrong to wear amulets?

THE FOURTH POINT:[14] 1. It would seem that it is not wrong to wear inscribed amulets about the neck. Sacred words should be no less efficacious when written than when spoken, and it is legitimate to utter them for the purpose of producing certain effects, for instance, to heal the sick, thus to say the *Our Father* or the *Hail Mary*; it is legitimate to call on the Lord's name according to Mark, *in thy Name they shall cast out devils, they shall speak with new tongues, they shall take up serpents.*[15] Therefore, it seems legitimate to wear sacred words on one's person, as a remedy for sickness or for any kind of distress.

2. Moreover, sacred words are no less effective on the human body than on snakes and other animals. Now certain incantations are effective in controlling snakes, or in healing other animals; it is written in the *Psalms, Their madness is according to the likeness of the serpent, like the death asp that stops its ears, which will not hear the voice of the charmers nor of the wizard that charms wisely.*[16] So it is lawful to wear sacred words as a remedy for human ills.

3. Moreover, God's word is no less holy than the relics of the saints. Augustine says that *God's word is of no less account than the body of Christ.*[17] To wear the relics of the saints for protection is lawful; equally so, then, to have recourse to Holy Writ, whether uttered or written, for one's protection.

4. On the other hand,[18] Chrysostom writes, *Some wear around their necks written passages from the Gospel. Yet is not the Gospel read in church and heard by all every day?*

---

11. Ia. 117, 3 ad 2.
12. *De doctrina Christiana* 2. PL 34, 52.
13. *Contra Faustum* IV, 2; XXII, 24. PL 42, 218, 417.
14. cf *Quodl.* XII, 9. 2. *In Rom.* I, *lect.* 6; *In I Cor.* 10, *lect.* 7.
15. *Mark* 16, 17–18.
16. *Psalms* 57, 5–6.
17. *Liber quinquaginta homiliae* 26. PL 39, 2319.
18. The *sed contra* usually anticipates the line that will be taken in the *responsio*. Here it goes to the opposite extreme and is answered as a fourth objection.

*How, then, if it does not help a man to have the Gospels in his ears, will he find salvation by wearing them around his neck? Besides, where is the power of the Gospel? In the shapes of the letters or in the understanding of its sense. If it is in the shapes of the letters, you do well to wear them round your neck; but if in the understanding, you would do better to bear the words in your heart.*[19]

REPLY: In every incantation or the wearing of written words, two points seem to call for caution. The first concerns what is said or written; if it implies invocation of the demonic, it is clearly superstitious and unlawful. Similarly, we should beware, it seems, of strange words we do not understand lest they conceal something unlawful. So Chrysostom says, *Many, after the example of the Pharisees (who lengthened their phylacteries), now invent and write Hebrew names of angels, and fasten them to their persons, for they stand for powers which seem fearsome to those who do not understand them.*[20] Again, one should take care lest a supposedly sacred word contain error, for then its effect could not be ascribed to God, who bears no witness to falsehood.

A second point for caution: besides the sacred words the inscription may contain emblems of vanity, for instance, signs other than that of the cross. Or our confidence may be committed to the style of writing or fashion in wearing them, or to some such nonsense, which has no connection with reverence for God. All this should be judged superstitious.

Otherwise such tokens are lawful. Hence it is written in the *Decretals*, *In blending together medicinal herbs, it is not lawful to make use of observances on incantations other than the Creed or the Lord's Prayer, so as to give honour to none but God, the Creator of all.*[21]

Hence: 1. It is lawful to pronounce divine words or to invoke the name of God if we do so to honour him alone from whom the benefit is hoped. But it is unlawful if done in connection with any vain observance.

2. Incantations, with snakes or other animals, are not unlawful if we attend only to the sacred words and divine power. Incantations, however, often imply unlawful observances, and rely on the demonic for their result, especially in the case of snakes; the serpent was the first instrument used by the devil to deceive man. And so a gloss says, *Note that Scripture does not commend everything from which it draws comparisons and literary allusions, as in the case of the unjust judge who scarcely heard the widow's request.*[22]

3. This same consideration applies in the wearing of relics. If it is out of confidence in God and the saints, whose relics they are, this is not wrong. But if account were taken of some irrelevance, for instance, that the locket is triangular and the like, which has no bearing on the reverence due to God and the saints, it would be superstitious and wrong.

4. Chrysostom is speaking of a case in which more attention is paid to the written characters than to the understanding of the words.

---

19. *Opus imperfectum in Matth.* 43. PG 56, 878–9. The passage in Matthew is 23, 5. This work is not now ascribed to Chrysostom.
20. Ibid.
21. Gratian, *Decretum* II, 26, 5, can. 3; ed cit, I, 1028.
22. Lombard. PL 191, 537; *Glossa ordinaria*. PL 113, 928; cf Augustine, *Enarr. in Psalm.* 57. PL 36, 679.

# 8

# AGRIPPA OF NETTESHEIM

*Three Books of Occult Philosophy* 1.1–2, translation James Freake

The German Heinrich Cornelius Agrippa of Nettesheim (b. 1486; d. 1535) was an itinerant scholar who wrote on various subjects. He is most known for his *De occulta philosophia* (written in 1509/1510, published during 1531 to 1533), a kind of summa of occult thinking, in which the concept of "natural magic" (*magia naturalis*) was of paramount importance. In this extensive work, Agrippa subsumed a vast variety of practices and conceptual patterns brought forward by Marsilio Ficino, Pico della Mirandola and others under the concept of "magic" (see the Introduction to Part I) – such as Ptolemaic astrology, alchemy, divination, the Plotinic idea of a world soul, "Hermetic" ideas such as the correspondence of the upper and the lower, "Kabbalistic" speculations about the occult property of words, letters, numbers and signs, and reflections on the order and names of intermediary beings. However, Agrippa avoided the term *magia* in the title of the work, probably in order to prevent problems with church authorities.

We present Chapters 1 and 2 from the first book of *De occulta philosophia*. In the first chapter, Agrippa claims that there is a "threefold world", referring to an "elementary" world (in Ptolemaic terms, this is the sub-lunar sphere, mainly corresponding to human life on the earthly surface), a "celestial" world (the super-lunar sphere – i.e., the celestial bodies), and an "intellectual" world (the human mind and soul, higher beings such as angels and demons, God and the world soul). Accordingly, the three books of the work focus on three different kinds of "magic" corresponding to these parts of the world: "natural magic", "celestial magic" and "ceremonial magic". Agrippa further claims that, through "magic", it is possible for humans to ascend through these worlds in order to reach God, "the Maker of all things". Thus, for Agrippa, the "magician" is a specialist in controlling the powers from these three spheres by applying the methods described in *De occulta philosophia*.

In the second chapter, Agrippa gives a more precise definition of "magic", regarding it as a "faculty of wonderful virtue" that includes a thorough knowledge of all aspects of nature. Accordingly, Agrippa maintains that "magic" is the "most perfect and chief science", even the "most absolute perfection of all most excellent philosophy". Quoting verses from Virgil, Agrippa explains the purposes of "natural philosophy" (equated with "natural magic"), "mathematical philosophy" (equated with "celestial magic" – i.e., astrology) and "theological philosophy" (equated with "ceremonial magic"). Note that the list of historical "magicians" in Chapter 2 is partly inspired by Pliny's history of "magic" in the *Historia Naturalis* (see Chapter 2 in this volume). Agrippa's final statement that one has to master natural philosophy, mathematics (i.e., astrology) and theology to become a successful "magician" again illustrates that the early modern concept of "magic" covers, in fact, all aspects of human knowledge.

Agrippa's *De occulta philosophia* had a lasting impact upon Western discourses on "magic", especially on later authors who advocated an affirmatory use of the concept – such as Helena Petrovna Blavatsky (see Chapter 10). Turning to modern academic discourse, the fifteenth chapter of the first book seems to anticipate aspects of what Frazer would later call "homeopathic magic" (see Chapter 12). Agrippa's *De occulta philosophia* was also read by Edward B. Tylor, who cites it in his *Primitive Culture* (see Chapter 11). However, Tylor rejects Agrippa's positive evaluation of "magic" – obviously so, for Tylor did not regard "magic" as the most superior part of philosophy, but rather as the most primitive "survival" of cultural evolution.

# THREE BOOKS OF OCCULT PHILOSOPHY 1.1–2

## CHAPTER 1: HOW MAGICIANS COLLECT VIRTUES FROM THE THREEFOLD WORLD, IS DECLARED IN THESE THREE BOOKS

Seeing there is a threefold world, elementary, celestial, and intellectual, and every inferior is governed by its superior, and receiveth the influence of the virtues thereof, so that the very original, and chief Worker of all cloth by angels, the heavens, stars, elements, animals, plants, metals, and stones convey from himself the virtues of his omnipotency upon us, for whose service he made, and created all these things: wise men conceive it no way irrational that it should be possible for us to ascend by the same degrees through each world, to the same very original world itself, the Maker of all things, and First Cause, from whence all things are, and proceed; and also to enjoy not only these virtues, which are already in the more excellent kind of things, but also besides these, to draw new virtues from above.

Hence it is that they seek after the virtues of the elementary world, through the help of physic, and natural philosophy in the various mixtions of natural things, then of the celestial world in the rays, and influences thereof, according to the rules of astrologers, and the doctrines of mathematicians, joining the celestial vertues to the former: moreover, they ratify and confirm all these with the powers of diverse intelligencies, through the sacred ceremonies of religion.

The order and process of all these I shall endeavor to deliver in these three books: whereof the first contains natural magic, the second celestial, and the third ceremonial. But I know not whether it be an unpardonable presumption in me, that I, a man of so little judgement and learning should in my very youth so confidently set upon a business so difficult, so hard, and intricate as this is. Wherefore, whatsoever things have here already, and shall afterwards be said by me, I would not have anyone assent to them, nor shall I myself, any farther than they shall be approved of by the universal Church, and the congregation of the faithful?

PART I: HISTORICAL SOURCES

## CHAPTER 2: WHAT MAGIC IS, WHAT ARE THE PARTS THEREOF, AND HOW THE PROFESSORS THEREOF MUST BE QUALIFIED

Magic is a faculty of wonderful virtue, full of most high mysteries, containing the most profound contemplation of most secret things, together with the nature, power, quality, substance, and virtues thereof, as also the knowledge of whole nature, and it doth instruct us concerning the differing, and agreement of things amongst themselves, whence it produceth its wonderful effects, by uniting the virtues of things through the application of them one to the other, and to their inferior suitable subjects, joining and knitting them together thoroughly by the powers, and virtues of the superior bodies.

This is the most perfect, and chief science, that sacred, and sublimer kind of philosophy, and lastly the most absolute perfection of all most excellent philosophy. For seeing that all regulative philosophy is divided into natural, mathematical, and theological: (Natural philosophy teacheth the nature of those things which are in the world, searching and enquiring into their causes, effects, times, places, fashions, events, their whole, and parts, also:

> *The number and the nature of those things,*
> *Called elements, what Fire, Earth, Air forth brings:*
> *From whence the heavens their beginnings had;*
> *Whence tide, whence rainbow in gay colours clad.*
> *What makes the clouds that gathered are, and black,*
> *To send forth lightnings, and a thundering crack;*
> *What doth the nightly flames, and comets make;*
> *What makes the Earth to swell, and then to quake:*
> *What is the seed of metals, and of gold*
> *What virtues, wealth, doth Nature's coffer hold.*[1]

All these things doth natural philosophy, the viewer of nature contain, teaching us according to *Virgil's* muse:

> *whence all things flow,*
> *Whence mankind, beast, whence fire, whence rain, and snow,*
> *Whence earthquakes are, why the whole ocean beats*
> *Over his banks, and then again retreats:*
> *Whence strength of herbs, whence courage, rage of brutes,*
> *All kinds of stone, of creeping things, and fruits.*[2]

But mathematical philosophy teacheth us to know the quantity of natural bodies, as extended into three dimensions, as also to conceive of the motion, and course of celestial bodies:

---

1. "*coffer hold*": This quote is not from Virgil, but I have been unable to locate its source.
2. "*and fruits*": The second and third lines of this quote are from the *Georgics* 2, lines 479–80. The other I cannot identify.

*as in great haste,*
*What makes the golden stars to march so fast;*
*What makes the Moon sometimes to mask her face,*
*The Sun also, as if in some disgrace.*[3]

And as *Virgil* sings:

*How the Sun doth rule with twelve Zodiac signs,*
*The orb that's measured round about with lines,*
*It doth the heaven's starry way make known,*
*And strange eclipses of the Sun, and Moon,*
*Arcturus also, and the Stars of Rain,*
*The Seven Stars likewise, and Charles his Wain,*
*Why winter Suns make towards the west so fast;*
*What makes the nights so long ere they be past?*[4]

All which is understood by mathematical philosophy:

*hence by the heavens we may foreknow*
*the seasons all; times for to reap and sow,*
*And when 'tis fit to launch into the deep,*
*And when to war, and when in peace to sleep,*
*And when to dig up trees, and them again to set;*
*that so they may bring forth amain.*[5]

Now theological philosophy, or divinity, teacheth what God is, what the mind, what an intelligence, what an angel, what a devil, what the soul, what religion, what sacred institutions, rites, temples, observations, and sacred mysteries are: it instructs us also concerning faith, miracles, the virtues of words and figures, the secret operations and mysteries of seals, and as *Apuleius* saith, it teacheth us rightly to understand, and to be skilled in the ceremonial laws, the equity of holy things, and rule of religions. But to recollect myself these three principal faculties magic comprehends, unites, and actuates; deservedly therefore was it by the ancients esteemed as the highest, and most sacred philosophy.

It was, as we find, brought to light by most sage authors, and most famous writers; amongst which principally *Zamolxis* and *Zoroaster* were so famous, that many believed they were the inventors of this science. Their track *Abbaris* the Hyperborean, Charmondas, *Damigeron, Eudoxus, Hermippus* followed: there were also other eminent, choice men, as *Mercurius Tresmegistus, Porphyrius, Iamblicus, Plotinus, Proclus, Dardanus, Orpheus* the

---

3. "*some disgrace*": Not Virgil, but again I cannot place it.
4. "*they the past*": A composite of *Georgics* 1, lines 231–32; *Georgics* 2, lines 477–78; and the *Aeneid* 1, lines 744–46.
5. "*forth amain*": *Georgics* 1, lines 252–56.

Thracian, *Gog* the Grecian, *Germa* the Babylonian, *Apollonius* of Tyana. *Osthanes* also wrote excellently in this art; whose books being as it were lost, *Democritus* of Abdera recovered, and set forth with his own commentaries. Besides *Pythagoras, Empedocles, Democritus, Plato*, and many other renowned philosophers traveled far by sea to learn this art: and being returned, published it with wonderful devoutness, esteeming of it as a great secret. Also it is well known that *Pythagoras*, and *Plato* went to the prophets of Memphis to learn it, and traveled through almost all Syria, Egypt, Judea, and the schools of the Chaldeans, that they might not be ignorant of the most sacred memorials, and records of magic, as also that they might be furnished with divine things.

Whosoever therefore is desirous to study in this faculty, if he be not skilled in natural philosophy, wherein are discovered the qualities of things, and in which are found the occult properties of every being, and if he be not skillful in the mathematics, and in the aspects, and figures of the stars, upon which depends the sublime virtue, and property of everything; and if he be not learned in theology, wherein are manifested those immaterial substances, which dispense, and minister all things, he cannot be possibly able to understand the rationality of magic. For there is no work that is done by mere magic, nor any work that is merely magical, that doth not comprehend these three faculties.

# 9

# DENIS DIDEROT

"Magie", *Encyclopédie, ou Dictionnaire raisonné des sciences, des arts et des metiers*,
translation Steve Harris

The *Encyclopédie, ou Dictionnaire raisonné des sciences, des arts et des métiers*, edited between 1751 and 1780 by Denis Diderot (b. 1713; d. 1784) and Jean Baptiste le Rond d'Alembert (b. 1717; d. 1783), is the first encyclopaedia published in French. Consisting of 35 volumes and more than 60,000 alphabetically arranged entries (apart from Diderot and d'Alembert, 142 other authors contributed to the work), the *Encyclopédie* epitomizes the political project of the Enlightenment. We present the entry for the French term *magie* written by Diderot.

This text again reflects the ambiguity of the historical concept of "magic". On the one hand, the general evaluation is harsh: Diderot regards "magic" as a "science equally illusory and contemptible", and as a "daughter of ignorance and pride". In a similar vein, Agrippa's *De occulta philosophia* (see Chapter 8) – one of Diderot's prime negative examples – is described as "a confused heap of obscure, ambiguous and inconclusive principles, practices which were generally arbitrary and childish". On the other hand, Diderot begins by stating that in some distant past, "magic" was the "study of wisdom" and only degenerated over time. Furthermore, he proposes a threefold distinction of "magic" – divine, natural and supernatural – that implies some positive aspects. "Divine magic" is characterized by the ability to know the plans of God, work miracles and read people's hearts. Here, Diderot seems to be inspired by biblical miracle-workers (but he completely ignores the recurrent attempts of Christian authors to separate "miracle" from "magic"). Diderot's view of "natural magic" still reflects core notions of the early modern discourse when he claims that it is the "in-depth study of nature and the amazing secrets that we find there", including sciences such as physics, astronomy, medicine, agriculture, navigation and mechanics. It is only his third category – "supernatural magic" – that he addresses with scorn. This category comprises astrology, divination, the invocation of demons or "spirits of the dead", the "discovery of hidden treasure", or "healing the most stubborn illnesses by mysterious means".

Diderot asserts that only his third category – "supernatural magic" – which he equates with Agrippa's "celestial magic" and "ceremonial magic", should be "properly called magic" as it "always takes offense, […] leads to pride, ignorance and the rejection of science". These polemics seem to reflect the emancipation of the eighteenth-century scientific discourse from the notion of *magia naturalis*. In fact, Diderot states that "Philosophy's ultimate task is to finally disabuse humanity of these imaginary humiliations." Thus, he ends by evaluating (supernatural) "magic" as completely illusory, based on fear, fantasy and error. In a similar vein, he points to former court trials against "magicians", arguing that these trials originated in "the unhappy passions of envy and vengeance" and that the accused merely functioned as "an unhappy sacrifice to the simplicity of some and the barbarism of others". Here, Diderot anticipates the main arguments of the "deviance theory" (see the General Introduction to this volume).

# "MAGIE", *ENCYCLOPÉDIE*

Magic, considered as the science of the first mages, was nothing but the study of wisdom; for at the time it was well-taken. But it is rare that Man is satisfied with the limits of knowledge, it is too simple for him. It is nearly impossible that a small number of learned people, in one era and in a country subject to a crass ignorance, would not quickly succumb to the temptation to appear greater than human. Thus, the mages of Chaldea and all the East, or rather their disciples (because it is with the latter that ideas are usually degenerated), attached themselves to astrology, divination, enchantment and curses; and soon the term "magic" became odious and inapt to designate a science equally illusory and contemptible. The daughter of ignorance and pride, this science stretches back into the depths of time. It would be difficult to determine its date of origin; intending to reduce the pains of humanity, it was born at the same time as our miseries. As a dark science, it is honoured in countries where barbarism and coarseness reign. The Lapps and, in general, savage peoples cultivate magic and make a great deal of it.

To write a complete treatise on magic, to consider it in its fullest sense, that is to say, in all the good and evil that it can do, one must distinguish between divine magic, natural magic and supernatural magic.

First, divine magic is nothing but the particular knowledge of the plans and visions of sovereign wisdom that God (in his grace) has revealed to holy men filled with his spirit; the supernatural power that He enables them to predict the future, to make miracles and to read, so to speak, the heart of those to whom they have been sent. We must believe they had such gifts; even if science, clarified by faith, has no better idea, it reveres it in silence. But is it still so? I do not know and I believe that it may be doubted. It does not depend on us acquiring this desirable magic, which does not comes neither from ordinary life nor from the will; it is a gift from God.

Second, by natural magic, we mean the in-depth study of nature and the amazing secrets that we find there; the inestimable benefits that this work has brought to humanity in nearly all the arts and sciences. These include physics, astronomy, medicine, agriculture, navigation, mechanics and, I would say even eloquence; because it is for the knowledge of nature and the inspiration which it fires the human spirit in particular, that the great masters are due for the impact which they had on their students, the passions which they have excited in them and the tears they have drawn from them.

This magic, praiseworthy in itself, was developed far back in antiquity. It is evidenced by Greek fire and some other discoveries made by those writers of which we have spoken. In several areas, the ancients have surpassed us in this type of magic, but the invasions by the northern peoples proved to have the most disastrous consequences for our Europe, including the shocking blows from which science and the fine arts have had such pain in overcoming.

Thus, for many centuries after Archimedes' glass sphere, Architras' flying wooden dove, the Emperor Leo's singing golden birds, Boetius' singing and flying bronze birds, hissing bronze serpents and other things, there was a country in Europe (but of neither of Vaucanson's century nor country), there was, I say, a country in which came to the point of burning Brioché and his puppets. A French knight who would walk around and see in the fair a mare who was clever enough to respond exactly to his signals, as we have seen as much in what follows: was saddened in Spain to see an animal subjected to the Inquisition who used all his resources to escape its clutches. There are innumerable examples of natural events which, through ignorance, were treated as black magic and evil. How were those who first spoke of the Antipodes and the New World treated?

But we are gradually recovering from this former attitude and one can say that the awareness of this so-called natural magic is, even in the eyes of the multitude, continually retreating. Under the light of science we are, happily, continuously discovering the secrets and systems of nature, supported by many sound experiences which show humanity of what it is capable itself and without magic. Thus, we see the compass, the telescope, the microscope and, in our own time, polyps and electricity. In chemistry and physics, the most beautiful and useful discoveries will immortalize our era and if Europe were to fall back into the barbarism from which it has finally emerged, we will seem like magicians to our barbarous successors.

Third, supernatural magic is which is properly called magic. This black magic, that always takes offense, that leads to pride, ignorance and the rejection of science; it is this which Agrippa included under the labels "celestial" and "ceremonial". It had no science but the name and nothing but a confused heap of obscure, ambiguous and inconclusive principles, practices which were generally arbitrary and childish, the uselessness of which is shown by the nature of things.

Agrippa, who was also a philosopher as well as a magician, used the term celestial magic to describe judicial astrology which attributed to spirits some domination over the planets, and to the planets some domination over men. He also claimed that different constellations influenced the tendencies, destiny and good or bad fortune of men. On these weak foundations, he built a ridiculous system, which does not dare appear these days except in the Liege Almanac and other similar books. These pathetic collections of material nourish popular errors and prejudices.

Ceremonial magic, according to Agrippa, is incontrovertibly the most odious of these fruitless sciences. It consists of the invocation of demons who respond according to an express or tacit agreement made with the powers of darkness. He claims they have the power to harm their enemies, to produce evil and pernicious effects which the unhappy victims of their furor cannot avoid.

Magic is divided into several branches, according to its differing objects and operations: cabals, spells, enchantment, evoking the spirit of the dead or of evil spirits, discovery of hidden treasure; as well as the greater secret arts: divination, prophecy, healing the most stubborn illnesses by mysterious means, attending a witches Sabbath, etc. Of what failings is the human mind not capable! It is shown in all these dreams.

Philosophy's ultimate task is to finally disabuse humanity of these imaginary humiliations. It has fought superstition, even joining with Theology (with which it has rarely made common cause). But finally in countries where people think, reflect and doubt, demons play a small role and diabolical magic remains discredited and held in contempt.

But let's not flatter our style of thinking here: we are a bit late for that; open the records of the smallest court of justice and you will find immense register of proceedings against sorcerers, magicians and enchanters. That the judiciary enriched themselves from the spoils and the confiscation of goods relating to alleged sorcerers is perhaps more illuminating than a funeral pyre. At least it is true that often the passion of the people often overwhelmed their credulity and led them to regard as a sorcerer or doctor of magic those who they would have not otherwise paid attention to. Similarly, according to the judicious remark of Apuleius (who had previously been accused of magic), "this crime", he said, "is not believed by those who accuse others, because if a man was quite convinced that another man could kill by magic, he would be afraid to irritate him by accusing him of such an abominable crime".

Leonora Galigaï, the wife of the famous Marshal of Ancre, provides a memorable example of a disastrous accusation of an imaginary crime, fomented by a secret passion and born out of a dangerous court intrigue. But there are few examples of this type better known than that of the famous Urbain Grandier, the priest and canon of Loudun, who was burnt alive as a magician in the year 629. It is appalling that a philosopher who was merely a friend of humanity would have to suffer the pain of being an unhappy sacrifice to the simplicity of some and the barbarism of others! How are we to understand someone cold-bloodedly condemned as a magician to perish in the flames, judged by the statement of Astaroth, devil of the order of seraphim, of d'Easas, de Celsus, d'Acaos, de Cédon, d'Asmodée, devils of the order of the throne; d'Alex, de Zabulon, Nephtalim, de Cham, d'Uriel, d'Ahaz, of the order of princes? How are we to understand the unhappy canon judged unmercifully on the word of those monks and nuns who said that he had raised the legions of infernal spirits? How is one not discomfited by seeing someone burned alive who is alleged to be magical, chased and defamed as a magician to the same pyre where a black fly of the order of those who call themselves bumblebees and who practiced on the head of Grandier were led by a monk who doubtlessly had read in the Council of Quieres that devils came to tempt a man at his death; taken, I say, for Beelzebub, lord of the flies, who flew around Grandier in order to take his soul to Hell? A puerile observation perhaps, but in the mouth of the monk, it was one of the least bad arguments that a barbarous mob could use to justify its excess, resulting from the absurd stories imposed on the disastrous credulity of simple people. What Horrors! Where will the human spirit not descend when it is blinded by the unhappy passions of envy and vengeance? One must certainly respect Gabriel Naudé for having generously undertaken the defense of great men accused of magic, but I think that they owe more to the rise of science which highlighted the vanity of the accusations than to the zeal of their advocate who, perhaps, had more courage than the cleverness or force of his arguments. If Naudé could have exonerated the great men from an imputation which evaporated in the light of common sense and reason: in spite of all his zeal, he had clearly failed. If he had undertaken to clear the wise men of antiquity entirely in this regard, then all their philosophy could not have sheltered them from the outrageous superstition of the magic they embraced.

I will not cite another example, save that of Cato. He had the idea that one could heal the most serious maladies by magic words. Here are those barbarous words, which, at least according to him, were a certain recipe to restore his ailing patients: *Incipe cantare in alto S: F. motas danata dardaries astotaries, dic una parite usque dum coeant*, etc. [Begin to chant over the affected areas, "dardaries, astotaries", and repeat until they come together.] This is from Alde Manuce's edition, since that of Henri Estienne, revised and corrected by Victorius, was considerably changed to the point that its obscurity became greatly attacked by the critics.

Everyone knows that the ancients put great significance to the magical word abracadabra. Q. Serenus, a famous doctor, claimed that a meaningless word written on paper and hung around the neck was a sure remedy for quarte fever. Undoubtedly, with such principles, this superstition was a complete pharmacy and the faith of the patient was his own best resource.

It is to this faith that one can and one must attribute the reports of remarkable recoveries that seemed to come from magic, but which, underneath, were nearly always pious frauds or the results of this superstition that could not triumph too frequently over good sense, reason and even science. Our prejudices, errors and follies help each other. Fear is the daughter of ignorance; the latter produces superstition, which is, in its turn, the mother of fantasy, a rich source of error, illusion, phantoms, an over-heated imagination which creates imps, werewolves, ghosts and demons, which all jostle together. How can any mind in this state not believe all the fantasies of magic? If fanaticism is pious and devout (and it is nearly always shown this way), it will see magic as part of the glory of God; at the least it will attribute to magic the privilege of saving and damning without appeal. There is no worse magic than that of the falsely devout. In conclusion, once could as well call the Sabbath the empire of the subterranean Amazons; at least there have always been more witches than wizards, we rightly attribute magic to the weak spirit or excessive curiosity of women. Daughters of Eve, they would lose their souls in order to know. But an anonymous writer (see Alector ou le Coq, Book II of the adepts) who would persuade the public that he is one of Satan's closest confidantes, attributes to demons a lewd spirit which justifies their predilection for sex and the favors which they are granted. But this rationale would justly apply to part of the human race for whom, ordinarily, one cannot win for losing.

# 10

# HELENA PETROVNA BLAVATSKY

*"Magic", Theosophical Glossary*

Helena Petrovna Blavatsky (b. 1831; d. 1891) was one of the most important voices of nascent Western Esotericism in the late nineteenth century. She was the leading figure of the Theosophical Society, which was founded in 1875 in New York with the intention of investigating "the hidden mysteries of Nature under every aspect possible, and the psychic and spiritual powers latent in man especially" (*The Key to Theosophy*, 1889 [reprint 2002], 39). Given this programme, it is not surprising that Blavatsky picked up positive interpretations of "magic" from previous authors such as Agrippa of Nettesheim (see Chapter 8) and used "magic" as a core concept in her own writings, including *Isis Unveiled* (1877), *The Secret Doctrine* (1888) or *The Key to Theosophy* (1889). In all these works, "magic" functions as a broad synthetic concept, signifying miraculous powers and hidden truths of existence – synonymous to Blavatsky's concepts of "Occultism" and "Esotericism". We present the entry "Magic" from the *Theosophical Glossary*, an encyclopaedic work elucidating the main concepts of *Theosophy* that was published posthumously in 1892.

Our text exemplifies the long and on-going history of positive interpretations of the concept of "magic" in Western history. "Magic" is introduced as a "great science" that operated as a "sacred science inseparable from religion" among the ancient Hindus and Egyptians. To underpin this idea, Blavatsky refers to (Pseudo-)Plato's *Alcibiades* I (see Chapter 1), arguing that "magic" would not have survived thousands of years of Egyptian and Indian history if it were a mere fraud. She claims that the Gods commanded by "magic practices" are, in fact, "the occult powers or potencies of Nature" – which seems to reflect the early modern conception of *magia naturalis* (see Chapter 8) with a psychological twist. "Magic" is then defined as "communicating with and directing supernal, supramundane Potencies" and distinguished into "*Theurgia, Goëtia* and natural *Magic*" – here, Blavatsky follows an article of the *Royal Masonic Cyclopaedia* (published in 1874 by Kenneth MacKenzie). Blavatsky's background criterion to separate these three facets of "magic" is a psychological one: while *Goëtia* (a derivate of Greek *goēteía*; see Chapters 3 and 6) corresponds to malevolent ritual intentions ("black magic"), both *Theurgia* and "natural magic" correspond to benevolent – for example, healing – purposes (compare also her article "Magic, white" in the *Theosophical Glossary*) with *Theurgia* marking the more elaborate, metaphysical part (the term *theurgia* goes back to Jamblichus Chalcidensis). The text ends with wistful remarks on the "low, miserable status of modern civilization" that, according to Blavatsky, lost sight of the true, divine "magic" of the ancients. Here, Blavatsky even seems to posit a model of cultural evolution, but unlike James G. Frazer (see Chapter 12) she suggests a decadence process from "magic" to modern "science" and "religion", implicitly criticizing the ostensibly soulless materialism and superficiality of the institutionalized religions of her lifetime.

With her writings, not least with her conception of "magic", Blavatsky strongly influenced the blossoming of Western Esotericism during the late nineteenth century. Her ideas were picked up by many subsequent authors and currents, including famous "magicians" such as the protagonists of the *Hermetic Order of the Golden Dawn*, Aleister Crowley or Gerald Brousseau Gardner. Thus, her writings can be regarded as an important link between ancient, early modern and modern affirmatory discourses of "magic". What is more, our text shows that at the very outset of modern academic discourse, strikingly different conceptions of "magic" have been brought forward in Europe that were, deliberately or out of mere ignorance, neglected by academic discourse. This points to a longstanding discursive "gap" between academic theorists of "magic" and Western "magicians" (i.e., ritual practitioners claiming the title) that has only recently been transcended by scholars who attempt uniting both identities (see, for example, Chapter 21 by Susan Greenwood).

## "MAGIC", *THEOSOPHICAL GLOSSARY*

*Magic.* The great "Science". According to Deveria and other Orientalists, "magic was considered as a sacred science inseparable from religion" by the oldest and most civilized and learned nations. The Egyptians, for instance, were one of the most sincerely religious nations, as were and still are the Hindus. "Magic consists of, and is acquired by the worship of the gods", said Plato. Could then a nation, which, owing to the irrefragable evidence of inscriptions and papyri, is proved to have firmly believed in magic for thousands of years, have been deceived for so long a time. And is it likely that generations upon generations of a learned and pious hierarchy, many among whom led lives of self-martyrdom, holiness and asceticism, would have gone on deceiving themselves and the people (or even only the latter) for the pleasure of perpetuating belief in "miracles"? Fanatics, we are told, will do anything to enforce belief in their god or idols. To this we reply: in such case, Brahmans and Egyptian Rekhget-amens (*q.v.*) or Hierophants would not have popularized *belief in the power of man by magic practices to command the services of the gods*: which gods, are in truth, but the occult powers or potencies of Nature, personified by the learned priests themselves, in which they reverenced only the attributes of the one unknown and nameless Principle. As Proclus the Platonist ably puts it: "Ancient priests, when they considered that there is a certain alliance and sympathy in natural things to each other, and of things manifest to occult powers, and discovered that all things subsist in all, *fabricated a sacred science from this mutual sympathy and similarity* [...] and applied for occult purposes, both celestial and terrene natures, by means of which, through a certain similitude, they deduced divine virtues into this inferior abode." Magic is the science of communicating with and directing supernal, supramundane Potencies, as well as of commanding those of the lower spheres; a practical knowledge of the hidden mysteries of nature known to only the few, because they are so difficult to acquire, without falling into sins against nature. Ancient and mediaeval mystics divided magic into three classes – *Theurgia*, *Goëtia* and natural *Magic*. "Theurgia has long since been appropriated as the peculiar sphere of the theosophists and metaphysicians", says Kenneth Mackenzie. Goëtia is *black* magic, and "natural (or white) magic has risen with healing in its wings to the proud position of an exact and progressive study". The comments added by our late learned Brother are remarkable. "The realistic desires of modern times have contributed to bring magic into disrepute and ridicule [...] Faith (in one's own self) is an essential element in magic, and existed long before other ideas which presume its pre-existence. It is said that it takes a wise man to make a fool; and a man's ideas must be exalted almost to madness, i.e., his brain susceptibilities must be increased far beyond the low, miserable status of modern civilization, before he can become a true magician; (for) a pursuit of this science implies a certain amount of isolation and *an abnegation of Self.*" A very great isolation, certainly, the achievement of which constitutes a wonderful phenomenon, a miracle in itself. Withal magic is not something *supernatural*. As explained by Jamblichus, "they through the sacerdotal theurgy announce that they are able to ascend *to more elevated and universal Essences*, and to those that are established above fate, *viz.*, to god and the demiurgus: neither employing matter, nor assuming any other things besides, except the observation of a sensible time". Already some are beginning to recognise the existence of subtle powers and influences in nature of which they have hitherto known nought. But as Dr Carter Blake truly remarks, "the nineteenth century is not that which has observed the genesis of new, nor the completion of old, methods of thought"; to which Mr Bonwick adds that "if the ancients knew but little of our mode of investigations into the secrets of nature, we know still less of their mode of research".

# PART II

## FOUNDATIONAL WORKS OF THE ACADEMIC DEBATE

PART II: FOUNDATIONAL WORKS OF THE ACADEMIC DEBATE

# INTRODUCTION

The formal difference between the historical (Part I) and the academic sources (Parts II to IV) presented in this volume is that the latter are written by academics (i.e., members of a modern university or college). The University of Berlin, founded in 1810 by Wilhelm von Humboldt, is often cited as an influential model of the modern university where research became the guiding force rather than lecturing. One of the luminaries of that university was Georg Wilhelm Friedrich Hegel (b. 1770; d. 1831), who was appointed to the chair of philosophy in 1816 and became its rector in 1830. At the university, Hegel delivered lecture series on many topics, including the philosophy of history and the philosophy of religion (published posthumously). In the latter lectures he devoted some attention to "*Zauberei*" ("sorcery", but rendered as "magic" in the English translation edited by Peter C. Hodgson [1987]). Randall Styers (2004: 66) reviews the impact of Hegel's lectures as follows: "The fundamental components of Hegel's account of magic will be rehearsed repeatedly throughout the nineteenth and twentieth centuries: magic marks the boundary of religion [...]; magic is largely a local, ethnic phenomenon; magic is based on unconstrained and arbitrary desire and wilfulness; magic lacks any notion of transcendence and universality; magic is linked essentially to non-European peoples, even though it maintains an inexplicable allure even in higher culture."

Hegel conceived history as an evolutionary process. In that process, "*Zauberei*" was at the threshold of "religion", being a form of primitive nature "religion" but not yet really qualifying as "religion" in a fuller sense. The account of civilization provided by the later Victorian anthropologists Edward B. Tylor (see Chapter 11) and James George Frazer (see Chapter 12) during the formative period of the modern academic discourse on "magic" was also evolutionary and likewise assigned "magic" to lower stages of cultural achievements. Incidentally, the appendix of the first volume of the third edition of Frazer's *The Golden Bough* (1906) contains excerpts from Hegel's *Lectures on the Philosophy of Religion*; Frazer made it clear, however, that his attention to Hegel's work was only alerted after having composed his own evolutionist scheme.

Tylor's successor as reader in anthropology at the University of Oxford, Robert Ranulph Marett (b. 1866; d. 1943), was one of the earliest critics of Tylor and Frazer. In his "Pre-animistic religion" (1909 [1899]), Marett advocates a "pre-animistic" phase in the evolution of religions, arguing that a "feeling of awe" – instead of Tylor's "belief in spiritual beings" – stood at the outset of religious evolution. In his article "From speech to prayer" (1909 [1904]), Marett engrosses this criticism by refuting the idea of "magic" as a "pseudo-science" based on a false "association of ideas", arguing instead that "primitive" people could well differentiate between the symbol and the symbolized. Instead of focusing on different types of thinking, Marett suggests that "magic" arose from strong emotions that led to the performance of impulsive symbolic actions and later evolved into more complex ritual sequences (for a similar argument, see Chapter 17 by Bronislaw Malinowski). Marett also refutes Frazer's mechanistic, deterministic understanding of the "spell", holding that it originally derived from the interaction with transcendent beings (i.e., in Tylor's and Frazer's words, "religion") where it "is generally a projection of the imperative will"

(Marett 1909: 58) of the practitioner. Accordingly, Marett rejects Frazer's opposition of spell ("magic") and prayer ("religion") but conjoins them in the necessarily fuzzy "sphere of the magico-religious" (e.g. 90, 131). This dissolution of a strict dichotomy between "magic" and "religion" influenced later authors who advocated a "magico-religious continuum" (see the Introduction to Part III).

In France, Marcel Mauss (see Chapter 13) and Émile Durkheim (Chapter 14) explored the relationship between "magic" and "religion" by emphasizing different social (rather than cognitive) processes involved. Durkheim's colleague Lucien Lévy-Bruhl (b. 1857; d. 1939), however, in his pivotal works *Les fonctions mentales dans les sociétés inférieures* (1910; 1926 translated as *How Natives Think*) and *La mentalité primitive* (1922; 1923 translated as *Primitive Mentality*) mainly followed in the footsteps of Frazer. Although he did not propose any novel theories or definitions of "magic", his controversial idea of "participation" – referring to the alleged worldview of "primitive mentality" that (contrary to "Western" mentality) does not differentiate between natural and supernatural, or cause and effect – was often picked up and interpreted in the conceptual framework of "magic" by later authors. While Lévy-Bruhl, particularly in his late work, stresses that the concept of "participation" could be applicable to both "magic" and "religion", and even to aspects of modern societies, later authors tended to exclusively associate it with "magic". This led to purporting the idea of there being a fundamentally different kind of "magical" worldview (see, for example, Chapter 15 in this volume by Gerardus van der Leeuw as well as Chapter 21 by Susan Greenwood; see also Wax and Wax 1963; van Baal 1963). However, Lévy-Bruhl's concept of "participation" was also severely criticized by important theorists of "magic", most importantly by Bronislaw Malinowski (see Chapter II of Malinowski 1948) and Edward E. Evans-Pritchard (see Evans-Pritchard 1934 and Chapter 16 in this volume).

Sigmund Freud (b. 1856; d. 1939) devoted some pages to "magic" in his work *Totem and Taboo* (1913). In Part III of this work, Freud discusses "Animism, magic, and the omnipotence of thought", classifying "magic" as the main technique of "animism" (Freud 2010: 91; "animism" is understood as "belief in souls and in demons": 102). Freud claims that "primitive" people believe in "magic" because they believe in the "omnipotence of thought" and Freud therefore compares the performance of "magical" rites to the actions of children and neurotics: while the child aims at fulfilling his wishes by hallucinating, and the neurotic by compulsive behaviour, the "magician" performs "motor hallucinations" (98). Freud follows the evolutionist paradigm and assumes a cultural evolution from "animism" to "religion" to "science", equating these stages to the developmental steps of the human psyche. According to Freud, the "animistic" ("magical") worldview corresponds to early forms of individual narcissism since the belief in the "omnipotence of thought" does not yet envisage external beings (such as the parents, or Gods in the context of "religion"). In this elaborated form, Freud's strikingly reductionist interpretation of "magic" was rarely adopted in the subsequent debate. However, psychoanalytical concepts and ideas repeatedly entered, in a somewhat reduced manner, anthropological narratives (see, for example, Malinowski 1948; Leach 1958; Lévi-Strauss 1963; Douglas 1966).

Last but not least, Max Weber (b. 1864; d. 1920) is one of the main theoreticians of the "formative period" not represented by a text in Part II (partly because he had little say on the later debate). Weber never proposed a coherent definition or theory of "magic". In passages on the sociology of religion from his posthumously published work *Economy and Society*, written between 1910 and 1914, Weber suggests a historical evolution from "magic" to "religion" and rather tentatively discusses criteria that could plausibly distinguish these concepts. Among others, he suggests that:

1. "Religion" implies the worship of "gods" by prayer and invocation whereas "magic" coerces "demons" by "magical formulae" (Weber 1964: 25).
2. "Religion" is based on regular cultic practice performed by "priests" as "professional functionaries" whereas "magicians" are "self-employed" (29).
3. "Religion" is accompanied by an on-going rationalization and systematization of theological issues, leading to the increased reflection on "other-worldly" matters and the establishment of complex ethical systems; "magic", on the other hand, is rarely systematized and usually lacks ethical considerations, or adopts only the (mostly mechanistic) notion of "taboo".

Yet, Weber more than once emphasizes that the boundary between "magic" and "religion" remains fluid; he even states that in the history of religions there "may be no instance in which it is possible to apply this differentiation absolutely" (28). Weber was probably the most prominent figure to emphasize the "magical" aspects of institutionalized religions, foremost of (Catholic) Christianity, holding that the "Catholic priest continues to practice something of this magical power in executing the miracle of the mass and in exercising the power of the keys" (29). In this regard, Weber's conviction that only "ascetic Protestantism completely eliminated magic" (269) seems to reflect his famous narrative of "disenchantment".

# 11

# EDWARD B. TYLOR

*Primitive Culture*

Due to his Quaker family background, Edward Burnett Tylor (b. 1832; d. 1917) never received a higher school or university degree. He discovered his interest in human culture during a journey to Mexico in 1856 that was arranged as a treatment of his tuberculosis, resulting in his first work *Anahuac: Or Mexico and the Mexicans, Ancient and Modern* (1861). Inspired by the growing literature on biological and cultural evolution, Tylor aimed at a more thorough explanation of cultural history in his second book *Researches into the Early History of Mankind and the Development of Civilization* (1865). His most influential work, however, was *Primitive Culture*, published in two volumes in 1871. Here, we find his most important contributions to academic discourse – the concepts of "animism" and of "survival". In recognition of his scientific merits, Tylor was first appointed a reader in anthropology (1884). In 1896, Tylor became the first professor of anthropology in England (University of Oxford).

We present an excerpt from chapter four of the first volume of *Primitive Culture* on "Survivals in culture". Tylor employs the term "survival" to signify and explain vestiges of former thoughts and practices (such as customs, games, riddles, sayings, etc.) that had lost their utility but were retained, even if poorly integrated, in contemporary culture. Tylor's rationale for classifying "magic" as a "survival" is an overall scheme of cultural evolution: "magic", he claims, belongs "in its main principle to the lowest known stages of civilization" and while "progressive races have been learning to submit their opinions to closer and closer experimental tests, occult science has been breaking down into the condition of a survival". This interpretation of "magic" as one of the most primitive "survivals" of cultural evolution significantly influenced later evolutionist theories – foremost that of Frazer (see Chapter 12).

In the framework of his evolutionist agenda, Tylor subsumes beliefs and practices from a huge variety of cultural–religious contexts under the concept of "magic": interpretation of dreams, clairvoyance and other forms of divination, astrology, healing rites, malevolent rites ("witchcraft"), alchemy, spiritism and spirit possession, or the belief in miracles (see the parts of Chapter 4 not reprinted here). In order to assign these very diverse beliefs and practices to the overall concept of "magic" and, furthermore, to explain their persistence over long periods of cultural history, Tylor maintains that they all share a similar principle of thought – namely, an erroneous "association of ideas": man, "having come to associate in thought those things which he found by experience to be connected in fact, proceeded erroneously to invert this action, and to conclude that association in thought must involve similar connexion in reality". Similarly, Tylor speaks of "analogical" thinking or "symbolic magic". In the second part of our excerpt, Tylor offers a variety of alternative explanations of the persistence of "magic" – this "whole monstrous farrago". Given these pejorative rhetorics and, in particular, the rationalistic impetus of his narrative, Tylor seems to be continuing the Enlightenment agenda (see Chapter 9).

## *PRIMITIVE CULTURE*

IN examining the survival of opinions in the midst of conditions of society becoming gradually estranged from them, and tending at last to suppress them altogether, much may be learnt from the history of one of the most pernicious delusions that ever vexed mankind, the belief in Magic. Looking at Occult Science from this ethnographic point of view, I shall instance some of its branches as illustrating the course of intellectual culture. Its place in history is briefly this. It belongs in its main principle to the lowest known stages of civilization, and the lower races, who have not partaken largely of the education of the world, still maintain it in vigour. From this level it may be traced upward, much of the savage art holding its place substantially unchanged, and many new practices being in course of time developed, while both the older and newer developments have lasted on more or less among modern cultured nations. But during the ages in which progressive races have been learning to submit their opinions to closer and closer experimental tests, occult science has been breaking down into the condition of a survival, in which state we mostly find it among ourselves.

The modern educated world, rejecting occult science as a contemptible superstition, has practically committed itself to the opinion that magic belongs to a lower level of civilization. It is very instructive to find the soundness of this judgment undesignedly confirmed by nations whose education has not advanced far enough to destroy their belief in magic itself. In any country an isolated or outlying race, the lingering survivor of an older nationality, is liable to the reputation of sorcery. It is thus with the Lavas of Burma, supposed to be the broken-down remains of an ancient cultured race, and dreaded as man-tigers;[1] and with the Budas of Abyssinia, who are at once the smiths and potters, sorcerers and werewolves, of their district.[2] But the usual and suggestive state of things is that nations who believe with the sincerest terror in the reality of the magic art, at the same time cannot shut their eyes to the fact that it more essentially belongs to, and is more thoroughly at home among, races less civilized than themselves. The Malays of the Peninsula, who have adopted Mohammedan religion and civilization, have this idea of the lower tribes of the land, tribes more or less of their own race, but who have remained in their early savage condition. The Malays have enchanters of their own, but consider them inferior to the

---
1. Bastian, Adolf. 1866. *Die Völker des oestlichen Asien*, vol. I. Leipzig, London, p119.
2. Pearce, Nathaniel. 1831. *The Life and Adventures of Nathaniel Pearce*, ed. by J. J. Halls, vol. I. London, p286.

sorcerers or poyangs belonging to the rude Mintira; to these they will resort for the cure of diseases and the working of misfortune and death to their enemies. It is, in fact, the best protection the Mintira have against their stronger Malay neighbours, that these are careful not to offend them for fear of their powers of magical revenge. The Jakuns, again, are a rude and wild race, whom the Malays despise as infidels and little higher than animals, but whom at the same time they fear extremely. To the Malay the Jakun seems a supernatural being, skilled in divination, sorcery, and fascination, able to do evil or good according to his pleasure, whose blessing will be followed by the most fortunate success, and his curse by the most dreadful consequences; he can turn towards the house of an enemy, at whatever distance, and beat two sticks together till that enemy will fall sick and die; he is skilled in herbal physic; he has the power of charming the fiercest wild beasts. Thus it is that the Malays, though they despise the Jakuns, refrain, in many circumstances, from ill-treating them.[3] In India, in long-past ages, the dominant Aryans described the rude indigenes of the land by the epithets of "possessed of magical powers, changing their shape at will".[4] To this day, Hindus settled in Chota-Nagpur and Singbhum firmly believe that the Mundas have powers of witchcraft, whereby they can transform themselves into tigers and other beasts of prey to devour their enemies, and can witch away the lives of man and beast; it is to the wildest and most savage of the tribe that such powers are generally ascribed.[5] In Southern India, again, we hear in past times of Hinduized Dravidians, the Sudras of Canara, living in fear of the demoniacal powers of the slave-caste below them.[6] In our own day, among Dravidian tribes of the Nilagiri district, the Todas and Badagas are in mortal dread of the Kurumbas, despised and wretched forest outcasts, but gifted, it is believed, with powers of destroying men and animals and property by witchcraft.[7] Northern Europe brings the like contrast sharply into view. The Finns and Lapps, whose low Tatar barbarism was characterized by sorcery such as flourishes still among their Siberian kinsfolk, were accordingly objects of superstitious fear to their Scandinavian neighbours and oppressors. In the middle ages the name of Finn was, as it still remains among seafaring men, equivalent to that of sorcerer, while Lapland witches had a European celebrity as practitioners of the black art. Ages after the Finns had risen in the social scale, the Lapps retained much of their old half-savage habit of life, and with it naturally their witchcraft, so that even the magic-gifted Finns revered the occult powers of a people more barbarous than themselves. Rühs writes thus early in the last century: "There are still sorcerers in Finland, but the skilfullest of them believe that the Lapps far excel them; of a well-experienced magician

---

3. *Journal of the Indian Archipelago and Eastern Asia*, vol. I. p328; vol. II. p273; see vol. IV. p425.
4. Muir, John. 1860. *Original Sanskrit Texts on the Origin and History of the People of India, Their Religion and Institutions*, Part II. London, p435.
5. Dalton, E. T. 1868. "The 'Kols' of Chota-Nagpore", *Transactions of the Ethnological Society of London*, vol. VI. p6; see p16.
6. Gardner, James. 1858–1860. *Faiths of the World: An Account of all Religions and Religious Sects, Their Doctrines, Rites, Ceremonies, and Customs*. Edinburgh, s.v. "Exorcism".
7. Shortt, John. 1869. "An Account of the Hill Tribes of the Neilgherries", *Transactions of the Ethnological Society of London*, vol. VI. pp247, 277; Sir W. Elliot. 1868. "On Ancient Sepulchral Remains in Southern India, and Particularly of Those in the Nilagiri Mountains", in *Congress of Prehistoric Archaeology: Transactions of the Third Session*. London and Norwich, p253.

they say, 'That is quite a Lapp', and they journey to Lapland for such knowledge."[8] All this is of a piece with the survival of such ideas among the ignorant elsewhere in the civilized world. Many a white man in the West Indies and Africa dreads the incantations of the Obi-man, and Europe ascribes powers of sorcery to despised outcast "races maudites", Gypsies and Cagots. To turn from nations to sects, the attitude of Protestants to Catholics in this matter is instructive. It was remarked in Scotland: "There is one opinion which many of them entertain, […] that a popish priest can cast out devils and cure madness, and that the Presbyterian clergy have no such power." So Bourne says of the Church of England clergy, that the vulgar think them no conjurers, and say none can lay spirits but popish priests.[9] These accounts are not recent, but in Germany the same state of things appears to exist still Protestants get the aid of Catholic priests and monks to help them against witchcraft, to lay ghosts, consecrate herbs, and discover thieves;[10] thus with unconscious irony judging the relation of Rome toward modern civilization.

The principal key to the understanding of Occult Science is to consider it as based on the Association of Ideas, a faculty which lies at the very foundation of human reason, but in no small degree of human unreason also. Man, as yet in a low intellectual condition, having come to associate in thought those things which he found by experience to be connected in fact, proceeded erroneously to invert this action, and to conclude that association in thought must involve similar connexion in reality. He thus attempted to discover, to foretell, and to cause events by means of processes which we can now see to have only an ideal significance. By a vast mass of evidence from savage, barbaric, and civilized life, magic arts which have resulted from thus mistaking an ideal for a real connexion, may be clearly traced from the lower culture which they are of, to the higher culture which they are in.[11] Such are the practices whereby a distant person is to be affected by acting on something closely associated with him – his property, clothes he has worn, and above all cuttings of his hair and nails. Not only do savages high and low like the Australians and Polynesians, and barbarians like the nations of Guinea, live in deadly terror of this spiteful craft – not only have the Parsis their sacred ritual prescribed for burying their cut hair and nails, lest demons and sorcerers should do mischief with them, but the fear of leaving such clippings and parings about lest their former owner should be harmed through them, has by no means died out of European folk-lore, and the German peasant, during the days between his child's birth and baptism, objects to lend anything out of the house, lest witchcraft should be worked through it on the yet unconsecrated baby.[12] As the

---

8. Rühs, Friedrich. 1809. *Finland und seine Bewohner*. Leipzig, p296; Bastian, Adolf. 1860. *Der Mensch in der Geschichte*, vol. III. Leipzig, p202.
9. Brand, John. 1777. *Observations on Popular Antiquities*, vol. III. London, pp81–3; see p313.
10. Wuttke, Adolf. 1860. *Der deutsche Volksaberglaube der Gegenwart*. Hamburg, p128; see p239.
11. For an examination of numerous magical arts, mostly coming under this category, see Tylor, Edward Burnett. 1865. *Researches into the Early History of Mankind and the Development of Civilization*. London, Chapters VI and X.
12. Stanbridge, William Edward. 1861. "Some Particulars of the General Characteristics, Astronomy, and Mythology of the Tribes in the Central Part of Victoria, Southern Australia", *Transactions of the Ethnological Society of London*, vol. I. p299; Ellis, William. 1853. *Polynesian Researches during a Residence*

negro fetish-man, when his patient does not come in person, can divine by means of his dirty cloth or cap instead,[13] so the modern clairvoyant professes to feel sympathetically the sensations of a distant person, if communication be made through a lock of his hair or any object that has been in contact with him.[14] The simple idea of joining two objects with a cord, taking for granted that this communication will establish connexion or carry influence, has been worked out in various ways in the world. In Australia, the native doctor fastens one end of a string to the ailing part of the patient's body, and by sucking at the other end pretends to draw out blood for his relief.[15] In Orissa, the Jeypore witch lets down a ball of thread through her enemy's roof to reach his body, that by putting the other end in her own mouth she may suck his blood.[16] When a reindeer is sacrificed at a sick Ostyak's tent door, the patient holds in his hand a cord attached to the victim offered for his benefit.[17] Greek history shows a similar idea, when the citizens of Ephesus carried a rope seven furlongs from their walls to the temple of Artemis, thus to place themselves under her safeguard against the attack of Croesus; and in the yet more striking story of the Kylonians, who tied a cord to the statue of the goddess when they quitted the asylum, and clung to it for protection as they crossed unhallowed ground; but by ill-fate the cord of safety broke and they were mercilessly put to death.[18] And in our own day, Buddhist priests in solemn ceremony put themselves in communication with a sacred relic, by each taking hold of a long thread fastened near it and around the temple.[19]

Magical arts in which the connexion is that of mere analogy or symbolism are endlessly numerous throughout the course of civilization. Their common theory may be readily made out from a few typical cases, and thence applied confidently to the general mass. The Australian will observe the track of an insect near a grave, to ascertain the direction where the sorcerer is to be found, by whose craft the man died.[20] The Zulu may be seen chewing a bit of wood, in order, by this symbolic act, to soften the heart of the man he wants to buy oxen from, or of the woman he wants for a wife.[21] The Obi-man of West Africa makes

---

of *Nearly Eight Years in the Society and Sandwich Islands*, vol I. London, p364; Wilson, John Leighton. 1856. *Western Africa: Its History, Condition and Prospects*. London, p215; Spiegel, Friedrich von (ed.). 1853. *Avesta: die heiligen Schriften der Parsen*, vol. I. Wien and Leipzig, p124; Wuttke. op cit. [*Der deutsche Volksaberglaube der Gegenwart*], p195; general references in Tylor. *op. cit.* [*Researches into the Early History of Mankind and the Development of Civilization*], p129.

13. Burton, Richard Francis. 1865. *Wit and Wisdom from West Africa*. London, p411.
14. Gregory, William. 1851. *Letters to a Candid Inquirer, on Animal Magnetism*, Philadelphia, p128.
15. Eyre, Edward John. 1845. *Journals of Expeditions of Discovery into Central Australia and Overland from Adelaide to King George's Sound in the Years 1840–1*, vol. II. London, p361; Collins, David. 1798. *An Account of the English Colony in New South Wales*, vol. I. London, pp561, 594.
16. Shortt, John. 1868. "A Contribution to the Ethnology of Jeypore", *Transactions of the Ethnological Society of London*, vol. VI. p278.
17. Bastian. *op. cit.* [*Der Mensch in der Geschichte*], p117.
18. See Grote, George. 1849. *A History of Greece*, vol. III. New York, pp113, 351.
19. Hardy, Robert Spence. 1850. *Eastern Monachism*. London, p241.
20. Oldfield, Augustus. 1865. "On the Aborigines of Australia", *Transactions of the Ethnological Society of London*, vol. III. p246.
21. Grout, Lewis. 1860. *Zulu-Land: Or Life Among the Zulu-Kafirs of Natal and Zulu-Land, South Africa*. London, p134.

his packet of grave-dust, blood, and bones, that this suggestive representation of death may bring his enemy to the grave.[22] The Bhond sets up the iron arrow of the War-god in a basket of rice, and judges from its standing upright that war must be kept up also, or from its falling that the quarrel may be let fall too; and when he tortures human victims sacrificed to the Earth-goddess, he rejoices to see them shed plentiful tears, which betoken copious showers to fall upon his land.[23] These are fair examples of the symbolic magic of the lower races, and they are fully rivalled in superstitions which still hold their ground in Europe. With quaint simplicity, the German cottager declares that if a dog howls looking downward, it portends a death; but if upward, then a recovery from sickness.[24] Locks must be opened and bolts drawn in a dying man's house, that his soul may not be held fast.[25] The Hessian lad thinks that he may escape the conscription by carrying a baby-girl's cap in his pocket – a symbolic way of repudiating manhood.[26] Modern Servians, dancing and singing, lead about a little girl dressed in leaves and flowers, and pour bowls of water over her to make the rain come.[27] Sailors becalmed will sometimes whistle for a wind; but in other weather they hate whistling at sea, which raises a whistling gale.[28] Fish, says the Cornishman, should be eaten from the tail towards the head, to bring the other fishes' heads towards the shore, for eating them the wrong way turns them from the coast.[29] He who has cut himself should rub the knife with fat, and as it dries, the wound will heal; this is a lingering survival from days when recipes for sympathetic ointment were to be found in the Pharmacopœia.[30] Fanciful as these notions are, it should be borne in mind that they come fairly under definite mental law, depending as they do on a principle of ideal association, of which we can quite understand the mental action, though we deny its practical results. The clever Lord Chesterfield, too clever to understand folly, may again be cited to prove this. He relates in one of his letters that the king had been ill, and that people generally expected the illness to be fatal, because the oldest lion in the Tower, about the king's age, had just died. "So wild and capricious is the human mind", he exclaims, by way of comment. But indeed the thought was neither wild nor capricious, it was simply such an argument from analogy as the educated world has at length painfully learnt to be worthless; but which, it is not too much to declare, would to this day carry considerable weight to the minds of four-fifths of the human race.

A glance at those magical arts which have been systematized into pseudo-sciences shows the same underlying principle. The art of taking omens from seeing and meeting

---

22. See specimen and description in the Christy Museum.
23. Macpherson, Samuel Charters. 1865. *Memorials of Service in India*. London, pp130, 363.
24. Wuttke. *op. cit.* [*Der deutsche Volksaberglaube der Gegenwart*], p31.
25. Hunt, Robert. 1865. *Popular Romances of the West of England* [2nd series]. London, p165; Brand. *op. cit.* [*Observations on Popular Antiquities*], vol. II, p231.
26. Wuttke. *op. cit.* [*Der deutsche Volksaberglaube der Gegenwart*], p100.
27. Grimm, Jacob. 1835. *Deutsche Mythologie*. Göttingen, p560.
28. Brand. *op. cit.* [*Observations on Popular Antiquities*], vol. III. p240.
29. Hunt. op cit. [*Popular Romances of the West of England*], p148.
30. Wuttke. *op. cit.* [*Der deutsche Volksaberglaube der Gegenwart*], p165; Brand. *op. cit.* [*Observations on Popular Antiquities*], vol. III. p305.

animals, which includes augury, is familiar to such savages as the Tupis of Brazil[31] and the Dayaks of Borneo,[32] and extends upward through classic civilization. The Maoris may give a sample of the character of its rules: they hold it unlucky if an owl hoots during a consultation, but a council of war is encouraged by prospect of victory when a hawk flies overhead; a flight of birds to the right of the war-sacrifice is propitious if the villages of the tribe are in that quarter, but if the omen is in the enemy's direction the war will be given up.[33] Compare these with the Tatar rules, and it is obvious that similar thoughts lie at the source of both. Here a certain little owl's cry is a sound of terror, although there is a white owl which is lucky; but of all birds the white falcon is most prophetic, and the Kalmuk bows his thanks for the good omen when one flies by on the right, but seeing one on the left turns away his face and expects calamity.[34] So to the negro of Old Calabar, the cry of the great kingfisher bodes good or evil, according as it is heard on the right or left.[35] Here we have the obvious symbolism of the right and left hand, the foreboding of ill from the owl's doleful note, and the suggestion of victory from the fierce swooping hawk, a thought which in old Europe made the bird of prey the warrior's omen of conquest. Meaning of the same kind appears in the "Angang", the omens taken from meeting animals and people, especially on first going out in the morning, as when the ancient Slaves held meeting a sick man or an old woman to bode ill-luck. Anyone who takes the trouble to go into this subject in detail, and to study the classic, medieval, and oriental codes of rules, will find that the principle of direct symbolism still accounts for a fair proportion of them, though the rest may have lost their early significance, or may have been originally due to some other reason, or may have been arbitrarily invented (as a considerable proportion of such devices must necessarily be) to fill up the gaps in the system. It is still plain to us why the omen of the crow should be different on the right or left hand, why a vulture should mean rapacity, a stork concord, a pelican piety, an ass labour, why the fierce conquering wolf should be a good omen, and the timid hare a bad one, why bees, types of an obedient nation, should be Lucky to a king, while flies, returning however often they are driven off, should be signs of importunity and impudence.[36] And as to the general principle that animals are ominous to those who meet them, the German peasant who says a flock of sheep is lucky but a herd of swine unlucky to meet, and the Cornish miner who turns

---

31. Gandavo, Pero de Magalhanes de. 1837. *Histoire de la province de Sancta-Cruz*. Paris, p125; D'Orbigny, Alcide Dessalines. 1839. *L'Homme Américain*, vol. II. Paris, p168.
32. St John, Spenser. 1862. *Life in the Forests of Far East*, vol. I. London, p202; *Journal of the Indian Archipelago and Eastern Asia*, vol. II. p357.
33. Yate, William. 1835. *An Account of New Zealand and the Formation and Progress of the Church Missionary Society's Mission in the Northern Island*. London, p90; Polack, Joel Samuel. 1838. *New Zealand: Being a Narrative of Travels and Adventures During a Residence in that Country Between the Years 1831 and 1837*, vol. I. London, p248.
34. Klemm, Gustav. 1844. *Allgemeine Cultur-Geschichte*, vol. III. Leipzig, p202.
35. Burton. op cit. [*Wit and Wisdom from West Africa*], p381.
36. See Agrippa von Nettesheim, H.C. 1533. *De Occulta Philosophia*, vol. I. chap. 63; Agrippa von Nettesheim, H.C. 1527. *De Incertitudine et Vanitate Scientiarum*, chap. 37; Grimm. *op. cit.* [*Deutsche Mythologie*], p1073; Hanusch, Ignaz Johann. 1842. *Die Wissenschaft des Slawischen Mythus*. Lemberg, p285; Brand. *op. cit.* [*Observations on Popular Antiquities*], vol. III. pp184–227.

away in horror when he meets an old woman or a rabbit on his way to the pit's mouth, are to this day keeping up relics of early savagery as genuine as any flint implement dug out of a tumulus.

[…]

Looking at the details here selected as fair samples of symbolic magic, we may well ask the question, is there in the whole monstrous farrago no truth or value whatever? It appears that there is practically none, and that the world has been enthralled for ages by a blind belief in processes wholly irrelevant to their supposed results, and which might as well have been taken just the opposite way. Pliny justly saw in magic a study worthy of his especial attention, "for the very reason that, being the most fraudulent of arts, it had prevailed throughout the world and through so many ages" (*eo ipso quod fraudulentissima artium plurimum in toto terrarum orbe plurimisque seculis valuit*). If it be asked how such a system could have held its ground, not merely in independence but in defiance of its own facts, a fair answer does not seem hard to give. In the first place, it must be borne in mind that occult science has not existed entirely in its own strength. Futile as its arts may be, they are associated in practice with other proceedings by no means futile. What are passed off as sacred omens, are often really the cunning man's shrewd guesses at the past and future. Divination serves to the sorcerer as a mask for real inquest, as when the ordeal gives him invaluable opportunity of examining the guilty, whose trembling hands and equivocating speech betray at once their secret and their utter belief in his power of discerning it. Prophecy tends to fulfil itself, as where the magician, by putting into a victim's mind the belief that fatal arts have been practised against him, can slay him with this idea as with a material weapon. Often priest as well as magician, he has the whole power of religion at his back; often a man in power, always an unscrupulous intriguer, he can work witchcraft and statecraft together, and make his left hand help his right. Often a doctor, he can aid his omens of life or death with remedy or poison, while what we still call "conjurers' tricks" of sleight of hand have done much to keep up his supernatural prestige. From the earliest known stages of civilization, professional magicians have existed, who live by their craft, and keep it alive. It has been said, that if somebody had endowed lecturers to teach that two sides of a triangle are together equal to the third, the doctrine would have a respectable following among ourselves. At any rate, magic, with an influential profession interested in keeping it in credit and power, did not depend for its existence on mere evidence.

And, in the second place, as to this evidence. Magic has not its origin in fraud, and seems seldom practised as an utter imposture. The sorcerer generally learns his time-honoured profession in good faith, and retains his belief in it more or less from first to last; at once dupe and cheat, he combines the energy of a believer with the cunning of a hypocrite. Had occult science been simply framed for purposes of deception, mere nonsense would have answered the purpose, whereas, what we find is an elaborate and systematic pseudo-science. It is, in fact, a sincere but fallacious system of philosophy, evolved by the human intellect by processes still in great measure intelligible to our own minds, and it had thus an original standing-ground in the world. And though the evidence of fact was dead against it, it was but lately and gradually that this evidence was brought fatally to bear. A general survey of the practical working of the system may be made somewhat thus.

A large proportion of successful cases belong to natural means disguised as magic. Also, a certain proportion of cases must succeed by mere chance. By far the larger proportion, however, are what we should call failures; but it is a part of the magician's profession to keep these from counting, and this he does with extraordinary resource of rhetorical shift and brazen impudence. He deals in ambiguous phrases, which give him three or four chances for one. He knows perfectly how to impose difficult conditions, and to lay the blame of failure on their neglect. If you wish to make gold, the alchemist in Central Asia has a recipe at your service, only, to use it, you must abstain three days from thinking of apes; just as our English folk-lore says, that if one of your eyelashes comes out, and you put it on your thumb, you will get anything you wish for, if you can only avoid thinking of foxes' tails at the fatal moment. Again, if the wrong thing happens, the wizard has at least a reason why. Has a daughter been born when he promised a son, then it is some hostile practitioner who has turned the boy into a girl; does a tempest come just when he is making fine weather, then he calmly demands a larger fee for stronger ceremonies, assuring his clients that they may thank him as it is, for how much worse it would have been had he not done what he did. And even setting aside all this accessory trickery, if we look at honest but unscientific people practising occult science in good faith, and face to face with facts, we shall see that the failures which condemn it in our eyes carry comparatively little weight in theirs. Part escape under the elastic pretext of a "little more or less", as the loser in the lottery consoles himself that his lucky number came within two of a prize, or the moon-observer points out triumphantly that a change of weather has come within two or three days before or after a quarter, so that his convenient definition of near a moon's quarter applies to four or, six days out of every seven. Part escape through incapacity to appreciate negative evidence, which allows one success to outweigh half-a-dozen failures. How few there are even among the educated classes now, who have taken in the drift of that memorable passage in the beginning of the "Novum Organum" – "The human understanding, when any proposition has been once laid down (either from general admission and belief, or from the pleasure it affords), forces everything else to add fresh support and confirmation; and although most cogent and abundant instances may exist to the contrary, yet either does not observe or despises them, or gets rid of and rejects them by some distinction, with violent and injurious prejudice, rather than sacrifice the authority of its first conclusions. It was well answered by him who was shown in a temple the votive tablets suspended by such as had escaped the peril of shipwreck, and was pressed as to whether he would then recognize the power of the gods, by an inquiry, 'But where are the portraits of those who have perished in spite of their vows?'"[37]

On the whole, the survival of symbolic magic through the middle ages and into our own times is an unsatisfactory, but not a mysterious fact. A once-established opinion, however delusive, can hold its own from age to age, for belief can propagate itself without reference to its reasonable origin, as plants are propagated from slips without fresh raising from the seed.

---

37. Bacon, Francis. 1620. *Novum Organum Scientarium*. The original story is that of Diagoras – see Cicero. *De Natura Deorum*, vol. III. 37; Diog. Laert. lib. vi., Diogenes, 6.

[…]

But the opinions drawn from old or worn-out culture are not to be left lying where they were shaped. It is no more reasonable to suppose the laws of mind differently constituted in Australia and in England, in the time of the cave-dwellers and in the time of the builders of sheet-iron houses, than to suppose that the laws of chemical combination were of one sort in the time of the coal-measures, and are of another now. The thing that has been will be; and we are to study savages and old nations to learn the laws that under new circumstances are working for good or ill in our own development. If it is needful to give an instance of the directness with which antiquity and savagery bear upon our modern life, let it be taken in the facts just brought forward on the relation of ancient sorcery to the belief in witchcraft which was not long since one of the gravest facts of European history, and of savage spiritualism to beliefs which so deeply affect our civilization now. No one who can see in these cases, and in many others to be brought before him in these volumes, how direct and close the connexion may be between modern culture and the condition of the rudest savage, will be prone to accuse students who spend their labour on even the lowest and most trifling facts of ethnography, of wasting their hours in the satisfaction of a frivolous curiosity.

# 12

# JAMES GEORGE FRAZER

*The Golden Bough*

James George Frazer (b. 1854; d. 1941) studied Classics and graduated in 1878 with a dissertation on *The Growth of Plato's Ideal Theory*. Around the 1880s, strongly influenced by Tylor (see Chapter 11), Frazer adopted the evolutionist agenda and subsequently focused on comparative religion, myth and anthropology. Frazer, a fellow at Trinity College, Cambridge, for almost all his life, has written extensively on a huge variety of topics; his most important work, however, is *The Golden Bough*, first published in two volumes in 1890, swelling up to twelve volumes in the third edition published between 1906 and 1915 (furthermore, a supplementary volume entitled *Aftermath* was published in 1936). The excerpt presented here is taken from the "abridged" (one-volume) edition of *The Golden Bough* (1922).

The text begins with Frazer's classical definition of "magic" that distinguishes two main principles – namely, the Law of Similarity and the Law of Contagion: "From the first of these principles […] the magician infers that he can produce any effect he desires merely by imitating it; from the second he infers that whatever he does to a material object will affect equally the person with whom the object was once in contact." Frazer assigns both principles to the superordinate concept of "sympathetic magic" as both "assume that things act on each other at a distance through a secret sympathy". Frazer categorically refutes the existence of this secret sympathy ("magic is […] a false science as well as an abortive art") and explains – like Tylor (see Chapter 11) – mankind's widespread and continuous belief in "magic" as a false "association of ideas".

In the second and third part of the excerpt, Frazer introduces his famous idea of a continuous evolution of three cultural stages. Mankind starts off with "magic", but at some point realizes its "inherent falsehood and barrenness" and moves on to assuming that "other beings […] brought about all the varied series of events which he had hitherto believed to be dependent on his own magic" – thence, "religion" arises. Frazer, moreover, claims that, if spirits or some higher beings are addressed, "magic", rather, "constrains or coerces instead of conciliating or propitiating them as religion would do". Finally, man realizes the fallacy of "religion" by "postulating […] an inflexible regularity in the order of natural events, which […] enables us to foresee their course with certainty and to act accordingly". As a result of this development, "religion, regarded as an explanation of nature, is displaced by science".

This "master narrative" had a lasting impact upon academic and non-academic discourses during the nineteenth to twenty-first centuries. Frazer's core ideas – his evolutionistic scheme; his two laws of "sympathetic magic"; his criteria to distinguish "magic", "religion" and "science"; even his conviction that "science" is self-evidently superior to "magic" – have been fundamentally questioned and often rejected by subsequent authors (see, e.g., Chapters 13, 14, 19 and 20). Yet, many contemporary encyclopaedias and popular science works still perpetuate his theory and terminology, and even academic authors continue to discuss his thoughts, partly using them as a point of reference for their own research (see Chapters 21 and 23).

# *THE GOLDEN BOUGH*

## CHAPTER III: SYMPATHETIC MAGIC

§ 1. *The Principles of Magic*. If we analyse the principles of thought on which magic is based, they will probably be found to resolve themselves into two: first, that like produces like, or that an effect resembles its cause; and, second, that things which have once been in contact with each other continue to act on each other at a distance after the physical contact has been severed. The former principle may be called the Law of Similarity, the latter the Law of Contact or Contagion. From the first of these principles, namely the Law of Similarity, the magician infers that he can produce any effect he desires merely by imitating it: from the second he infers that whatever he does to a material object will affect equally the person with whom the object was once in contact, whether it formed part of his body or not. Charms based on the Law of Similarity may be called Homoeopathic or Imitative Magic. Charms based on the Law of Contact or Contagion may be called Contagious Magic. To denote the first of these branches of magic the term Homoeopathic is perhaps preferable, for the alternative term Imitative or Mimetic suggests, if it does not imply, a conscious agent who imitates, thereby limiting the scope of magic too narrowly. For the same principles which the magician applies in the practice of his art are implicitly believed by him to regulate the operations of inanimate nature; in other words, he tacitly assumes that the Laws of Similarity and Contact are of universal application and are not limited to human actions. In short, magic is a spurious system of natural law as well as a fallacious guide of conduct; it is a false science as well as an abortive art. Regarded as a system of natural law, that is, as a statement of the rules which determine the sequence of events throughout the world, it may be called Theoretical Magic: regarded as a set of precepts which human beings observe in order to compass their ends, it may be called Practical Magic. At the same time it is to be borne in mind that the primitive magician knows magic only on its practical side; he never analyses the mental processes on which his practice is based, never reflects on the abstract principles involved in his actions. With him, as with the vast majority of men, logic is implicit, not explicit: he reasons just as he digests his food in complete ignorance of the intellectual and physiological processes which are essential to the one operation and to the other. In short, to him magic is always an art, never a science; the very idea of science is lacking in his undeveloped mind. It is for the philosophic student to trace the train of thought which underlies the magician's practice; to draw out the few simple threads of which the tangled skein is composed; to disengage the abstract principles from their concrete applications; in short, to discern the spurious science behind the bastard art.

If my analysis of the magician's logic is correct, its two great principles turn out to be merely two different misapplications of the association of ideas. Homoeopathic magic is founded on the association of ideas by similarity: contagious magic is founded on the association of ideas by contiguity. Homoeopathic magic commits the mistake of assuming that things which resemble each other are the same: contagious magic commits the mistake of assuming that things which have once been in contact with each other are always in contact. But in practice the two branches are often combined; or, to be more exact, while homoeopathic or imitative magic may be practised by itself, contagious magic will generally be found to involve an application of the homoeopathic or imitative principle. Thus generally stated the two things may be a little difficult to grasp, but they will readily become intelligible when they are illustrated by particular examples. Both trains of thought are in fact extremely simple and elementary. It could hardly be otherwise, since they are familiar in the concrete, though certainly not in the abstract, to the crude intelligence not only of the savage, but of ignorant and dull-witted people everywhere. Both branches of magic, the homoeopathic and the contagious, may conveniently be comprehended under the general name of Sympathetic Magic, since both assume that things act on each other at a distance through a secret sympathy, the impulse being transmitted from one to the other by means of what we may conceive as a kind of invisible ether, not unlike that which is postulated by modern science for a precisely similar purpose, namely, to explain how things can physically affect each other through a space which appears to be empty.

It may be convenient to tabulate as follows the branches of magic according to the laws of thought which underlie them:

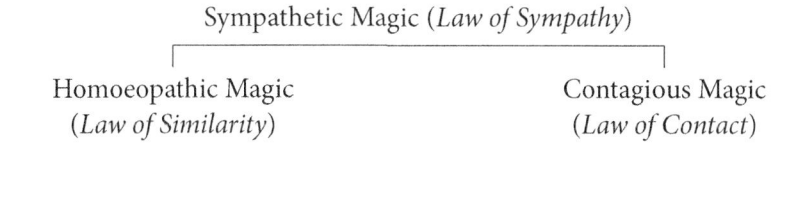

Sympathetic Magic (Law of Sympathy)

| Homoeopathic Magic | Contagious Magic |
| --- | --- |
| (*Law of Similarity*) | (*Law of Contact*) |

[…]

## CHAPTER IV: MAGIC AND RELIGION

The examples collected in the last chapter may suffice to illustrate the general principles of sympathetic magic in its two branches, to which we have given the names of Homoeopathic and Contagious respectively. In some cases of magic which have come before us we have seen that the operation of spirits is assumed, and that an attempt is made to win their favour by prayer and sacrifice. But these cases are on the whole exceptional; they exhibit magic tinged and alloyed with religion. Wherever sympathetic magic occurs in its pure unadulterated form it assumes that in nature one event follows another necessarily and invariably without the intervention of any spiritual or personal agency. Thus its fundamental conception is identical with that of modern science; underlying the whole system is a faith, implicit but real and firm, in the order and uniformity of nature. The magician does not doubt that the same causes will always produce the same effects, that the performance of the proper ceremony, accompanied by the appropriate spell, will inevitably be attended by the desired result, unless, indeed, his incantations should chance to be thwarted and foiled by the more potent charms of another sorcerer. He supplicates no higher power: he sues the favour of no fickle and wayward being: he abases himself before no awful deity. Yet his power, great as he believes it to be, is by no means arbitrary and unlimited. He can wield it only so long as he strictly conforms to the rules of his art, or to what may be called the laws of nature as conceived by him. To neglect these rules, to break these laws in the smallest particular, is to incur failure, and may even expose the unskilful practitioner himself to the utmost peril. If he claims a sovereignty over nature, it is a constitutional sovereignty rigorously limited in its scope and exercised in exact conformity with ancient usage. Thus the analogy between the magical and the scientific conceptions of the world is close. In both of them the succession of events is assumed to be perfectly regular and certain, being determined by immutable laws, the operation of which can be foreseen and calculated precisely; the elements of caprice, of chance, and of accident" are banished from the course of nature. Both of them open up a seemingly boundless vista of possibilities to him who knows the causes of things and can touch the secret springs that set in motion the vast and intricate mechanism of the world. Hence the strong attraction which magic and science alike have exercised on the human mind; hence the powerful stimulus that both have given to the pursuit of knowledge. They lure the weary enquirer, the footsore seeker, on through the wilderness of disappointment in the present by their endless promises of the future: they take him up to the top of an exceeding high mountain and show him, beyond the dark clouds and rolling mists at his feet, a vision of the celestial city, far off, it may be, but radiant with unearthly splendour, bathed in the light of dreams.

The fatal flaw of magic lies not in its general assumption of a sequence of events determined by law, but in its total misconception of the nature of the particular laws which govern that sequence. If we analyse the various cases of sympathetic magic which have been passed in review in the preceding pages, and which may be taken as fair samples of the bulk, we shall find, as I have already indicated, that they are all mistaken applications of one or other of two great fundamental laws of thought, namely, the association of ideas by similarity and the association of ideas by contiguity in space or time. A mistaken association of similar ideas produces homoeopathic or imitative magic: a mistaken association of contiguous ideas produces contagious magic. The principles of association are excellent in themselves, and indeed absolutely essential to the working of the human mind. Legitimately applied they yield science; illegitimately applied they yield magic, the bastard sister of science. It is therefore a truism, almost a tautology, to say that all magic is necessarily false and barren; for were it ever to become true and fruitful, it would no longer be magic but science. From the earliest times man has been engaged in a search for general rules whereby to turn the order of natural phenomena to his own advantage, and in the long search he has scraped together a great hoard of such maxims, some of them golden and some of them mere dross. The true or golden rules constitute the body of applied science which we call the arts; the false are magic.

If magic is thus next of kin to science, we have still to enquire how it stands related to religion. But the view we take of that relation will necessarily be coloured by the idea which we have formed of the nature of religion itself; hence a writer may reasonably be expected to define his conception of religion before he proceeds to investigate its relation to magic. There is probably no subject in the world about which opinions differ so much as the nature of religion, and to frame a definition of it which would satisfy everyone must obviously be impossible. All that a writer can do is, first, to say clearly what he means by religion, and afterwards to employ the word consistently in that sense throughout his work. By religion, then, I understand a propitiation or conciliation of powers superior to man which are believed to direct and control the course of nature and of human life. Thus defined, religion consists of two elements, a theoretical and a practical, namely, a belief in powers higher than man and an attempt to propitiate or please them. Of the two, belief clearly comes first, since we must believe in the existence of a divine being before we can attempt to please him. But unless the belief leads to a corresponding practice, it is not a religion but merely a theology; in the language of St. James, "faith, if it hath not works, is dead, being alone." In other words, no man is religious who does not govern his conduct in some measure by the fear or love of God. On the other hand, mere practice, divested of all religious belief, is also not religion. Two men may behave in exactly the same way, and yet one of them may be religious and the other not. If the one acts from the love or fear of God, he is religious; if the other acts from the love or fear of man, he is moral or immoral according as his behaviour comports or conflicts with the general good. Hence belief and practice or, in theological language, faith and works are equally essential to religion, which cannot exist without both of them. But it is not necessary that religious practice should always take the form of a ritual; that is, it need not consist in the offering of sacrifice, the recitation of prayers, and other outward ceremonies. Its aim is to please the deity, and if the deity is one who delights in charity and mercy and purity more than in oblations of blood, the chanting of hymns, and the fumes of incense, his worshippers will best please him, not by prostrating themselves before him, by intoning his praises, and by filling his temples with costly gifts, but by being pure and merciful and charitable towards men, for in so doing they will imitate, so far as human infirmity allows, the perfections of the divine nature. It was this ethical side of religion which the Hebrew prophets, inspired with a noble ideal of God's goodness and holiness, were never weary of inculcating. Thus Micah says: "He hath shewed thee, O man, what is good; and what doth the Lord require of thee, but to do justly, and to love mercy, and to walk humbly with thy God?" And at a later time much of the force by which Christianity conquered the world was drawn from the same high conception of God's moral nature and the duty laid on men of conforming themselves to it. "Pure religion and undefiled", says St. James, "before God and the Father is this, To visit the fatherless and widows in their affliction, and to keep himself unspotted from the world."

But if religion involves, first, a belief in superhuman beings who rule the world, and, second, an attempt to win their favour, it clearly assumes that the course of nature is to some extent elastic or variable, and that we can persuade or induce the mighty beings who control it to deflect, for our benefit, the current of events from the channel in which they would otherwise flow. Now this implied elasticity or variability of nature is directly opposed to the principles of magic as well as of science, both of which assume that the processes of nature are rigid and invariable in their operation, and that they can as little be turned from their course by persuasion and entreaty as by threats and intimidation. The distinction between the two conflicting views of the universe turns on their answer to the crucial question, Are the forces which govern the world conscious and personal, or unconscious and impersonal? Religion, as a conciliation of the superhuman powers, assumes the former member of the alternative. For all conciliation implies that the being conciliated is a conscious or personal agent, that his conduct is in some measure uncertain, and that he can be prevailed upon to vary it in the desired direction by a judicious appeal to his interests, his appetites, or his emotions. Conciliation is never employed towards things which are regarded as inanimate, nor towards persons whose behaviour in the particular circumstances is known to be determined with absolute certainty. Thus in so far as religion assumes the world to be directed by conscious agents who may be turned from their purpose by persuasion, it stands in fundamental antagonism to magic as well as to science, both of which take for granted that the course of nature is determined, not by the passions or caprice of personal beings, but by the operation of immutable laws acting mechanically. In magic, indeed, the assumption is only implicit, but in science it is explicit. It is true that magic often deals with spirits, which are personal agents of the kind assumed by religion; but whenever it does so in its proper form, it treats them exactly in the same fashion as it treats inanimate agents, that is, it constrains or coerces instead of conciliating or propitiating them as religion would do. Thus it assumes that all personal beings, whether human or divine, are in the last resort subject to those impersonal forces which control all things, but which nevertheless can be turned to account by anyone who knows how to manipulate them by the appropriate ceremonies and spells. In ancient Egypt, for example, the magicians claimed the power of compelling even the highest gods to do their bidding, and actually threatened them with destruction in case of disobedience. Sometimes, without going quite so far as that, the wizard declared that he would scatter the bones of Osiris or reveal his sacred legend, if the god proved contumacious. Similarly in India at the present day the great Hindoo trinity itself of Brahma, Vishnu, and Siva is subject to the sorcerers, who, by means of their spells, exercise such an ascendency over the mightiest deities, that these are bound submissively to execute on earth below, or in heaven above, whatever commands their masters the magicians may please to issue. There is a saying everywhere current in India: "The whole universe is subject to the gods; the gods are subject to the spells (*mantras*); the spells to the Brahmans; therefore the Brahmans are our gods."

This radical conflict of principle between magic and religion sufficiently explains the relentless hostility with which in history the priest has often pursued the magician. The haughty self-sufficiency of the magician, his arrogant demeanour towards the higher powers, and his unabashed claim to exercise a sway like theirs could not but revolt the priest, to whom, with his awful sense of the divine majesty, and his humble prostration in presence of it, such claims and such a demeanour must have appeared an impious and blasphemous usurpation of prerogatives that belong to God alone. And sometimes, we may suspect, lower motives concurred to whet the edge of the priest's hostility. He professed to be the proper medium, the true intercessor between God and man, and no doubt his interests as well as his feelings were often injured by a rival practitioner, who preached a surer and smoother road to fortune than the rugged and slippery path of divine favour.

Yet this antagonism, familiar as it is to us, seems to have made its appearance comparatively late in the history of religion. At an earlier stage the functions of priest and sorcerer were often combined or, to speak perhaps more correctly, were not yet differentiated from each other. To serve his purpose man wooed the good-will of gods or spirits by prayer and sacrifice, while at the same time he had recourse to ceremonies and forms of words which he hoped would of themselves bring about the desired result without the help of god or devil. In short, he performed religious and magical rites simultaneously; he uttered prayers and incantations almost in the same breath, knowing or recking little of the theoretical inconsistency of his behaviour, so long as by hook or crook he contrived to get what he wanted. Instances of this fusion or confusion of magic with religion have already met us in the practices of Melanesians and of other peoples.

The same confusion of magic and religion has survived among peoples that have risen to higher levels of culture. It was rife in ancient India and ancient Egypt; it is by no means extinct among European peasantry at the present day. With regard to ancient India we are told by an eminent Sanscrit scholar that "the sacrificial ritual at the earliest period of which we have detailed information is pervaded with practices that breathe the spirit of the most primitive magic". Speaking of the importance of magic in the East, and especially in Egypt, Professor Maspero remarks that "we ought not to attach to the word magic the degrading idea which it almost inevitably calls up in the mind of a modern. Ancient magic was the very foundation of religion. The faithful who desired to obtain some favour from a god had no chance of succeeding except by laying hands on the deity, and this arrest could only be effected by means of a certain number of rites, sacrifices, prayers, and chants, which the god himself had revealed, and which obliged him to do what was demanded of him."

Among the ignorant classes of modern Europe the same confusion of ideas, the same mixture of religion and magic, crops up in various forms. Thus we are told that in France "the majority of the peasants still believe that the priest possesses a secret and irresistible power over the elements. By reciting certain prayers which he alone knows and has the right to utter, yet for the utterance of which he must afterwards demand absolution, he can, on an occasion of pressing danger; arrest or reverse for a moment the action of the eternal laws of the physical world. The winds, the storms, the hail, and the rain are at his command and obey his will. The fire also is subject to him, and the flames of a conflagration are extinguished at his word". For example, French peasants used to be, perhaps are still, persuaded that the priests could celebrate, with certain special rites, a Mass of the Holy Spirit, of which the efficacy was so miraculous that it never met with any opposition from the divine will; God was forced to grant whatever was asked of Him in this form, however rash and importunate might be the petition. No idea of impiety or irreverence attached to the rite in the minds of those who, in some of the great extremities of life, sought by this singular means to take the kingdom of heaven by storm. The secular priests generally refused to say the Mass of the Holy Spirit; but the monks, especially the Capuchin friars, had the reputation of yielding with less scruple to the entreaties of the anxious and distressed. In the constraint thus supposed by Catholic peasantry to be laid by the priest upon the deity we seem to have an exact counterpart of the power which the ancient Egyptians ascribed to their magicians. Again, to take another example, in many villages of Provence the priest is still reputed to possess the faculty of averting storms. It is not every priest who enjoys this reputation; and in some villages, when a change of pastors takes place, the parishioners are eager to learn whether the new incumbent has the power (*pouder*), as they call it. At the first sign of a heavy storm they put him to the proof by inviting him to exorcise the threatening clouds; and if the result answers to their hopes, the new shepherd is assured of the sympathy and respect of his flock. In some parishes, where the reputation of the curate in this respect stood higher than that of his rector, the relations between the two have been so strained in consequence that the bishop has had to translate the rector to another benefice. Again, Gascon peasants believe that to revenge themselves on their enemies bad men will sometimes induce a priest to say a mass called the Mass of Saint Sécaire. Very few priests know this mass, and three-fourths of those who do know it would not say it for love or money. None but wicked priests dare to perform the gruesome ceremony, and you may be quite sure that they will have a very heavy account to render for it at the last day. No curate or bishop, not even the archbishop of Auch, can pardon them; that right belongs to the pope of Rome alone. The Mass of Saint Sécaire may be said only in a ruined or deserted church, where owls mope and hoot, where bats flit in the gloaming, where gypsies lodge of nights, and where toads squat under the desecrated altar. Thither the bad priest comes by night with his light of love, and at the first stroke of eleven he begins to mumble the mass backwards, and ends just as the clocks are knelling the midnight hour. His leman acts as clerk. The host he blesses is black and has three points; he consecrates no wine, but instead he drinks the water of a well into which the body of an unbaptized infant has been flung. He makes the sign of the cross, but it is on the ground and with his left foot. And many other things he does which no good Christian could look upon without being struck blind and deaf and dumb for the rest of his life. But the man for whom the mass is said withers away little by little, and nobody can say what is the matter with him; even the doctors can make nothing of it. They do not know that he is slowly dying of the Mass of Saint Sécaire.

Yet though magic is thus found to fuse and amalgamate with religion in many ages and in many lands, there are some grounds for thinking that this fusion is not primitive, and that there was a time when man trusted to magic alone for the satisfaction of such wants as transcended his immediate animal cravings. In the first place a consideration of the fundamental notions of magic and religion may incline us to surmise that magic is older than religion in the history of humanity. We have seen that on the one hand magic is nothing but a mistaken application of the very simplest and most elementary processes of the mind, namely the association of ideas by virtue of resemblance or contiguity; and that on the other hand religion assumes the operation of conscious or personal agents, superior to man, behind the visible screen of nature. Obviously the conception of personal agents is more complex than a simple recognition of the similarity or contiguity of ideas; and a theory which assumes that the course of nature is determined by conscious agents is more abstruse and recondite, and requires for its apprehension a far higher degree of intelligence and reflection, than the view that things succeed each other simply by reason of their contiguity or resemblance. The very beasts associate the ideas of things that are like each other or that have been found together in their experience; and they could hardly survive for a day if they ceased to do so. But who attributes to the animals a belief that the phenomena of nature are worked by a multitude of invisible animals or by one enormous and prodigiously strong animal behind the scenes? It is probably no injustice to the brutes to assume that the honour of devising a theory of this latter sort must be reserved for human reason. Thus, if magic be deduced immediately from elementary processes of reasoning, and be, in fact, an error into which the mind falls almost spontaneously, while religion rests on conceptions which the merely animal intelligence can hardly be supposed to have yet attained to, it becomes probable that magic arose before religion in the evolution of our race, and that man essayed to bend nature to his wishes by the sheer force of spells and enchantments before he strove to coax and mollify a coy, capricious, or irascible deity by the soft insinuation of prayer and sacrifice. The conclusion which we have thus reached deductively from a consideration of the fundamental ideas of magic and religion is confirmed inductively by the observation that among the aborigines of Australia, the rudest savages as to whom we possess accurate information, magic is universally practised, whereas religion in the sense of a propitiation or conciliation of the higher powers seems to be nearly unknown. Roughly speaking, all men in Australia are magicians, but not one is a priest; everybody fancies he can influence his fellows or the course of nature by sympathetic magic, but nobody dreams of propitiating gods by prayer and sacrifice.

But if in the most backward state of human society now known to us we find magic thus conspicuously present and religion conspicuously absent, may we not reasonably conjecture that the civilised races of the world have also at some period of their history passed through a similar intellectual phase, that they attempted to force the great powers of nature to do their pleasure before they thought of courting their favour by offerings and prayer – in short that, just as on the material side of human culture there has everywhere been an Age of Stone, so on the intellectual side there has everywhere been an Age of Magic? There are reasons for answering this question in the affirmative. When we survey the existing races of mankind from Greenland to Tierra del Fuego, or from Scotland to Singapore, we observe that they are distinguished one from the other by a great variety of religions, and that these distinctions are not, so to speak, merely coterminous with the broad distinctions of race, but descend into the minuter subdivisions of states and commonwealths, nay, that they honeycomb the town, the village, and even the family, so that the surface of society all over the world is cracked and seamed, sapped and mined with rents and fissures and yawning crevasses opened up by the disintegrating influence of religious dissension. Yet when we have penetrated through these differences, which affect mainly the intelligent and thoughtful part of the community, we shall find underlying them all a solid stratum of intellectual agreement among the dull, the weak, the ignorant, and the superstitious, who constitute, unfortunately, the vast majority of mankind. One of the great achievements of the nineteenth century was to run shafts down into this low mental stratum in many parts of the world, and thus to discover its substantial identity everywhere. It is beneath our feet – and not very far beneath them – here in Europe at the present day, and it crops up on the surface in the heart of the Australian wilderness and wherever the advent of a higher civilisation has not crushed it under ground. This universal faith, this truly Catholic creed, is a belief in the efficacy of magic. While religious systems differ not only in different countries, but in the same country in different ages, the system of sympathetic magic remains everywhere and at all times substantially alike in its principles and practice. Among the ignorant and superstitious classes of modern Europe it is very much what it was thousands of years ago in Egypt and India, and what it now is among the lowest savages surviving in the remotest corners of the world. If the test of truth lay in a show of hands or a counting of heads, the system of magic might appeal, with far more reason than the Catholic Church, to the proud motto, "*Quod semper, quod ubique, quod ab omnibus*," as the sure and certain credential of its own infallibility.

It is not our business here to consider what bearing the permanent existence of such a solid layer of savagery beneath the surface of society, and unaffected by the superficial changes of religion and culture, has upon the future of humanity. The dispassionate observer, whose studies have led him to plumb its depths, can hardly regard it otherwise than as a standing menace to civilisation. We seem to move on a thin crust which may at any moment be rent by the subterranean forces slumbering below. From time to time a hollow murmur underground or a sudden spurt of flame into the air tells of what is going on beneath our feet. Now and then the polite world is startled by a paragraph in a newspaper which tells how in Scotland an image has been found stuck full of pins for the purpose of killing an obnoxious laird or minister, how a woman has been slowly roasted to death as a witch in Ireland, or how a girl has been murdered and chopped up in Russia to make those candles of human tallow by whose light thieves hope to pursue their midnight trade unseen. But whether the influences that make for further progress, or those that threaten to undo what has already been accomplished, will ultimately prevail; whether the impulsive energy of the minority or the dead weight of the majority of mankind will prove the stronger force to carry us up to higher heights or to sink us into lower depths, are questions rather for the sage, the moralist, and the statesman, whose eagle vision scans the future, than for the humble student of the present and the past. Here we are only concerned to ask how far the uniformity, the universality, and the permanence of a belief in magic, compared with the endless variety and the shifting character of religious creeds, raises a presumption that the former represents a ruder and earlier phase of the human mind, through which all the races of mankind have passed or are passing on their way to religion and science.

If an Age of Religion has thus everywhere, as I venture to surmise, been preceded by an Age of Magic, it is natural that we should enquire what causes have led mankind, or rather a portion of them, to abandon magic as a principle of faith and practice and to betake themselves to religion instead. When we reflect upon the multitude, the variety, and the complexity of the facts to be explained, and the scantiness of our information regarding them, we shall be ready to acknowledge that a full and satisfactory solution of so profound a problem is hardly to be hoped for, and that the most we can do in the present state of our knowledge is to hazard a more or less plausible conjecture. With all due diffidence, then, I would suggest that a tardy recognition of the inherent falsehood and barrenness of magic set the more thoughtful part of mankind to cast about for a truer theory of nature and a more fruitful method of turning her resources to account. The shrewder intelligences must in time have come to perceive that magical ceremonies and incantations did not really effect the results which they were designed to produce, and which the majority of their simpler fellows still believed that they did actually produce. This great discovery of the inefficacy of magic must have wrought a radical though probably slow revolution in the minds of those who had the sagacity to make it. The discovery amounted to this, that men for the first time recognised their inability to manipulate at pleasure certain natural forces which hitherto they had believed to be completely within their control. It was a confession of human ignorance and weakness. Man saw that he had taken for causes what were no causes, and that all his efforts to work by means of these imaginary causes had been vain. His painful toil had been wasted, his curious ingenuity had been squandered to no purpose. He had been pulling at strings to which nothing was attached; he had been marching, as he thought, straight to the goal, while in reality he had only been treading in a narrow circle. Not that the effects which he had striven so hard to produce did not continue to manifest themselves. They were still produced, but not by him. The rain still fell on the thirsty ground: the sun still pursued his daily, and the moon her nightly journey across the sky: the silent procession of the seasons still moved in light and shadow, in cloud and sunshine across the earth: men were still born to labour, and sorrow, and still, after a brief sojourn here, were gathered to their fathers in the long home hereafter. All things indeed went on as before, yet all seemed different to him from whose eyes the old scales had fallen. For he could no longer cherish the pleasing illusion that it was he who guided the earth and the heaven in their courses, and that they would cease to perform their great revolutions were he to take his feeble hand from the wheel. In the death of his enemies and his friends he no longer saw a proof of the resistless potency of his own or of hostile enchantments; he now knew that friends and foes alike had succumbed to a force stronger than any that he could wield, and in obedience to a destiny which he was powerless to control.

Thus cut adrift from his ancient moorings and left to toss on a troubled sea of doubt and uncertainty, his old happy confidence in himself and his powers rudely shaken, our primitive philosopher must have been sadly perplexed and agitated till he came to rest, as in a quiet haven after a tempestuous voyage, in a new system of faith and practice, which seemed to offer a solution of his harassing doubts and a substitute, however precarious, for that sovereignty over nature which he had reluctantly abdicated. If the great world went on its way without the help of him or his fellows, it must surely be because there were other beings, like himself, but far stronger, who, unseen themselves, directed its course and brought about all the varied series of events which he had hitherto believed to be dependent on his own magic. It was they, as he now believed, and not he himself, who made the stormy wind to blow, the lightning to flash, and the thunder to roll; who had laid the foundations of the solid earth and set bounds to the restless sea that it might not pass; who caused all the glorious lights of heaven to shine; who gave the fowls of the air their meat and the wild beasts of the desert their prey; who bade the fruitful land to bring forth in abundance, the high hills to be clothed with forests, the bubbling springs to rise under the rocks in the valleys, and green pastures to grow by still waters; who breathed into man's nostrils and made him live, or turned him to destruction by famine and pestilence and war. To these mighty beings, whose handiwork he traced in all the gorgeous and varied pageantry of nature, man now addressed himself, humbly confessing his dependence on their invisible power, and beseeching them of their mercy to furnish him with all good things, to defend him from the perils and dangers by which our mortal life is compassed about on every hand, and finally to bring his immortal spirit, freed from the burden of the body, to some happier world, beyond the reach of pain and sorrow, where he might rest with them and with the spirits of good men in joy and felicity for ever.

In this, or some such way as this, the deeper minds may be conceived to have made the great transition from magic to religion. But even in them the change can hardly ever have been sudden; probably it proceeded very slowly, and required long ages for its more or less perfect accomplishment. For the recognition of man's powerlessness to influence the course of nature on a grand scale must have been gradual; he cannot have been shorn of the whole of his fancied dominion at a blow. Step by step he must have been driven back from his proud position; foot by foot he must have yielded, with a sigh, the ground which he had once viewed as his own. Now it would be the wind, now the rain, now the sunshine, now the thunder, that he confessed himself unable to wield at will; and as province after province of nature thus fell from his grasp, till what had once seemed a kingdom threatened to shrink into a prison, man must have been more and more profoundly impressed with a sense of his own helplessness and the might of the invisible beings by whom he believed himself to be surrounded. Thus religion, beginning as a slight and partial acknowledgment of powers superior to man, tends with the growth of knowledge to deepen into a confession of man's entire and absolute dependence on the divine; his old free bearing is exchanged for an attitude of lowliest prostration before the mysterious powers of the unseen, and his highest virtue is to submit his will to theirs: *In la sua volontade è nostra pace*. But this deepening sense of religion, this more perfect submission to the divine will in all things, affects only those higher intelligences who have breadth of view enough to comprehend the vastness of the universe and the littleness of man. Small minds cannot grasp great ideas; to their narrow comprehension, their purblind vision, nothing seems really great and important but themselves: Such minds hardly rise into religion at all. They are, indeed, drilled by their betters into an outward conformity with its precepts and a verbal profession of its tenets; but at heart they cling to their old magical superstitions, which may be discountenanced and forbidden, but cannot be eradicated by religion, so long as they have their roots deep down in the mental framework and constitution of the great majority of mankind.

The reader may well be tempted to ask, How was it that intelligent men did not sooner detect the fallacy of magic? How could they continue to cherish expectations that were invariably doomed to disappointment? With what heart persist in playing venerable antics that led to nothing, and mumbling solemn balderdash that remained without effect? Why cling to beliefs which were so flatly contradicted by experience? How dare to repeat experiments that had failed so often? The answer seems to be that the fallacy was far from easy to detect, the failure by no means obvious, since in many, perhaps in most cases, the desired event did actually follow, at a longer or shorter interval, the performance of the rite which was designed to bring it about; and a mind of more than common acuteness was needed to perceive that, even in these cases, the rite was not necessarily the cause of the event. A ceremony intended to make the wind blow or the rain fall, or to work the death of an enemy, will always be followed, sooner or later, by the occurrence it is meant to bring to pass; and primitive man may be excused for regarding the occurrence as a direct result of the ceremony, and the best possible proof of its efficacy. Similarly, rites observed in the morning to help the sun to rise, and in spring to wake the dreaming earth from her winter sleep, will invariably appear to be crowned with success, at least within the temperate zones; for in these regions the sun lights his golden lamp in the east every morning, and year by year the vernal earth decks herself afresh with a rich mantle of green. Hence the practical savage, with his conservative instincts, might well turn a deaf ear to the subtleties of the theoretical doubter, the philosophic radical, who presumed to hint that sunrise and spring might not, after all, be direct consequences of the punctual performance of certain daily or yearly ceremonies, and that the sun might perhaps continue to rise and trees to blossom though the ceremonies were occasionally intermitted, or even discontinued altogether. These sceptical doubts would naturally be repelled by the other with scorn and indignation as airy reveries subversive of the faith and manifestly contradicted by experience. "Can anything be plainer", he might say, "than that I light my two penny candle on earth and that the sun then kindles his great fire in heaven? I should be glad to know whether, when I have put on my green robe in spring, the trees do not afterwards do the same? These are facts patent to everybody, and on them I take my stand. I am a plain practical man, not one of your theorists and splitters of hairs and choppers of logic. Theories and speculation and all that may be very well in their way, and I have not the least objection to your indulging in them, provided, of course, you do not put them in practice. But give me leave to stick to facts; then I know where I am." The fallacy of this reasoning is obvious to us, because it happens to deal with facts about which we have long made up our minds. But let an argument of precisely the same calibre be applied to matters which are still under debate, and it may be questioned whether a British audience would not applaud it as sound, and esteem the speaker who used it a safe man – not brilliant or showy, perhaps, but thoroughly sensible and hard-headed. If such reasonings could pass muster among ourselves, need we wonder that they long escaped detection by the savage?

[…]

For the present we have journeyed far enough together, and it is time to part. Yet before we do so, we may well ask ourselves whether there is not some more general conclusion, some lesson, if possible, of hope and encouragement, to be drawn from the melancholy record of human error and folly which has engaged our attention in this book.

If then we consider, on the one hand, the essential similarity of man's chief wants everywhere and at all times, and on the other hand, the wide difference between the means he has adopted to satisfy them in different ages, we shall perhaps be disposed to conclude that the movement of the higher thought, so far as we can trace it, has on the whole been from magic through religion to science. In magic man depends on his own strength to meet the difficulties and dangers that beset him on every side. He believes in a certain established order of nature on which he can surely count, and which he can manipulate for his own ends. When he discovers his mistake, when he recognises sadly that both the order of nature which he had assumed and the control which he had believed himself to exercise over it were purely imaginary, he ceases to rely on his own intelligence and his own unaided efforts, and throws himself humbly on the mercy of certain great invisible beings behind the veil of nature, to whom he now ascribes all those far-reaching powers which he once arrogated to himself. Thus in the acuter minds magic is gradually superseded by religion, which explains the succession of natural phenomena as regulated by the will, the passion, or the caprice of spiritual beings like man in kind, though vastly superior to him in power.

But as time goes on this explanation in its turn proves to be unsatisfactory. For it assumes that the succession of natural events is not determined by immutable laws, but is to some extent variable and irregular, and this assumption is not borne out by closer observation. On the contrary, the more we scrutinise that succession the more we are struck by the rigid uniformity, the punctual precision with which, wherever we can follow them, the operations of nature are carried on. Every great advance in knowledge has extended the sphere of order and correspondingly restricted the sphere of apparent disorder in the world, till now we are ready to anticipate that even in regions where chance and confusion appear still to reign, a fuller knowledge would everywhere reduce the seeming chaos to cosmos. Thus the keener minds, still pressing forward to a deeper solution of the mysteries of the universe, come to reject the religious theory of nature as inadequate, and to revert in a measure to the older standpoint of magic by postulating explicitly, what in magic had only been implicitly assumed, to wit, an inflexible regularity in the order of natural events, which, if carefully observed, enables us to foresee their course with certainty and to act accordingly. In short, religion, regarded as an explanation of nature, is displaced by science.

But while science has this much in common with magic that both rest on a faith in order as the underlying principle of all things, readers of this work will hardly need to be reminded that the order presupposed by magic differs widely from that which forms the basis of science. The difference flows naturally from the different modes in which the two orders have been reached. For whereas the order on which magic reckons is merely an extension, by false analogy, of the order in which ideas present themselves to our minds, the order laid down by science is derived from patient and exact observation of the phenomena themselves. The abundance, the solidity, and the splendour of the results already achieved by science are well fitted to inspire us with a cheerful confidence in the soundness of its method. Here at last, after groping about in the dark for countless ages, man has hit upon a clue to the labyrinth, a golden key that opens many locks in the treasury of nature. It is probably not too much to say that the hope of progress – moral and intellectual as well as material – in the future is bound up with the fortunes of science, and that every obstacle placed in the way of scientific discovery is a wrong to humanity.

Yet the history of thought should warn us against concluding that because the scientific theory of the world is the best that has yet been formulated, it is necessarily complete and final. We must remember that at bottom the generalisations of science or, in common parlance, the laws of nature are merely hypotheses devised to explain that ever-shifting phantasmagoria of thought which we dignify with the high-sounding names of the world and the universe. In the last analysis magic, religion, and science are nothing but theories of thought; and as science has supplanted its predecessors, so it may hereafter be itself superseded by some more perfect hypothesis, perhaps by some totally different way of looking at the phenomena – of registering the shadows on the screen – of which we in this generation can form no idea. The advance of knowledge is an infinite progression towards a goal that for ever recedes. We need not murmur at the endless pursuit:

*Fatti non foste a viver come bruti*
*Ma per seguir virtute e conoscenza.*

Great things will come of that pursuit, though we may not enjoy them. Brighter stars will rise on some voyager of the future – some great Ulysses of the realms of thought – than shine on us. The dreams of magic may one day be the waking realities of science. But a dark shadow lies athwart the far end of this fair prospect. For however vast the increase of knowledge and of power which the future may have in store for man, he can scarcely hope to stay the sweep of those great forces which seem to be making silently but relentlessly for the destruction of all this starry universe in which our earth swims as a speck or mote. In the ages to come man may be able to predict, perhaps even to control, the wayward courses of the winds and clouds, but hardly will his puny hands have strength to speed afresh our slackening planet in its orbit or rekindle the dying fire of the sun. Yet the philosopher who trembles at the idea of such distant catastrophes may console himself by reflecting that these gloomy apprehensions, like the earth and the sun themselves, are only parts of that unsubstantial world which thought has conjured up out of the void, and that the phantoms which the subtle enchantress has evoked to-day she may ban to-morrow. They too, like so much that to common eyes seems solid, may melt into air, into thin air.

Without dipping so far into the future, we may illustrate the course which thought has hitherto run by likening it to a web woven of three different threads – the black thread of magic, the red thread of religion, and the white thread of science, if under science we may include those simple truths, drawn from observation of nature, of which men in all ages have possessed a store. Could we then survey the web of thought from the beginning, we should probably perceive it to be at first a chequer of black and white, a patchwork of true and false notions, hardly tinged as yet by the red thread of religion. But carry your eye farther along the fabric and you will remark that, while the black and white chequer still runs through it, there rests on the middle portion of the web, where religion has entered most deeply into its texture, a dark crimson stain, which shades off insensibly into a lighter tint as the white thread of science is woven more and more into the tissue. To a web thus chequered and stained, thus shot with threads of diverse hues, but gradually changing colour the farther it is unrolled, the state of modern thought, with all its divergent aims and conflicting tendencies, may be compared. Will the great movement which for centuries has been slowly altering the complexion of thought be continued in the near future? Or will a reaction set in which may arrest progress and even undo much that has been done? To keep up our parable, what will be the colour of the web which the Fates are now weaving on the humming loom of time? will it be white or red? We cannot tell. A faint glimmering light illumines the backward portion of the web. Clouds and thick darkness hide the other end.

# 13

# MARCEL MAUSS AND HENRI HUBERT

"A General Theory of Magic", translation Robert Brain

Marcel Mauss (b. 1872; d. 1950) and Henri Hubert (b. 1872; d. 1927) were close collaborators of Émile Durkheim (Mauss was, furthermore, Durkheim's nephew) and regularly contributed articles to his journal *L'Année sociologique*. Their famous "Essai sur la nature et la fonction du sacrifice" ("Essay on the nature and function of sacrifice") was published in the second issue of this journal (1898). In the seventh issue of the *L'Année sociologique* (1902/1903), Mauss and Hubert published the text we present here, their "Esquisse d'une théorie générale de la magie" ("Outline of a general theory of magic").

With their theory, Mauss and Hubert seek to refute Frazer's concept of "sympathetic magic" (see Chapter 12). They claim that:

1. "Sympathetic" rites and beliefs are not restricted to "magic" as "there are sympathetic practices in religion".
2. Frazer's distinction of coercive ("magical") versus submissive ("religious") rites is not satisfactory as "Religious rites may also constrain."
3. Frazer's idea that "religion" addresses transcendent beings while "magic" would be mostly mechanistic is misleading as "spirits and even gods may be involved in magic".

Due to these perceived inconsistencies in Frazer's theory, Mauss and Hubert argue that "magic" should not be defined "in terms of the structure of its rites, but by the circumstances in which these rites occur". This is mirrored in their own definition of "magic": "A magical rite is *any rite which does not play a part in organized cults* – it is private, secret, mysterious and approaches the limit of a prohibited rite."

While Durkheim – who proposes a similar definition in his *Elementary Forms* (see Chapter 14) – excludes "magic" from his investigation due to its "asocial" character, Mauss and Hubert aim at further elaborating its nature in their "Esquisse". In particular, they attempt to demonstrate that "magic" – its definition as a private, individualistic, asocial practice notwithstanding – is a social phenomenon and "created and qualified by the collectivity". They propose two reasons for the social nature of "magic": on the one hand, all of its elements are derived from collective – often religious (as in the case of demonology) or scientific (as in the case of alchemy) –

traditions. On the other, the belief in "magic" is itself a necessarily societal phenomenon and the precondition for individual "magicians" to exist. This argument is grounded in their "constructivist" understanding of social beliefs: "We have seen how, in some societies, a patient who is deserted by the magician dies. We have seen him cured through trust and confidence. It is a kind of comfort which a collective, traditional power of suggestion can provide." Mauss and Hubert conclude that, by means of tradition and social belief, "magic" – this "most childish of skills" – has nevertheless become a powerful factor in cultural history.

## "A GENERAL THEORY OF MAGIC"

We suggest, provisionally, that magic has been sufficiently distinguished in various societies from other systems of social facts. This being the case we have reason to believe that magic not only forms a distinct class of phenomena but that it is also susceptible to clear definition. We shall have to provide this definition for ourselves, since we cannot be content to accept facts as "magical" simply because they have been so called by the actors themselves or observers. The points of view of such people are subjective, hence not necessarily scientific. A religion designates the remnants of former cults as "magical" even when the rites are still being performed in a religious manner; this way of looking at things has even been followed by scholars – a folklorist as distinguished as Skeat considers the old agrarian rites of the Malays as magical. As far as we are concerned, magic should be used to refer to those things which society as a whole considers magical and not those qualified as such by a single segment of society only. However we are also aware that some societies are not very coherent in their notions of magic and, even if they are, this has only come about gradually. Consequently, we are not very optimistic about suddenly discovering an ideal definition of our subject; this must await the conclusion of our analysis of the relations between magic and religion.

In magic we have officers, actions and representations: we call a person who accomplishes magical actions a *magician*, even if he is not a professional; *magical representations* are those ideas and beliefs which correspond to magical actions; as for these actions, with regard to which we have defined the other elements of magic, we shall call them *magical rites*. At this stage it is important to distinguish between these activities and other social practices with which they might be confused.

In the first place, magic and magical rites, as a whole, are traditional facts. Actions which are never repeated cannot be called magical. If the whole community does not believe in the efficacy of a group of actions, they cannot be magical. The form of the ritual is eminently transmissible and this is sanctioned by public opinion. It follows from this that strictly individual actions, such as the private superstitions of gamblers, cannot be called magical.

The kind of traditional practices which might be confused with magical activities include legal actions, techniques and religious ritual. Magic has been linked with a system of jural obligations, since in many places there are words and gestures which are binding sanctions. It is true that legal actions may often acquire a ritual character and that contracts, oaths and trials by ordeal are to a certain extent sacramental. Nevertheless, the fact remains that although they contain ritual elements they are not magical rites in themselves. If they assume a special kind of efficacy or if they do more than merely establish contractual relations between persons, they cease to be legal actions and do become magical or religious rites. Ritual acts, on the contrary, are essentially thought to be able to produce much more than a contract: rites are eminently effective; they are creative; they *do* things. It is through these qualities that magical ritual is recognizable as such. In some cases even, ritual derives its name from a reference to these effective characteristics: in India the word which best corresponds to our word ritual is *karman*, action; sympathetic magic is the *factum, krtyâ,* par excellence. The German word *Zauber* has the same etymological meaning; in other languages the words for magic contain the root *to do.*

However, human skill can also be creative and the actions of craftsmen are known to be effective. From this point of view the greater part of the human race has always had difficulty in distinguishing techniques from rites. Moreover, there is probably not a single activity which artists and craftsmen perform which is not also believed to be within the capacity of the magician. It is because their ends are similar that they are found in natural association and constantly join forces. Nevertheless, the extent of their co-operation varies. Magic, in general, aids and abets techniques such as fishing, hunting and farming. Other arts are, in a manner of speaking, entirely swamped by magic. Medicine and alchemy are examples: for a long period technical elements were reduced to a minimum and magic became the dominant partner; they depended on magic to such an extent that they seemed to have grown from it. Medicine, almost to our own days, has remained hedged in by religious and magical taboos, prayers, incantations and astrological predictions. Furthermore, a doctor's drugs and potions and a surgeon's incisions are a real tissue of symbolic, sympathetic, homeopathic and antipathetic actions which are really thought of as magical. The effectiveness of the rites is not distinguished from that of the techniques; they are considered to be one and the same.

It is all the more confusing when the traditional character of magic is found to be bound up with the arts and crafts. The successive gestures of an artisan may be as uniformly regulated as those of a magician. Nevertheless, the arts and crafts have been universally distinguished from magic; there has always been an intangible difference in method between the two activities. As far as techniques are concerned, the effects are considered to be produced through a person's skill. Everyone knows that the results are achieved directly through the co-ordination of action, tool and physical agent. Effect follows on immediately from cause. The results are homogeneous with the means: the javelin flies through the air because it is thrown and food is cooked by means of fire. Moreover, traditional techniques are controllable by experience which is constantly putting the value of technical beliefs to the test. The whole existence of these skills depends on a continued perception of this homogeneity between cause and effect. If an activity is both magical and technical at the same time, the magical aspect is the one which fails to live up to this definition. Thus, in medical practices, words, incantations, ritual and astrological observances are magical; this is the realm of the occult and of the spirits, a world of ideas which imbues ritual movements and gestures with a special kind of effectiveness, quite different from their mechanical effectiveness. It is not really believed that the gestures themselves bring about the result. The effect derives from something else, and usually this is not of the same order. Let us take, for example, the case of a man who stirs the water of a spring in order to bring rain. This is the peculiar nature of rites which we might call *traditional actions whose effectiveness is sui generis.*

So far we have managed to define only ritual, not magical ritual, and we must now attempt to distinguish it from religious rites. Frazer, as we have seen, proposed his own criteria. The first is that magical rites are sympathetic rites. But this is not sufficient. There are not only magical rites which are not sympathetic, but neither is sympathy a prerogative of magic, since there are sympathetic practices in religion. During the festival of Succoth, when the great priest in the temple of Jerusalem poured water onto the altar, hands held high above his head, he was obviously performing a sympathetic rite destined to bring about rain. When, during a holy sacrifice, a Hindu officiant prolongs or shortens at will the life of the sacrificial victim, following the peregrination which accompanies the libation, the ritual is still eminently sympathetic. In both cases the symbolism is perfectly clear; the ritual appears to act by itself. However, in each of these rituals the dominant character is religious. The officiants, the atmosphere of the place, the presence of divinities, the gravity of the actions, the aims of the people attending the rite – all leave no doubt in our minds on this score. Sympathetic rites may therefore, be either magical or religious.

The second criterion proposed by Frazer is that a magical rite normally acts on its own, that is, constrains, while a religious rite worships and conciliates. The former has an automatic, immediate reaction; the latter acts indirectly through a kind of respectful persuasion – here the agent is a spiritual intermediary. However, this is far from satisfactory as an explanation. Religious rites may also constrain and, in most of the ancient religions, the god was unable to prevent a rite from accomplishing its end if it had been faultlessly executed. Nor is it true – as we shall see later – that all magical rites have a direct action, since spirits and even gods may be involved in magic. Finally, spirits, gods and devils do not always automatically obey the orders of a magician; the latter is often forced to supplicate to them.

We shall, therefore, have to find other criteria. To find them we shall look at the various aspects one after the other.

Among rites, there are some which are certainly religious in nature; these include ritual which is solemn, public, obligatory, regular – for example, festivals and sacraments. And yet there are rites of this kind which Frazer refused to accept as religious. As far as he was concerned, all the ceremonies of the Australian aborigines, and most of their initiation rites, are magical because of the sympathetic ritual involved. In fact, the ritual of the Arunta clans, known as the *intichiuma* – the tribal initiatory rites – have precisely that degree of importance, seriousness and holiness which the idea of religion evokes. The totemic species and ancestors present during the course of the ritual are, in fact, of the same order as those respected and feared forces, the presence of which Frazer himself takes as indicative of the religious nature of a rite. These are the very forces invoked during the ceremonies.

On the other hand, rites do exist which are consistently magical. These are the evil spells or *maléfices*, and we find them regularly qualified as such by both law and religion. The casting of evil spells is illicit and expressly prohibited and punished. This prohibition marks the formal distinction between magical and religious rites. It is the fact of prohibition itself which gives the spell its magical character. There are religious rites which are equally maleficent, such as certain cases of *devotio*, the imprecations made against a communal enemy, against persons violating tombs or breaking oaths, and all those death rites sanctioned by ritual taboos. We might go so far as to say that there are evil spells which are evil only in so far as people fear them. The fact of their being prohibited provides a delimitation for the whole sphere of magical action.

We have, in other words, two extremes which form the differing poles of magic religion: the pole of sacrifice and the pole of evil spells. Religion has always created a kind of ideal towards which people direct their hymns, vows, sacrifices, an ideal which is bolstered by prescriptions. These are areas which are avoided by magic, since association with evil as an aspect of magical rites always provides humanity with a rough general notion of magic. Between these two poles we have a confused mass of activities whose specific nature is not immediately apparent. These are practices which are neither prescribed nor proscribed in any special way. We have religious practices which are private and voluntary, as well as magical practices which are licit. On the one hand, we have the occasional actions of private cults; on the other, there are magical practices associated with technical skills, such as those of the medical profession. A European peasant who exorcizes the mice from his field, an Indian who prepares his war medicine, or a Finn who incants over his hunting weapons – they all aim at ends which are perfectly above board and perform actions which are licit. There is the same connexion between magical and domestic cults in Melanesia, where magic acts in a series of rites involving their ancestors. Far from denying the possibility of confusing magic and religion we should like to stress the fact, reserving our explanation for the situation until later. For the moment we are happy enough to accept Grimm's definition that magic is a "kind of religion, used in the lower spheres of domestic life". However, while the continuity between magic and religion is of great interest, we must, for the moment, begin to classify our data. In order to do this we shall enumerate a certain number of external characteristics by which they can be recognized. This interrelationship between magic and religion has not prevented people from noting the difference between the two types of rite and hence from practising them in such a way as to show that they are aware of the difference. We must, therefore, look for these signs, which will enable us to make some kind of classification.

First of all, magical and religious rites often have different agents; in other words, they are not performed by one and the same person. By way of exception, a priest performing a magical rite does not adopt the normal comportment of his profession: he turns his back to the altar, he performs with his left hand what he usually does with his right, and so on and so forth.

There are also many other signs which should be grouped together. First there is the choice of place where the magical ceremony is to be performed. This is not generally inside a temple or at some domestic shrine. Magical rites are commonly performed in woods, far away from dwelling places, at night or in shadowy corners, in the secret recesses of a house or at any rate in some out-of-the-way place. Where religious rites are performed openly, in full public view, magical rites are carried out in secret. Even when magic is licit, it is done in secret, as if performing some maleficent deed. And even if the magician has to work in public he makes an attempt to dissemble: his gestures become furtive and his words indistinct. The medicine man and the bone-setter, working before the assembled gathering of a family, mutter their spells, cover up their actions and hide behind simulated or real ecstasies. Thus, as far as society is concerned, the magician is a being set apart and he prefers even more to retire to the depths of the forest. Among colleagues too he nearly always tries to keep himself to himself. In this way he is reserving his powers. Isolation and secrecy are two almost perfect signs of the intimate character of a magical rite. They are always features of a person or persons working in a private capacity; both the act and the actor are shrouded in mystery.

In fact, however, the various characteristics we have so far revealed only reflect the irreligiosity of magical rites. They are anti-religious and it is desired that they be so. In any case, they do not belong to those organized systems which we call cults. Religious practices, on the contrary, even fortuitous and voluntary ones, are always predictable, prescribed and official. They *do* form part of a cult. Gifts presented to gods on the occasion of a vow, or an expiatory sacrifice offered during illness, are regular kinds of homage. Although performed in each case voluntarily, they are really obligatory and inevitable actions. Magical rites, on the other hand, while they may occur regularly (as in the case of agricultural magic) and fulfil a need when they are performed for specific ends (such as a cure), are always considered unauthorized, abnormal and, at the very least, not highly estimable. Medical rites, however useful and licit they may be made to appear, do not involve the same degree of solemnity, nor the same idea of an accomplished duty, as do expiatory sacrifices or vows made to a curative divinity. When somebody has recourse to a medicine man, the owner of a spirit-fetish, a bone-mender or a magician, there is certainly a need, but no moral obligation is involved.

Nevertheless, there are examples of cults which are magical. There was the Hecate cult of Ancient Greece, the cult of Diana and the devil in the magic of the Middle Ages and the whole cult devoted to one of the greatest Hindu divinities, Rudra-Shiva. These, however, are examples of secondary developments and quite simply prove that magicians have themselves set up a cult which was modelled along the lines of religious cults.

We have thus arrived at a provisionally adequate definition of magical phenomena. A magical rite is *any rite which does not play a part in organized cults* – it is private, secret, mysterious and approaches the limit of a prohibited rite. With this definition, and taking into consideration the other elements of magic which we have mentioned, we have the first hint of its special qualities. It will be noticed that we do not define magic in terms of the structure of its rites, but by the circumstances in which these rites occur, which in turn determines the place they occupy in the totality of social customs.

[…]

At first sight, the facts we have collected together may seem very disparate. Some tend to merge magic with technology and science, while others assimilate it to religion. In fact, it should be placed somewhere between the two, but it cannot be defined by its aims, processes or its ideas. Up to the present, our studies have shown that the subject is even more ambiguous, more indeterminate than ever. It resembles non-religious techniques in its practical aspects, in the automatic nature of so many of its actions, in the false air of experiment inherent in some of its important notions. But it is very different from techniques when we come to consider special agencies, spirit intermediaries and cult activities. Here it has more in common with religion because of the elements it has borrowed from this sphere. There are almost no religious rites which lack their magical equivalent. Magic has even developed the idea of orthodoxy as we see in the διαβολαί, those magical accusations dealing with impure rites in Greco-Egyptian magic. However, apart from the antipathy which magic shows towards religion and vice versa (an antipathy, moreover, which is neither universal nor constant), its incoherence and the important role played by pure fancy make it a far cry from the image we have learnt to associate with religion.

Nonetheless, the unity of the whole magical system now stands out with greater clarity. This is the first gain to be made from our incursions into the subject and our long discussions. We have reason to believe that magic does form a real whole. Magicians share the same characteristics, and the effects of their magical performances – in spite of an infinite diversity – always betray much in common. Very different processes can be associated together as complex types and ceremonies. Quite disparate notions fuse and harmonize without the whole losing anything of its incoherent and dislocated aspects. The parts do, in fact, form a whole.

At the same time the whole adds up to much more than the number of its parts. The different elements which we have dealt with consecutively are, in fact, present simultaneously. Although our analysis has abstracted them they are very intimately and necessarily combined in the whole. We considered it sufficient to define magicians and magical representations by stating that the former are the agents of magical rites, while the latter are those representations which correspond to them – we considered them together in relation to magical rites. We are not in the least surprised that our fore-runners have preferred to consider magic solely as a series of actions. We might also have defined magical elements in relation to the magician. Each presupposes the other. There is no such thing as an inactive, honorary magician. To qualify as a magician you must make magic; conversely, anyone who makes magic is, at least for the moment, a magician. There are part-time magicians who revert immediately to their status of layman as soon as the rite is accomplished. As for representations, they have no life outside ritual. Most of them offer little of theoretical interest to the magician and he rarely formulates them. They have solely a practical interest, and as far as magic is concerned they are expressed almost entirely through actions. The people who first reduced them to systems were philosophers, not magicians. It was esoteric philosophy which promulgated a theory of magical representation. Magic itself did not even attempt to codify its demonology. In Christian Europe, as well as in

India, it was religion which classified demons. Outside ritual, demons exist only in fairy tales and church dogma. In magic, therefore, we have no pure representations and magical mythology is embryonic and thin. While in religion ritual and its like on the one hand, and myths and dogmas on the other, have real autonomy, the constituents of magic are by their very nature inseparable.

Magic is a living mass, formless and inorganic, and its vital parts have neither a fixed position nor a fixed function. They merge confusedly together. The very important distinction between representation and rite sometimes disappears altogether until we are left with the mere utterance of a representation which thereby becomes the rite: the *venenum veneno vincitur* is an incantation. The spirits which the sorcerer possesses or which possess the sorcerer may become confused with his soul or his magical powers. Spirits and sorcerers sometimes have the same name. The energy or force behind the rite – that of the spirit and the magician – is usually one and the same thing. The normal condition of magic is one involving an almost total confusion of powers and roles. As a result, one of its constituent features may disappear without the nature of the whole changing. There are magical rites which fail to correspond to any conscious idea. The action of spell-binding is a case in point, as well as many imprecations. Conversely, there are cases where representations absorb the ritual, as in genealogical charms, where the utterance of natures and causes constitutes the rite. In sum, the functions of magic are not specialized. Magical life is not compartmentalized like religion. It has not led to the growth of any autonomous institutions like sacrifice and priesthood. And, since magical facts cannot be divided up into categories, we have been forced to think in terms of abstract elements. Magic is everywhere in a diffuse state. In each case we are confronted with a whole, which, as we have pointed out, is more than the sum of its parts. In this way we have shown that magic as a whole has an objective reality – that it is *some* thing. But what kind of thing is it?

We have already gone beyond the bound of our provisional definition by establishing that the diverse elements of magic are created and qualified by the collectivity. This is our second, noteworthy advance. The magician often qualifies professionally through being a member of an association of magicians. In the final count, however, he always receives this quality from society itself. His actions are ritualistic, repeated according to the dictates of tradition. As for representations, some are borrowed from other spheres of social life: the idea of spirit beings, for example. Further research will be required, involving religion directly, if we are to find out whether this idea is the result of individual experience or not. Other representations are not derived from the observations or reflections of individuals, nor does their application allow any individual initiative, since they are remedies and formulas which are imposed by tradition and which are used quite uncritically.

While elements of a magical system are collective in nature, can the same be said for the whole? In other words, is there some basic aspect of magic which is not the object of representations or the fruit of collective activities? Is it not, in fact, absurd or even contradictory to suppose that magic could ever be, in essence, a collective phenomenon, when, in order to compare it with religion, we have chosen, from among all its characteristics, those which set it apart from the regular life of society? We have seen that it is practised by individuals, that it is mysterious, isolated, furtive, scattered and broken up, and, finally, that it is arbitrary and voluntary in nature. Magic is as anti-social as it can be, if by "social" we primarily imply obligation and coercion. Is it social in the sense of being, like a crime, secret, illegitimate and forbidden? This is not quite true, at least not exclusively so, since magic is not exactly the reverse side of religion, in the way that crime is the reverse side of the law. It must be social in the manner of a special function of society. But in what way should we think of it? How are we to conceive the idea of a collective phenomenon, where individuals would remain so perfectly independent of each other?

There are two types of special functions in society which we have already mentioned in relation to magic. They are science and technology on the one hand, and religion on the other. Is magic a kind of universal art or possibly a class of phenomena analogous to religion? In art or science the principles and methods of action are elaborated collectively and transmitted by tradition. It is for these reasons that science and the arts can be called collective phenomena. Moreover, both art and science satisfy common needs. But, given these facts, each individual is able to act on his own. Using his own common sense, he goes from one element to the next and thence to their application. He is free: he may even start again at the beginning, adapting or rectifying, according to his technique or skill, at any stage, all at his own risk. Nothing can take away his control. Now, if magic were of the same order as science or technology, the difficulties we previously observed would no longer exist, since science and technology are not collective in every single essential aspect, and, while they may have social functions and society is their beneficiary and their vehicle, their sole promoters are individuals. But it is difficult to assimilate to magic the sciences or arts, since its manifestations can be described without once encountering similar creative or critical faculties among its individual practitioners.

It only remains now to compare magic with religion; and here we are faced with formidable difficulties. We still uphold, in fact, that religion in all its aspects is essentially a collective phenomenon. Everything is done by the group or under pressure from the group. Beliefs and practices, by their very nature, are obligatory. In analysing a rite which we took as a type – that is, sacrifice – we established that society was present and immanent everywhere; that society itself was the real actor in the ceremonial drama. We even went so far as to maintain that the sacred objects of sacrifice were social things *par excellence*. Religious life, like sacrifice, permits no individual initiative, and invention is admitted only under the form of revelation. The individual feels constantly subordinate to forces which are outside his power – forces which incite him to action. If we are able to demonstrate that within the field of magic there are similar powers to those existing in religion, we shall have shown that magic has the same collective character as religion. All that will then remain to be done will be to show how these collective forces are produced – in face of the isolation which magicians insist on – and we shall thereby conclude that these individuals have merely appropriated to themselves the collective forces of society.

[...]

Throughout the course of history magic has provoked states of collective sentiment, from which it derives stimulus and fresh vigour. The witchcraft epidemics of the Middle

Ages provide one of the best examples of the extent to which fantastic social passion can be excited. While the Inquisition certainly burned more innocent people than real witches, it also served to generate them. On everyone's mind was imprinted the idea of magic and this exercised a terrible fascination. With startling swiftness it brought about mass conversions. Moreover, during witch trials, witches sought each other out, brought together and recruited proselytes and acolytes. Such initiative comes only with a sense of group feeling. There must be at least two persons before risking suspect experiments. United, they become aware of a sense of mystery which affords them protection. In an account of the life of the witch Marie-Anne de la Ville – tried and condemned in 1711 – we can read how men specialized in the unearthing of buried treasure grouped themselves around her and refurbished their faith through their mutual activities. However, no magical group, however large, is sufficient unto itself. Each time the members are deceived they need to have their optimism rekindled through the faith of new recruits. In this way the magician of Moulins, whom we have already mentioned as the carpenter Jean Michel, found his faith renewed by contact with his judge's belief, and out came his confessions – from the sheer pleasure of speaking magic.

In this way, the magician receives continual encouragement from outside. Magical beliefs which are active in certain corners of our society and which were quite general a century ago, are the most alive, the most real indications of a state of social unrest and social consciousness, in which there floats a whole crowd of vague ideas, hopes and vain fears, giving form to the remnants of the former category of *mana*. In society there is an inexhaustible source of diffuse magic which the magician uses to his own advantage. Everything happens as though society, from a distance, formed a kind of huge magical conclave around him. This is the reason why the magician lives in a kind of specialized atmosphere which follows him everywhere – if we can express ourselves like this. However cut off from the real world he may seem to others, it does not appear the same to him. His individual consciousness is deeply affected by this social sentiment. As a magician he is no longer himself. If he thinks about his condition, he may come to the conclusion that his magical powers are quite separate from him. He merely has access to them or acts as a kind of depository for them. And if he lacks power, his individual knowledge is useless. Prospero is not Ariel's master. He took over his magical power, when he freed him from the tree where he had been imprisoned by the sorceress Sycorax, on certain conditions and for a certain time. When he gives him back to the elements, to nature and the world, he is nothing but an ordinary mortal and may as well burn his books:

> Now my charms are all o'erthrown,
> And what strength I have's mine own;
> Which is most faint […]

Throughout its existence, magic has never forgotten its social origins. Each of its elements, agents, rites and representations not only perpetuate the memory of this original collective state, but even help in their reproduction in an attenuated form. Every day society, in a manner of speaking, ordains new magicians, experiences rites, listens to fresh tales, which are always the same. In spite of the fact that there are constant interruptions, society's creation of magic is no less continuous. In communal life, these emotions, impressions, impulses are ceaselessly produced and give rise to the idea of *mana*. People's habits are continually disturbed by things which trouble the calm ordering of life: drought, wealth, illness, war, meteors, stones with special shapes, abnormal individuals, etc. At each shock, at each perception of the unusual, society hesitates, searches, waits. Ambroise Paré himself believed in the universal virtues of the Bezoar stone, which the Emperor Rudolph received from the King of Portugal. These are attitudes which turn the abnormal into *mana*, that is, magic or things produced from magic. Moreover, everything magical is effective, because the expectations engender and pursue a hallucinatory reality. We have seen how, in some societies, a patient who is deserted by the magician dies. We have seen him cured through trust and confidence. It is a kind of comfort which a collective, traditional power of suggestion can provide. The world of magic is full of the expectations of successive generations, their tenacious illusions, their hopes in the form of magical formulas. Basically it is nothing more than this, but it is this which gives it an objectivity far superior to that which it would have if it were nothing more than a tissue of false individual ideas, an aberrant and primitive science.

However, while we have this basis of social phenomena, it is a remarkable fact that as soon as magic becomes separated from religion, only individual phenomena arise. Having found social phenomena at the basis of magic, which we earlier defined by its individualistic features, it will be convenient to return to this latter aspect now. While it is impossible to understand magic without taking into consideration the magical group, we can, on the other hand, easily grasp how the magical group resolves itself into individuals. In the same way, it is easy to understand how the public and collective needs of a small primitive group ceded later to very general individual needs. It is also easy to grasp the fact that, once definitive suggestions like education and tradition existed, magic was able to live on as an individual phenomenon.

Magical knowledge seems to have been passed on from individual to individual, just as in the teaching of science and techniques. The means of transmitting magical rites among the Cherokee are instructive on this score. There existed a whole body of magical scholarship and schools of magicians. In order to pass on magical knowledge to individuals, magic had to make it intelligible to individuals. Then there developed experimental or dialectical theory which naturally enough neglected the unconscious collective facts. The Greek alchemists and their successors, our modern magicians, tried to deduce it from philosophical principles. Moreover, all magical systems, even the most primitive or popular, justify their remedies by reference to past experience. And magical systems have developed through objective researches and genuine experiences. They have progressively benefited from discoveries which have been both true and false. In this way, the relative role of the collectivity in magic has been whittled down. It diminished because the collectivity banished everything of an irrational or an *a priori* nature. In this way, magic began to approximate to the sciences and finally came to resemble them in so far as it claimed to result from experimental researches and logical deductions made by individuals. In this as well, magic more and more came to resemble technology, which itself responds to the same positive and individual needs. Except for its traditional character, magic has tried to cast off all collective aspects. Everything involving theoretical and practical achievements now becomes the work of individuals, and it is exploited only by individuals.

[…]

Magic is, therefore, a social phenomenon. It only remains for us to show what place it holds among the other social phenomena, religion excepted, since we shall return to that later. Its relationships with law and custom, with economy and aesthetics, and also with language, however fascinating they may be, do not concern us here. Between these types of facts and magic we have a mere exchange of influences. Magic has no genuine kinship with anything apart from religion on the one hand and science and technology on the other.

We have said that magic tends to resemble technology, as it becomes more individualistic and specialized in the pursuit of its varied aims. Nevertheless, these two series of facts contain more than an external similarity: there is a functional identity, since, as we pointed out in our definition, both have the same aims. While religion is directed towards more metaphysical ends and is involved in the creation of idealistic images, magic has found a thousand fissures in the mystical world from whence it draws its forces, and is continually leaving it in order to take part in everyday life and play a practical role there. It has a taste for the concrete. Religion, on the other hand, tends to be abstract. Magic works in the same way as do our techniques, crafts, medicine, chemistry, industry, etc. Magic is essentially the art of doing things, and magicians have always taken advantage of their know-how, their dexterity, their manual skill. Magic is the domain of pure production, *ex nihilo*. With words and gestures it does what techniques achieve by labour. Fortunately, the magical art has not always been characterized by gesticulations into thin air. It has dealt with material things, carried out real experiments and even made its own discoveries.

Nevertheless, we could say that it is still a very simple craft. All efforts are avoided by successfully replacing reality by images. A magician does nothing, or almost nothing, but makes everyone believe that he is doing everything, and all the more so since he puts to work collective forces and ideas to help the individual imagination in its belief. The art of the magician involves suggesting means, enlarging on the virtues of objects, anticipating effects, and by these methods fully satisfying the desires and expectations which have been fostered by entire generations in common. Magic gives form and shape to those poorly co-ordinated or impotent gestures by which the needs of the individual are expressed, and because it does this through ritual, it renders them effective.

We must admit that these actions are the prefiguration of techniques. Magic is both an *opus operatum* from the magician's point of view, and an *opus inoperans* from the technical point of view. Since magic is the most childish of skills, it is possibly also the oldest. In fact, the history of technology proves that there is a genealogical link between techniques and magic. By virtue of its mystical character, magic even contributed to the growth of techniques. Magic protected techniques; behind magic they were able to make progress. Magic lent its clear authority and efficacy to those practical, if timid, efforts of the magician-craftsman. Without the support of magic, these efforts and tests would have been considered complete failures and stamped out. Certain techniques with complex objectives, unsure steps and delicate methods – such as pharmacy, medicine, surgery, metallurgy, enamel work (the last two are the heirs of alchemy) – could not have survived, unless magic had proffered help and made them last by actually absorbing them. We feel justified in saying that medicine, pharmacy, alchemy and astrology all developed within the discipline of magic, around a kernel of discoveries which were purely technical and as basic as possible. We hazard the suggestion that other more ancient techniques, simpler perhaps and separated at an earlier stage from magic, were also merged into magic at the very beginnings of mankind. Hewitt tells us that the local clan of the Woivorung, apart from owning a flint quarry where tribes in the vicinity come to get their tool supplies, also furnish the bard-magicians. This fact may be a fortuitous one. Nevertheless, it seems to shed some light on the way our first tools were invented and made. We feel that techniques are like seeds which bore fruit in the soil of magic. Later, magic was dispossessed. Techniques gradually discarded everything coloured by mysticism. Procedures which still remain have changed more and more in meaning. Mystical virtues were once attributed to them. They no longer possess anything but an automatic action. Likewise, in our own time, medical massage has taken over from the tricks of the bone-setter.

Magic is linked to science in the same way as it is linked to technology. It is not only a practical art, it is also a storehouse of ideas. It attaches great importance to knowledge – one of its mainsprings. In fact, we have seen over and over again how, as far as magic is concerned, knowledge is power. But while religion, because of its intellectual character, has a tendency toward metaphysics, magic – which we have shown to be more concerned with the concrete – is concerned with understanding nature. It quickly set up a kind of index of plants, metals, phenomena, beings and life in general, and became an early store of information for the astronomical, physical and natural sciences. It is a fact that certain branches of magic, such as astrology and alchemy, were called applied physics in Greece. That is why magicians received the name of φύσικοι and that the word φυσικός was a synonym for magic.

Magicians have sometimes even attempted to systematize their knowledge and, by so doing, derive principles. When such theories are elaborated in magician colleges, it is done by rational and individual procedures. In their doctrinal studies magicians tried to discard as many mystical elements as they could, and thus it was that magic took on the character of a genuine science. This is what happened during the last period of Greek magic. "I wish to give you an idea of the mind of the ancients", said the alchemist, Olympiodore, "to tell you, as philosophers, they spoke the language of philosophers and applied the tenets of philosophy to their art by means of science": καὶ παρεισηνεγκαν τῇ τεχνῇ διὰ τῆς σοφίας τὴν φιλοσοφίαν (Olympiodore, ii, 4; P. E. M. Berthelot, *Coll. des anciens alchimistes grecs*, Paris, 1887, I, p86).

It is obvious that a certain section of science has been elaborated by magicians, particularly in primitive societies. Magicians, who were also alchemists, astrologers and doctors in Greece, India and elsewhere, were the founders and exponents of astronomy, physics and natural history. It is possible to suppose, as we did for technology, that other, more simple sciences had similar genealogical connexions with magic. Mathematicians certainly owed a lot to researches carried out concerning magic squares and the magical properties of numbers and figures. This treasury of ideas, amassed by magic, was a capital store which science for a long time exploited.

Magic served science and magicians served scholars. In primitive societies, sorcerers are the only people who have the leisure to make observations on nature, to reflect and dream about these matters. They do so as part of their profession. It is possible to believe that it was also in these schools of magic that a scientific tradition and methods of intellectual scholarship were developed. In the lower strata of civilization, magicians are scholars and scholars are magicians. Shape-changing bards of the Australian tribes are both scholars and magicians. So are the following figures in Celtic literature: Amairgen, Taliessin, Talhwiarn, Gaion, the prophets, astrologers, astronomers and physicians, who seemed to have gained their knowledge of nature and its laws from the cauldron of the witch Ceridwen.

Though we may feel ourselves to be very far removed from magic, we are still very much bound up with it. Our ideas of good and bad luck, of quintessence, which are still familiar to us, are very close to the idea of magic itself. Neither technology, science, nor the directing principles of our reason are quite free from their original taint. We are not being daring, I think, if we suggest that a good part of all those non-positive mystical and poetical elements in our notions of force, causation, effect and substance could be traced back to the old habits of mind in which magic was born and which the human mind is slow to throw off.

We are confident that, for this reason, we shall find magical origins in those early forms of collective representations which have since become the basis for individual understanding. Thus, as we said in the beginning, our work has not been merely a chapter in religious sociology, but is also a contribution to the study of collective representations. General sociology may even gain some profit – and we hope this may be so – since we believe that we have shown, with regard to magic, how a collective phenomenon can assume individual forms.

# 14

# ÉMILE DURKHEIM

*The Elementary Forms of Religious Life*, translation Karen E. Fields

Émile Durkheim (b. 1858; d. 1917), the descendent of a long line of rabbis, is a founding figure of French sociology. In a letter from 1907, Durkheim reports that "it was not until 1895 that I achieved a clear view of the essential role played by religion in social life" (Lukes 1973: 237). Possibly, this "revelation" was occasioned by his reading of the Robertson Smith's *Lectures on the Religion of the Semites* (1889). His interest in religion first resulted in an essay "On the definition of religious phenomena" (1899). As a footnote to his definition ("religious phenomena is the name given to obligatory beliefs as well as the practices relating to given objects in such beliefs" [Durkheim 1994: 92]), Durkheim points to a clear distinction between "religious rites proper and magical rites" – the latter are "not directed towards the gods or sacred things" (Durkheim 1994: 99).

His main work on "religion" came out in 1912. In contrast to his books on the division of labour (1893) and on suicide (1897) that addressed problems of contemporary society and were based on contemporary evidence, in *The Elementary Forms of Religious Life* Durkheim adopted a different strategy: in order to analyse and to explain religion, in general, this work studies "the simplest and most primitive" religion currently known – namely, "totemism" among the Aranda in Central Australia.

Our first excerpt is from the initial section on the definition of "religion". "Magic" enters the stage as a problem – namely, as a potentially overlapping "order of things", "domain" or "institution", the separate existence of which Durkheim takes for granted. Fundamental shared features notwithstanding, the aversion of "religion" for "magic" requires a line of demarcation. This is collectivity or sociality: "religion" is the matter of groups and religion binds individuals together into a lasting moral body or community, but *"There is no Church of magic."*

In the third part of *The Elementary Forms*, Durkheim discusses "the main ritual attitudes", divided into negative and positive forms. The former refers to rites of separation and prohibition, the latter to varieties of exchange with sacred things. For the negative rituals, Durkheim separates "magic" from religion. In the case of "magic", the interdiction operates purely mechanically, out of a sense of physical necessity, but does not involve a sense of sin (*"there is no magical sin"*). Moreover, "magical" prohibitions are based on a simple sense of property; they are not based on respect for sacred things, but on utilitarian, hygienic and medical considerations.

Our third excerpt is taken from Durkheim's discussion of positive rituals. One group of these, the memetic rituals, are "composed of movements and cries intended to mimic the behaviour or traits of the animal whose reproduction is hoped for" (Durkheim 1995: 355). The main principles of these resemble "sympathetic magic" (Frazer), particularly the principle "like is like", which Durkheim seeks to explain. The passage ends on an inversion of Frazer's scheme: "magic" is full of religious elements because it derives from religion – not historically, though, but in a contextual and complementary sense.

## *THE ELEMENTARY FORMS OF RELIGIOUS LIFE*

Now we have a first criterion of religious beliefs. No doubt, within these two fundamental genera, there are secondary species that are themselves more or less incompatible with each other.[1] But characteristically, the religious phenomenon is such that it always assumes a bipartite division of the universe, known and knowable, into two genera that include all that exists but radically exclude one another. Sacred things are things protected and isolated by prohibitions; profane things are those things to which the prohibitions are applied and that must keep at a distance from what is sacred. Religious beliefs are those representations that express the nature of sacred things and the relations they have with other sacred things or with profane things. Finally, rites are rules of conduct that prescribe how man must conduct himself with sacred things.

When a certain number of sacred things have relations of coordination and subordination with one another, so as to form a system that has a certain coherence and does not belong to any other system of the same sort, then the beliefs and rites, taken together, constitute a religion. By this definition, a religion is not necessarily contained within a single idea and does not derive from a single principle that may vary with the circumstances it deals with, while remaining basically the same everywhere. Instead, it is a whole formed of separate and relatively distinct parts. Each homogeneous group of sacred things, or indeed each sacred thing of any importance, constitutes an organizational centre around which gravitates a set of beliefs and rites, a cult of its own. There is no religion, however unified it may be, that does not acknowledge a plurality of sacred things. Even Christianity, at least in its Catholic form, accepts the Virgin, the angels, the saints, the souls of the dead, etc. – above and beyond the divine personality (who, besides, is both three and one). As a rule, furthermore, religion is not merely a single cult either but is made up of a system of cults that possess a certain autonomy. This autonomy is also variable. Sometimes the cults are ranked and subordinated to some dominant cult into which they are eventually absorbed; but sometimes as well they simply exist side by side in confederation. The religion to be studied in this book will provide an example of this confederate organization.

---

1. Later I will show how, for example, certain species of sacred things between which there is incompatibility exclude one another as the sacred excludes the profane (Bk. III, Chap. 5, § 4).

At the same time, we can explain why groups of religious phenomena that belong to no constituted religion can exist: because they are not or are no longer integrated into a religious system. If, for specific reasons, one of those cults just mentioned should manage to survive while the whole to which it belonged has disappeared, it will survive only in fragments. This is what has happened to so many agrarian cults that live on in folklore. In certain cases, what persists in that form is not even a cult, but a mere ceremony or a particular rite.[2]

Although this definition is merely preliminary, it indicates the terms in which the problem that dominates the science of religions must be posed. If sacred beings are believed to be distinguished from the others solely by the greater intensity of the powers attributed to them, the question of how men could have imagined them is rather simple: Nothing more is needed than to identify those forces that, through their exceptional energy, have managed to impress the human mind forcefully enough to inspire religious feelings. But if, as I have tried to establish, sacred things are different in nature from profane things, if they are different in their essence, the problem is far more complex. In that case, one must ask what led man to see the world as two heterogeneous and incomparable worlds, even though nothing in sense experience seems likely to have suggested the idea of such a radical duality.

## IV

Even so, this definition is not yet complete, for it fits equally well two orders of things that must be distinguished even though they are akin: magic and religion. Magic, too, is made up of beliefs and rites. Like religion, it has its own myths and dogmas, but these are less well developed, probably because, given its pursuit of technical and utilitarian ends, magic does not waste time in pure speculation. Magic also has its ceremonies, sacrifices, purifications, prayers, songs, and dances. Those beings whom the magician invokes and the forces he puts to work are not only of the same nature as the forces addressed by religion but very often are the same forces. In the most primitive societies, the souls of the dead are in essence sacred things and objects of religious rites, but at the same time, they have played a major role in magic. In Australia,[3] as well as in Melanesia,[4] in ancient Greece as well as among Christian peoples,[5] the souls, bones, and hair of the dead figure among the tools most often used by the magician. Demons are also a common instrument of magical influence. Now, demons are also surrounded by prohibitions; they too are separated and

---

2. This is the case, for example, of certain marriage and funeral rites.
3. See [Sir Baldwin] Spencer and [Francis James] Gillen, *The Native Tribes of Central Australia* [London, Macmillan, 1889], pp534ff., and *Northern Tribes of Central Australia* [London, Macmillan, 1904], p463; [Alfred William] Howitt, *Native Tribes of South East Australia* [London, Macmillan, 1904], pp359–61.
4. See [Robert Henry] Codrington, *The Melanesians* [*Studies in Their Anthropology and Folklore*, Oxford, Clarendon Press, 1891], Chap. 12
5. See Hubert, Henri. 1877. "Magia", in Daremberg, Charles and Saglio, Edmond (eds.). *Dictionnaire des antiquités Greques et Romaines*. Paris.

live in a world apart. Indeed, it is often difficult to distinguish them from gods proper.[6] Besides, even in Christianity, is not the devil a fallen god? And apart from his origins, does he not have a religious character, simply because the hell of which he is the keeper is an indispensable part in the machinery of the Christian religion? The magician can invoke regular and official deities. Sometimes these are gods of a foreign people: For example, the Greek magicians called upon Egyptian, Assyrian, or Jewish gods. Sometimes they are even national gods: Hecate and Diana were objects of a magic cult. The Virgin, the Christ, and the saints were used in the same manner by Christian magicians.[7]

Must we therefore say that magic cannot be rigorously differentiated from religion – that magic is full of religion and religion full of magic and, consequently, that it is impossible to separate them and define the one without the other? What makes that thesis hard to sustain is the marked repugnance of religion for magic and the hostility of magic to religion in return. Magic takes a kind of professional pleasure in profaning holy things,[8] inverting religious ceremonies in its rites,[9] On the other hand, while religion has not always condemned and prohibited magic rites, it has generally regarded them with disfavor. As messieurs Hubert and Mauss point out, there is something inherently antireligious about the maneuvers of the magician.[10] So it is difficult for these two institutions not to oppose one another at some point, whatever the relations between them. Since my intention is to limit my research to religion and stop where magic begins, discovering what distinguishes them is all the more important.

Here is how a line of demarcation can be drawn between these two domains.

Religious beliefs proper are always shared by a definite group that professes them and that practices the corresponding rites. Not only are they individually accepted by all members of that group, but they also belong to the group and unify it. The individuals who comprise the group feel joined to one another by the fact of common faith. A society whose members are united because they imagine the sacred world and its relations with the profane world in the same way, and because they translate this common representation into identical practices, is what is called a Church. In history we do not find religion without Church. Sometimes the Church is narrowly national; sometimes it extends beyond frontiers; sometimes it encompasses an entire people (Rome, Athens, the Hebrews); sometimes it encompasses only a fraction (Christian denominations since the coming of Protestantism); sometimes it is led by a body of priests; sometimes it is more or less without any official directing body.[11] But wherever we observe religious life, it has a definite group as its basis. Even so-called private cults, like the domestic cult or a

---

6. For example, in Melanesia the *tindalo* is a spirit that is sometimes religious and sometimes magical (Codrington, *The Melanesians*, pp125ff., 194ff.).
7. See Hubert and Mauss, "Esquisse d'une théorie générale de la magie", *AS*, vol. VII [1902–03], pp83–4.
8. For example, the Host is profaned in the Black Mass.
9. See Hubert, "Magia", in *Dictionnaire des antiquités*.
10. Hubert and Mauss, "Esquisse", p19.
11. Certainly it is rare for each ceremony not to have its director at the moment it is conducted; even in the most crudely organized societies, there generally are men designated, due to the importance of their social role, to exercise a directive influence upon religious life (for example, the heads of local groups in certain Australian societies). But this attribution of functions is nevertheless very loose.

corporate cult, satisfy this condition: They are always celebrated by a group, the family or the corporation. And, furthermore, even these private religions often are merely special forms of a broader religion that embraces the totality of life.[12] These small Churches are in reality only chapels in a larger Church and, because of this very scope, deserve all the more to be called by that name.[13]

Magic is an entirely different matter. Granted, magic beliefs are never without a certain currency. They are often widespread among broad strata of the population, and there are even peoples where they count no fewer active followers than religion proper. But they do not bind men who believe in them to one another and unite them into the same group, living the same life. *There is no Church of magic.* Between the magician and the individuals who consult him, there are no durable ties that make them members of a single moral body, comparable to the ties that join the faithful of the same god or the adherents of the same cult. The magician has a clientele, not a Church, and his clients may have no mutual relations, and may even be unknown to one another. Indeed, the relations they have with him are generally accidental and transient, analogous to those of a sick man with his doctor. The official and public character with which the magician is sometimes invested makes no difference. That he functions in broad daylight does not join him in a more regular and lasting manner with those who make use of his services.

It is true that, in certain cases, magicians form a society among themselves. They meet more or less periodically to celebrate certain rites in common in some instances; the place held by witches' meetings in European folklore is well known. But these associations are not at all indispensable for the functioning of magic. Indeed, they are rare and rather exceptional. To practice his art, the magician has no need whatever to congregate with his peers. He is more often a loner. In general, far from seeking company, he flees it. "He stands aloof, even from his colleagues."[14] By contrast, religion is inseparable from the idea of Church. In this first regard, there is already a fundamental difference between magic and religion. Furthermore, and above all, when magic societies of this sort are formed, they never encompass all the adherents of magic. Far from it. They encompass only the magicians. Excluded from them are the laity, as it were – that is, those for whose benefit the rites are conducted, which is to say those who are the adherents of regular cults. Now, the magician is to magic what the priest is to religion. But a college of priests is no more a religion than a religious congregation that worships a certain saint in the shadows of the cloister is a private cult. A Church is not simply a priestly brotherhood; it is a moral community made up of all the faithful, both laity and priests. Magic ordinarily has no community of this sort.[15]

---

12. In Athens, the gods addressed by the domestic cult are only specialized forms of the gods of the City (Ζεὺς κτήσιος, Ζεὺς ἑρκεῖος). [Zeus, protector of property, Zeus, the household god. Trans.] Similarly, in the Middle Ages, the patrons of brotherhoods are saints of the calendar.
13. For the name of Church ordinarily applies only to a group whose common beliefs refer to a sphere of less specialized things.
14. Hubert and Mauss, "Esquisse", p18.
15. [William] Robertson Smith had already shown that magic is opposed to religion as the individual is to the social ([*Lectures on*] *the Religion of the Semites*, 2nd ed. [London, A. & C. Black; 1894], pp264–5).

But if one includes the notion of Church in the definition of religion, does one not by the same stroke exclude the individual religions that the individual institutes for himself and celebrates for himself alone? There is scarcely any society in which this is not to be found. As will be seen below, every Ojibway has his personal *manitou* that he chooses himself and to which he bears specific religious obligations; the Melanesian of the Banks Islands has his *tamaniu*;[16] the Roman has his *genius*;[17] the Christian has his patron saint and his guardian angel, and so forth. All these cults seem, by definition, to be independent of the group. And not only are these individual religions very common throughout history, but some people today pose the question whether such religions are not destined to become the dominant form of religious life – whether a day will not come when the only cult will be the one that each person freely practices in his innermost self.[18]

But, let us put aside these speculations about the future for a moment. If we confine our discussion to religions as they are in the present and as they have been in the past, it becomes obvious that these individual cults are not distinct and autonomous religious systems but simply aspects of the religion common to the whole Church of which the individuals are part. The patron saint of the Christian is chosen from the official list of saints recognized by the Catholic Church, and there are canonical laws that prescribe how each believer must conduct this private cult. In the same way, the idea that every man necessarily has a protective genie is, in different forms, at the basis of a large number of American religions, as well as of Roman religion (to cite only these two examples). As will be seen below, that idea is tightly bound up with the idea of soul, and the idea of soul is not among those things that can be left entirely to individual choice. In a word, it is the Church of which he is a member that teaches the individual what these personal gods are, what their role is, how he must enter into relations with them, and how he must honor them. When one analyzes the doctrines of that Church systematically, sooner or later one comes across the doctrines that concern these special cults. Thus there are not two religions of different types, turned in opposite directions, but the same ideas and principles applied in both cases – here, to circumstances that concern the group as a whole, and there, to the life of the individual. Indeed, this unity is so close that, among certain peoples,[19] the ceremonies during which the believer first enters into communication with his protective genie are combined with rites whose public character is incontestable, namely, rites of initiation.[20]

---

16. [Robert Henry] Codrington, "Notes on the Customs of Mota, Bank Islands", *RSV*, vol. XVI [1880], p136.
17. [Augusto] Negrioli, *Dei Genii presso i Romani*, [Bologna, Ditto Nicola Zanichelli, 1900].
18. This is the conclusion at which [Herbert] Spencer arrives in his *Ecclesiastical Institutions* [Part VI of *The Principles of Sociology*, New York, D. Appleton, 1886], Chap. 16. It is also the conclusion of [Auguste] Sabatier, in his *Esquisse d'une philosophie de la religion d'après la Psychologie et l'Histoire*, [Paris, Fischbacher, 1897], and that of the entire school to which he belongs.
19. Among numerous Indian peoples of North America, in particular.
20. However, that factual point does not settle the question of whether external and public religion is anything other than the development of an interior and personal religion that would be the primitive phenomenon, or whether, on the other hand, the personal religion is the extension, inside individual consciousnesses, of the exterior one. The problem will be taken up directly below (Bk. II, Chap. 5, §2. Cf. Bk. II, Chap. 6 and Bk. II, Chap. 7, §1). For now I merely note that the individual cult presents itself to the observer as an element and an appendage of the collective cult.

What remains are the present-day aspirations toward a religion that would consist entirely of interior and subjective states and be freely constructed by each one of us. But no matter how real those aspirations, they cannot affect our definition: This definition can be applied only to real, accomplished facts, not to uncertain possibilities. Religions can be defined as they are now or as they have been, not as they may be tending more or less vaguely to become. It is possible that this religious individualism is destined to become fact; but to be able to say in what measure, we must first know what religion is, of what elements it is made, from what causes it results, and what function it performs – all questions whose answers cannot be preordained, for we have not crossed the threshold of research. Only at the end of this study will I try to look into the future.

We arrive thus at the following definition: *A religion is a unified system of beliefs and practices relative to sacred things, that is to say, things set apart and forbidden – beliefs and practices which unite into one single moral community called a Church, all those who adhere to them.* The second element thus holds a place in my definition that is no less essential than the first: In showing that the idea of religion is inseparable from the idea of a Church, it conveys the notion that religion must be an eminently collective thing.[21]

[...]

But prohibitions are of different kinds, and it is important to distinguish them. We need not treat every sort of prohibition in this chapter.

To begin, aside from those that belong to religion, there are others that belong to magic. What both have in common is that they define certain things as incompatible and prescribe the separation of the things so defined. But there are also profound differences. First, the punishments are not the same in the two cases. Certainly, as will be pointed out below, the violation of religious prohibitions is often thought automatically to cause physical disorders from which the guilty person is thought to suffer and which are considered punishment for his action. But even when that really does occur, this spontaneous and automatic sanction does not stand alone. It is always supplemented by another that requires human intervention. Either a punishment properly so-called is added (if it does not actually precede the automatic sanction), and that punishment is purposely inflicted by human beings; or, at the very least, there is blame and public disapproval. Even when sacrilege has already been punished by the sickness or natural death of its perpetrator, it is also denounced. It offends opinion, which reacts against it, and it places the culprit

---

21. It is there that my definition picks up the one I proposed some time ago in the *Année sociologique*. In that work, I defined religious beliefs exclusively by their obligatory character; but that obligation evidently arises, as I showed, from the fact that those beliefs belong to a group that imposes them on its members. Thus the two definitions partly overlap. If I have thought it necessary to propose a new one, it is because the first was too formal and went too far in downplaying the content of religious representations. In the discussions that follow, we will see the point of having placed in evidence immediately what is characteristic of this content. In addition, if the imperative character is indeed a distinctive feature of religious beliefs, it has infinite gradations; consequently, it is not easily perceptible in some cases. There arise difficulties and troublesome questions that are avoided if this criterion is replaced by the one I have used above.

in a state of sin. By contrast, a magical prohibition is sanctioned only by the tangible consequences that the forbidden act is held to produce with a kind of physical necessity. By disobeying, one takes risks like those a sick person takes by not following the advice of his doctor; but in this case disobedience does not constitute sin and does not produce indignation. In magic, there is no such thing as sin.

In addition, the fact that the sanctions are not the same is part and parcel of a profound difference in the nature of the prohibitions. A religious prohibition necessarily involves the idea of the sacred. It arises from the respect evoked by the sacred object, and its purpose is to prevent any disrespect. By contrast, magic prohibitions presuppose an entirely secular idea of property – nothing more. The things that the magician recommends keeping separated are things that, because of their characteristic properties, cannot be mixed or brought near one another without danger. Although he may ask his clients to keep their distance from certain sacred things, he does not do so out of respect for those things or out of fear that they may be profaned (since, as we know, magic thrives on profanations). He does so only for reasons of secular utility. In short, religious prohibitions are categorical imperatives and magic ones are utilitarian maxims, the earliest form of hygienic and medical prohibitions. Two orders of facts that are so different cannot be studied at the same time, and under the same rubric, without confusion. Here we need concern ourselves only with religious prohibition.

[...]

All of these rites belong to the same category. The principle on which they are based is one of those on which what is commonly (and improperly[22]) called sympathetic magic is based.

This principle may usually be subdivided into two.[23]

The first can be stated in this way: *Whatever touches an object also touches everything that has any relationship of proximity or solidarity with that object.* Thus, whatever affects the part affects the whole; any force exerted on an individual is transmitted to his neighbors, his kin, and everything with which he is united in any way at all. All these cases are simply applications of the law of contagion, which we studied earlier. A good or bad state or quality is transmitted contagiously from one subject to another that has any relationship with the first.

The second principle is usually summarized in this formula: *Like produces like.* The depiction of a being or a state produces that being or state. This is the maxim that the rites just described put into operation, and its characteristic traits can be grasped best when they occur. The classic example of bewitchment, which is generally presented as the typical application of this same precept, is much less significant. Indeed, the phenomenon

---

22. I will explain the nature of this impropriety below (p517).
23. On this classification see [James George] Frazer, *Lectures on the Early History of Kingship*, [London, Macmillan, 1905], pp37ff.; [Henri] Hubert and [Marcel] Mauss, ["Esquisse d'une] theorie générale de la magie", [*AS*, vol. VII, 1902–03], pp61ff.

in bewitchment is largely a mere transfer. The idea of the image is associated in the mind with the idea of the model. As a result, the effects of any action on the statuette are passed on contagiously to the person whose traits it mimics. In relation to the original, the image plays the role of the part in relation to the whole; it is an agent of transmission. Thus it is believed that one can obtain the same result by burning the hair of the person one wants to get at. The only difference between these two kinds of operation is that, in one, the communication is done by means of similarity, and in the other, by means of contiguity.

The rites that concern us are a different case. They presuppose not merely the passage of a given state or quality from one object into another but the creation of something altogether new. The very act of depicting the animal gives birth to that animal and creates it – in imitating the noise of the wind or the falling water, one causes the clouds to form and dissolve into rain, and so forth. In both kinds of rites, resemblance undoubtedly has a role but a very different one. In bewitchment, resemblance only guides the force exerted in a particular way; it orients a power that is not its own in a certain direction. In the rites just considered, it acts by itself and is directly efficacious. Besides, contrary to the usual definitions, what really differentiates the two principles of the magic called sympathetic and its corresponding practices is not that contiguity acts in some cases and resemblance in others, but that, in the first, there is merely contagious communication and, in the second, production and creation.[24]

Thus to explain the mimetic rites is to explain the second of these principles, and vice versa.

I will not tarry long over the explanation that the anthropological school has put forward, notably Tylor and Frazer. They call upon the association of ideas, just as they do to account for the contagiousness of the sacred. "Homeopathic magic", says Frazer, who prefers this term to that of "mimetic magic", "rests on the association of ideas by similarity, and contagious magic on the association of ideas by contiguity. Homeopathic magic errs by taking things that resemble one another as identical."[25] But this is to misunderstand the specific character of the practices under discussion. From one point of view, Frazer's formula could be applied somewhat justifiably to the case of bewitchment.[26] In that context, it actually is two distinct things – the image and the model it represents more or less schematically – that are assimilated to one another because of their partial resemblance. But only the image is given in the mimetic rites we have just studied, and as for the model, there is none, since the new generation of the totemic species is still no more than a hope, and an uncertain hope at that. Thus there can be no question of assimilation, mistaken or not; there is creation, in the full sense of the word, and how the association

---

24. I say nothing about the so-called law of contrariety. As Hubert and Mauss have shown, the contrary produces its contrary only by means of its like (*Theorie générale de la magie*, p70).
25. [Frazer], *Lectures on the Early History of Kingship*, p39.
26. It is applicable in the sense that there really is an amalgamation of the statuette and the person bewitched. But this amalgamation is far from being a mere product of the association of ideas by similarity. As I have shown, the true determining cause of the phenomenon is the contagiousness that is characteristic of religious forces.

of ideas could ever lead one to believe in this creation is not clear. How could the mere fact of representing the movements of an animal produce certainty that the animal will be reborn in abundance?

The general properties of human nature cannot explain such odd practices. Instead of considering the principle on which they rest in its general and abstract form, let us put it back into the moral milieu to which it belongs and in which we have just observed it. Let us reconnect it with the set of ideas and feelings that are the origin of the rites in which it is applied, and we will be in a better position to discern its causes.

The men who gather for these rites believe they really are animals or plants of the species whose name they bear. They are conscious of an animal or plant nature, and in their eyes that nature constitutes what is most essential and most excellent about themselves. When they are assembled, then, their first act must be to affirm to one another this quality that they ascribe to themselves and by which they define themselves. The totem is their rallying sign. For this reason, as we have seen, they draw it on their bodies, and they try to emulate it by their gestures, cries, and carriage. Since they are emus or kangaroos, they will behave like the animals of the same name. By this means, they witness to one another that they are members of the same moral community, and they take cognizance of the kinship that unites them. The rite not only expresses this kinship but also makes or remakes it, for this kinship exists only insofar as it is believed, and the effect of all these collective demonstrations is to keep alive the beliefs on which it rests. So although these jumps, cries, and movements of all kinds are bizarre and grotesque in appearance, in reality they have a meaning that is human and profound. The Australian seeks to resemble his totem just as the adherent of more advanced religions seeks to resemble his God. For both, this is a means of communing with the sacred, that is, with the collective ideal that the sacred symbolizes. It is an early form of the ὁμοίωσις τῷ θεῷ [Imitation of God].

Still, this first cause applies to what is most specific to the totemic beliefs, and if it was the only cause, the principle of like produces like would not have lived beyond totemism. Since there is perhaps no religion in which rites derived from it are not to be found, another cause must have combined with that one.

In fact, the very general purpose of the ceremonies in which we have seen it applied is not only the one I have just mentioned, fundamental though it is, for they also have a more immediate and conscious purpose: to bring about the reproduction of the totemic species. The idea of this necessary reproduction haunts the minds of the faithful; they concentrate the force of their attention and will on this goal. Now a single concern cannot haunt an entire group of men to that extent and not become externalized in tangible form. Since all are thinking of an animal or plant to whose destinies the clan is allied, this thinking in common is inevitably manifested outwardly by movements, and the ones most singled out for this role are those that represent the animal or plant in one of its most characteristic forms. There are no movements that as closely resemble the idea that fills consciousnesses at that moment, since they are its direct and almost automatic translation. The people do their best to imitate the animal; they cry out like it; they jump like it; they mimic the settings in which the plant is daily used. All of these processes of representation are so many ways of outwardly marking the goal to which everyone aspires and of saying, calling on, and imagining the thing they want to bring about.[27] Nor is this the need of any one era or caused by the beliefs of any one religion. It is quintessentially human. This is why, even in religions very different from the one we are studying, once the faithful are gathered together to ask their gods for an outcome that they fervently desire, they are virtually compelled to depict it. To be sure, speech is one means of expressing it, but movement is no less natural. Springing from the body just as spontaneously, it comes even before speech or, in any case, at the same time.

But even if we can thus understand how these movements found their way into the ceremony, we must still explain the power that is ascribed to them. If the Australian repeats them regularly at each new season, it is because he thinks they are required for the success of the rite. Where could he have gotten the idea that imitating an animal makes it reproduce?

Such an obvious error seems barely intelligible so long as we see in the rite only the physical purpose it apparently has. But we know that apart from its presumed effect on the totemic species, it has a profound influence on the souls of the faithful who take part. The faithful come away from it with an impression of well-being whose causes they do not see clearly but that is well founded. They feel that the ceremony is good for them; and in it they do indeed remake their moral being. How would this kind of euphoria not make them feel that the rite has succeeded, that it actually was what it set out to be, that it achieved its intended goal? And since the reproduction of the totemic species is the only goal that is consciously pursued, it seems to be achieved by the methods used, the efficacy of which stands thereby demonstrated. In this way, men came to ascribe creative virtues to movements that are empty in themselves. The power of the rite over minds, which is real, made them believe in its power over things, which is imaginary; the efficacy of the whole led men to believe in that of each part, taken separately. The genuinely useful effects brought about by the ceremony as a whole are tantamount to an experimental justification of the elementary practices that comprise it, though in reality all these practices are in no way indispensable to its success. Moreover, the fact that they can be replaced by others of a very different nature, without change in the final result, proves that they do not act by themselves. Indeed, it seems there are Intichiumas made up of offerings only and without mimetic rites; others are purely mimetic and without offerings. Nevertheless, both are thought to be equally efficacious. Thus if value is attached to these various manipulations, it is not because of value intrinsic to them but because they are part of a complex rite whose overall utility is felt.

We can understand that way of thinking all the more easily since we can observe it in our midst. Especially among the most cultivated peoples and *milieux*, we often come upon believers [*croyants*] who, while having doubts about the specific power ascribed by dogma to each rite taken separately, nonetheless persist in their religious practice. They are not certain that the details of the prescribed observances can be rationally justified, but they feel that it would be impossible to emancipate themselves from those without

---

27. On the causes of this outward manifestation, see above, pp231ff.

falling into moral disarray, from which they recoil. Thus the very fact that faith has lost its intellectual roots among them reveals the profound causes that underlie it. This is why the faithful [*fideles*] are in general left indifferent by the facile criticisms that a simplistic rationalism has sometimes levelled against ritual prescriptions. The true justification of religious practices is not in the apparent ends they pursue but in their invisible influence over consciousnesses and in their manner of affecting our states of mind. Similarly, when preachers undertake to make a convert, they focus less upon directly establishing, with systematic evidence, the truth of some particular proposition or the usefulness of such and such observance, than upon awakening or reawakening the sense of moral support that regular celebration of the cult provides. In this way, they create a predisposition toward believing that goes in advance of proof, influences the intellect to pass over the inadequacy of the logical arguments, and leads it to go, as if on its own, beyond the propositions the preachers want to get it to accept. This favorable prejudice, this leap toward believing, is precisely what faith is made of; and it is faith that gives the rites authority in the eyes of the believer – no matter who he is, the Christian or the Australian. The Christian is superior only in his greater awareness of the psychic process from which belief results. He knows that salvation comes "by faith alone."

Because such is the origin of faith, it is in a sense "impervious to experience."[28] If the periodic failures of the Intichiuma do not shake the confidence the Australian has in his rite, it is because he holds with all the strength of his soul to those practices he comes to for the purpose of renewing himself periodically. He could not possibly deny them in principle without causing a real upheaval of his entire being, which resists. But however great that resistance might be, it does not radically distinguish the religious mentality from the other forms of human mentality, even from those other forms that we are most in the habit of opposing to it. In this regard, the mentality of the savant differs only in degree from the foregoing. When a scientific law has the authority of numerous and varied experiments, to reject it too easily upon discovery of one single fact that seems to contradict it is contrary to all method. It is still necessary to ensure that this fact has only one interpretation and cannot be accounted for without abandoning the proposition that seems discredited. The Australian does no differently when he puts down the failure of an Intichiuma to evildoing somewhere, or the abundance of a harvest that comes too soon to some mystic Intichiuma celebrated in the beyond.

He has even less grounds for doubting his rite on the strength of a contrary fact, since its value is, or seems to be, established by a larger number of facts that accord with it. To begin with, the moral efficacy of the ceremony is real and directly felt by all who take part; therein is a constantly repeated experience whose import no contradictory experience can weaken. What is more, physical efficacy itself finds at least apparent confirmation in the results of objective observation. It is in fact normal for the totemic species to reproduce itself regularly. Thus, in the great majority of cases, everything happens as if the ritual movements truly have brought about the hoped-for results. Failures are not the rule. Not

---

28. [Lucien] Lévy-Bruhl, *Les Fonctions mentales dans les sociétés inférieures* [Paris, F. Alcan, 1910], pp61–68.

surprisingly, since the rites, especially the periodic ones, demand only that nature take its regular course, it seems most often to obey them. In this way, if the believer happens to seem resistant to certain lessons from experience, he does so by relying on other experiences that seem to him more conclusive. The researcher does this more methodically but acts no differently.

Thus magic is not, as Frazer held,[29] a primary datum and religion only its derivative. Quite the contrary, the precepts on which the magician's art rests were formed under the influence of religious ideas, and only by a secondary extension were they turned to purely secular applications. Because all the forces of the universe were conceived on the model of sacred forces, the contagiousness inherent in the sacred forces was extended to them all, and it was believed that, under certain conditions, all the properties of bodies could transmit themselves contagiously. Similarly, once the principle that like produces like took form to satisfy definite religious needs, it became detached from its ritual origins and, through a kind of spontaneous generalization, became a law of nature.[30] To comprehend these fundamental axioms of magic, we must resituate them in the religious *milieux* in which they were born and which alone permits us to account for them. When we see those axioms as the work of isolated individuals, lone magicians, we wonder how human minds imagined them, since nothing in experience could have suggested or verified them. In particular, we cannot understand how such a deceptive craft could have abused men's trust for so long. The problem disappears if the faith men have in magic is only a special case of religious faith in general, if it is itself the product, or at least the indirect product, of a collective effervescence. In other words, using the phrase "sympathetic magic" to denote the collection of practices just discussed is not altogether improper. Although there are sympathetic rites, they are not peculiar to magic. Not only are they found in religion as well, but it is from religion that magic received them. Thus, all we do is court confusion if, by the name we give those rites, we seem to make them out to be something specifically magical.

Hence the results of my analysis strongly resemble those Hubert and Mauss obtained when they studied magic directly.[31] They showed magic to be something altogether different from crude industry, based on crude science. They have brought to light a whole background of religious conceptions that lie behind the apparently secular mechanisms used by the magician, a whole world of forces the idea of which magic took from religion. We can now see why magic is so full of religious elements: It was born out of religion.

---

29. [James George Frazer], *Golden Bough*, 2nd. ed. vol. I [London, Macmillan, 1900], pp69–75.
30. I do not mean to say that there was a time when religion existed without magic. Probably, as religion was formed, certain of its principles were extended to nonreligious relations, and in this way, a more or less developed magic came to complement it. Even if these two systems of ideas and practices do not correspond to distinct historical phases, nevertheless there is a definite relationship of derivation between them. This is all I have set out to establish.
31. [Mauss and Hubert, *Theorie générale de la magie*], pp108ff.

# PART III

# MID-TWENTIETH-CENTURY APPROACHES TO MAGIC

PART III: MID-TWENTIETH-CENTURY APPROACHES TO MAGIC

# INTRODUCTION

In Part II we have seen that the formative period of the academic debate yielded very diverse definitions and theories of "magic". Whereas Frazer imagined the "magician" to perform "sympathetic" rites for the sake of his community, Durkheim labelled communal rites "religious" (or "mimetic") and instead shaped the image of the "magician" as an antisocial, egoistic and individualistic service provider at the margins of society. Bronislaw Malinowski tried to synthesize some of Frazer's and Durkheim's ideas within his own functionalist interpretation of the magic–religion–science triad (see Chapter 17) but thereby complicated matters even more – now "the increase ceremonies of the Arunta are classed as religion by Durkheim but magic by Frazer, and Trobriand garden rituals, which Malinowski terms magic, would be religion according to Durkheim" (Hammond 1970: 1351). The fact that already the early scholarly discourse put forth not only inconsistent but even contradictory definitions of "magic" has been one of the major obstacles of the debate and forced later authors to engage in various coping strategies.

One of these strategies was to deny a clear-cut distinction between "magic" and "religion" (or "science", respectively) and instead advocate a continuum between these concepts, thereby following Marett's criticism of Frazer and his idea of the "sphere of the magico-religious" (see the Introduction to Part II). Ruth Benedict, in her article "Religion" (1938), picked up this idea and distinguished the poles of "animism" (where the supernatural is personified) and "animatism" (where the supernatural is impersonal – for example, an attribute of a material object). Accordingly, "religion" is characterized by "two poles" of behaviour (Benedict 1938: 647) and "magic" comes into play as a "technique of religion" (637) – namely of the "animatist" pole, where it refers to the ritual manipulation of things and objects. William Goode enhanced the continuum model by positing eleven patterns of distinction between the two poles "magic" and "religion" that had been postulated by various earlier scholars (Goode 1949). Adopting Weber's idea of the ideal type, Goode claimed that a specific source may never be completely assigned to one of the two poles but classed somewhere in between and may not have to match all eleven patterns. That made it possible to synthesize various earlier definitions, but at the same time undermined the pursuit of a clear-cut distinction between "magic" and "religion". Murray and Rosalie Wax hence criticized Goode's model as being practically useless for anthropological research (Wax and Wax 1963: 500). Another later author, the historian of religions Harald Biezais, completely dismantled the continuum model by postulating an "essential identity" of "magic" and "religion", thereby rejecting any attempts of differentiation (Biezais 1978).

Our text by Gerardus van der Leeuw (see Chapter 15) documents another line of thought – namely, the phenomenology of religion. Scholars associated with that approach tended to follow the intellectualist perspective of Tylor and Frazer and regarded the exercise of power over the world as the essence of "magic". Rudolf Otto, for example, in his *The Idea of the Holy* (first published in German in 1917), discusses various experiences of the "numinous" and assigns "magic" (most often he uses German "*Zauber*", which can also be translated as "sorcery" or "charm") to the beginnings of religious evolution, holding that the "magical is nothing but a suppressed and dimmed form of the numinous" (Otto

1939: 69). While identifying early "magic" as "modes of behaviour exhibiting some simple analogy and carried out quite unreflectively" (121), thereby recalling Frazer's concept of "sympathetic magic" (see Chapter 12), Otto argues that it later evolved into a more complex, personalized pattern of attributing events to "operations of force" that Otto labels "daemonic" (123). As these "demons" also evoked feelings of "uncanniness" and "shuddering" (123), as in "religion", "magic" represents to Otto a "vestibule at the threshold of the real religious feeling, an earliest stirring of the numinous consciousness" (126). This is mirrored by van der Leeuw's claim that "magic" essentially aims at influencing or controlling the world and that it is not distinct from "religion", but "one specific type of religion" (see Chapter 15). Mircea Eliade likewise sympathized with the "intellectualist" approach of Tylor and Frazer (see, e.g., Eliade 1959: 9–10, 216–17). However, while brushing upon the topic in many writings and even dealing with various historical discourses of "magic" (see, e.g., Eliade 1978, 1988), Eliade nowhere in his work gives a precise definition or novel theoretical account.

A more original direction was taken in the late 1940s by the Italian historian of religions Ernesto de Martino. In his *Il mondo magico: prolegomeni a una storia del magismo* (1948; translated 1972 as *Primitive Magic: The Psychic Powers of Shamans and Sorcerers*), de Martino emphatically rejects the "rationalistic" theories of Tylor, Frazer, Levy-Bruhl and others (even Hegel; see de Martino 1988 [1972]: 199–201); instead, he advocates a novel approach to "magic" influenced by contemporary philosophy. De Martino holds that human life is fragile and that humans aim at keeping "presence" (de Martino 1988 [1972]: 70) – that is, at "being-here" (76) free of existential threats and in stable relations with the world. "Magic" comes into play when there is a crisis of this "presence" (i.e., the threat of not "being-here") and, as a ritual technique, works by recalibrating and stabilizing the "presence" by giving symbolic shapes to this threat, by establishing a relationship with these symbolic shapes, and by indicating their controllability; de Martino labels this the "existential drama of magic" (72). Therefore, the "main interest of the magic world is [...] to master and consolidate the elementary being-within-the-world or presence of the individual" (150) and the cultural persistence of "magic" is explained by the inevitable fragility of human life.

However, despite these various attempts of recalibrating the category, the mid-twentieth century also witnessed harsh criticisms. Robert Lowie completely dismantled Frazer's and Durkheim's definitions in his standard work *Primitive Religion*, arriving at the conclusion that: "In short, Frazer's argument breaks down at every point" (Lowie 1925 [reprint 1997]: 147) and that "The sociological distinction between magic and religion is untenable" (151). Two other leading anthropologists of the mid-twentieth century, Alfred Radcliffe Brown and Clyde Kluckhohn, likewise pronounced serious concerns about the validity and utility of the concept of "magic" in anthropological research (Radcliffe-Brown 1952: 138; Kluckhohn 1953: 518). Olof Pettersson enhanced these criticisms by stating that the "scientific debate over the relation between 'magic' and 'religion' is a *discussion of an artificial problem created by defining religion on the ideal pattern of Christianity*. The elements of man's beliefs and ceremonies concerning the supernatural powers which did not coincide with this ideal type of religion was – and is – called 'magic'. There is always a tendency to mock the unfamiliar in other man's faith and worship. 'Magic' became – and still becomes – a refuse-heap for the elements which are not sufficiently 'valuable' to get a place within 'religion'" (Pettersson 1957: 119 [original emphasis]). In a similar vein, Malinowski's fieldwork monographs were criticized by later scholars who pointed to various misunderstandings and the potential valuelessness of the magic–science–religion triad to interpret his findings (see, e.g., Lee 1949; Bidney 1953: 162f; Goody 1961; Wax and Wax 1963; Philsooph 1971). However, the debate on the "refuse-heap" (Pettersson 1957) continued. Claude Lévi-Strauss attempted a structuralist explanation of "magic" in his article "The sorcerer and his magic", where he stresses the "symbolic function" of "magic" within culturally construed realities (Lévi-Strauss 1963: 184), a point he further elaborated upon in *The Savage Mind* (1966: e.g., 221f). Mary Douglas, in a chapter entitled "Magic and miracle" in her book *Purity and Danger* (1966), likewise calls into question several major accounts (from Tylor to Lévi-Strauss). Douglas holds that European notions of primitive "magic" had unfortunate consequences for the study of religion\s and reframes the debate on "magic" into a new theory of ritual, but she still continues to talk of "magic" and argues that "far from being meaningless, it is primitive magic which gives meaning to existence" (Douglas 1966: 73). Implicitly, Douglas raises the issue of ethnocentrism (see the General Introduction to this volume), a main concern of the subsequent debate.

Rituals and "magic" have also been the main topic of the "rationality debate" that discussed – mainly on the grounds of Evans-Pritchard's seminal study *Witchcraft, Oracles and Magic among the Azande* (see Chapter 16) – various epistemological problems implied in the scholarly attribution of rationality (or, more often, the absence of this attribution) to ritual practices or beliefs in non-Western cultures. Apart from Horton (see Chapter 18) and Tambiah (see Chapter 19) who reinterpreted the magic–science dyad in different ways, numerous other scholars participated in that debate. Jack Goody, for example, while discussing the works of Evans-Pritchard and Malinowski, arrives at the conclusion that the concept of "symbolic behaviour" (that includes "ritual" and "magic") has most often served as a "residual category to which 'meaning' is assigned by the observer in order to make sense of otherwise irrational, pseudo-rational or non-rational behaviour" (Goody 1961: 157). In a similar vein, Peter Winch questioned the possibility of "objectively" evaluating the rationality of non-Western cultures and stressed the relativity and language-dependence of truth claims (Winch 1964). This argument was further elaborated upon by I. C. Jarvie and Joseph Agassi, who differentiated various types of rationality (Jarvie and Agassi 1967, 1973), and John D. Peel, who, more disillusioned, argued that the concept of "magic" should not operate as part of sociological vocabulary any more (Peel 1969: 83–4). However, other scholars such as J. H. Beattie (Beattie 1966, 1970), Barry Barnes (Barnes 1973) and Steven Lukes (Lukes 1973) nevertheless advocated the idea of independent, transcultural criteria for "truth" and thereby also continued to embrace the concept of "magic".

# 15

# GERARDUS VAN DER LEEUW

*Religion in Essence and Manifestation*, translation J. E. Turner

Gerardus van der Leeuw (b. 1890; d. 1950) studied theology and Egyptology. In 1916, he became a pastor in the Dutch Reformed Church and in 1918 he was appointed to the chair of General History of Religion and History of Theological Doctrine in Groningen (The Netherlands). Van der Leeuw is the author of some 80 books, almost 800 articles and 400 book reviews, but his lasting reputation is built on his contributions to the phenomenology of religion, as witnessed in his massive handbook *Religion in Essence and Manifestation* (originally written and first published in 1933 in German under the title *Phänomenologie der Religion*). A substantially revised version of this seminal treatise was published posthumously in 1956. Ultimately, van der Leeuw's phenomenology is a theological project; Christianity is assigned a particular position in his book and the last chapter of the main text ends on a religious note.

The notion of power is a cornerstone of van der Leeuw's understanding of religion; the first chapters of his *Religion in Essence and Manifestation* provide a discussion of power as the key to "the object of religion" (i.e., its primal agency as perceived by religious people). In the first chapter, van der Leeuw briefly touches on "magic", where he rejects sweeping identifications of "magic" with potency. Even though "Magic is certainly manifested in power" and "Power may be employed in magic", "to employ power [...] is not in itself to act magically" (van der Leeuw 1986: 25).

Van der Leeuw discusses "magic" mainly in Chapter 82 (in Part IV of the book, entitled "The world") presented here. His discussion shows van der Leeuw's broad range of readings covering such diverse fields as psychology, philosophy, ethnography and literature; the impact of the French philosopher/sociologist/anthropologist Lévy-Bruhl (b. 1857; d. 1939) and his ideas on a "primitive mentality" – adopted and defended by van der Leeuw in various publications – are felt, in particular; but van der Leeuw emphasizes the continuity and presence of that mentality among the contemporaries. From Lévy-Bruhl he takes the notion of "participation", interpreted here as deep-rooted, "eternal" attitude of a non-objectivist sharing relationship with the world that allows for a two-way mutual influence between humans and the world. "I can influence the world [...], just as the world can affect me, in a way that is justified by neither logic nor facts, but which constitutes a very real struggle at the closest possible range. I shall call this contest the *magical attitude*; and the armistice that follows the struggle [...] I shall call the *mythical form-conferring attitude*. The former is concerned with Powers, the latter with Will and Form, but both alike are conditioned by participation." The "magical" attitude is one of protest and lies at the root of idealism and human liberation, but it is also autistic and van der Leeuw's analysis is imbued with comparisons with children, dream states and mental disorders. To van der Leeuw, "magic" is not distinct from religion, but "one specific type of religion".

## RELIGION IN ESSENCE AND MANIFESTATION

1. In Chapter 8 I showed that for primitive man the modern concept of "world" does not really exist, and that far from regarding his environment as an object, he immediately constitutes it his own "conjoint world"; and in this principle the essential feature of the religious *Weltanschauung* has already been expressed. I may now repeat this, however, in the sense that a "religious *Weltanschauung*" is never merely a "point of view", but is always a *participation*, a *sharing*. For out of his own particular environment everyone constructs a world for himself which he believes himself able to dominate; there is therefore no one single world, but just as many *worlds* as there are human beings. Thus what holds good of the child is true universally: and "it should be the fundamental principle of every psychology, as contrasted with theories of knowledge, that for conscious experience reality is never a constant, but that it changes with the individual's psychical organization, and indeed with his stage of development; it must then be definitely stated, at the outset, that every child lives in a world quite different from ours".[1] In this sense the world is "objective mind";[2] the human spirit does not direct itself towards a world that is given to it, but allows what meets it to become part of itself, after it has sufficiently modified it. The "world" is therefore an essentially "celebrated", not merely an "accepted" but a dominated world.[3]

2. Herein lies the truth of the principle of participation, of sharing, advanced by Lévy-Bruhl. Things do not encounter each other "solidly in space", but have some share in one another and may mingle with, and appear in place of, each other. Accordingly, man does not conduct himself "objectively" towards the "world": he participates in it, just as it does in him. His path to the world, therefore, is neither that of contemplation, nor reflection, nor presenting himself as a subject and so forming a "substratum", but of existing as oriented *towards* the world. Man's domination of the world is thus a domination exerted always from within.

This participation, still further, is an attitude deeply rooted in human nature; it is not a disposition that requires to be overcome, but is the perfectly natural mental outlook even of "modern" man, thoroughly accustomed as he is to theoretical and practical knowledge

---

1. Spranger, Eduard. 1924. *Psychologie des Jugendalters*. Leipzig: Quelle & Meyer, p32.
2. cf. Spranger, Eduard. 1921 [1910]. *Lebensformen: geisteswissenschaftliche Psychologie und Ethik der Persönlichkeit*. Halle (Saale): Niemeyer, pp17 f.
3. *cf.* Heidegger, *op. cit.* [Heidegger, Martin. 1927. *Sein und Zeit*. Halle: Niemeyer], p87.

and to objective observation and experiment.[4] As Lévy-Bruhl himself profoundly observes on this subject: "Now the need of participation assuredly remains something more imperious and more intense, even among peoples like ourselves, than the thirst for knowledge and the desire for conformity with the claims of reason. It lies deeper within us and its source is more remote."[5] This mental attitude, therefore, which neither dissects nor abstracts, neither infers nor analyses, but deals with the whole, grasps it concretely, connects together its essentials and experiences "participation", is ours to-day just as much as it is that of primitive man. In the case of the latter, certainly, it has a wider range of control, although so-called "primitives" are obviously "modern" also, and are quite familiar with analytical and logical thought! But for us too it is the actual way to the world:[6] not indeed as "lazy thinking", as Thurnwald would regard it, but existing as oriented towards the world in contrast to merely observing it. The self, that is to say, is a partner with the world and the world with the self.[7]

This relationship (to continue) results in events in the world, equally with man's own activities, being dominated by "mystical" factors; I shall employ this expression, which was coined by Lévy-Bruhl, although I believe myself that it involves some misapprehension, and I would therefore prefer to restrict the terms "mysticism" and "mystical" to the phenomenon previously described in Chapter 75.[8] As regards the facts, however, Lévy-Bruhl is perfectly correct. When, for example, Graebner attempts to invalidate his assertion by showing that "the Australian does not conceive the natural as supernatural, but conversely the supernatural as natural", and that the magic power he employs is thought of as "grossly material",[9] this only indicates that the ethnologist has failed to perceive how our own antithesis between supernatural and natural, as this has gradually developed in Western European thought, does not exist at all in primitive and religious thought. That the primitive mind understands everything supernatural in some natural sense is indeed quite correct; but then his "naturalness" is far more "supernatural", more "mystical" or (still better) more numinous, than our "supernaturalness". And that Power is conceived as material is equally true; but we observed much earlier that the contrast between the

---

4. cf. Marett, Robert Ranulph. 1932. *Faith, Hope and Charity in Primitive Religion*. Oxford: Clarendon Press, p86.
5. Lévy-Bruhl, Lucien. 1926. *How Natives Think*. London: Allen & Unwin, p. 385; cf. the remarkable discussion of Lévy-Bruhl's ideas in Bulletin 29, *Société française de philosophie*, 1929, no 3. Nothing is more significant of the low philosophic level of the historical and ethnological sciences than the misunderstanding of Lévy-Bruhl's views, exhibited by investigators in the most diverse fields. In this respect the urgent necessity becomes obvious of an understanding between psychology and phenomenology, on the one hand, and on the other the so-called pure historic, anthropological and ethnological sciences, which today, almost without exception, set out, without being aware of so doing, from the most extraordinary epistemological, psychological and metaphysical principles.
6. Thurnwald, Richard. 1928. *Bequemes Denken: Entwicklung und Gestaltung sozialer Gebilde bei Naturvölkern*. Paris: Nourry.
7. cf. Danzel, Theodor Wilhelm. 1922. "Die psychologischen Grundlagen der Mythologie", *Archiv für Religionswissenschaft*, 21, p432.
8. cf. Werner, Heinz. 1926. *Einführung in die Entwicklungspsychologie*. Leipzig: Barth, p270.
9. Graebner, Fritz. 1924. *Das Weltbild der Primitiven*. München: Reinhardt, p16.

material and the spiritual is far from being so fundamental as our current popular psychology would gladly believe it to be.[10]

I can influence the world therefore, just as the world can affect me, in a way that is justified by neither logic nor facts, but which constitutes a very real struggle at the closest possible range. I shall call this contest the *magical attitude*; and the armistice that follows the struggle, which is itself however also one kind of domination preluding a new combat, I shall call the *mythical form-conferring attitude*. The former is concerned with Powers, the latter with Will and Form, but both alike are conditioned by participation. For without participation there is no struggle: and similarly without proximity. This magical attitude, however, is not a structure of the spiritual life merely of the past, of which only meagre vestiges now persist for us; nor, again, is it a degeneration nor childish malady; it is neither "primitive science" nor elementary technique.[11] It is, on the contrary, a primal attitude very deeply grounded in human nature, as vital among ourselves as it ever was, in fact an eternal structure. This is evident, too, in the recurring predominance under certain conditions of the magical attitude. Children will be considered later, while Storch has discussed the reasoning of the mentally disordered and compiled remarkable examples of the magical attitude of mind, and has explicitly placed these parallel to "primitive" data. "As an underlying current of waking day-thinking there lies ready prepared, in every man, magical-archaic experience; but this comes into serious conflict with ordinary rational thinking only in specific schizoid types";[12] thus to victims of schizophrenic megalomania "the world, from being a differentiated objectivity, again becomes the immediate content of his own existence[13] [...] instead of being an object of objective consciousness, the world of things then becomes a mere modification of self-feeling".[14] One patient, for instance, "calls herself 'the goddess', relating how she has been placed in the domain of the sun and that the end of the world has been revealed to her, but that her joy in life could not be killed, as she wished to devour the time following the end of the world". We curtly describe this mental attitude as megalomania, but we must not forget that this mania subsists in the blood of us all without exception – this mania to dominate the world – and that anyone who had entirely relinquished this madness could no longer live. It is essentially human not to accept the given world, but to manipulate it until it has been adjusted to one's own life. "The world

---

10. K. Hidding has recently given an excellent description of so-called primitive mentality in his Hidding, Klaas Aldert Hendrik. 1933. *Gebruiken en godsdienst der Soendaneezer*. Bandung: Drukkerij A.C. Nix, p3.
11. Of a completely different opinion are Allier (Magic is degeneration), Lindworsky (primitives think rationally, but know nothing about the conditions of natural processes: magic is ignorance), Boas (feeling predominates among primitives), Bartlett (predominance of the play instinct); I have discussed these views elsewhere in Leeuw, Gerardus van der. 1928. *La Structure de la mentalité primitive*. Strasbourg: Impr. Alsacienne. Closely akin to my own ideas is Mayer-Gross, Willy. 1927. "Zur Frage der psychologischen Eigenart der sog. Naturvölker", *International Congress of Psychology, Proceedings and Papers* VIII, pp206 ff.
12. Storch, Alfred. 1922. *Das archaisch-primitive Erleben und Denken der Schizophrenen*. Berlin: Springer, pp88 f.
13. Storch. *Ibid.* [*Das archaisch-primitive Erleben und Denken der Schizophrenen*], p74.
14. Storch. *Ibid.* [*Das archaisch-primitive Erleben und Denken der Schizophrenen*].

was not, till it I did create."[15] Thus a condition of struggle always prevails, whose victorious conclusion implies the decline of world power into that of the individual.[16]

3. He who thus assumes the magical attitude, according to Salomon Reinach's fine simile, resembles the conductor dominating his orchestra; and it may well be that he believes that he himself produces the uproar! The best parallel to the person who is magically disposed, however, is Chanticleer, who thinks that his crowing makes the sun rise, and who suffers the most tragic disillusioning when, one morning, the sun is there "of itself!" So man too assumes the offensive against the powers:[17] he overcomes them by the main force of his own will: he creates them as it were. The purely magical attitude, which of course nowhere actually exists, is therefore that of God, of the Creator:

> At my command, upon yon primal Night,
> The starry hosts unveiled their glorious light.[18]

In magic, then, the dictum *eritis sicut Deus* – "ye shall be as gods" – attains full reality; and in truth magical thinking is not literally thought "but willing".[19]

It is, therefore, never legitimate to set "religion" and "magic" in any definitely adverse relationship, as though religion were the successor of magic, the latter being non-religious and the former never magical. Magic itself is religion simply because it is concerned with powers; certainly it requires no "god", but a "godless" act may very well be religious. Magic differs, however, from all other forms of religion in that the desire to dominate the world belongs to its essential nature. Not every religion has this aim; nevertheless it is adopted by very many non-magical religions, only with other methods. Thus I can concede neither the antithesis between religion and magic as social-antisocial, nor as ethical-scientific, nor again that magic is anterior to religion:[20] wherever there is religion there is magic, even though the magical stream does not always follow the main channel of religion; similarly, wherever there is magic there is religion, although it can be only one specific

---

15. Goethe, Johann Wolfgang von. 1832. *Faust: der Tragödie zweiter Teil*, Act 2.
16. Cassirer, *op. cit.*, II [Cassirer, Ernst. 1925. *Philosophie der symbolischen Formen. Teil II: Das mythische Denken*. Berlin: Cassirer], 94: "Thus the ego exercises an almost limitless domination over reality in the magical world survey; it draws all reality back into itself."
17. Reinach, Salomon. 1909. *Orpheus: histoire générale des religions*. Paris: Picard, p32 f. [English translation 1923: *Orpheus: A History of Religions*. London: Heinemann, p23.]
18. Goethe. op cit. [*Faust: der Tragödie zweiter Teil*] Act 2 (Swanwick).
19. Prinzhorn, Hans. 1923. *Bildnerei der Geisteskranken: ein Beitrag zur Psychologie und Psychopathologie der Gestaltung* [2. Auflage]. Berlin: Springer, p311.
20. cf. W. Otto's admirable observations on these problems: *Archiv für Religionswissenschaft*, 12, 1909, pp544 ff.; cf. Clemen, Carl. 1921. *Wesen und Ursprung der Magie, Archiv für Religionspsychologie*, II–III; Beth, Karl. 1914. *Religion und Magie bei den Naturvölkern*. Leipzig: Teubner; Bertholet, Alfred. 1927. "Das Wesen der Magie", in: *Nachrichten der Gesellschaft der Wissenschaften zu Göttingen*. p23; Thurnwald, Richard. 1929. "Zauber", in Ebert, Max (ed.). *Lexikon der Vorgeschichte*. Berlin: De Gruyter, pp485, 498 ff. Vierkandt, Alfred. 1907. "Die Anfänge der Religion und Zauberei", in *Globus: Illustrierte Zeitschrift für Länder und Völkerkunde* 92, p64.

type of religion. Saintyves, therefore, is quite correct: magic is an art, knowledge, a cult, only it deals with mystery.[21]

The magical attitude, then, is certainly religious: nevertheless it demands nothing "supernatural"; and the extent to which scholars of to-day take for granted the application of modern concepts to primitive religion, and in fact to religion in general, is astonishing. If I shoot an arrow at an enemy directly opposite me, this is to our modes of thought certainly a disagreeable, but perfectly logical, action. But if I aim my arrow at an opponent who is in another town a hundred miles away, then our logic ceases and we speak of an action grounded on the "supernatural", for whose results the supernatural may well be responsible. In primitive consciousness, however, these two acts are by no means so different: in any case we require a superior and numinous power for the success of both alike.[22] This is the truth in those theories of magic which emphasize the close relationship of ordinary *technique* to magical processes,[23] although the derivation of magical activity from primitive *technique*, attempted by Vierkandt,[24] has little force; and with his usual keen penetration Nietzsche has perceived the essential feature here: "when one rows, it is not the rowing that moves the boat, but rowing is only a magical ceremony by which one compels a *daemon* to move the boat" (I should myself substitute a "power"). "All maladies, even death itself, are the result of magical influences. Illness and death never happen naturally; *the whole conception of 'natural sequence' is lacking* […] when a man shoots with a bow, there is still always present an irrational hand and strength […] man is the *rule*, nature is irregularity."[25] To this I need add nothing.

But what really lends the magical attitude its intrinsic human interest is its character of protest: Preuss has observed how, in magical thinking, man opposed animal *instinct*, and so rose above himself; how too, in magic, lie the roots of all idealism and the possibility of the liberation of the human spirit.[26] Magical man, then, makes a "world", his own world, out of the "environment" of the animal; and thus magic was the earliest mode of uniting individual objects within one all-inclusive world-picture.[27]

This magical attitude, still further, appears even more clearly in the simplest examples than in complicated magic rituals. Lévy-Bruhl alludes, for instance, to the rite of reversing an action (*renverser un acte*): in certain tribes stepping over anyone is strictly prohibited and whoever inadvertently does so must nullify his action by once again stepping over the person concerned, only this time "in the reverse direction".[28] That is a magical action

---

21. Saintyves, Pierre. 1914. *La Force magique: du mana des primitifs au dynamisme scientifique*. Paris: Nourry, pp9, 14.
22. *cf.* Arbmann, *op. cit.* [Arbmann, Ernst. 1931. "Seele und Mana", *Archiv für Religionswissenschaft* 29. pp293–394], 352.
23. Söderblom, Nathan. 1916. *Das Werden des Gottesglaubens, Untersuchungen über die Anfänge der Religion*. Leipzig, pp68 ff.;Vierkandt. loc. cit., *op. cit.* [*Die Anfänge der Religion und Zauberei*], pp21 ff., 40 f.
24. cf. Beth, *op. cit.* [*Religion und Magie bei den Naturvölkern*], p84.
25. Nietzsche, Friedrich Wilhelm. 1910. *Human, All Too Human I*. Edinburgh, pp117, 118 (Foulis Edition).
26. Geistige Kultur [Preuss, Konrad Theodor. 1914. *Die geistige Kultur der Naturvölker*. Leipzig: Hinrichs], p8.
27. Kretschmer, Ernst. 1922. *Medizinische Psychologie*. Leipzig: Georg Thieme Verlag, p34.
28. Lévy-Bruhl, Lucien. 1935. *Primitives and the Supernatural*. New York: Haskell House Publishers, p381.

which many of us will recognize from our own youthful experience: a compulsive action consisting, for example, in not striking the right foot with the left without making this good immediately by touching the left foot with the right one. In this simple act, however, there lies a mastery of the world which permits whatever has happened to be modified, or even to be made retrogressive. Here then man raises his protest, utters his "Nevertheless", *tenses* his own will against what is simply given to him. It is thus not at all astonishing that a certain relationship exists between idealism and magic. We have already quoted the Bachelor in Goethe's *Faust*; we can also cite Amiel, who correctly discerned a magical tendency in Schleiermacher's *Monologues*: "The tameless liberty, the divine dignity of the individual spirit, expanding till it admits neither any limit nor anything foreign to itself, and conscious of a strength instinct with creative force."[29]

This domination of the world by will has, however, one essential condition: before the world can be thus controlled it must be transferred inwards, and man must take it into himself: he can actually dominate it only when it has in this way become an inner realm. For this reason all magic is autism, or "living within oneself".[30] "From the sensuous data of the environment the autistic-self-sufficient schizophrene makes for himself a totally different and more abundantly filled world, which he does not secure nor bring into accord with other people by means of any logical conventions, but which remains just raw material for his own fancies, caprices and needs. The actual environment, as such, is depreciated; it demands no recognition – it may be either utilized, or excluded, wholly at will."[31] And what is here asserted about mental disorder holds good almost precisely for magical man in general.[32] Man does not trouble himself at all about "reality": he dominates it creatively, since he immures himself against it; he erects a kingdom internally, a divine service in his own soul. Wherever any settled limits are given between man and the world, between object and subject, severe conflicts arise as in mental disease, or again in the contest between the artist and the world; and wherever these do not exist, as with primitive peoples, the magician receives his own official status, while everyone participates somehow or other in magical procedure. As Kretschmer correctly observes, myths and dogmas do not consider the world as it actually is, but deal with it wholly at will and make it into a world as it should be. In the fairy tale the idea that simultaneously expresses, and fulfils, a wish holds good even to-day, and the entire rite, the celebration, is quite incomprehensible apart from this autistic attitude: it is man himself who settles his own conditions. Thus primitive man firmly believes that unless certain words are recited and certain actions performed, it will not rain; and quite similarly, "only if you tidy up your chest of drawers now will you get your summer holiday", thinks the magically disposed child, who likewise lives in her own world. "When my dearest friend was very ill", said the same child, "I believed I could

---

29. *Journal*, 1 Feb. 1852 [Amiel, Henry-Frederic. 1890. *Amiel's Journal; the Journal in Time of Henri-Frederic Amiel*. Transl. Mary A. Ward. London].
30. In fuller detail cf. Leeuw. *op. cit.* [*La Structure de la mentalité primitive*].
31. Prinzhorn. *op. cit.* [*Bildnerei der Geisteskranken*], p55.
32. In my Structure I have discussed the problem, which is scarcely pertinent here, of how it is that the same attitude arises in so widely diverse types of people as the mentally deranged, primitives, children, artists, etc. In any case we must be most cautious in making phylogenetic generalizations.

## PART III: MID-TWENTIETH-CENTURY APPROACHES TO MAGIC

save her only by going up and down the street six times every day", and naturally with a most scrupulous avoidance of the gaps in the paving-stones![33] "Children stand nearer to the world of magic: the problem of the possibility of things does not torment them, and although their thoughts are not debarred from the experience of reality, still they remain outside its domain; they are autistic, and live within themselves, not because they are turned away from the world but simply because they have not yet attained an adequate relationship to the real." In these terms H. C. Rümke[34] presents the essence of this mental attitude and, at the same time, reveals the reason why the norm that governs the life both of children and of primitives leads among modern adults to illness.[35]

When it is considered from the standpoint of its object, the world, the autistic "living within oneself" that characterizes the subject of experience appears as "catathymia" – a term employed by Kretschmer to describe that state of mind in which everything is perceived in accordance with one's own subjective mood, so that objective reality is to that degree distorted. Consequently the "world" becomes regarded entirely as one's own domain and experienced merely "in accord with human subjectivity", with its desires and demands. One catatonic patient, for example, crawled under his bed and tried to lift it with all his strength: that was the way in which he wanted "to lead the earth nearer to God",[36] while another person similarly afflicted would fall out of bed "in order to keep the world rotating, so that the wheel should go on turning".[37] For in all such cases the "world" lies within while, conversely, nothing whatever is perceived outside except the self: another patient felt fatigued and thought that her own strength was exhausted by the farmers working in the fields![38] I cannot agree with Kretschmer, however, in seeking the principle of this "catathymia" merely in feeling;[39] while this view is certainly not wholly incorrect, still in the wish for domination, in the emotional craving, the will is also manifested, and this has formed itself on the lines of the "wholly other". Once again then: magical man *protests*.

This "catathymic" attitude, again, extends to the entire Universe: the "underworld" becomes Hades, hell: heaven the abode of the blessed, the desert the resort of demons;[40] in all conditions, and in every event, man perceives himself. He is Power: he is God. It may be, however, that in him Faust's yearning is manifested:

---

33. Additional examples in Zeininger, Karl. 1929. *Magische Geisteshaltung im Kindesalter und ihrer Bedeutung für die religiöse Entwicklung*. Leipzig: J. A. Barth.
34. *Geneeskundige bladen uit kliniek en laboratorium voor de praktijk* 1927, 26. Reeks, X, p. 329; cf. also *Journal für Psychologie und Neurologie*, 1928, pp5–6, 29.
35. Prinzhorn. *op. cit*. [*Bildnerei der Geisteskranken*], pp298 f. This by no means implies that primitive thought corresponds in every respect to that of children.
36. Storch. *op. cit*. [*Das archaisch-primitive Erleben und Denken der Schizophrenen*], p73.
37. Storch. *op. cit*. [*Das archaisch-primitive Erleben und Denken der Schizophrenen*], p8; cf. pp69, 80, and the characteristic case in Jaspers, Karl. 1920 [1913]. *Allgemeine Psychopathologie*. Berlin: Springer, p. 400.
38. Storch. *op. cit*. [*Das archaisch-primitive Erleben und Denken der Schizophrenen*], p41.
39. According to Kretschmer, causal thought connects things together in accordance with the principle of frequency, but magical thinking on the basis of the principle of community of feeling; *op. cit*. [*Medizinische Psychologie*], 34.
40. cf. Danzel. *op. cit*. [*Die psychologischen Grundlagen der Mythologie*], pp436 ff.; Werner. *op. cit*. [*Einführung in die Entwicklungspsychologie*], p62.

> Could I my pathway but from magic free,
> And quite unlearn the spells of sorcery,
> Stood I, Oh Nature, man alone 'fore thee,
> Then were it worth the trouble man to be![41]

This indeed the Greeks were able to do, since in the Homeric structure of their spirit they were the first to discover "Nature" in its modern sense.[42] Their religion (so far, of course, as it was Homeric and not mystical-Platonic) was that of the given, of quiescent Being, and as such it maintains a quite specific position among religions.[43]

A quite different victory over magic consists in the idea of *creation*. Magic is certainly by no means disavowed: but God, Who utters His creative word, is now the sole magician; and man's word, which is essentially an answer, can never possess magical power. But God speaks "So let it be!" and it is: He speaks again, and a second creation consummates the marvel of rebirth: He speaks "the word only, and my servant shall be healed".[44] Here, then, there is neither "acceptance" nor self-sufficient "celebration", but only receiving.

4. The second mode of creative domination, as has already been observed, may be understood as a quiescent pause following on the convulsive magical attainment of mastery. Man now retires from the world to a certain distance; and at first he seems to desire only to contemplate. Hence the static aspect of the mythical world: it wholly disregards time and, as it were, immobilizes it;[45] its forms are eternal, immutable. Every human passion, every desire, every thought, has there, in the realm of myth, its "eternal aspect".[46]

But this apparently contemplative domination is nonetheless control: man endows the world powers with form so that he can overcome them more effectively, even though in a manner wholly different from his magical attitude. Thus the form-imparting individual,[47] who invokes and evokes events as myths,[48] has adopted an attitude directly opposed to that of the magical individual. The latter absorbed the world within himself: but the other type of man ejects the world from himself. He projects experienced power into the external world; his own love assumes the form of the Cyprian goddess, his yearning becomes the Garden of Eden and his guilt the fall.[49] His death again, together with his hope of resurrection, he experiences "dually" (the dual experience of form!) in the myth of Light, and his dread in demonic figures.

---

41. Goethe. op cit. [*Faust: der Tragödie zweiter Teil*], Act 5.
42. Otto, Walter F. 1929. *Die Götter Griechenlands: das Bild des Göttlichen im Spiegel des griechischen Geistes*. Bonn: Cohen, p47.
43. Leeuw, Gerardus van der. 1938. *Religion in Essence and Manifestation*. London, Chap. 95.
44. Matt. viii. 8.
45. Leeuw. *op. cit.* [*Religion in Essence and Manifestation* ], Chap. 55, 60.
46. Otto, *op. cit.* [*Die Götter Griechenlands*].
47. Leeuw. *op. cit.* [*Religion in Essence and Manifestation* ], Chap. 17.
48. Leeuw. *op. cit.* [*Religion in Essence and Manifestation* ], Chap. 60.
49. cf. Danzel. *op. cit.* [*Die psychologischen Grundlagen der Mythologie*].

Flight from the self, still further, corresponds to autism, to the passionate search for the self. "The poet draws the world within himself, in order to transfer it 'outwardly' afresh in the manifold forms of his work: the youth who has withdrawn from the world, into the depths of his own soul, attempts to bring its riches to light once more by writing poems."[50] Similarly, "primitive man has created a world for himself which, although it is for us only a product of imagination, implies for him a very concrete reality; but he thus elicits from his own soul all the possibilities that he has experienced. He peoples field and forest with the figures of his desires, his dread, his hope and his woe."[51] This is the animistic tendency of humanity, which here we encounter afresh, and in this sense spirits and gods are indeed "exponents of feeling".[52] "Under the pressure of a hostile world man, unsatisfied with a refuge in his inner being, creates a life apart from his own, a 'thou', in which he finds anew his own hate and his own love. Thus the two tendencies, of magical autism and of mythical endowment with form, correspond to and complete each other. They are both present simultaneously: now the one, and again the other, predominates. Only the attitude of the mentally disordered (the schizophrene) halts at the magical method, and hence it turns into a blind alley. But we too are just as much 'mythologists' as 'primitive man'",[53] and are distinguished from him only by being conscious of the abyss separating our "primitive" from our logically grounded knowledge. It is true that Storch maintains that poetical images and metaphors hold their place in our own thought only as parallels or comparisons, or that these figures emerge only when our ideas relax.[54] But I believe that when Chesterton describes the Law of Gravitation as "that mad and quickening rush by which all earth's creatures fly back to her heart when released", he is expounding a genuinely vital "animistic" idea[55] which, despite its lack of scientific precision, exactly expresses the essence of the situation. For the time is past when poetry could be disposed of as merely playful comparison and religion as a similarly playful notion.

The form of myth, therefore, is that of experience; and whoever wishes to understand myth must first of all discover in it not any "explanation" of certain natural phenomena, but an attaining of mastery over the world which, although certainly less forcible than the magical method, would still wrest from the "thou" what magic had extorted from the powers. In this connection, too, the newer mythological method is fully justified in its endeavour to understand the cult, in the first instance, in order to comprehend myths.[56] For what lives in myth subsists already in sacred action, in the "celebration" of the event, and conversely!

Like magic, still further, the mythical endowment with form comes to an end that is, however, never ultimate. Probably, therefore, we shall never be able to remove magic

---

50. cf. Spranger. *op. cit.* [*Psychologie des Jugendalters*], p68.
51. Leeuw. *op. cit.* [*La Structure de la mentalité primitive*], pp19 f.
52. Wilamowitz [Wilamowitz-Möllendorf, Ulrich von. 1931. *Der Glaube der Hellenen. Band 1.* Berlin: Weidmann].
53. cf. Tillich, Paul. 1929. *Religiöse Verwirklichung.* Berlin: Furche-Verlag, pp96 ff.
54. Tillich. *op. cit.* [*Religiöse Verwirklichung*], p11.
55. Leeuw. *op. cit.* [*La Structure de la mentalité primitive*], pp20 f.
56. Leeuw. *op. cit.* [*Religion in Essence and Manifestation*], Chap. 60.

completely from our path, just as we are scarcely ever likely to discontinue spontaneous creation of form or ignore the traditionally given. Essentially, however, mythical endowment with form does reach its end where nothingness is the goal of all powerfulness. Mysticism, particularly the Hindu type, can instruct us on this point.[57] For where the void, or nullity, is to be attained in a "modeless mode", there every form without exception disappears. But the mythical form also comes to an end where an all-embracing form is given to faith,[58] which is not intended to subserve any acquisition of power but is itself that of a servitor. The belief in Incarnation, therefore, may essentially (that is, theologically and eschatologically) dispense with every form.

5. The two paths to the world, finally, with which we have thus become familiar, are actually only *one* road with two rails. Once again, however, this does not involve humanity following this road to its end until it notices that it raises a dilemma, and then striking another road such as that of science, of mysticism or of faith, as evolutionists and phylogenists are inclined to maintain. For we travel both roads now, just as previously and as always. But we are not restricted to them; and at this point the simile of the two roads ends: it must now be replaced by that of strata. The spiritual life of man then consists of different levels, one of which is at the same moment the most deeply situated and the most important: that is the dual level of autism and myth, wherein "participation" is the fundamental law. Above this stratum others are deposited that are more or less based upon it.

To these other levels (to continue) the magical-mythical domination of the world is related in the same way as is dream life to waking consciousness. From recent psychology, then, we learn that dream experience is in no degree less "real" than is daily life. The study of dreams is in fact a no less reliable path to the secret of life than is the investigation of waking consciousness; and Wilhelm Raabe observes that "we raise a corner of the curtain over the great mystery of the world when we reflect, and carefully consider the fact that stupid people and the poor in spirit may have the most marvellous and the most intelligent dreams; just as talented and strange as those of clever people, equally by day and by night".[59] Here again, therefore, we approach more closely to primitive feeling than to that of the nineteenth century when we regard dream facts as being valid of life, though not of waking life, just as Kamchadalc tribesmen do who tell a young girl whom they desire that they have already won her favours in their dreams, whereupon the girl yields.[60] Similarly for primitive man his wife's infidelity, of which he has merely dreamt, is regarded as established;[61] while in Gaboon "a dream is more conclusive than a witness".[62] We must concede then that here a consciousness of reality is experienced, and this not only in the

---

57. Leeuw. *op. cit.* [*Religion in Essence and Manifestation* ], Chap. 75.
58. Leeuw. *op. cit.* [*Religion in Essence and Manifestation* ], Chap. 80.
59. Raabe, Wilhelm. 1920. "Das Odfeld", in *Sämtliche Werke, Band 4*. Berlin: Klemm, p90.
60. Lévy-Bruhl, Lucien. 1923. *Primitive Mentality*. London: Allen & Unwin, p115.
61. Thurnwald, Richard. 1927. *Die Lüge in psychologischer, philosophischer, juristischer, pädagogischer, historischer, soziologischer, sprach- und literaturwissenschaftlicher und entwicklungsgeschichtlicher Betrachtung*, in Lippmann, Otto and Plaut, Paul (eds.). Leipzig: Barth, p 398.
62. Lévy-Bruhl. *op. cit.* [*Primitive Mentality*], p101.

magical attitude. Thus the dream differs from waking consciousness in three respects: (1) "the supporting pillar of conscious experience, while we are awake, the tension between subject and object" disappears;[63] (2) the dream orders events in a way which compared with the experience of the day is asyntactic: it has a loose or "diffuse structure",[64] its images being arranged in accord with the feelings, anxieties and desires of the dreamer, as in the previously defined "catathymia";[65] (3) the dream world is sharply separated from daily reality: it is mythical, having neither past nor future.[66]

The dream itself, of course, is not within the religious category; nevertheless it is life: life is a dream, the dream a life. And it displays life to us in rendering the domination of the world first of all possible in the magical-mythical manner; and also by the way in which it appears in its profoundest depths at the very frontier of the mechanized consciousness. In Prospero's words:

> We are such stuff
> As dreams are made on, and our little life
> Is rounded with a sleep.

---

63. Storch, *op. cit.* [*Das archaisch-primitive Erleben und Denken der Schizophrenen*], p25; not, however, in the manner of mysticism, since the dream lacks the element of passion.
64. Werner. *op. cit.* [*Einführung in die Entwicklungspsychologie*], p41.
65. Kretschmer, *op. cit.* [*Medizinische Psychologie*], pp57 f.
66. Kretschmer, *op. cit.* [*Medizinische Psychologie*], pp64 ff.; Binswanger, Ludwig. 1928. *Wandlungen in der Auffassung und Deutung des Traumes von den Griechen bis zur Gegenwart*. Berlin: Springer; Leeuw. *op. cit.* [*La Structure de la mentalité primitive*].

# 16

# EDWARD E. EVANS-PRITCHARD

*Witchcraft, Oracles and Magic among the Azande*

Edward E. Evans-Pritchard (b. 1902; d. 1973) was one of the most important British anthropologists of his time. Trained by Malinowski (see Chapter 17) and influenced, foremost, by Alfred R. Radcliffe-Brown, Evans-Pritchard was professor of social anthropology at the University of Oxford from 1946 until 1970. His fieldwork among the native population of Anglo-Egyptian Sudan resulted in several anthropological classics such as *Witchcraft, Oracles and Magic among the Azande* (1937), *The Nuer* (1940), *Kinship and Marriage among the Nuer* (1951) and the late yet highly influential *Theories of Primitive Religion* (1965). His *Witchcraft, Oracles and Magic*, of which we present an excerpt, was widely discussed beyond the boundaries of anthropology during the so-called "rationality debate" of the 1960s and 1970s.

The excerpt begins with introductory remarks on some basic concepts used in *Witchcraft, Oracles and Magic*, including the important distinction of "mystical", "common-sense" and "scientific notions" that underlies Evans-Pritchard's interpretation of the Zande belief in "witchcraft". By "witchcraft", Evans-Pritchard refers to the Zande habit of attributing experiences of misfortune to *mangu*, a substance or organ that allegedly resides in the bodies of some members of their society and has the power to emanate by night and "devour the soul of its victim". According to Evans-Pritchard, this pattern of explaining misfortune is ubiquitous in Zande culture and accompanied by a complex ritual sequence of identifying the "witch" (mostly by the ritual "enquiry" of venomed chicken that operate as oracles) and applying ritual counter-measures against the assumed aggressor. Note that Evans-Pritchard uses the term "witchcraft" to denote the Zande belief in *mangu*, the term "magic" to signify the abovementioned ritual counter-measures (in Zande language: *ngua*), and the term "sorcery" when referring to other, mostly malevolent rites that were avoided and condemned by the Zande themselves (*gbegbere ngua*).

To Evans-Pritchard, the Zande belief in "witchcraft" is a "mystical" form of thinking as it attributes to "phenomena supra-sensible qualities which, or part of which, are not derived from observation or cannot be logically inferred from it, and which they do not possess". Although he therefore asserts that "witchcraft […] is not an objective reality" and that "witches, as Azande conceive them, cannot exist", Evans-Pritchard regards the Zande concept of "witchcraft" as an "intellectually coherent system" mostly based on observation and rational reasoning – in this way, he went beyond contemporary narratives of "primitive mentality" (Lévy-Bruhl). Yet, the adherence of the Azande to the concept of "witchcraft" was a challenge to Evans-Pritchard's enquiring mind; at the end of the excerpt, he gives as many as twenty-two reasons for the Azande's alleged indifference towards criticism and scrutinization. This "immunity to falsification" was one of the big issues during the "rationality debate" of the 1960s and 1970s and led, for example, Robin Horton to differentiate between open and closed societies (see Chapter 18). Evans-Pritchard's analysis also provoked later authors to argue that Western science could not operate as an objective standpoint from which to evaluate the rationality of non-Western cultures (see Winch 1964).

# WITCHCRAFT, ORACLES AND MAGIC AMONG THE AZANDE

In classifying Zande notions and behaviour I have made use of further categories to which some students may object. I will ask them not to deliver judgement here but to withhold their opinions till they have read the book. In any case, such are the meanings I attach to the terms, and if any one wishes to attach different meanings to them or to class the facts under different headings he is at liberty to do so. Terms are only labels which help us to sort out facts of the same kind from facts which are different, or are in some respects different. If the labels do not prove helpful we can discard them. The facts will be the same without their labels.

*MYSTICAL NOTIONS.* These are patterns of thought that attribute to phenomena supra-sensible qualities which, or part of which, are not derived from observation or cannot be logically inferred from it, and which they do not possess.

*COMMON SENSE NOTIONS.* These are patterns of thought that attribute to phenomena only what men observe in them or what can logically be inferred from observation. So long as a notion does not assert something which has not been observed, it is not classed as mystical even though it is mistaken on account of incomplete observation. It still differs from mystical notions in which supra-sensible forces are always posited.

*SCIENTIFIC NOTIONS.* Science has developed out of common sense but is far more methodical and has better techniques of observation and reasoning. Common sense uses experience and rules of thumb. Science uses experiment and rules of Logic. Common sense observes only some links in a chain of causation. Science observes all, or many more, of the links. In this place we need not define scientific notions more clearly because Azande have none, or very few, according to where we draw the line between common sense and science. The term is introduced because we need a judge to whom we can appeal for a decision when the question arises whether a notion shall be classed as mystical or common sense. Our body of scientific knowledge and Logic are the sole arbiters of what are mystical, common-sense, and scientific notions. Their judgements are never absolute.

*RITUAL BEHAVIOUR.* Any behaviour that is accounted for by mystical notions. There is no objective nexus between the behaviour and the event it is intended to cause. Such behaviour is usually intelligible to us only when we know the mystical notions associated with it.

*EMPIRICAL BEHAVIOUR.* Any behaviour that is accounted for by common-sense notions. Such behaviour is usually intelligible to us without explanation if we see the whole of it and its effects.

These definitions will be sufficient for our purposes at the commencement of our study. A much more detailed classification could be made. Also a social fact is generally complex and can seldom be placed wholly in any one analytical category. We can reconsider our categories when the facts have been described. We will create new tools when the need for them is felt. Moreover, our categories are intended to class only certain notions – those that assert or assume facts that can be said to be in accord with experience or otherwise – and not all notions. It is an *ad hoc* classification for descriptive purposes.

[...]

I have described some of the prominent characteristics of witchcraft in Zande thought. Others will be developed in this and the following chapters. It is an inevitable conclusion from Zande descriptions of witchcraft that it is not an objective reality. The physiological condition which is said to be the seat of witchcraft, and which I believe to be nothing more than food passing through the small intestine, is an objective condition, but the qualities they attribute to it and the rest of their beliefs about it are mystical. Witches, as Azande conceive them, cannot exist.

The concept of witchcraft nevertheless provides them with a natural philosophy by which the relations between men and unfortunate events are explained and a ready and stereotyped means of reacting to such events. Witchcraft beliefs also embrace a system of values which regulate human conduct.

Witchcraft is ubiquitous. It plays its part in every activity of Zande life; in agricultural, fishing, and hunting pursuits; in domestic life of homesteads as well as in communal life of district and court; it is an important theme of mental life in which it forms the background of a vast panorama of oracles and magic; its influence is plainly stamped on law and morals, etiquette and religion; it is prominent in technology and language; there is no niche or corner of Zande culture into which it does not twist itself. If blight seizes the ground-nut crop it is witchcraft; if the bush is vainly scoured for game it is witchcraft; if women laboriously bale water out of a pool and are rewarded by but a few small fish it is witchcraft; if termites do not rise when their swarming is due and a cold useless night is spent in waiting for their flight it is witchcraft; if a wife is sulky and unresponsive to her husband it is witchcraft; if a prince is cold and distant with his subject it is witchcraft; if a magical rite fails to achieve its purpose it is witchcraft; if, in fact, any failure or misfortune falls upon any one at any time and in relation to any of the manifold activities of his life it may be due to witchcraft. Those acquainted either at first hand or through reading with the life of an African people will realize that there is no end to possible misfortunes, in routine tasks and leisure hours alike, arising not only from miscalculation, incompetence, and laziness, but also from causes over which the African, with his meagre scientific knowledge, has no control. The Zande attributes all these misfortunes to witchcraft unless there is strong evidence, and subsequent oracular confirmation, that sorcery or one of those evil agents which I mentioned in the preceding section has been at work, or unless they are clearly to be attributed to incompetence, breach of a taboo, or failure to observe a moral rule.

When a Zande speaks of witchcraft he does not speak of it as we speak of the weird witchcraft of our own history. Witchcraft is to him a commonplace happening and he seldom passes a day without mentioning it. Where we talk about the crops, hunting, and our neighbours' ailments the Zande introduces into these topics of conversation the subject of witchcraft. To say that witchcraft has blighted the ground-nut crop, that witchcraft has scared away game, and that witchcraft has made so-and-so ill is equivalent to saying in terms of our own culture that the ground-nut crop has failed owing to blight, that game is scarce this season, and that so-and-so has caught influenza. Witchcraft participates in all misfortunes and is the idiom in which Azande speak about them and in which they explain them. Witchcraft is a classification of misfortunes which while differing from each other in other respects have this single common character, their harmfulness to man.

Unless the reader appreciates that witchcraft is quite a normal factor in the life of Azande, one to which almost any and every happening may be referred, he will entirely misunderstand their behaviour towards it. To us witchcraft is something which haunted and disgusted our credulous forefathers. But the Zande expects to come across witchcraft at any time of the day or night. He would be just as surprised if he were not brought into daily contact with it as we would be if confronted by its appearance. To him there is nothing miraculous about it.

It is expected that a man's hunting will be injured by witches, and he has at his disposal means of dealing with them. When misfortunes occur he does not become awestruck at the play of supernatural forces. He is not terrified at the presence of an occult enemy. He is, on the other hand, extremely annoyed. Someone, out of spite, has ruined his ground-nuts or spoilt his hunting or given his wife a chill, and surely this is cause for anger! He has done no one harm, so what right has any one to interfere in his affairs? It is an impertinence, an insult, a dirty, offensive trick! It is the aggressiveness and not the eerieness of these actions which Azande emphasize when speaking of them, and it is anger and not awe which we observe in their response to them.

Witchcraft is not less anticipated than adultery. It is so intertwined with everyday happenings that it is part of a Zande's ordinary world. There is nothing remarkable about a witch – you may be one yourself, and certainly many of your closest neighbours are witches. Nor is there anything awe-inspiring about witchcraft. We do not become psychologically transformed when we hear that someone is ill – we expect people to be ill – and it is the same with Azande. They expect people to be ill, i.e. to be bewitched, and it is not a matter for surprise or wonderment.

## II

But is not Zande belief in witchcraft a belief in mystical causation of phenomena and events to the complete exclusion of all natural causes? The relations of mystical to common-sense thought are very complicated and raise problems that confront us on every page of this book. Here I wish to state the problem in a preliminary manner and in terms of actual situations.

I found it strange at first to live among Azande and listen to naive explanations of misfortunes which, to our minds, have apparent causes, but after a while I learnt the idiom of their thought and applied notions of witchcraft as spontaneously as themselves in situations where the concept was relevant. A boy knocked his foot against a small stump of wood in the centre of a bush path, a frequent happening in Africa, and suffered pain and inconvenience in consequence. Owing to its position on his toe it was impossible to keep the cut free from dirt and it began to fester. He declared that witchcraft had made him knock his foot against the stump. I always argued with Azande and criticized their statements, and I did so on this occasion I told the boy that he had knocked his foot against the stump of wood because he had been careless, and that witchcraft had not placed it in the path, for it had grown there naturally. He agreed that witchcraft had nothing to do with the stump of wood being in his path but added that he had kept his eyes open for stumps, as indeed every Zande does most carefully, and that if he had not been bewitched he would have seen the stump. As a conclusive argument for his view he remarked that all cuts do not take days to heal but, on the contrary, close quickly, for that is the nature of cuts. Why, then, had his sore festered and remained open if there were no witchcraft behind it? This, as I discovered before long, was to be regarded as the Zande explanation of sickness. Thus, to give a further example, I had been feeling unfit for several days, and I consulted Zande friends whether my consumption of bananas could have had anything to do with my indisposition and I was at once informed that bananas do not cause sickness, however many are eaten, unless one is bewitched. I have described at length Zande notions of disease in Part IV, so I shall record here a few examples of witchcraft being offered as an explanation for happenings other than illness.

Shortly after my arrival in Zandeland we were passing through a government settlement and noticed that a hut had been burnt to the ground on the previous night. Its owner was overcome with grief as it had contained the beer he was preparing for a mortuary feast. He told us that he had gone the previous night to examine his beer. He had lit a handful of straw and raised it above his head so that light would be cast on the pots, and in so doing he had ignited the thatch. He, and my companions also, were convinced that the disaster was caused by witchcraft.

One of my chief informants, Kisanga, was a skilled woodcarver, one of the finest carvers in the whole kingdom of Gbudwe. Occasionally the bowls and stools which he carved split during the work, as one may well imagine in such a climate. Though the hardest woods be selected they sometimes split in process of carving or on completion of the utensil even if the craftsman is careful and well acquainted with the technical rules of his craft. When this happened to the bowls and stools of this particular craftsman he attributed the misfortune to witchcraft and used to harangue me about the spite and jealousy of his neighbours. When I used to reply that I thought he was mistaken and that people were well disposed towards him he used to hold the split bowl or stool towards me as concrete evidence of his assertions. If people were not bewitching his work, how would I account for that? Likewise a potter will attribute the cracking of his pots during firing to witchcraft. An experienced potter need have no fear that his pots will crack as a result of error. He selects the proper clay, kneads it thoroughly till he has extracted all grit and pebbles, and builds it up slowly and carefully. On the night before digging out his clay he abstains from sexual intercourse. So he should have nothing to fear. Yet pots sometimes break, even when they are the handiwork of expert potters, and this can only be accounted for by witchcraft. It is broken – there is witchcraft, says the potter simply. Many similar situations in which witchcraft is cited as an agent are instanced throughout this and following chapters.

## III

In speaking to Azande about witchcraft and in observing their reactions to situations of misfortune it was obvious that they did not attempt to account for the existence of phenomena, or even the action of phenomena, by mystical causation alone. What they explained by witchcraft were the particular conditions in a chain of causation which related an individual to natural happenings in such a way that he sustained injury. The boy who knocked his foot against a stump of wood did not account for the stump by reference to witchcraft, nor did he suggest that whenever anybody knocks his foot against a stump it is necessarily due to witchcraft, nor yet again did he account for the cut by saying that it was caused by witchcraft, for he knew quite well that it was caused by the stump of wood. What he attributed to witchcraft was that on this particular occasion, when exercising his usual care, he struck his foot against a stump of wood, whereas on a hundred other occasions he did not do so, and that on this particular occasion the cut, which he expected to result from the knock, festered whereas he had had dozens of cuts which had not festered. Surely these peculiar conditions demand an explanation. Again, if one eats a number of bananas this does not in itself cause sickness. Why should it do so? Plenty of people eat bananas but are not sick in consequence, and I myself had often done so in the past. Therefore my indisposition could not possibly be attributed to bananas alone. If bananas alone had caused my sickness, then it was necessary to account for the fact that they had caused me sickness on this single occasion and not on dozens of previous occasions, and that they had made only me ill and not other people who were eating them. Again, every year hundreds of Azande go and inspect their beer by night and they always take with them a handful of straw in order to illuminate the hut in which it is fermenting. Why then should this particular man on this single occasion have ignited the thatch of his hut? I present the Zande's explicit line of reasoning – not my own. Again, my friend the wood-carver had made scores of bowls and stools without mishap and he knew all there was to know about the selection of wood, use of tools, and conditions of carving. His bowls and stools did not split like the products of craftsmen who were unskilled in their work, so why on rare occasions should his bowls and stools split when they did not split usually and when he had exercised all his usual knowledge and care? He knew the answer well enough and so, in his opinion, did his envious, backbiting neighbours. In the same way, a potter wants to know why his pots should break on an occasion when he uses the same material and technique as on other occasions; or rather he already knows, for the reason is known in advance, as it were. If the pots break it is due to witchcraft.

We must understand, therefore, that we shall give a false account of Zande philosophy if we say that they believe witchcraft to be the sole cause of phenomena. This proposition is not contained in Zande patterns of thought, which only assert that witchcraft brings a man into relation with events in such a way that he sustains injury.

My old friend Ongosi was many years ago injured by an elephant while out hunting, and his prince, Basongoda, consulted the oracles to discover who had bewitched him. We must distinguish here between the elephant and its prowess, on the one hand, and the fact that a particular elephant injured a particular man, on the other hand. The Supreme Being, not witchcraft, created elephants and gave them tusks and a trunk and huge legs so that they are able to pierce men and fling them sky high and reduce them to pulp by kneeling on them. But whenever men and elephants come across one another in the bush these dreadful things do not happen. They are rare events. Why, then, should this particular man on this one occasion in a life crowded with similar situations in which he and his friends emerged scatheless have been gored by this particular beast? Why he and not someone else? Why on this occasion and not on other occasions? Why by this elephant and not by other elephants? It is the particular and variable conditions of an event and not the general and universal conditions that witchcraft explains. Fire is hot, but it is not hot owing to witchcraft, for that is its nature. It is a universal quality of fire to burn, but it is not a universal quality of fire to burn *you*. This may never happen; or once in a lifetime, and then only if you have been bewitched.

In Zandeland sometimes an old granary collapses. There is nothing remarkable in this. Every Zande knows that termites eat the supports in course of time and that even the hardest woods decay after years of service. Now a granary is the summerhouse of a Zande homestead and people sit beneath it in the heat of the day and chat or play the African hole-game or work at some craft. Consequently it may happen that there are people sitting beneath the granary when it collapses and they are injured, for it is a heavy structure made of beams and clay and may be stored with eleusine as well. Now why should these particular people have been sitting under this particular granary at the particular moment when it collapsed? That it should collapse is easily intelligible, but why should it have collapsed at the particular moment when these particular people were sitting beneath it? Through years it might have collapsed, so why should it fall just when certain people sought its kindly shelter? We say that the granary collapsed because its supports were eaten away by termites. That is the cause that explains the collapse of the granary. We also say that people were sitting under it at the time because it was in the heat of the day and they thought that it would be a comfortable place to talk and work. This is the cause of people being under the granary at the time it collapsed. To our minds the only relationship between these two independently caused facts is their coincidence in time and space. We have no explanation of why the two chains of causation intersected at a certain time and in a certain place, for there is no interdependence between them.

Zande philosophy can supply the missing link. The Zande knows that the supports were undermined by termites and that people were sitting beneath the granary in order to escape the heat and glare of the sun. But he knows besides why these two events occurred at a precisely similar moment in time and space. It was due to the action of witchcraft. If there had been no witchcraft people would have been sitting under the granary and it would not have fallen on them, or it would have collapsed but the people would not have been sheltering under it at the time. Witchcraft explains the coincidence of these two happenings.

## IV

I hope I am not expected to point out that the Zande cannot analyse his doctrines as I have done for him. In fact I never obtained an explanatory text on witchcraft, though I was able to obtain in the form of texts clear statements on dozens of other subjects. It is no use saying to a Zande "now tell me what you Azande think about witchcraft" because the subject is too general and indeterminate, both too vague and too immense, to be described concisely. But it is possible to extract the principles of their thought from dozens of situations in which witchcraft is called upon to explain happenings and from dozens of other situations in which failure is attributed to some other cause. Their philosophy is explicit, but is not formally stated as a doctrine. A Zande would not say "I believe in natural causation but I do not think that that fully explain coincidences, and it seems to me that the theory of witchcraft offers a satisfactory explanation of them", but he expresses his thought in terms of actual and particular situations. He says "a buffalo charges", "a tree falls", "termites are not making their seasonal flight when they are expected to do so", and so on. Herein he is stating empirically ascertained facts. But he also says "a buffalo charged and wounded so-and-so", "a tree fell on so-and-so and killed him", "my termites refuse to make their flight in numbers worth collecting but other people are collecting theirs all right", and so on. He tells you that these things are due to witchcraft, saying in each instance, "So-and-so has been bewitched." The facts do not explain themselves or only partly explain themselves. They can only be explained fully if one takes witchcraft into consideration.

One can only obtain the full range of a Zande's ideas about causation by allowing him to fill in the gaps himself, otherwise one will be led astray by linguistic conventions. He tells you "So-and-so was bewitched and killed himself" or even simply that "So-and-so was killed by witchcraft." But he is telling you the ultimate cause of his death and not the secondary causes. You can ask him "How did he kill himself?" and he will tell you that he committed suicide by hanging himself from the branch of a tree. You can also ask "Why did he kill himself?" and he will tell you that it was because he was angry with his brothers. The cause of his death was hanging from a tree, and the cause of his hanging from a tree was his anger with his brothers. If you then ask a Zande why he should say that the man was bewitched if he committed suicide on account of his anger with his brothers, he will tell you that only crazy people commit suicide, and that if everyone who was angry with his brothers committed suicide there would soon be no people left in the world, and that if this man had not been bewitched he would not have done what he did do. If you persevere and ask why witchcraft caused the man to kill himself the Zande will reply that he supposes someone hated him, and if you ask him why someone hated him your informant will tell you that such is the nature of men.

For if Azande cannot enunciate a theory of causation in terms acceptable to us they describe happenings in an idiom that is explanatory. They are aware that it is particular circumstances of events in their relation to man, their harmfulness to a particular person, that constitutes evidence of witchcraft. Witchcraft explains *why* events are harmful to man and not *how* they happen. A Zande perceives how they happen just as we do. He does not see a witch charge a man, but an elephant. He does not see a witch push over a granary, but termites gnawing away its supports. He does not see a psychical flame igniting thatch, but an ordinary lighted bundle of straw. His perception of how events occur is as clear as our own.

Zande notions of causality will interest us throughout this book and repeated attention is given to them in my account of oracles and magic. I shall only mention briefly in this place that the variability, we may almost say the inconsistency, of witchcraft as a cooperating cause in the production of phenomena is amply illustrated by Zande use of oracles. Therein we see how a particular site may be inauspicious for building a homestead or digging a game-pit or planting eleusine and maize, while neighbouring sites have no witchcraft hanging over them so that all a Zande has to do is to cope with natural difficulties: density of brushwood, poverty or hardness of soil, and excess or absence of moisture. The difference between two sites may be simply that while witchcraft is a future factor in the exploitation of the one it will be absent in the exploitation of the other. Witchcraft is a variable factor in time as well as in space and gives peculiar value to particular times as it does to particular places or persons. A project that has to be abandoned owing to the discovery that it is in advance a failure because of the inevitable presence of witchcraft on its horizon may be resumed a week or two later with confidence if the poison oracle declares that it sees no witchcraft ahead. Or, again, the oracles may declare that it is all right for a certain person to undertake a venture while another must at all costs refrain from doing so, since witchcraft is not a factor in the one case but is a factor in the other. Witchcraft is a causative factor in the production of harmful phenomena in particular places, at particular times, and in relation to particular persons. It is not a necessary link in a sequence of events but something external to them that participates in them and gives them a peculiar value.

V

Zande belief in witchcraft in no way contradicts empirical knowledge of cause and effect. The world known to the senses is just as real to them as it is to us. We must not be deceived by their way of expressing causation and imagine that because they say a man was killed by witchcraft they entirely neglect the secondary causes that, as we judge them, were the true causes of his death. They are foreshortening the chain of events, and in a particular social situation are selecting the cause that is socially relevant and neglecting the rest. If a man is killed by a spear in war, or by a wild beast in hunting, or by the bite of a snake, or from sickness, the reaction is the same and it is not directed in different modes of expression by the different modes of death. In every case witchcraft is the socially relevant cause, since it is the only one which allows intervention and determines social behaviour. If a buffalo kills a man you can do nothing about it as far as the buffalo is concerned. But, though surely enough the buffalo has killed him, it would not have killed him if it had not been for the operation of witchcraft at the same time, and witchcraft is a social fact, a person. In a number of co-operating causes this single one is selected and spoken of as the cause of death because it is the ideological pivot around which swings the lengthy social procedure from death to vengeance.

Belief in death from natural causes and belief in death from witchcraft are not mutually exclusive. On the contrary, they supplement one another, the one accounting for what the other does not account for. Besides, death is not only a natural fact but also a social fact. It is not simply that the heart ceases to beat and the lungs to pump air in an organism, but it is also the destruction of a member of a family and kin, of a community and tribe. Death leads to consultation of oracles, magic rites, and revenge. Among the causes of death witchcraft is the only one that has any significance for social behaviour. The attribution of misfortune to witchcraft does not exclude what we call its real causes but is superimposed on them and gives to social events their moral value.

As a matter of fact Zande thought expresses the notion of natural and mystical causation quite clearly by using a hunting metaphor to define their relations. Azande always say of witchcraft that it is the *umbaga* or second spear. When Azande kill game there is a division of meat between the man who first speared the animal and the man who plunged a second spear into it. These two are considered to have killed the beast and the owner of the second spear is called the *umbaga*. Hence if a man is killed by an elephant Azande say that the elephant is the first spear and that witchcraft is the second spear and that together they killed the man. If a man spears another in war the slayer is the first spear and witchcraft is the second spear and together they killed him.

[...]

Hence we see that witchcraft has its own logic, its own rules of thought, and that these do not exclude natural causation. Belief in witchcraft is quite consistent with human responsibility and a rational appreciation of nature. First of all a man must carry out an activity according to traditional rules of technique, which consist of knowledge checked by trial and error in each generation. It is only if he fails in spite of adherence to these rules that people will impute his lack of success to witchcraft. Three short examples in addition to those already mentioned will suffice to illustrate the relations between witchcraft and technical efficiency. I had accompanied Kisanga to the stream which ran near by our settlement to watch him preparing malted grain for beer-making. After eleusine has been threshed the seed is placed in baskets and immersed in water for a time. It is then laid out on banana-leaves to germinate, and while this process is taking place more leaves are put over it to protect it from the sun. When Kisanga had covered the malted grain with leaves he took his spear and prepared to accompany me home, saying as he did so, "There is no more question of the sun – it is only witchcraft that can harm it now." He had worked efficiently and he knew that the grain would be all right if its success depended on his knowledge and skill, but if someone bewitched it – well, he could not answer for that. Also in connexion with beer-making a man said to me: "Witchcraft does not spoil beer in the stream but only in the pots", which means "beer does not get spoilt while it is being soaked but only when it is being brewed". This statement was not agreed to by all present, but is an illuminating expression of opinion none the less.

I once consulted an old Zande where to sow my ground-nuts, and I followed his advice. Later I went with him to see how these young plants were progressing, and as they did not seem to be very healthy I ventured to suggest that perhaps the soil was exhausted or was not the right kind of soil in which to plant ground-nuts, and he replied, "The soil is excellent, only witchcraft might spoil them". He knew from experience that so long as there was no interference from witchcraft that kind of soil produced good ground-nuts and that as far as human knowledge went he had advised me well. The ground-nuts flourished.

From generation to generation Azande regulate their economic activities according to a transmitted body of knowledge, in their building and crafts no less than their agricultural and hunting pursuits. They have a sound working knowledge of nature in so far as it concerns their welfare. Beyond this point it has for them no scientific interest or sentimental appeal. It is true that their knowledge is empirical and incomplete and that it is not transmitted by any systematic teaching but is handed over from one generation to another slowly and casually during childhood and early manhood. Yet it suffices for their everyday tasks and seasonal pursuits. When in spite of it they fail, the reason for their failure is known in advance – it is due to witchcraft.

Nevertheless, public opinion only attributes failure to witchcraft when all possibility of technical error has been eliminated. It is easy to see that this must be the case, for technical rules are in themselves a recognition of technical errors, and the rules could never be maintained unless errors were attributed to human responsibility. No Zande youth would ever learn to fashion a pot, weave a hat, make a spear, or carve a bowl if he attributed all his errors to witchcraft, for a man becomes a good craftsman by perceiving his own errors and those of others.

## VII

The question may be asked whether Azande distinguish between causation by witchcraft and causation in which neither witchcraft nor any other mystical agency participates. It is often asked whether primitive peoples distinguish between the natural and the supernatural, and the query may be here answered in a preliminary manner in respect to the Azande.

The question as it stands may mean, do primitive peoples distinguish between the natural and the supernatural in the abstract? We have a notion of an ordered world conforming to what we call natural laws, but some people in our society believe that mysterious things can happen which cannot be accounted for by reference to natural laws and which therefore are held to transcend them, and we call these happenings supernatural. To us supernatural means very much the same as abnormal or extraordinary. Azande certainly have no such notions of reality. They have no conception of "natural" as we understand it, and therefore neither of the "supernatural" as we understand it. What we call supernatural we raise to a different plane, even thought of spacially, from the plane of the natural. But witchcraft is to Azande an ordinary and not an extraordinary, even though it may in some circumstances be an infrequent, event. It is a normal, and not an abnormal, happening. But if they do not give to the natural and supernatural the meanings which educated Europeans give to them they nevertheless distinguish between them. For our question may be formulated, and should be formulated, in a different manner. We ought rather to ask whether primitive peoples perceive any difference between the happenings which we, the observers of their culture, class as natural and the happenings which we class as mystical. Azande undoubtedly perceive a difference between what we consider the workings of nature on the one hand and the workings of magic and ghosts and witchcraft on the other hand, though in the absence of a formulated doctrine of natural law they do not, and cannot, express the difference as we express it.

The Zande notion of witchcraft is incompatible with our ways of thought. But it must also be said that even to the Azande there is something peculiar about the action of witchcraft. Normally it can be perceived only in dreams. It is not an evident notion but transcends sensory experience. They do not profess to understand witchcraft entirely. They know that it exists and works evil, but they have to guess at the manner in which it works. Indeed, I have frequently been struck when discussing witchcraft with Azande by the doubt they express about the subject, not only in what they say, but even more in their manner of saying it, both of which contrast with their ready knowledge, fluently imparted, about social events and economic techniques. They fell out of their depth in trying to describe the way in which witchcraft accomplishes its ends. That it kills people is obvious, but how it kills them cannot be known precisely. They tell you that perhaps if you were to ask an older man or a witch-doctor he might give you more information. But the older men and the witch-doctors can tell you little more than youth and laymen. They only know what the others know: that the soul of witchcraft goes by night and devours the soul of its victim. Only witches themselves understand these matters fully. In truth Azande experience feelings about witchcraft rather than ideas, for their intellectual concepts of it are weak and they know better what to do when attacked by it than how to explain it. Their response is action and not analysis.

I anticipate here what I shall develop more fully in the Part on magic by saying that my impression in discussing magical rites with Azande was the same as that received in discussions about witchcraft. I noted the same uncertainty and the same feeling that they were dealing with things only part of whose action was visible, the invisible part being accounted for by an inherent power which is mysterious not only for us but also for them.

This is the *mbisimo* or the soul of a thing. They do not clearly understand how witches kill people, but "people say that the witch sends the soul of his witchcraft to eat the soul of the flesh of a man". They know likewise that magic will kill people, but if you inquire from them how it kills them they will say simply, "I do not know exactly, but I suppose that the soul of the medicine tracks down a man and slays him." They believe that when a man dies he in some way becomes the totem animal of his clan. But how? They do not rightly know, but "the soul of a man changes itself into an animal".

We find the same difficulty in seeking to translate their ideas about oracles, for though in action and speech they appear to personify them and to treat them as though they possessed minds, yet there is no pattern of thought which the observer can evoke in which such a belief is enunciated. Here again the answer to a question by a European – for it is we who question them about their beliefs and by our innovations challenge them; they enact them and feel little urge to explain them – is that the soul of the oracle hears what is said to it and makes replies.

Above all, we have to be careful to avoid in the absence of native doctrine constructing a dogma which we would formulate were we to act as Azande do. There is no elaborate and consistent representation of witchcraft that will account in detail for its workings, nor of nature which expounds its conformity to sequences and functional interrelations. The Zande actualizes these beliefs rather than intellectualizes them, and their tenets are expressed in socially controlled behaviour rather than in doctrines. Hence the difficulty of discussing the subject of witchcraft with Azande, for their ideas are imprisoned in action and cannot be cited to explain and justify action.

[…]

It may be asked why Azande do not perceive the futility of their magic. It would be easy to write at great length in answer to this question, but I will content myself with suggesting as shortly as possible a number of reasons. It will be evident to the reader that some of these reasons only apply to the use of important medicines, others to all magic and to mystical beliefs in general:

(1) Magic is very largely employed against mystical powers, witchcraft, and sorcery. Since its action transcends experience it cannot easily be contradicted by experience.
(2) Witchcraft, oracles, and magic form an intellectually coherent system. Each explains and proves the others. Death is proof of witchcraft. It is avenged by magic. The achievement of vengeance-magic is proved by the poison oracle. The accuracy of the poison oracle is determined by the king's oracle, which is above suspicion.
(3) Azande often observe that a medicine is unsuccessful, but they do not generalize their observations. Therefore the failure of a single medicine does not teach them that all medicines of this type are foolish. Far less does it teach them that all magic is useless.
(4) Scepticism, far from being smothered, is recognized, even inculcated. But it is only about certain medicines and certain magicians. By contrast it tends to support other medicines and magicians.

(5) The results which magic is supposed to produce actually happen after rites are performed. Vengeance-magic is made and a man dies. Hunting-magic is made and animals are speared.

(6) Contradictions between their beliefs are not noticed by Azande because the beliefs are not all present at the same time but function in different situations. They are therefore not brought into opposition.

(7) Each man and kinship group acts without cognizance of the actions of others. People do not pool their ritual experiences. For one family a death is the starting-point of vengeance, while for another family the same death is the conclusion of vengeance. In the one case the dead man is believed to have been slain by a witch. In the other case he is himself a witch who has fallen a victim to vengeance-magic. A man is sick after beer-drinking and believes that his host has made sorcery against him. His host believes that the man is sick because he bewitched the eleusine from which the beer was brewed. Normally these beliefs do not clash. Both are possible interpretations, and each man accepts the one advantageous to himself.

(8) A Zande is born into a culture with ready-made patterns of belief which have the weight of tradition behind them. It seldom occurs to him to question them. He accepts them, like those around him, with more or less faith according to their importance and his upbringing. Many of his beliefs being axiomatic, a Zande finds it difficult to understand that other peoples do not share them.

(9) The experience of an individual counts for little against accepted opinion. If it contradicts a belief this does not show that the belief is unfounded, but that the experience is peculiar or inadequate.

(10) The failure of any rite is accounted for in advance by a variety of mystical notions – e.g. witchcraft, sorcery, and taboo. Hence the perception of error in one mystical notion in a particular situation merely proves the correctness of another and equally mystical notion.

(11) Magic is only made to produce events which are likely to happen in any case – e.g. rain is produced in the rainy season and held up in the dry season; pumpkins and bananas are likely to flourish – they usually do so. Magic is not asked to achieve what is unlikely to occur.

(12) Not too much is claimed for magic. Generally, in the use of productive magic it is only claimed that success will be greater by the use of magic than it would have been if no magic had been used. It is not claimed that without the aid of magic a man must fail – e.g. a man will catch many termites, even though he does not use termite-medicines.

(13) Magic is seldom asked to produce a result by itself, but is associated with empirical action that does in fact produce it – e.g. a prince gives food to attract followers and does not rely on magic alone. A man makes beer by approved methods and only uses medicines to hasten the brew, not in the place of it.

(14) Men are sometimes compelled to perform magic as part of their social obligations – e.g. to use vengeance-magic on the death of a kinsman.

(15) Success is often expressed in terms of magic – e.g. a successful hunter gets a reputation for magic. People therefore attribute his success to his magic whether he possesses medicines or not.
(16) Political authority supports vengeance-magic. (Lesser medicines are seldom backed by sanctions other than the feeling of failure to conform to the behaviour of those around one, and the feeling that one has not taken every precaution).
(17) Azande do not possess sufficient knowledge to understand the real causes of things – e.g. germination of crops, disease, &c. Having no clocks, they cannot perceive that placing a stone in a tree in no way retards sunset. Moreover, they are not experimentally inclined.
(18) Not being experimentally inclined, they do not test the efficacy of their medicines. A man who uses termite-medicines uses them always and therefore cannot perceive that the results would be the same if he did not use them.
(19) There are always stories circulating which tell of the achievement of magic. A man's belief is backed by other people's experience contained in these stories. In certain myths and folk-tales the efficacy of magic is vouched for in olden times. Their fathers would not have used medicines unless their value was certain.
(20) Most Zande medicines come to them from foreign peoples, and Azande believe that foreigners know much more about magic than they do. Foreign medicines are vouched for by the peoples who use them.
(21) The place occupied by the more important medicines in a sequence of events protects them from exposure as frauds. Magic is made against unknown witches, adulterers, and thieves. On the death of a man the poison oracle determines whether he died as a victim to the magic. If the oracles were first consulted to discover the criminal, and then magic were made against him, the magic would soon be seen to be unsuccessful.
(22) Zande beliefs are generally vaguely formulated. A belief to be easily contradicted by experience and to be easily shown to be out of harmony with other beliefs must be clearly stated and intellectually developed – e.g. the Zande concept of a soul of medicine is so vague that it cannot clash with experience.

# 17

# BRONISLAW MALINOWSKI

"Magic, Science and Religion"

The scholarly education of Bronislaw Kaspar Malinowski (b. 1884; d. 1942) is characterized by both interdisciplinarity (he studied mathematics, physics, philosophy, psychology, economics and anthropology) and internationality (born in Krakow, Poland, he studied in Krakow, Leipzig and London). Malinowski spent most of his teaching career at the London School of Economics where he was professor of anthropology between 1922 and 1938.

Malinowski is most known for his fieldwork in Melanesia and his seminal contributions to the method of "participant observation" (some regard Malinowski as the inventor of this method). His works *Argonauts of the Western Pacifics* (1922) and *Coral Gardens and Their Magic* (1935), where he recollects and analyses his fieldwork experiences in the framework of his "functionalist" theory, exerted a major influence on the later debate on "magic".

The excerpt is taken from his article "Magic, Science and Religion" that was posthumously published in 1948. In this text, Malinowski adopts and combines a variety of former approaches, while adding some new perspectives. By contrasting "magic" with "science", Malinowski follows in the footsteps of Frazer (see Chapter 12): "magic" is a fraudulent "pseudo-science" and is characterized by a false "association of ideas". Malinowski rejects, however, Frazer's evolutionism: "magic", "science" and "religion" can exist side by side by complementing instead of replacing one another (such as, Malinowski claims, in the case of the Trobriand Islands). While opposing "magic" and "religion", Malinowski adopts Durkheim's conceptualization of "religion" as a constitutive and stabilizing force of the community (see Chapter 14). He defines "magic" as a "practical art consisting of acts which are only means to a definite end expected to follow later on", whereas "religion" is understood as a "body of self-contained acts being themselves the fulfilment of their purpose" – such as collective rites based on myth or other complex patterns of belief.

Malinowski adds to these established theorems a psychological explanation of the origin of "magic". Influenced by Robert R. Marett (1909) and, in particular, by Sigmund Freud's *Totem and Taboo* (1913), Malinowski claims that "magic" evolved as a "substitute action" in situations of crisis and threat that confronted people with their lack of power and knowledge, leading to anxiety, anger and distress. Their "obsessive desire" in these situations led to a "spontaneous enactment of the desired end in a practical impasse", expressed by impulsive words and actions (some of these later evolve into traditionalized patterns of "magical" actions). Malinowski suggests that through these enactments some *katharsis* takes place, implying the conviction that "the desired end seems nearer satisfaction". The cultural function of "magic" is thus to enable "man to carry out with confidence his important tasks, to maintain his poise and his mental integrity in fits of anger, in the throes of hate, of unrequited love, of despair and anxiety". With this "psychological" and at the same time "functionalist" explanation, Malinowski rejects theories that associate "magic" with the impersonal concept of *mana* and "intellectualist" approaches that disregard the factor of emotion.

## "MAGIC, SCIENCE AND RELIGION"

Magic – the very word seems to reveal a world of mysterious and unexpected possibilities! Even for those who do not share in that hankering after the occult, after the short cuts into "esoteric truth", this morbid interest, nowadays so freely ministered to by stale revivals of half-understood ancient creeds and cults, dished up under the names of "theosophy", "spiritism" or "spiritualism", and various pseudo-"sciences", -ologies and -isms – even for the clear scientific mind the subject of magic has a special attraction. Partly perhaps because we hope to find in it the quintessence of primitive man's longings and of his wisdom – and that, whatever it might be, is worth knowing. Partly because "magic" seems to stir up in everyone some hidden mental forces, some lingering hopes in the miraculous, some dormant beliefs in man's mysterious possibilities. Witness to this is the power which the words *magic, spell, charm, to bewitch*, and *to enchant*, possess in poetry, where the inner value of words, the emotional forces which they still release, survive longest and are revealed most clearly.

Yet when the sociologist approaches the study of magic, there where it still reigns supreme, where even now it can be found fully developed – that is, among the Stone Age savages of today – he finds to his disappointment an entirely sober, prosaic, even clumsy art, enacted for purely practical reasons, governed by crude and shallow beliefs, carried out in a simple and monotonous technique. This was already indicated in the definition of magic given above when in order to distinguish it from religion we described it as a body of purely practical acts, performed as a means to an end. Such also we have found it when we tried to disentangle it from knowledge and from practical arts, in which it is so strongly enmeshed, superficially so alike that it requires some effort to distinguish the essentially different mental attitude and the specifically ritual nature of its acts. Primitive magic – every field anthropologist knows it to his cost – is extremely monotonous and unexciting, strictly limited in its means of action, circumscribed in its beliefs, stunted in its fundamental assumptions. Follow one rite, study one spell, grasp the principles of magical belief, art and sociology in one case, and you will know not only all the acts of the tribe, but, adding a variant here and there, you will be able to settle as a magical practitioner in any part of the world yet fortunate enough to have faith in that desirable art.

PART III: MID-TWENTIETH-CENTURY APPROACHES TO MAGIC

## 1. THE RITE AND THE SPELL

Let us have a look at a typical act of magic, and choose one which is well-known and generally regarded as a standard performance – an act of black magic. Among the several types which we meet in savagery, witchcraft by the act of pointing the magical dart is, perhaps, the most widespread of all. A pointed bone or a stick, an arrow or the spine of some animal, is ritually, in a mimic fashion, thrust, thrown, or pointed in the direction of the man to be killed by sorcery. We have innumerable recipes in the oriental and ancient books of magic, in ethnographic descriptions and tales of travelers, of how such a rite is performed. But the emotional setting, the gestures and expressions of the sorcerer during the performance, have been but seldom described. Yet these are of the greatest importance. If a spectator were suddenly transported to some part of Melanesia and could observe the sorcerer at work, not perhaps knowing exactly what he was looking at, he might think that he had either to do with a lunatic or else he would guess that here was a man acting under the sway of uncontrolled anger. For the sorcerer has, as an essential part of the ritual performance, not merely to point the bone dart at his victim, but with an intense expression of fury and hatred he has to thrust it in the air, turn and twist it as if to bore it in the wound, then pull it back with a sudden jerk. Thus not only is the act of violence, or stabbing, reproduced, but the passion of violence has to be enacted.

We see thus that the dramatic expression of emotion is the essence of this act, for what is it that is reproduced in it? Not its end, for the magician would in that case have to imitate the death of the victim, but the emotional state of the performer, a state which closely corresponds to the situation in which we find it and which has to be gone through mimetically.

I could adduce a number of similar rites from my own experience, and many more, of course, from other records. Thus, when in other types of black magic the sorcerer ritually injures or mutilates or destroys a figure or object symbolizing the victim, this rite is, above all, a clear expression of hatred and anger. Or when in love magic the performer has really or symbolically to grasp, stroke, fondle the beloved person or some object representing her, he reproduces the behavior of a heartsick lover who has lost his common sense and is overwhelmed by passion. In war magic, anger, the fury of attack, the emotions of combative passion, are frequently expressed in a more or less direct manner. In the magic of terror, in the exorcism directed against powers of darkness and evil, the magician behaves as if himself overcome by the emotion of fear, or at least violently struggling against it. Shouts, brandishing of weapons, the use of lighted torches, form often the substance of this rite. Or else in an act, recorded by myself, to ward off the evil powers of darkness, a man has ritually to tremble, to utter a spell slowly as if paralyzed by fear. And this fear gets hold also of the approaching sorcerer and wards him off.

All such acts, usually rationalized and explained by some principle of magic, are *prima facie* expressions of emotion. The substances and paraphernalia used in them have often the same significance. Daggers, sharp-pointed lacerating objects, evil-smelling or poisonous substances, used in black magic; scents, flowers, inebriating stimulants, in love magic; valuables, in economic magic – all these are associated primarily through emotions and not through ideas with the end of the respective magic.

Besides such rites, however, in which a dominant element serves to express an emotion, there are others in which the act does forecast its result, or, to use Sir James Frazer's expression, the rite imitates its end. Thus, in the black magic of the Melanesians recorded by myself, a characteristic ritual way of winding-up the spell is for the sorcerer to weaken the voice, utter a death rattle, and fall down in imitation of the rigor of death. It is, however, not necessary to adduce any other examples, for this aspect of magic and the allied one of contagious magic has been brilliantly described and exhaustively documented by Frazer. Sir James has also shown that there exists a special lore of magical substances based on affinities, relations, on ideas of similarity and contagion, developed with a magical pseudo-science.

But there are also ritual proceedings in which there is neither imitation nor forecasting nor the expression of any special idea or emotion. There are rites so simple that they can be described only as an immediate application of magical virtue, as when the performer stands up and, directly invoking the wind, causes it to rise. Or again, as when a man conveys the spell to some material substance which afterwards will be applied to the thing or person to be charmed. The material objects used in such ritual are also of a strictly appropriate character – substances best fitted to receive, retain, and transmit magical virtue, coverings designed to imprison and preserve it until it is applied to its object.

But what is the magical virtue which figures not only in the last-mentioned type of act but in every magical rite? For whether it be an act expressing certain emotions or a rite of imitation and foreshadowing or an act of simple casting, one feature they have always in common: the force of magic, its virtue, must always be conveyed to the charmed object. What is it? Briefly, it is always the power contained in the spell, for, and this is never sufficiently emphasized, the most important element in magic is the spell. The spell is that part of magic which is occult, handed over in magical filiation, known only to the practitioner. To the natives knowledge of magic means knowledge of spell, and in an analysis of any act of witchcraft it will always be found that the ritual centers round the utterance of the spell. The formula is always the core of the magical performance.

The study of the texts and formulas of primitive magic reveals that there are three typical elements associated with the belief in magical efficiency. There are, first, the phonetic effects, imitations of natural sounds, such as the whistling of the wind, the growling of thunder, the roar of the sea, the voices of various animals. These sounds symbolize certain phenomena and thus are believed to produce them magically. Or else they express certain emotional states associated with the desire which is to be realized by means of the magic.

The second element, very conspicuous in primitive spells, is the use of words which invoke, state, or command the desired aim. Thus the sorcerer will mention all the symptoms of the disease which he is inflicting, or in the lethal formula he will describe the end of his victim. In healing magic the wizard will give word pictures of perfect health and bodily strength. In economic magic the growing of plants, the approach of animals, the arrival of fish in shoals are depicted. Or again the magician uses words and sentences which express the emotion under the stress of which he works his magic, and the action which gives expression to this emotion. The sorcerer in tones of fury will have to repeat such verbs as "I break – I twist – I burn – I destroy", enumerating with each of them the various parts of the body and internal organs of his victim. In all this we see that the spells are built very much on the same pattern as the rites and the words selected for the same reasons as the substances of magic.

Thirdly there is an element in almost every spell to which there is no counterpart in ritual. I mean the mythological allusions, the references to ancestors and culture heroes from whom this magic has been received. And that brings us to perhaps the most important point in the subject, to the traditional setting of magic.

## 2. THE TRADITION OF MAGIC

Tradition, which, as we have several times insisted, reigns supreme in primitive civilization, gathers in great abundance round magical ritual and cult. In the case of any important magic we invariably find the story accounting for its existence. Such a story tells when and where it entered the possession of man, how it became the property of a local group or of a family or clan. But such a story is not the story of its origins. Magic never "originated", it never has been made or invented. All magic simply "was" from the beginning an essential adjunct of all such things and processes as vitally interest man and yet elude his normal rational efforts. The spell, the rite, and the thing which they govern are coeval.

Thus, in Central Australia, all magic existed and has been inherited from the *alcheringa* times, when it came about like everything else. In Melanesia all magic comes from a time when humanity lived underground and when magic was a natural knowledge of ancestral man. In higher societies magic is often derived from spirits and demons, but even these, as a rule, originally received and did not invent it. Thus the belief in the primeval natural existence of magic is universal. As its counterpart we find the conviction that only by an absolutely unmodified immaculate transmission does magic retain its efficiency. The slightest alteration from the original pattern would be fatal. There is, then, the idea that between the object and its magic there exists an essential nexus. Magic is the quality of the thing, or rather, of the relation between man and the thing, for though never man-made it is always made for man. In all tradition, in all mythology, magic is always found in the possession of man and through the knowledge of man or man-like being. It implies the performing magician quite as much as the thing to be charmed and the means of charming. It is part of the original endowment of primeval humanity, of the *mura-mura* or *alcheringa* of Australia, of the subterrestrial humanity of Melanesia, of the people of the magical Golden Age all the world over.

Magic is not only human in its embodiment, but also in its subject matter: it refers principally to human activities and states, hunting, gardening, fishing, trading, love-making, disease, and death. It is not directed so much to nature as to man's relation to nature and to the human activities which affect it. Moreover, the effects of magic are usually conceived not as a product of nature influenced by the charm, but as something specially magical, something which nature cannot produce, but only the power of magic. The graver forms of disease, love in its passionate phases, the desire for a ceremonial exchange and other similar manifestations in the human organism and mind, are the direct product of the spell and rite. Magic is thus not derived from an observation of nature or knowledge of its laws, it is a primeval possession of man to be known only through tradition and affirming man's autonomous power of creating desired ends.

Thus, the force of magic is not a universal force residing everywhere, flowing where it will or it is willed to. Magic is the one and only specific power, a force unique of its kind, residing exclusively in man, let loose only by his magical art, gushing out with his voice, conveyed by the casting forth of the rite.

It may be here mentioned that the human body, being the receptacle of magic and the channel of its flow, must be submitted to various conditions. Thus the magician has to keep all sorts of taboos, or else the spell might be injured, especially as in certain parts of the world, in Melanesia for instance, the spell resides in the magician's belly, which is the seat of memory as well as of food. When necessary it is summoned up to the larynx, which is the seat of intelligence, and thence sent forth by the voice, the main organ of the human mind. Thus, not only is magic an essentially human possession, but it is literally and actually enshrined in man and can be handed on only from man to man, according to very strict rules of magical filiation, initiation, and instruction. It is thus never conceived as a force of nature, residing in things, acting independently of man, to be found out and learned by him, by any of those proceedings by which he gains his ordinary knowledge of nature.

### 3. *MANA* AND THE VIRTUE OF MAGIC

The obvious result of this is that all the theories which lay *mana* and similar conceptions at the basis of magic are pointing altogether in the wrong direction. For if the virtue of magic is exclusively localized in man, can be wielded by him only under very special conditions and in a traditionally prescribed manner it certainly is not a force such as the one described by Dr Codrington: "This *mana* is not fixed in anything and can be conveyed in almost anything." *Mana* also "acts in all ways for good and evil [...] shows itself in physical force or in any kind of power and excellence which a man possesses." Now it is clear that this force as described by Codrington is almost the exact opposite of the magical virtue as found embodied in the mythology of savages, in their behaviour, and in the structure of their magical formulas. For the real virtue of magic, as I know it from Melanesia, is fixed only in the spell and in its rite, and it cannot be "conveyed in" anything, but can be conveyed only by its strictly defined procedure. It never acts "in all ways", but only in ways specified by tradition. It never shows itself in physical force, while its effect upon the powers and excellences of man are strictly limited and defined.

And again, the similar conception found among the North American Indians cannot have anything to do with the specialized concrete virtue of magic. For of the *wakan* of the Dakota we read "all life is *wakan*. So also is everything which exhibits power, whether in action, as the winds and drifting clouds, or in passive endurance, as the boulder by the wayside [...] It embraces all mystery, all secret power, all divinity." Of the *orenda*, a word taken from the Iroquois, we are told: "This potence is held to be the property of all things

[...] the rocks, the waters, the tides, the plants and the trees, the animals and man, the wind and the storms, the clouds and the thunders and the lightnings [...] by the inchoate mentality of man, it is regarded as the efficient cause of all phenomena, all the activities of his environment."

After what has been established about the essence of magical power, it hardly needs emphasizing that there is little in common between the concepts of the *mana* type and the special virtue of magical spell and rite. We have seen that the keynote of all magical belief is the sharp distinction between the traditional force of magic on the one hand and the other forces and powers with which man and nature are endowed. The conceptions of the *wakan, orenda,* and *mana* class which include all sorts of forces and powers, besides that of magic, are simply an example of an early generalization of a crude metaphysical concept such as is found in several other savage words also, extremely important for our knowledge of primitive mentality but, as far as our present data go, opening only a problem as to the relation between the early concepts of "force", "the supernatural", and "the virtue of magic". It is impossible to decide, with the summary information at our disposal, what is the primary meaning of these compound concepts: that of physical force and that of supernatural efficiency. In the American concepts the emphasis seems to be on the former, in the Oceanic on the latter. What I want to make clear is that in all the attempts to understand native mentality it is necessary to study and describe the types of behavior first and to explain their vocabulary by their customs and their life. There is no more fallacious guide of knowledge than language, and in anthropology the "ontological argument" is specially dangerous.

It was necessary to enter into this problem in detail, for the theory of *mana* as the essence of primitive magic and religion has been so brilliantly advocated and so recklessly handled that it must be realized first that our knowledge of the *mana*, notably in Melanesia, is somewhat contradictory, and especially that we have hardly any data at all showing just how this conception enters into religious or magical cult and belief.

One thing is certain: magic is not born of an abstract conception of universal power, subsequently applied to concrete cases. It has undoubtedly arisen independently in a number of actual situations. Each type of magic, born of its own situation and of the emotional tension thereof, is due to the spontaneous flow of ideas and the spontaneous reaction of man. It is the uniformity of the mental process in each case which has led to certain universal features of magic and to the general conceptions which we find at the basis of man's magical thought and behaviour. It will be necessary to give now an analysis of the situations of magic and the experiences which they provoke.

## 4. MAGIC AND EXPERIENCE

So far we have been dealing mainly with native ideas and with native views of magic. This has led us to a point where the savage simply affirms that magic gives man the power over certain things. Now we must analyze this belief from the point of view of the sociological observer. Let us realize once more the type of situation in which we find magic. Man, engaged in a series of practical activities, comes to a gap; the hunter is disappointed by his quarry, the sailor misses propitious winds, the canoe builder has to deal with some material of which he is never certain that it will stand the strain, or the healthy person suddenly feels his strength failing. What does man do naturally under such conditions, setting aside all magic, belief and ritual? Forsaken by his knowledge, baffled by his past experience and by his technical skill, he realizes his impotence. Yet his desire grips him only the more strongly; his anxiety, his fears and hopes, induce a tension in his organism which drives him to some sort of activity. Whether he be savage or civilized, whether in possession of magic or entirely ignorant of its existence, passive inaction, the only thing dictated by reason, is the last thing in which he can acquiesce. His nervous system and his whole organism drive him to some substitute activity. Obsessed by the idea of the desired end, he sees it and feels it. His organism reproduces the acts suggested by the anticipations of hope, dictated by the emotion of passion so strongly felt.

The man under the sway of impotent fury or dominated by thwarted hate spontaneously clenches his fist and carries out imaginary thrusts at his enemy, muttering imprecations, casting words of hatred and anger against him. The lover aching for his unattainable or irresponsive beauty sees her in his visions, addresses her, and entreats and commands her favors, feeling himself accepted, pressing her to his bosom in his dreams. The anxious fisherman or hunter sees in his imagination the quarry enmeshed in the nets, the animal attained by the spear; he utters their names, describes in words his visions of the magnificent catch, he even breaks out into gestures of mimic representation of what he desires. The man lost at night in the woods or the jungle, beset by superstitious fear, sees around him the haunting demons, addresses them, tries to ward off, to frighten them, or shrinks from them in fear, like an animal which attempts to save itself by feigning death.

These reactions to overwhelming emotion or obsessive desire are natural responses of man to such a situation, based on a universal psycho-physiological mechanism. They engender what could be called extended expressions of emotion in act and in word, the threatening gestures of impotent anger and its maledictions, the spontaneous enactment of the desired end in a practical impasse, the passionate fondling gestures of the lover, and so on. All these spontaneous acts and spontaneous works make man forecast the images of the wished-for results, or express his passion in uncontrollable gestures, or break out into words which give vent to desire and anticipate its end.

And what is the purely intellectual process, the conviction formed during such a free outburst of emotion in words and deeds? First there surges a clear image of the desired end, of the hated person, of the feared danger or ghost. And each image is blended with its specific passion, which drives us to assume an active attitude towards that image. When passion reaches the breaking point at which man loses control over himself, the words which he utters, his blind behavior, allow the pent-up physiological tension to flow over. But over all this outburst presides the image of the end. It supplies the motive-force of the reaction, it apparently organizes and directs words and acts towards a definite purpose. The substitute action in which the passion finds its vent, and which is due to impotence, has subjectively all the value of a real action, to which emotion would, if not impeded, naturally have led.

As the tension spends itself in these words and gestures the obsessing visions fade away, the desired end seems nearer satisfaction, we regain our balance, once more at harmony with life. And we remain with a conviction that the words of malediction and the gestures of fury have traveled towards the hated person and hit their target; that the imploration of love, the visionary embraces, cannot have remained unanswered, that the visionary attainment of success in our pursuit cannot have been without a beneficial influence on the pending issue. In the case of fear, as the emotion which has led us to frenzied behavior gradually subsides, we feel that it is this behavior that has driven away the terrors. In brief, a strong emotional experience, which spends itself in a purely subjective flow of images, words, and acts of behavior, leaves a very deep conviction of its reality, as if of some practical and positive achievement, as if of something done by a power revealed to man. This power, born of mental and physiological obsession, seems to get hold of us from outside, and to primitive man, or to the credulous and untutored mind of all ages, the spontaneous spell, the spontaneous rite, and the spontaneous belief in their efficiency must appear as a direct revelation from some external and no doubt impersonal sources.

When we compare this spontaneous ritual and verbiage of overflowing passion or desire with traditionally fixed magical ritual and with the principles embodied in magical spells and substances, the striking resemblance of the two products shows that they are not independent of each other. Magical ritual, most of the principles of magic, most of its spells and substances, have been revealed to man in those passionate experiences which assail him in the impasses of his instinctive life and of his practical pursuits, in those gaps and breaches left in the ever-imperfect wall of culture which he erects between himself and the besetting temptations and dangers of his destiny. In this I think we have to recognize not only one of the sources but the very fountainhead of magical belief.

To most types of magical ritual, therefore, there corresponds a spontaneous ritual of emotional expression or of a forecast of the desired end. To most features of magical spell, to the commands, invocations, metaphors, there corresponds a natural flow of words, in malediction, in entreaty, in exorcism, and in the descriptions of unfulfilled wishes. To every belief in magical efficiency there can be laid in parallel one of those illusions of subjective experience, transient in the mind of the civilized rationalist, though even there never quite absent, but powerful and convincing to the simple man in every culture, and, above all, to the primitive savage mind.

Thus the foundations of magical belief and practice are not taken from the air, but are due to a number of experiences actually lived through, in which man receives the revelation of his power to attain the desired end. We must now ask: What is the relation between the promises contained in such experience and their fulfillment in real life? Plausible though the fallacious claims of magic might be to primitive man, how is it that they have remained so long unexposed?

The answer to this is that, first, it is a well-known fact that in human memory the testimony of a positive case always overshadows the negative one. One gain easily outweighs several losses. Thus the instances which affirm magic always loom far more conspicuously than those which deny it. But there are other facts which endorse by a real or apparent testimony the claims of magic. We have seen that magical ritual must have originated from a revelation in a real experience. But the man who from such an experience conceived, formulated, and gave to his tribesmen the nucleus of a new magical performance – acting, be it remembered, in perfect good faith – must have been a man of genius. The men who inherited and wielded his magic after him, no doubt always building it out and developing it, while believing that they were simply following up the tradition, must have been always men of great intelligence, energy, and power of enterprise. They would be the men successful in all emergencies. It is an empirical fact that in all savage societies magic and outstanding personality go hand in hand. Thus magic also coincides with personal success, skill, courage, and mental power. No wonder that it is considered a source of success.

This personal renown of the magician and its importance in enhancing the belief about the efficiency of magic are the cause of an interesting phenomenon: what may be called the *current mythology* of magic. Round every big magician there arises a halo made up of stories about his wonderful cures or kills, his catches, his victories, his conquests in love. In every savage society such stories form the backbone of belief in magic, for, supported as they are by the emotional experiences which everyone has had himself, the running chronicle of magical miracles establishes its claims beyond any doubt or cavil. Every eminent practitioner, besides his traditional claim, besides the filiation with his predecessors, makes his personal warrant of wonder-working.

Thus myth is not a dead product of past ages, merely surviving as an idle narrative. It is a living force, constantly producing new phenomena, constantly surrounding magic by new testimonies. Magic moves in the glory of past tradition, but it also creates its atmosphere of ever-nascent myth. As there is the body of legends already fixed, standardized, and constituting the folklore of the tribe, so there is always a stream of narratives in kind to those of the mythological time. Magic is the bridge between the golden age of primeval craft and the wonder-working power of today. Hence the formulas are full of mythical allusions, which, when uttered, unchain the powers of the past and cast them into the present.

With this we see also the role and meaning of mythology in a new light. Myth is not a savage speculation about origins of things born out of philosophic interest. Neither is it the result of the contemplation of nature – a sort of symbolical representation of its laws. It is the historical statement of one of those events which once for all vouch for the truth of a certain form of magic. Sometimes it is the actual record of a magical revelation coming directly from the first man to whom magic was revealed in some dramatic occurrence. More often it bears on its surface that it is merely a statement of how magic came into the possession of a clan or a community or a tribe. In all cases it is a warrant of its truth, a pedigree of its filiation, a charter of its claims to validity. And as we have seen, myth is the natural result of human faith, because every power must give signs of its efficiency, must act and be known to act, if people are to believe in its virtue. Every belief engenders its mythology, for there is no faith without miracles, and the main myth recounts simply the primeval miracle of the magic.

Myth, it may be added at once, can attach itself not only to magic but to any form of social power or social claim. It is used always to account for extraordinary privileges or duties, for great social inequalities, for severe burdens of rank, whether this be very high or very low. Also the beliefs and powers of religion are traced to their sources by mythological accounts. Religious myth, however, is rather an explicit dogma, the belief in the nether world, in creation, in the nature of divinities, spun out into a story. Sociological myth, on the other hand, especially in primitive cultures, is usually blended with legends about the sources of magical power. It can be said without exaggeration that the most typical, most highly developed, mythology in primitive societies is that of magic, and the function of myth is not to explain but to vouch for, not to satisfy curiosity but to give confidence in power, not to spin out yarns but to establish the flowing freely from present-day occurrences, frequently similar validity of belief. The deep connection between myth and cult, the pragmatic function of myth in enforcing belief, has been so persistently overlooked in favor of the etiological or explanatory theory of myth that it was necessary to dwell on this point.

## 5. MAGIC AND SCIENCE

We have had to make a digression on mythology since we found that myth is engendered by the real or imaginary success of witchcraft. But what about its failures? With all the strength which magic draws from the spontaneous belief and spontaneous ritual of intense desire or thwarted emotion, with all the force given it by the personal prestige, the social power and success common in the magician and practitioner – still there are failures and breakdowns, and we should vastly underrate the savage's intelligence, logic, and grasp of experience if we assumed that he is not aware of it and that he fails to account for it.

First of all, magic is surrounded by strict conditions: exact remembrance of a spell, unimpeachable performance of the rite, unswerving adhesion to the taboos and observances which shackle the magician. If any one of these is neglected, failure of magic follows. And then, even if magic be done in the most perfect manner, its effects can be equally well undone: for against every magic there can be also counter-magic. If magic, as we have shown, is begotten by the union of man's steadfast desire with the wayward whim of chance, then every desire, positive or negative, may – nay, must – have its magic. Now in all his social and worldly ambitions, in all his strivings to catch good fortune and trap propitious luck, man moves in an atmosphere of rivalry, of envy, and of spite. For luck, possessions, even health, are matters of degree and of comparison, and if your neighbor owns more cattle, more wives, more health, and more power than yourself, you feel dwarfed in all you own and all you are. And such is human nature that a man's desire is as much satisfied by the thwarting of others as by the advancement of himself. To this sociological play of desire and counter-desire, of ambition and spite, of success and envy, there corresponds the play of magic and counter-magic, or of magic white and black.

In Melanesia, where I have studied this problem at first hand, there is not one single magical act which is not firmly believed to possess a counter-act which, when stronger, can completely annihilate its effects. In certain types of magic, as for instance, that of health and disease, the formulas actually go in couples. A sorcerer who learns a performance by which to cause a definite disease will at the same time learn the formula and the rite which can annul completely the effects of his evil magic. In love, again, not only does there exist a belief that, when two formulas are performed to win the same heart, the stronger will override the weaker one, but there are spells uttered directly to alienate the affections of the sweetheart or wife of another. Whether this duality of magic is as consistently carried out all the world over as in the Trobriands it is difficult to say, but that the twin forces of white and black, of positive and negative, exist everywhere is beyond doubt. Thus the failures of magic can always be accounted for by the slip of memory, by slovenliness in performance or in observance of a taboo, and, last not least, by the fact that someone else has performed some counter-magic.

We are now in a position to state more fully the relation between magic and science already outlined above. Magic is akin to science in that it always has a definite aim intimately associated with human instincts, needs, and pursuits. The magic art is directed towards the attainment of practical aims. Like the other arts and crafts, it is also governed by a theory, by a system of principles which dictate the manner in which the act has to be performed in order to be effective. In analyzing magical spells, rites, and substances we have found that there are a number of general principles which govern them. Both science and magic develop a special technique. In magic, as in the other arts, man can undo what he has done or mend the damage which he has wrought. In fact, in magic, the quantative equivalents of black and white seem to be much more exact and the effects of witchcraft much more completely eradicated by counter-witchcraft than is possible in any practical art or craft. Thus both magic and science show certain similarities, and, with Sir James Frazer, we can appropriately call magic a pseudo-science.

And the spurious character of this pseudo-science is not hard to detect. Science, even as represented by the primitive knowledge of savage man, is based on the normal universal experience of everyday life, experience won in man's struggle with nature for his subsistence and safety, founded on observation, fixed by reason. Magic is based on specific experience of emotional states in which man observes not nature but himself, in which the truth is revealed not by reason but by the play of emotions upon the human organism. Science is founded on the conviction that experience, effort, and reason are valid; magic on the belief that hope cannot fail nor desire deceive. The theories of knowledge are dictated by logic, those of magic by the association of ideas under the influence of desire. As a matter of empirical fact the body of rational knowledge and the body of magical lore are incorporated each in a different tradition, in a different social setting and in a different type of activity, and all these differences are clearly recognized by the savages. The one constitutes the domain of the profane; the other, hedged round by observances, mysteries, and taboos, makes up half of the domain of the sacred.

## 6. MAGIC AND RELIGION

Both magic and religion arise and function in situations of emotional stress: crises of life, lacunae in important pursuits, death and initiation into tribal mysteries, unhappy love and unsatisfied hate. Both magic and religion open up escapes from such situations and such impasses as offer no empirical way out except by ritual and belief into the domain of the supernatural. This domain embraces, in religion, beliefs in ghosts, spirits, the primitive forebodings of providence, the guardians of tribal mysteries; in magic, the primeval force and virtue of magic. Both magic and religion are based strictly on mythological tradition, and they also both exist in the atmosphere of the miraculous, in a constant revelation of their wonder-working power. They both are surrounded by taboos and observances which mark off their acts from those of the profane world.

Now what distinguishes magic from religion? We have taken for our starting-point a most definite and tangible distinction: we have defined, within the domain of the sacred, magic as a practical art consisting of acts which are only means to a definite end expected to follow later on; religion as a body of self-contained acts being themselves the fulfillment of their purpose. We can now follow up this difference into its deeper layers. The practical art of magic has its limited, circumscribed technique: spell, rite, and the condition of the performer form always its trite trinity. Religion, with its complex aspects and purposes, has no such simple technique, and its unity can be seen neither in the form of its acts nor even in the uniformity of its subject matter, but rather in the function which it fulfills and in the value of its belief and ritual. Again, the belief in magic, corresponding to its plain practical nature, is extremely simple. It is always the affirmation of man's power to cause certain definite effects by a definite spell and rite. In religion, on the other hand, we have a whole supernatural world of faith: the pantheon of spirits and demons, the benevolent powers of totem, guardian spirit, tribal all-father, the vision of the future life, create a second supernatural reality for primitive man. The mythology of religion is also more varied and complex as well as more creative. It usually centres round the various tenets of belief, and it develops them into cosmogonies, tales of culture heroes, accounts of the doings of gods and demigods. In magic, important as it is, mythology is an ever-recurrent boasting about man's primeval achievements.

Magic, the specific art for specific ends, has in every one of its forms come once into the possession of man, and it had to be handed over in direct filiation from generation to generation. Hence it remains from the earliest times in the hands of specialists, and the first profession of mankind is that of a wizard or witch. Religion, on the other hand, in primitive conditions is an affair of all, in which everyone takes an active and equivalent part. Every member of the tribe has to go through initiation, and then himself initiates others. Everyone wails, mourns, digs the grave and commemorates, and in due time everyone has his turn in being mourned and commemorated. Spirits are for all, and everyone becomes a spirit. The only specialization in religion – that is, early spiritualistic mediumism – is not a profession but a personal gift. One more difference between magic and religion is the play of black and white in witchcraft, while religion in its primitive stages has but little of the contrast between good and evil, between the beneficent and malevolent powers. This is due also to the practical character of magic, which aims at direct quantitative results, while early religion, though essentially moral, has to deal with fateful, irremediable happenings and supernatural forces and beings, so that the undoing of things done by man does not enter into it. The maxim that fear first made gods in the universe is certainly not true in the light of anthropology.

In order to grasp the difference between religion and magic and to gain a clear vision of the three-cornered constellation of magic, religion, and science, let us briefly realize the cultural function of each. The function of primitive knowledge and its value have been assessed already and indeed are not difficult to grasp. By acquainting man with his surroundings, by allowing him to use the forces of nature, science, primitive knowledge, bestows on man an immense biological advantage, setting him far above all the rest of creation. The function of religion and its value we have learned to understand in the survey of savage creeds and cults given above. We have shown there that religious faith establishes, fixes, and enhances all valuable mental attitudes, such as reverence for tradition, harmony with environment, courage and confidence in the struggle with difficulties and at the prospect of death. This belief, embodied and maintained by cult and ceremonial, has an immense biological value, and so reveals to primitive man truth in the wider, pragmatic sense of the word.

What is the cultural function of magic? We have seen that all the instincts and emotions, all practical activities, lead man into impasses where gaps in his knowledge and the limitations of his early power of observation and reason betray him at a crucial moment. Human organism reacts to this in spontaneous outbursts, in which rudimentary modes of behavior and rudimentary beliefs in their efficiency are engendered. Magic fixes upon these beliefs and rudimentary rites and standardizes them into permanent traditional forms. Thus magic supplies primitive man with a number of ready-made ritual acts and beliefs, with a definite mental and practical technique which serves to bridge over the dangerous gaps in every important pursuit or critical situation. It enables man to carry out with confidence his important tasks, to maintain his poise and his mental integrity in fits of anger, in the throes of hate, of unrequited love, of despair and anxiety. The function of magic is to ritualize man's optimism, to enhance his faith in the victory of hope over fear. Magic expresses the greater value for man of confidence over doubt, of steadfastness over vacillation, of optimism over pessimism.

Looking from far and above, from our high places of safety in developed civilization, it is easy to see all the crudity and irrelevance of magic. But without its power and guidance early man could not have mastered his practical difficulties as he has done, nor could man have advanced to the higher stages of culture. Hence the universal occurrence of magic in primitive societies and its enormous sway. Hence do we find magic an invariable adjunct of all important activities. I think we must see in it the embodiment of the sublime folly of hope, which has yet been the best school of man's character.[1]

---

1. The most important works on Primitive Religion, Magic and Knowledge, referred to in the text, directly or implicitly, are:
Lang, Andrew. 1898. *The Making of Religion*. London.
Lang, Andrew. 1901. *Magic and Religion*. London.
McLennan, John Furguson. 1886. *Studies in Ancient History*. London.
Smith, William Robertson. 1889. *Lectures on the Religion of the Semites*. London.
Tylor, Edward Burnett. 1903 [1871]. *Primitive Culture: Researches into the Development of Mythology, Philosophy, Religion, Language, Art and Custom* [4th ed.], in two volumes. London: Routledge.

These, though out of date as regards material and some of their conclusions, are still inspiring and deserve study. Entirely fresh and representing the most modern points of view are the classical works of J. G. Frazer:

Frazer, James George. 1910. *Totemism and Exogamy: A Treatise on Certain Early Forms of Superstition and Society*, in 4 volumes. London: Macmillan.

Frazer, James George. 1906–1915. *The Golden Bough: A Study in Magic and Religion* [3rd ed.], in 12 volumes (also abridged edition, 1 vol.). London: Macmillan.

Frazer, James George. 1919. *Folk-Lore in the Old Testament: Studies in Comparative Religion and Law*, in 3 volumes. London: Macmillan.

Frazer, James George. 1913. *The Belief in Immortality and the Worship of the Dead*, in 3 volumes. London: Macmillan.

With Frazer's works should be read the two excellent contributions of Crawley:

Crawley, Alfred Ernest. 1902. *The Mystic Rose: A Study of Primitive Marriage and of Primitive Thought in Its Bearing on Marriage*. London: Macmillan.

Crawley, Alfred Ernest. 1905. *The Tree of Life: A Study of Religion*. London: Hutchinson & Co.

Also on the subject of the history of morals, the two extremely important works:

Hobhouse, Leonard Trelawny, 1915 [1906]. *Morals in Evolution: A Study in Comparative Ethics* [2nd ed.]. London: Chapman & Hall.

Westermarck, Edward. 1905. *The Origin and Development of the Moral Ideas*, in 2 volumes. London: Macmillan.

Further:

Brinton, Daniel Garrison. 1899 [1897]. *Religions of Primitive Peoples* [3rd ed.]. New York.

Durkheim, Émile. 1912. *Les formes élementaires de la vie religieuse*. Paris: Alcan. (Also English translation).

Ehrenreich, Paul. 1910. *Die Allgemeine Mythologie und ihre ethnologischen Grundlagen*. Leipzig: Hinrichs.

Gennep, Arnhold van. 1909. *Les rites de passage*. Paris: Nourry.

Harrison, Jane Ellen. 1912. *Themis: A Study of the Social Origins of Greek Religion*. Cambridge: Cambridge University Press.

Hubert, Henri and Mauss, Marcel. 1909. *Mélanges d'histoire des religions*. Paris: Alcan.

King, Irving. 1910. *The Development of Religion: A Study in Anthropology and Social Psychology*. New York: Macmillan.

Lowie, Robert Harry. 1925. *Primitive Religion*. London: Oxford University Press.

Marett, Robert Ranulph. 1909. *The Threshold of Religion*. London: Methuen.

Preuss, Konrad Theodor. 1904. *Der Ursprung der Religion und Kunst*. Braunschweig: Friedrich Viehweg.

Schmidt, Wilhelm. 1912. *Der Ursprung der Gottesidee: Eine historisch-kritische und positive Studie*. Münster/W.: Aschendorff.

An encyclopedic survey of facts and opinions will be found in:

Hastings, James. 1908. *Encyclopedia of Religion and Ethics*. Edinburgh: Clark, is excellent and indispensable to the serious student.

Wundt, Wilhelm. 1900. *Völkerpsychologie: eine Untersuchung der Entwicklungsgesetze von Sprache, Mythus und Sitte*. Leipzig, 1904 ff.

Primitive Knowledge in particular is discussed by:

Boas, Franz. 1911. *The Mind of Primitive Man*. New York: Macmillan.

Goldenweiser, Alexander A. 1921. *Early Civilization: An Introduction to Anthropology*. London: Harrap.

Lévy-Bruhl, Lucien. 1910. *Les fonctions mentales dans les sociétés inférieures*. Paris: Alcan.

Thurnwald, R. 1922. "Psychologie des Primitiven Menschen", in *Handbuch der vergleichenden Psychologie*. Band 1. Abteilung 2, G. Kafka (ed), 147–320. Munich: Reinhardt. Cf. also:

Kroeber, Alfred Louis. 1923. *Anthropology*. New York: Harcourt, Brace & Co.
Lowie, Robert Harry. 1920. *Primitive Society*. New York: Oxford University Press.

For fuller information upon the natives of Melanesia, who loom largely in the foregoing descriptions:
cf. Codrington, Robert Henry. 1891. *The Melanesians*. Oxford.
Malinowski, Bronislaw. 1915. "The Natives of Mailu", *Transactions of the Royal Society of South Australia* 39: 494–706.
Malinowski, Bronislaw. 1916. "Baloma", *Journal of the Royal Anthropological Institute* 46: 354–430.
Malinowski, Bronislaw. 1922. *Argonauts of the Western Pacific: An Account of Native Enterprise and Adventure in the Archipelagoes of Melanesia New Guinea*. London: London School of Economics and Political Science.
Seligman, Charles G. 1910. *The Melanesians of British New Guinea*. Cambridge: Cambridge University Press.
Thurnwald, Richard. 1912. *Forschungen auf den Solomo-Inseln und den Bismarck-Archipel*, in 2 volumes. Berlin: Reimer.
Thurnwald, Richard. 1921. *Die Gemeinde der Bánaro*. Stuttgart: Enke.

And three articles in *Psyche*: "Psychology of sex and the foundations of kinship in primitive society", *Psyche*, vol. III [1923], pp98–128; "Psychoanalysis and anthropology", *Psyche*, vol. IV [1924], pp293–332); "Complex and myth in mother-right", *Psyche*, vol. V [1925], pp194–216.

# 18

# ROBIN HORTON

"African Traditional Thought and Western Science. Part II"

Robin Horton (b. 1932) is an anthropologist who did his main ethnographic work among the Kalabari in Nigeria (see his *The Gods as Guests* [1960], which ends on observing the "truncation of religious practice" [71] as a result the Pax Britannica and the spread of Christianity). Horton worked at several Nigerian universities. With Meyer Fortes he co-authored a book on *Oedipus and Job in West African Religion* (1959); but Horton's main writing took the form of articles, the most important of which are collected in his book *Patterns of Thought in Africa and the West: Essays on Magic, Religion and Science* (1993), where he also defends some of his arguments against critics.

Together with Ruth Finnegan he edited the influential volume *Modes of Thought* (1973) on the question of whether Western and non-Western thinking are fundamentally different. Much of Horton's work focuses on this issue; but as he explains in the introduction to his *Patterns of Thought*, he is interested in the modern West mainly as a contrasting case to African cultures and religions and to illuminate the questions of universality and uniqueness of different styles of thinking. Reflecting on Western thought also made it clear to him how strongly anthropolgal work was shaped by Western educational and ideological background assumptions. Against theological and symbolist approaches, which, in Horton's view, divide human thought into two main categories – the expressive and the instrumental – he sided with the intellectualist or pragmatist tradition that emphasizes the quest for practical control and explanatory schemes. According to Horton, "many of the religious beliefs of preliterate cultures *are* primarily explanatory in intent" (1993 [1968]: 58). He therefore defends the thesis that there is "a deep-seated similarity between much of the world's religious thought, past and present, and the theoretical thought of modern science" (1993: 347).

The excerpt is taken from an essay, originally published in 1967, in which Horton unfolds some key arguments pertaining to this thesis. In the first part of this paper he sets out a number of general propositions about "the nature and function of theoretical thinking" (1993 [1967]: 197), whether in Western science or African thought. Our excerpt covers the first major section of Part II of the article that deals with points of difference between traditional (African) and (modern Western) scientific thinking. The main difference, for Horton, is the absence or presence of a positive awareness of theoretical alternatives and two related distinctions: the extent to which beliefs are held sacred, and the degree of anxiety felt about theoretical alternatives. Horton lays out a series of distinctions relating to the absence/presence of alternatives and the anxiety felt about these. "Magic" enters the stage when he deals with different attitudes to words (which appear bound with reality in Africa but separated from reality in science). He frames his argument within Karl Popper's distinction between open and closed societies. In his later work, Horton abandoned this idea and instead distinguished between traditionalist and progressive concepts of time and between consensual and competitive modes of theorizing (1993: 13).

## "AFRICAN TRADITIONAL THOUGHT AND WESTERN SCIENCE"

In Part I of this paper, I pushed as far as it would go the thesis that important continuities link the religious thinking of traditional Africa and the theoretical thinking of the modern West. I showed how this view helps us make sense of many otherwise puzzling features of traditional religious thinking. I also showed how it helps us to avoid certain rather troublesome red herrings which lie across the path towards understanding the crucial differences between the traditional and the scientific outlook.

In Part II, I shall concentrate on these differences. I shall start by isolating one which strikes me as the key to all the others, and will then go on to suggest how the latter flow from it.

What I take to be the key difference is a very simple one. It is that in traditional cultures there is no developed awareness of alternatives to the established body of theoretical tenets; whereas in scientifically oriented cultures, such an awareness is highly developed. It is this difference we refer to when we say that traditional cultures are "closed" and scientifically oriented cultures "open".[1]

One important consequence of the lack of awareness of alternatives is very clearly spelled out be Evans-Pritchard in his pioneering work on Azande witchcraft beliefs. Thus he says:

> I have attempted to show how rhythm, mode of utterance, content of prophecies, and so forth, assist in creating faith in witch-doctors, but these are only some of the ways in which faith is supported, and do not entirely explain belief. Weight

---

1. Philosophically minded readers will notice here some affinities with Karl Popper, who also makes the transition from a "closed" to an "open" predicament crucial for the take-off from tradition to science. For me, however, Popper obscures the issue by packing too many contrasts into his definitions of "closed" and "open". Thus, for him, the transition from one predicament to the other implies not just a growth in the awareness of alternatives, but also a transition from communalism to individualism, and from ascribed status to achieved status. Bus as I hope to show in this essay, it is the awareness of alternatives which is crucial for the take-off into science. Not individualism or achieved status: for there are lots of societies where both of the latter are well developed, but which show no signs whatever of take-off. In the present context, therefore, my own narrower definitions of "closed" and "open" seems more appropriate.

of tradition alone can do that [...] There is no incentive to agnosticism. All their beliefs hang together, and were a Zande to give up faith in witch-doctorhood, he would have to surrender equally his faith in witchcraft and oracles [...] In this web of belief every strand depends upon every other strand, *and a Zande cannot get out of its meshes because it is the only world he knows. The web is not an external structure in which he is enclosed. It is the texture of his thought and he cannot think that his thought is wrong.*[2]

And again:

And yet Azande do not see that their oracles tell them nothing! Their blindness is not due to stupidity, for they display great ingenuity in explaining away the failures and inequalities of the poison oracle and experimental keenness in testing it. It is due rather to the fact that their intellectual ingenuity and experimental keenness are conditioned by patterns of ritual behaviour and mystical belief. Within the limits set by these patterns, they show great intelligence, but it cannot operate beyond these limits. Or, to put it in another way; *they reason excellently in the idiom of their beliefs, but they cannot reason outside, or against their beliefs because they have no other idiom in which to express their thoughts.*[3]

Yet again, writing more generally of "closed" societies in a recent book, he says:

Everyone has the same sort of religious beliefs and practices, and their generality, or collectivity, gives them an objectivity which places them over and above the psychological experience of any individual, or indeed of all individuals [...] *Apart from positive and negative sanctions, the mere fact that religion is general means, again in a closed society, that it is obligatory, for even if there is no coercion, a man has no option but to accept what everybody gives assent to, because he has no choice, any more than of what language he speaks. Even were he to be a sceptic, he could express his doubts only in terms of the beliefs held by all around him.*[4]

In other words, absence of any awareness of alternatives makes for an absolute acceptance of the established theoretical tenets, and removes any possibility of questioning them. In these circumstances, the established tenets invest the believer with a compelling force. It is this force which we refer to when we talk of such tenets as sacred.

A second important consequence of lack of awareness of alternatives is vividly illustrated by the reaction of an Ijo man to a missionary who told him to throw away his old gods. He said: "Does your God really want us to climb to the top of a tall palm tree, then take off our hands and let ourselves fall?" Where the established tenets have an absolute

---

2. Evans-Pritchard, Edward E. 1958 (1937). *Witchcraft, Oracles and Magic among the Azande*. Oxford, p194.
3. *Ibid.* [*Witchcraft, Oracles and Magic among the Azande*], p338.
4. Evans-Pritchard, Edward E. 1965. *Theories of Primitive Religion*. Oxford, p55.

and exclusive validity for those who hold them, any challenge to them is a threat of chaos, of the cosmic abyss, and therefore evokes intense anxiety.

With developing awareness of alternatives, the established theoretical tenets come to seem less absolute in their validity, and lose something of their sacredness. At the same time, a challenge to these tenets is no longer a horrific threat of chaos. For just as the tenets themselves have lost some of their absolute validity, a challenge to them is no longer a threat of absolute calamity. It can now be seen as nothing more threatening than an intimation that new tenets might profitably be tried. Where these conditions begin to prevail, the stage is set for change from a traditional to a scientific outlook.

Here, then, we have two basic predicaments: the "closed" – characterized by lack of awareness of alternatives, sacredness of beliefs, and anxiety about threats to them; and the "open" – characterized by awareness of alternatives, diminished sacredness of beliefs, and diminished anxiety about threats to them.

Now, as I have said, I believe all the major differences between traditional and scientific outlooks can be understood in terms of these two predicaments. In substantiating this, I should like to divide the differences into two groups: A, those directly connected with the presence or absence of a vision of alternative; and B, those directly connected with the presence or absence of anxiety about threats to the established beliefs.

## DIFFERENCES CONNECTED WITH THE PRESENCE OR ABSENCE OF A VISION OF ALTERNATIVES

### (a) Magical versus non-magical attitude to words

A central characteristic of nearly all the traditional African world-views we know of is an assumption about the power of words, uttered under appropriate circumstances, to bring into being the events or states they stand for.

The most striking examples of this assumption are to be found in creation mythologies where the supreme being is said to have formed the world out of chaos by uttering the names of all things in it. Such mythologies occur most notably in Ancient Egypt and among the peoples of the Western Sudan.

In traditional African cultures, to know the name of a being or thing is to have some degree of control over it. In the invocation of spirits, it is essential to call their names correctly; and the control which such correct calling gives is one reason why the true or "deep" names of gods are often withheld from strangers, and their utterance forbidden to all but a few whose business it is to use them in ritual. Similar ideas lie behind the very widespread traditional practice of using euphemisms to refer to such things as dangerous diseases and wild animals. for it is thought that use of the real names might secure their presence. Yet again, it is widely believed that harm can be done to a man by various operations performed on his name – for instance, by writing his name on a piece of paper and burning it.

Through a very wide range of traditional African belief and activity, it is possible to see an implicit assumption as to the magical power of words.

Now if we take into account what I have called the basic predicament of the traditional thinker, we can begin to see why this assumption should be so deeply entrenched in his daily life and thought. Briefly, no man can make contact with reality save through a screen of words. Hence no man can escape the tendency to see a unique and intimate link between words and things. For the traditional thinker this tendency has an overwhelming power. Since he can imagine no alternatives to his established system of concepts and words, the latter appear bound to reality in an absolute fashion. There is no way at all in which they can be seen as varying independently of the segments of reality they stand for. Hence they appear so integrally involved with their referents that any manipulation of the one self-evidently affects the other.

The scientist's attitude to words is, of course, quite opposite. He dismisses contemptuously any suggestion that words could have an immediate, magical power over the things they stand for. Indeed, he finds magical notions amongst the most absurd and alien trappings of traditional thought. Though he grants an enormous power to words, it is the indirect one of bringing control over things through the functions of explanation and prediction.

Why does the scientist reject the magician's view of words? One easy answer is that he has come to know better: magical behaviour has been found not to produce the results it claims to. Perhaps. But what scientist has ever bothered to put magic to the test? The answer is, none; because there are deeper grounds for rejection – grounds which make the idea of testing beside the point.

To see what these grounds are, let us return to the scientist's basic predicament – to his awareness of alternative idea-systems whose ways of classifying and interpreting the world are very different from his own. Now this changed awareness gives him two intellectual possibilities. Both are eminently thinkable; but one is intolerable, the other hopeful.

The first possibility is simply a continuance of the magical world-view. If ideas and words are inextricably bound up with reality, and if indeed they shape it and control it, then, a multiplicity of idea-systems means a multiplicity of realities, and a change of ideas means a change of things. But whereas there is nothing particularly absurd or inconsistent about this view, it is clearly intolerable in the extreme. For it means that the world is in the last analysis dependent on human whim, that the search for order is a folly, and that human beings can expect to find no sort of anchor in reality.

The second possibility takes hold as an escape from this horrific prospect. It is based on the faith that while ideas and words change, there must be some anchor, some constant reality. This faith leads to the modern view of words and reality as independent variables. With its advent, words come "unstuck from" reality and are no longer seen as acting magically upon it. Intellectually, this second possibility is neither more nor less respectable than the first. But it has the great advantage of being tolerable whilst the first is horrific.

That the outlook behind magic still remains an intellectual possibility in the scientifically oriented cultures of the modern West can be seen from its survival as a nagging undercurrent in the last 300 years of Western philosophy. This undercurrent generally goes under the labels of "Idealism" and "Solipsism"; and under these labels it is not immediately recognizable. But a deeper scrutiny reveals that the old outlook is there all right – albeit in a strange guise. True, Idealism does not say that words create, sustain, and have power over that which they represent. Rather, it says that material things are "in the mind". That is, the mind creates, sustains, and has power over matter. But the second view is little more than a post-Cartesian transposition of the first. Let me elaborate. Both in traditional African cosmologies and in European cosmologies before Descartes, the modern distinction between "mind" and "matter" does not appear. Although everything in the universe is underpinned by spiritual forces, what moderns would call "mental activities" and "material things" are both part of a single reality, neither material nor immaterial. Thinking, conceiving, saying, etc. are described in terms or organs like heart and brain and actions like the uttering of words. Now when Descartes wrote his philosophical works, he crystallized a half-way phase in the transition from a personal to an impersonal cosmological idiom. Whilst "higher" human activities still remained under the aegis of a personalized theory, physical and biological events were brought under the aegis of impersonal theory. Hence thinking, conceiving, saying, etc. became manifestations of "mind", whilst all other happenings became manifestations of "matter". Hence whereas before Descartes we have "words over things", after him we have "mind over matter" – just a new disguise for the old view.

What I have said about this view being intellectually respectable but emotionally intolerable is borne out by the attitude to it of modern Western philosophers. Since they are duty bound to explore all the alternative possibilities of thought that lie within the grasp of their imaginations, these philosophers mention, nay even expound, the doctrines of Idealism and Solipsism. Invariably, too, they follow up their expositions with attempts at refutation. But such attempts are, just as invariably, a farce. Their character is summed up in G. E. Moore's desperate gesture, when challenged to prove the existence of a world outside his mind, of banging his hand with his fist and exclaiming: "It is there!" A gesture of faith rather than of reason, if ever there was one!

With the change from the "closed" to the "open" predicament, then, the outlook behind magic becomes intolerable; and to escape from it people espouse the view that words vary independently of reality. Smug rationalists who congratulate themselves on their freedom from magical thinking would do well to reflect on the nature of this freedom!

# 19

# STANLEY J. TAMBIAH

"Form and Meaning of Magical Acts: A Point of View"

Stanley J. Tambiah (b. 1929) is a social anthropologist from Sri Lanka who taught at the Universities of Ceylon (Sri Lanka), Cambridge, Chicago and Harvard. He conducted fieldwork mainly in Sri Lanka and Thailand and published various books on the religious and ethnic conflicts of modern Thailand. Tambiah is particularly known for his book *Magic, Science and Religion and the Scope of Rationality* (1990), where he discusses and refutes several of the major theorists of the debate and stresses the ethnocentricity and ineffectiveness of the scholarly habit to oppose "magic", "science" and "religion". His most original contributions to the endeavour of "defining magic" stem, however, from the "rationality debate" of the 1960s and 1970s, where he was one of the main protagonists. Tambiah's article "Form and meaning of magical acts: A point of view", of which we present the last two chapters, appeared in one of the mouthpieces of this debate, Robin Horton's and Ruth Finnegan's *Modes of Thought: Essays on Thinking in Western and Non-Western Societies* (1973).

In an earlier article on "The magical power of words" (1968), Tambiah advocates a *linguistic turn* in the study of rituals. While focusing on the role of verbal actions (and their relation to other types of actions) in ritual, he argues that the often metaphoric and metonymic use of language in "magical" rites is intended to imitate or simulate practical actions. Words therefore operate as one of the main ritual mediators of the "imperative transfer" of effects to which ("magical") rites are mostly devoted. Words spoken in ("magical") rites, hence, differ from ordinary language in so far as their function is not communication but action; this would explain the often-attested ritual efficacy of words.

In the first part of "Form and meaning of magical acts", Tambiah discusses various aspects of Evans-Pritchard's *Witchcraft, Oracles and Magic among the Azande* (see Chapter 16), arguing that Evans-Pritchard partly misunderstood Zande "witchcraft" due to his purely "scientific" interpretation of analogy. In our excerpt, Tambiah then proposes a more appropriate conceptualization of "magic" (which he mainly equalizes with "ritual"). Tambiah applies Austin's theory of "speech acts" to the investigation of ("magical") rites and distinguishes between "locutionary" (words refer to things and can therefore be true or false), "illocutionary" (words actually do something – that is, alter the status of unwed persons during a marriage ceremony) and "perlocutionary acts" (words aim at achieving something – that is, through convincing or persuading others). The crux of this manoeuvre is that Tambiah mainly interprets both speech and material acts in ("magical") rites as "illocutionary" (or "performative") acts. For this reason, "magic" is not comparable to "science"; scholars doing that (such as Evans-Pritchard or Horton, who are criticized accordingly) commit, so to speak, a category mistake as "it is *inappropriate* to subject these performative rites to verification, to test whether they are true or false in a referential or assertive sense or whether the act has effected a result in terms of the logic of 'causation' as this is understood in science". In line with this argument, Tambiah, in the end of the article, addresses the problem of ethnocentrism.

# "FORM AND MEANING OF MAGICAL ACTS"

## HOW TO UNDERSTAND RITUAL (WHICH INCLUDES "MAGIC")?

I have perhaps so far only indicated negatively how "magic" should not be viewed and not positively how it might be viewed in terms of a new perspective. I have argued that to view magic as an attempt at science that failed (or more crudely a "bastard science" in the manner of Frazer, or more sophisticatedly as a "closed" system of thought that allows for no verification and falsification of its principles *a la* Popper) is to assert that in their magic and ritual[1] the primitives tried to achieve results through "causal" reasoning and failed. I have also argued that while it is the case that much primitive magic is based on analogical thought and action as is Western science, the difference between them is that whereas in science the use of an analogy is closely linked to prediction and verification, and its adequacy judged in terms of inductive support, or of meeting standards of probability criteria, or standing up to tests of falsifiability and the like, the semantics of a magical rite *are* not necessarily to be judged in terms of such "true/false" criteria of science but on different standards and objectives. The corresponding objectives *in* (magical) ritual are "persuasion", "conceptualization", "expansion of meaning" and the like, and the criteria of adequacy are better conveyed by notions such as "validity", "correctness", "legitimacy", and "felicity" of the ceremony performed.

It is this latter assertion that I wish to elucidate now. In my essay on "The magical power of words"[2] I took some steps towards understanding the form and meaning of ritual in terms of its inner semantic frame and outer pragmatic frame. My starting point with regard to the former was that most "magical rites" (as indeed most rituals) combine word and deed and that the rite is devoted to an "imperative transfer" of effects, which some might phrase as the "telic" and others as the "illocutionary" or "performative" nature of the rite.[3] The semantics of the transfer itself, the logic of construction of the transfer, in the

---
1. For me magic is embedded in ritual.
2. *Man*, N.S., 3, 1968.
3. J. L. Austin. 1962. *How To Do Things with Words*, Clarendon Press, Oxford; R. Finnegan. 1969. "How to do things with words: Performative utterances among the Limba of Sierra Leone", *Man*, N.S., 4.

Trobriand case depends on (1) metaphorical and analogical transfers by word mediated by realistic contact transfer through objects used as "transformers", and (2) on imperative verbal transfer of energy to a "whole" through the metonymical naming of the parts. One of the points I made was that the same laws of association that apply to ordinary language apply to magical language – I reiterate this because one reader at least has managed to misunderstand my effort and thinks I tried to deal with the special character of "magical" utterances,[4] thereby also not appreciating my critique of the theory of "magical" language held by Ogden and Richards, Malinowski, and others. But fortunately, in compensation, Finnegan has led me to Austin,[5] whose ideas I shall exploit in an attempt to formulate a perspective, according to my own design, for viewing the form and meaning of ritual.

In Austin's *How to do things with words* the chief topic of elaboration is what he calls the "performative" or "illocutionary" act, in which the uttering of the sentence cannot merely be described as saying something, but is, or is a part of, the *doing of an action*. When in a marriage ceremony the man says "I do take this woman to be my lawful wedded wife" (or some such formula), or the man says in a will "I give and bequeath", to utter these sentences in the appropriate circumstances "is not to *describe* my doing of what I should be said in so uttering to be doing or to state I am doing it: it is to do it".[6]

What ultimately I think Austin arrives at towards the end of his exercise is a classification of speech acts, "the issuing of utterances in a speech situation", which makes any stating "performing an act". (This is close to Malinowski's approach of seeing speech as part of action.)[7] How many senses may there be in which to say something is to do something, or in saying something we do something, or even by saying something we do something? The following classification of speech acts may help to answer the question:

(1) To perform *a locutionary act*: to utter a sentence with a certain sense and reference (an assertion, a descriptive statement of fact) which is *true or false in a referential sense*.

(2) To perform *an illocutionary act*: this relates to an utterance which has *a certain conventional force*, a performative act *which does something* (as implied in promising, ordering, apologizing, warning etc.). Usually the explicit illocutionary utterance is reducible or analysable into a form with a verb in the first person singular present indicative active (i.e. the "I", the "active" and the "present" seem appropriate). These statements cannot be subject *to the true – false test*, but are *normatively judged* as "happy"/"unhappy", valid/invalid, correct/defective etc.

(3) To perform *a perlocutionary act*: this refers to what we bring about or achieve *by saying something* (as connoted by convincing, persuading, misleading etc.). It refers to both the intended and unintended *consequence* upon the hearer of words uttered by the speaker. (By saying it I convinced him.)

---

4. Finnegan, *op. cit.*, p549.
5. Austin, *op. cit.*
6. *Ibid.*, p6.
7. See Tambiah, *op. cit.* [*The Magical Power of Words*], pp185 ff.

These three are analytically separate but in reality not exclusive categories: both locutionary and illocutionary acts can have consequences listed as perlocutionary; and an illocutionary act can have referring and predicating elements together with the performative.[8] We could perhaps say that an imperative illocutionary act attempts to get the world to conform to words, whereas "true" when ascribed to illocutions attributes success in getting words to conform to the world.

Now adapting these ideas for our purposes, we can say that ritual acts and magical rites are of the "illocutionary" or "performative" sort, which simply by virtue of being enacted (under the appropriate conditions) achieve a change of state, or do something effective (e.g. an installation ceremony undergone by the candidate makes him a "chief"). This performative aspect of the rite should be distinguished from its locutionary (referential, information-carrying) and perlocutionary (consequences for the participants) features.

It was quite evident to Austin that, while he focused on the role of speech in illocutionary acts, the utterance was not the sole thing necessary if the illocutionary act was to be deemed to have been performed, and also that *actions other than speech* whether physical or mental were entailed for the full realization of the performance. Indeed it is even possible at the other extreme to enact a performative act without uttering words at all – a hypothetical example would be the establishing of blood brotherhood by the physical exchange of blood (without an exchange of words).

The vast majority of ritual and magical acts combine word and deed. Hence it is appropriate to say that they use words in a performative or illocutionary manner, just as the action (the manipulation of objects and persons) is correspondingly performative.

I shall attempt to formalize in a few words the essentials of what I see as the form and meaning of magical ritual acts. The rite usually consists of a close interweaving of *speech* (in the form of utterances and spells) and *action* (consisting of the manipulation of objects). The *utterance* can be analysed with respect to its "predicative" and "illocutionary" frames. In terms of predication and reference the words exploit analogical associations, comparisons and transfers (through simile, metaphor, metonym etc.). The illocutionary force and power by which the deed is directed and enacted is achieved through use of words commanding, ordering, persuading and the like: "Whistle, whistle, I send you after a thief", so commands an Azande spell. And a Trobriand spell combines both metaphor and illocutionary force by urging the *taytu yam* to throw out foliage like the spider spinning its web:[9]

The spider covers up, the spider covers up [...]
The open space, the open space between thy branches, O taytu the spider covers up,

---

8. It is for this reason that J. R. Searle prefers a different classification in terms of the elements of speech acts (*Speech Acts: An Essay in the Philosophy of Language,* University Press, Cambridge, 1969, Ch. 2), although, and this is what is important for us, he too preserves the essential distinction between an *assertion* which is a very special kind of commitment to the *truth* of a proposition (usually in terms of empirical verification), and the *illocutionary* act (which contains Austin's performative verbs) and which in contrast is appropriately subject to judgements of success, defectiveness and felicity of performance (*Ibid.*, p54).
9. B. Malinowski. 1965. *Coral Gardens and Their Magic,* Vol. 1. Bloomington, IN: Indiana University Press, p148.

[…] Shoot up, O head of my taytu
[…] Make mop upon mop of leaves, O head of my taytu.

The action can be similarly analysed. The objects manipulated are chosen analogically on the basis of similarity and difference to convey meaning. From the performative perspective, the action consists of an operation done on an object-symbol to make an imperative and realistic transfer of its properties to the recipient. Or to put it differently, two objects are seen as having resemblances and differences, and an attempt is made to transfer the desirable quality of one to the other which is in a defective state.

Now it is clear that the words and action closely combine to form an amalgam which is the magical or ritual *act*. The interrelation between the two media – speech and object manipulation – can take different forms.[10] What I want to emphasize here is that this way of looking at "magical art" breaks through the Saussurean *langue/parole* distinction. On the one hand, the magical act bears predicative and referential *langue-type* meanings and on the other it is a performative act. Both frames are co-existent, and it is as a *performative* or "illocutionary" act directed by analogical reasoning that magic gets its distinctiveness.

Now it is *inappropriate* to subject these performative rites to verification, to test whether they are true or false in a referential or assertive sense or whether the act has effected a result in terms of the logic of "causation" as this is understood in science. Let me illustrate the point by considering the Thai rite of blessing a new house by Buddhist monks (so that evil spirits may be driven out and prosperity result) through the recitation of sacred verses and the performance of certain acts. Several conditions have to be satisfied if a performance of this rite is not, to use Austin's word, to become an "infelicity": that there exists a conventional procedure properly enacted only by authorized persons, e.g. monks, householders etc.; that, in this particular instance, the monks who took part were entitled to conduct the ceremony, and that the actual ceremony was executed both correctly and completely.

Quite another set of conditions relates to the *bona fides* of the actors. For example, the rite is intended for beneficiaries who expect to conduct themselves in certain ways and who have the right intentions. In fulfilment of this, it is necessary that the participants, in the actual rite performed, satisfy these expectations and actually so conduct themselves subsequently.

Now suppose that after the performance of the rite it is found that one or more of these conditions were not fulfilled – the monks may have been bogus, the ceremony incorrectly performed, or the householder never intended to live in the house with his family but planned to use it for an illicit purpose – we cannot in these circumstances say that the rite

---

10. I cannot go into this question here, but it may be indicated that the relation between the media may be (1) equal and "redundant", (2) "unequal", one medium being dominant and the other subsidiary, (3) "complementary", and "linked", e.g. the words being "metaphorical", and action "metonymical", and, finally, (4) separate and discontinuous. These kinds of relation are not necessarily exclusive, and any complex rite may express all relations not only between these two media but between them and others as well, such as music, dancing, use of diagrams, food presentations, etc.

itself was false or empirically ineffective in a causal sense. The ceremony *itself* cannot ever be said to have been proved to be false or untrue or ineffective; however, any particular enactment of it may be said to be void, unworthy or defective. A bigamist who on false pretences has gone through a second marriage ceremony, does not on that account make the institution of marriage false, wrong or ineffective; what can be said is that he has undergone the ceremony in bad faith and that he has not properly "married" a second time.

The conclusions therefore are that (1) while to particular instances of ritual enactments of the illocutionary or performative type *normative* judgements of efficacy (legitimacy, defectiveness, propriety, etc.) may be applied, it is inappropriate to judge their efficacy in terms of *verification statements* and inductive rules, and (2) while ritual in general as an institution cannot be declared to be defective, particular instances of it may be so declared, if the proper conditions of performance were not met. It is at this point that I wish to join issue with Evans-Pritchard first and then Robin Horton afterwards.

Evans-Pritchard in his classic study of Zande witchcraft, oracles and magic, having elucidated the coherence and close linkage of these systems of belief, felt it necessary to ask how they fitted into the observer-imposed ritual/empirical categories and how they related to Zande "practical" day-to-day activity. More pointedly, Evans-Pritchard, naturally interested in a "European" intellectual problem, asked how magic, which was oriented to achieving effects, compared with Western empiricism based on canons of proof and experimentation. Evans-Pritchard gave various reasons why the Azande did not disbelieve in magic even when the expected or wished-for magical effect did not materialize. His answer was that although Azande may be sceptical about the skills and knowledge of particular witch doctors or their poor medicines or the correct performance of particular performances, and the like, their belief in the efficacy of the system itself was not thereby assailed. Now, whereas Evans-Pritchard gave this as evidence of why Zande magic cannot be empirically proven wrong, he did not perhaps fully appreciate that the answers he received were appropriate to all conventional performative and illocutionary acts – particular performances may for various reasons be "unhappy" or "incorrect" and therefore inefficacious while the convention itself is unassailable.

Robin Horton compounds the "error" in his challenging essays, suggestively entitled "African traditional thought and Western science".[11] On the one hand Horton argues that African traditional thought (with its supernatural entities couched in a personal idiom) and Western science (with its concepts couched in an impersonal idiom) are similar in that reference to theoretical entities is used to link events in the visible, tangible world (natural effects) to their antecedents in the same world (natural causes). On the other hand, however – and here is the sting – this same African thought-system whose aim is explanatory and predictive (just like science) refuses to subject itself (like good science) to falsifiability and other verification tests. Indeed African traditional thought (just as Evans-Pritchard elucidated it) is a "closed system"; the believer cannot get outside the web of his thought, he cannot be agnostic, there is no vision of alternatives; furthermore it portrays

---

11. *Africa*, 37, 1967.

unreflective thinking, i.e. traditional thought lacks logic and philosophy and reflection upon the rules of explanation. Evans-Pritchard's demonstration is driven home in traditional thought by a process of *secondary elaboration*; other current beliefs are utilized in such a way as to "excuse" each failure as it occurs and thus the major theoretical assumptions are protected even in the face of negative evidence. By comparison the collective memory of the European scientific community is littered with the wreckage of discarded theories [...] true, but Horton's enthusiasm for Popper's idealizations may benefit from some of Kuhn's scepticism.

I think it is possible to differ from Horton on the basic assumptions of the comparisons between traditional and scientific thought. One does not deny that traditional societies reflect the patterns he enumerates. But I think it is fundamentally mistaken to say that African religion and ritual are concerned with the same intellectual tasks that science in Western society is concerned with: this is a case of analogy abused. The net result of such comparative pursuit is to land oneself where Frazer found himself – magical rituals are like science with the difference that they are mistaken and false.

My counter-argument is that to view most ritual and magical acts as if they were directed to the purposes of scientific activity – to discover natural causes, predict empirical consequences in terms of a theory of causation – is inappropriate and not productive of maximum understanding. Analogical thought of Western science and of primitive ritual have different implications. Like "illocutionary" and "performative" acts ritual acts have consequences, effect changes, structure situations not in the idiom of "Western science" and "rationality" but in terms of convention and normative judgement, and as solutions of existential problems and intellectual puzzles. These orders of thought and action after all are to be found in Western societies as well – they co-exist with science and thrive outside its field of action or relevance. (It would be interesting to know what Horton thinks is the relation between science and religion in Western society.)

But returning to the problem of magic itself: have I merely evaded answering what magic is by embedding it in ritual and seeing it as an analogical *cum* performative act? By and large I think this is a correct representation of it. But I must also go on to say that in so far as magical rites try to effect a transfer they are often geared to achieving practical results – such as cure of disease or production of a fine harvest, etc. – as much as they are geared to effecting social results. Although we should not judge their *raison d'être* in terms of applied science, we should however recognize that many (but not all) magical rites are elaborated and utilized precisely in those circumstances where non-Western man has not achieved that special kind of "advanced" scientific knowledge which can control and act upon reality to an extent that reaches beyond the realm of his own practical knowledge. Let us not forget what Evans-Pritchard's conclusion was. Zande rites were most "mystical" where the diseases they dealt with were the most acute and chronic. These rites then are on a different wave length from scientific technology; or at least in primitive societies it is better to assimilate witchcraft and magic to "ritual" rather than to "applied science".

Let us also not forget one of Evans-Pritchard's most pregnant observations, that the Zande belief in witchcraft does not exclude "empirical knowledge of cause and effect" but that it provides a social and cultural method of acting upon the world: "In every case witchcraft is the socially relevant cause, since it is the only one which *allows intervention and determines social behaviour*".[12] Thus through ritual man imposes meaning on the world, anticipates the future, retrospectively "rationalizes" the past and effects results.

It is perhaps because magic and applied science are so to say on different wave lengths, yet may (partially) overlap over the ground they cover, that the results of the spread of modern science and technology in so-called "traditional" societies are complex, inconsistent and non-linear. An effective pesticide may over time render a "magical rite" for killing pests redundant and unnecessary. But a sacrifice which creates the cosmos persists because it "creates" the world in a sense that is different from that known in the laboratory. How does one understand the Hindu theory of sacrifice which asserts claims vaster than the causal act itself? And in the new urban communities of developing societies, "drugs" may replace traditional "medicines", but scientific "scepticism" and "prediction" do not replace astrology, or consulting of oracles or of diviners, for the guidance of human actions and for providing meaning in perplexing situations.

But what may be true of non-Western societies may not be true of Western civilization in its recent past. And hereby possibly hangs a tale.

## THE RELEVANCE OF EUROPEAN EXPERIENCE

In certain respects the history and experience of Western civilization are unique. There is the possibility that, perhaps because the Western anthropologist himself is so naturally grounded in his own civilization, he may at times project it as a potentially universal experience. Let me clarify. If Western anthropologists faced with certain ritual procedures of non-Western societies view them as "magic" that is empirically false and doomed to concede to the claims of science, they are right as far as their own history is concerned, irrespective of the truth of the assertion elsewhere. There is no denying that in Europe there is some kind of developmental sequence by which out of more "primitive" notions and "magical" practices more "scientific" notions and experimentation were born. The process was by no means linear but it is true that alchemy gave way to chemistry, astrology to astronomy, leechcraft to medicine, etc. It is also to be borne in mind that old concepts from Greek natural philosophy (such as "atoms", "species", "force", "attraction") and from Greek medicine (especially the Hippocratic corpus) still persist (in form) although they have been transformed (in meaning) in the process. Somewhere in the middle of the transition it is very plausible that science differentiated out of magic, while magic itself was at the same time making "empirical" claims. It may very well be that the Western experience is a *privileged* case of transition from "magic" to "science".

It is further possible that the outlines of similar transitions and developments can also be discerned in other great literate civilizations like China and India. For example, the relation between early Vedic ritual and cosmological ideas and the concepts of classical

---

12. Evans-Pritchard, Edward E. *op. cit.* [*Witchcraft, Oracles and Magic among the Azande*], p93 (my italics, S. J. T.).

Indian medicine of later times is comparable to the development in Europe, although the trend may not have gone as far. Filliozat who has examined the question with great scholarship (and who is interesting in that he thinks Indian medical ideas may have influenced the Greeks rather than vice versa) came to the conclusion that between the ideas of Vedic times and later periods of Indian developments in the field of medicine there were both discontinuities and continuities:

> Classical Indian medicine claims to explain by means of a coherent system the pathogeny and applies its therapeutics as a function of its theories; its design is entirely scientific, even though many of its doctrines are, in fact, erroneous. It cannot, therefore, have its bases in the pathology and the therapeutics of the Veda. It does not, however, follow that the classical medical texts are not rich in Vedic souvenirs. We have seen that a number of Vedic names of diseases are explained by naturally climbing back from their meaning in classical medicine to the sense possessed by them in the Veda. But in the Veda, we have not found the prefiguration of ulterior pathological doctrines.[13]

We should heed this warning in our comparative studies. By simply naming rituals of non-Western societies as "magic", and the substances they use as "medicines" and "drugs", we cannot thereby attribute to the phenomena so named, by virtue of that naming, characteristics that may be peculiar to one's own contemporary civilization. It is only a short step from here to go on to measure these same ritual practices and ideas as equivalent to, but of course misguided and falling short of, empirical science. It is not that such a perspective is wrong but that it may hide from view the positive, persuasive and creative, though "non-scientific", features of analogical thought and action expressed in magical rites. The dangers of excessive historical universalization should be kept in view. The rise of industry, capitalism and experimental science in Europe in recent centuries found its counterpart in sociological theorizing in Weber's doctrine of growing "rationality" and "rationalization" in Western civilization – an inevitable historical process towards efficiency of social forms like bureaucracy, towards pragmatic orientation whereby means were closely linked to ends, and towards the generation of context-free, neutral and universal constructs and principles. I am merely indicating that this is a particular historical experience which need not and should not be universalized if it entails automatic projections of how things traditional inevitably become things rational.

---

13. J. Filliozat. 1964. *The Classical Doctrine in Indian Medicine: Its Origin and Greek Parallels*, Munshiram Manoharlal, Delhi, p137.

# 20

# EDMUND R. LEACH

*Culture and Communication: The Logic by which Symbols Are Connected*

(Sir) Edmund R. Leach (b. 1910; d. 1989) is acknowledged as one of the towering figures of British social anthropology of his time (Tambiah 2002). Leach did most of his ethnographic work in South Asia (Burma, Ceylon and Thailand).

In 1958, Leach published an essay on hairdressing rituals in which he discussed the remarkable convergence of ethnographic evidence and psychoanalytical arguments, even though the latter are considered methodologically and theoretically inadequate in social anthropology. At the end of his essay, he observes "that magical potency, regarded as a social category, is something which inheres in 'circumcision' symbols, but that each symbolization is effective because for each individual the ritual situation is felt to signify 'castration'" (Leach 1958: 162).

Writing on "magic" in *A Dictionary of the Social Sciences* from 1964, Leach emphasizes the following key definitional characteristics of "magic": "The core of the magic act is that it rests on empirically untested belief and that it is an effort at control. The first aspect distinguishes it from science, the second from religion" (Leach 1964: 398).

Our excerpt is taken from Leach's later *Culture and Communication: The Logic by which Symbols Are Connected* (1976), in which he provides a more original approach to "magic". For Leach, culture *is* communication and his book, written for undergraduates, seeks to explore ways to decode communication as a way of analysing culture. This analysis derives its inspiration from structuralism.

In the first chapters, Leach introduces several distinctions, which he draws on when addressing the various issues discussed in the book such as "magic". For Leach, communication is dyadic: a "message-bearing entity $A$ conveys information about message $B$" (Leach 1976: 12). A first distinction is that between indexes and signals: a signal $A$ causes or automatically triggers a response $B$, whereas an index $A$ merely indicates a message $B$. There are two main types of indexes: in a natural index $A$ is selected for $B$ on the basis of natural association (smoke as a [natural] index of fire), while the relation between $A$ and $B$ is completely arbitrary in the case of a signum. There are two main types of signa: symbols and signs. A signum is a sign, in Leach's vocabulary, when there is some kind of intrinsic contextual relationship between $A$ and $B$. Consider the letter sequence APPLE for a particular fruit in the context of the English language or the crown as a sign for sovereignty in the context of monarchic systems. These relations are typically metonymical (a part standing for the whole; contiguity). A signum is a symbol, when *A* and *B* have no prior intrinsical contextual relationship – such as when a brewery uses a crown as a symbol for a brand of beer (or think of the serpent as indicating evil). These relations are typically metaphorical (extrinsic association). The varieties of these distinctions allow for ambiguity in the ways in which concepts in the mind are linked, via "sense-images", to objects or events in the external world. This helps to explain the functioning of "magic": "magical acts are *indices*; the magician treats them as *signals*".

In a later book, which provides "an egocentric and historical point of view" on social anthropology (1982: 7), Leach claims that politics, law and religion are words with "a quite specific institutional reference", whereas the words kinship, magic, myth and ritual "are devoid of any general agreed meaning and are not tied in with any clearly identifiable set of representative social roles" (132). The general assumption that these "English language categories together form a unified matrix from which the sub-divisions of a scholarly discourse can be developed" results in numerous "paradoxes" (132). As a result, "after a lifetime's career as a professional anthropologist, I have almost reached the conclusion that the word has no meaning whatsoever" (133). In the glossary to the book he states: "Few contemporary social anthropologists would confidentially assert that they can distinguish magical from non-magical acts [...] The performances which are described as 'magic' in ethnographic literature are ones in which [the] [...] symbolic component is very pronounced but they do not form a distinct class of actions" (Leach 1982: 235).

## *CULTURE AND COMMUNICATION*

The performances which anthropologists classify as magic and sorcery provide excellent examples of the ambiguities I have been discussing and of the mixture of metonymic and metaphoric association which is characteristic of all modes of human communication.

The point that I want to get across to you in this section is that, with slight modification, the technique of analysis which Levi-Strauss applied so successfully to the interpretation of myth can be made to throw light on the logical mystification of "magic".

Perhaps the first point to emphasise here is that ambiguity needs to be distinguished from error.

Earlier in this century anthropologists took it for granted that the manifest technological inferiority of primitive societies was the consequence of a general mental incapacity. Belief in magic was a symptom of this inferiority; it provided evidence that all primitive peoples are essentially childish and mentally confused.

The most generally accepted version of this theory was that of Sir James Frazer. In effect, Frazer held that "expressive acts which purport to alter the state of the world by metaphysical means" are mistaken attempts at "technical acts which alter the state of the world by physical means". He declared that magic is "bastard science"; its fundamental quality is erroneous belief about cause and effect. He then went on to distinguish two major types of the erroneous cause/effect nexus: (1) homoeopathic magic depending upon "the law of similarity"; (2) contagious magic depending upon "the law of contact".

In so far as Frazer was wrong he was wrong in an interesting way. In the first place he assumed that the magician's mistake is to confuse expressive acts with technical acts, whereas the general consensus of most recent anthropologists is that what the magician usually does is to interpret an index as a signal, after the fashion of Pavlov's dog [...] On the other hand, as Jakobson noticed a long while back (Jakobson and Halle, 1956, pp80–1), Frazer's distinction between homoeopathic and contagious magic is essentially the same as that between metaphoric and metonymic association. Frazer's bastard scientist–magician plays around with iconic symbols (which depend upon metaphor) and signs (which depend upon metonymy).

Frazer's failure to distinguish between purported signals and purported technical acts is an error but it is not easy to demonstrate that it is error except by specific examples. The essence of the matter is that when magical performance is observed in action it is palpably quite different in kind from straightforward technical action. If a Sinhalese peasant wants to drive a stake into the ground, he takes a hammer and does just that; if he wants to stop a charging elephant he will (or should) stand stock still and recite a magical formula!

The essential difference between the two types of performance is that whereas the primitive *technician* is always in direct mechanical contact with the object which he seeks to change, the *magician* purports to change the state of the world by action at a distance. The argument about *sense-images* in Section 3 in relation to Fig. 2 (p19) is relevant here as is also the statement at p23 that *signals* are automatic trigger response mechanisms. In terms of Fig. 1 (p12) magical acts are *indices*; the magician treats them as signals.

This marginal slither by which technical action is confused with expressive action, and symbolic communication with signal communication, deserves the anthropologist's close attention.

In ordinary day-to-day affairs the only way that I can make things happen at a distance (in the absence of a mechanical connecting link) is to issue verbal (i.e. symbolic) instructions to a trained agent, human or animal. My verbal instruction is an expressive rather than a technical action, but if my agent responds to my message *as if it were a signal* (i.e. in an automatic fashion like Pavlov's dog) the existence of the intermediate linkage through the agent becomes irrelevant. The effect is as if I myself had performed a technical action at a distance.

Notice that in situations of this sort the effect of the verbal command will only be reliable if it conforms to a conventional habitual mode, i.e. if the symbolic instructions can be treated as signs (cf. p20). On the other hand if the verbal commands are of a *completely*, habitual kind, like the "words" which are shouted by a sergeant major on a parade ground, it does not really matter what the words are; the noise itself can be treated as a signal. This is the general point. Where symbols are treated as signs, they can always very easily be perceived as signals.

It is thus very significant that the types of performance which anthropologists distinguish as magic invariably include a verbal (or sign language) component – the spell. It is the spell which is supposed to make the magical performance effective at a distance. This is a fallacy, but it is fallacy of a complicated sort.

Consider the following prototype example which might well come from Frazer:

> A sorcerer gains possession of a specimen of hair from the head of his intended victim X. The sorcerer destroys the hair to the accompaniment of spells and ritual. He predicts that, as a consequence, the victim X will suffer injury.

What is the "logic" of the sorcerer's fallacy?

In terms of Fig. 1 (p12) the connections are as follows: The sorcerer treats the hair growing on the head of X as a metonymic sign for X. He further assumes that if he destroys the sign he will damage X. This is perfectly "reasonable". In the expressions "A stands for APPLE" and "Crown stands for Kingship", A and Crown are metonymic signs for APPLE and KINGSHIP respectively. If you destroy the sign elements the residues are damaged: -PPLE and "royal regalia without a headpiece" are indecipherable.

Now when the hair is growing on the head of the potential victim it is indeed a "metonymic sign for X" in a genuine sense: the sign and the thing signified are contiguous; if the hair were destroyed, X would indeed be damaged. But by the time the hair has come into the sorcerer's possession the only continuing link with its origin is a verbal label "this is the hair of X". The label is now a metonymic sign for the hair, but the hair and X are separated; the link between the label and X is only metaphoric. In so far as a sense-image of X is generated in the mind of the sorcerer by the presence of the hair it entails the distinction […] between proper names which are symbolic of the individual so named and category words, e.g. pig, hair, which are normally signs for the category indicated.

In summary, in terms of the specifications of Fig. 1 (p12) the sorcerer makes a triple error. He first mistakes a metaphoric symbol (i.e. the verbal label "this is the hair of X") for a metonymic sign. He then goes on to treat the imputed sign as if it were a natural index, and finally he interprets the supposed natural index as a signal capable of triggering off automatic consequences at a distance.

You may perhaps think that this is a quite absurdly complicated, jargon-loaded way of describing what is quite obvious. I agree. But the mental associations of magical procedure are complicated and the logical errors are not nearly so self-evident as is sometimes thought to be the case. If you want to trace out just where the "mistakes" occur you need to examine the chain of associations very carefully. Notice the similarities between my prototype anthropological example and the following more familiar situations:

## CASE 1. *POLITICAL SORCERY*

In many parts of contemporary Latin America, Africa and Asia the normal method of changing the political regime is by military *coup*. In the great majority of instances the bloodshed involved is negligible. The insurrection is completed in a few hours and the leaders of the defeated government retire to a comfortable exile abroad. The form of such coups is quite standardised: it consists of a military assault on the Presidential Palace. In many cases it is later reported that the President himself was absent at the time. Newspaper and radio proclamations (spells) by the usurping military play a large part in the procedure.

The main difference between this kind of operation and that of my prototype sorcerer is that the intended victim's *hair* is replaced by the intended victim's *Presidential Palace*. The *coup* is an expressive rather than a technical act but in nine cases out of ten it achieves the desired result. You should not assume that magic and sorcery never work!

## CASE 2. *TECHNO-MAGIC IN THE HOME*

You go into a room and notice on the wall a knob of a familiar kind. You take this to be a sign that the room is wired for electricity. Through long experience you have come to believe that you can treat the sign as a signal. You press the knob in the expectation that a light will come on somewhere in the room.

Most of the complex string of assumptions which lie at the back of your expectation could only be verified with considerable difficulty. It is habit rather than technical knowledge which persuades us to treat light switches as signals. And in point of fact, were it not for the absence of a verbal spell, it would be difficult to distinguish your light switching behaviour from an act of magic.

I am not suggesting that we *should* treat light switching as an act of magic, but only that, if Sir James Frazer had been consistent, he should have to have done so! The action is technical in intention and may be technical in its consequences, but the actual form of the action is expressive.

Because our day-to-day behaviour is full of logical ambiguities of this kind it is worth going to some trouble to get this business of signals, signs and symbols sorted out.

The distinctions are not mere pedantry. Admittedly the three types of communication dyad are constantly getting mixed up, but it is valuable to have the formal distinctions clear in your minds because it is by means of such distinctions and by refusing to admit that there is any ambiguity that we manage to perceive the world as we do.

If you doubt this, try to work out in *detail* just why you feel that the sorcerer's hocus-pocus with his intended victim's hair is "magic" but that fiddling with an electric light switch is not.

# PART IV

## CONTEMPORARY VOICES

PART IV: CONTEMPORARY VOICES

# INTRODUCTION

Our selection of sources could create the mistaken impression that there was a gap in discussions on "magic" from the mid-1970s to the present. In fact, the production of ideas and interpretations did not slow down and we find several on-going threads of thoughts in different disciplines – discourses that to a great extent appear to operate in isolation from each other (some main developments will be highlighted in the following). Part IV presents original contributions by five contemporary authors who, from different theoretical backgrounds and based on different empirical materials, have published monographs on "magic" in the first decade of the twenty-first century: Kimberly B. Stratton on the ancient Mediterranean, Christopher I. Lehrich on early modern Europe and Randall Styers on the modern academic discourse about "magic", while Jesper Sørensen has attempted an explanation of "magic" in the light of findings from the cognitive sciences and Susan Greenwood interprets "magical" experience as a form of consciousness, imagination and participation.

"Magic" continues to be a main concern for anthropologists, even if they often use "sorcery" or "witchcraft" as basic terms. Bruce Kapferer's (1997) phenomenology of Sri Lankan "sorcery" practices, for example, where he highlights their existential and human dimensions, their creative contextual relevance for daily life, their cosmogonic symbolism and constructive social agency, and also gives critical remarks on the very concept of "sorcery", could be made relevant for analyses of "magical" practice. Broader terms such as "marvels" have been suggested to cover extraordinary phenomena (Shanafelt 2004), but we also find anthropologists who use the concept of "magic" largely as a trope. Nowhere in his acclaimed surreal ethnography *The Magic of the State* (1997) does Michael Taussig explicitly spell out anything vaguely resembling a definition of "magic". On another occasion, however, reflections on ethnographies of tricks and their exposure yield "another theory of magic" (Taussig 1998, reprinted 2003 and in 2006). Taussig suggests that there is no contradiction between trickery and reality, but that "reality is infused with trickery and that magic is a quality of Realism for dealing with the power of the ways of the world" (1998: 251). Accordingly, "magic" "is efficacious not despite the trick but on account of its exposure" (222). As it turns out that there is no pure, unmediated reality behind the veil and since revelation and concealment are mutually mediated, reality "is no less magical than magic" (251). With Alfred Gell we turn from trickery to technology. For Gell, "magic" provides a kind of symbolic commentary on technical strategies, or "magic" even is an ideal kind of technology: the "apotheosis of ideal, costless production" (Gell 1988: 9). Inspired by evolutionary anthropology, some scholars have tried to move beyond the traditional problem of false beliefs or falsified claims by interpreting "magic" as the acceptance of unverifiable communicative claims grounded in some supernatural authority; the acceptance of such claims is a ritual device that serves to promote social cooperation and to avoid conflict, even in the case of malevolent rites (Palmer et al. 2010). The anthropological debate about African "witchcraft" is still ubiquitous, resulting almost yearly in voluminous collections of essays or readers on the topic; elucidating what "witchcraft" precisely is, however, remains a complicated topic that is today even hampered by the adoption and reinterpretation of the term by African natives (Moore and Sanders 2001:

3–6). Contemporary anthropologists, against the cliché that "magic" properly belongs to primitive cultures or has been superseded in modern European history (Thomas 1971), not only stress the continuity of "magic" in "modern" times but even argue that modern societies have produced their own kinds of "magic" (see, in particular, Meyer and Pels 2003). Our text by Susan Greenwood (see Chapter 21) illustrates, furthermore, the contemporary trend to ground scholarship in personal experiences of "magical" practice. In general, while there is no dearth of ideas on "magic", the prominent anthropologists mentioned here rarely engage with each other's work so that one can hardly speak of something like a coherent debate.

While in contemporary anthropology we rarely find fundamental doubts as to the validity of the category of "magic", for historians of religion the apparent failures of providing a convincing distinction between "magic" and "religion" (see the General Introduction to this volume) has caused some embarrassment, as did its ethnocentrism and the conspicuous multiplicity of definitions of "magic". To solve these problems, Hendrik S. Versnel (1991), in a widely quoted article, resorts to a provisional, broad, polythetical definition of "magic" based on a common-sense collection of features, which he, however, only alludes to in his article. Einar Thomassen (1999) also votes for keeping the category by giving it a more precise meaning – namely, as a type of "anomalous" religious ritual: "magical" rituals are both dependent upon "normal", or official/legitimate, ritual practice and appropriate these rituals (such as prayers or invocations) "for personal ends, offsetting the balance between the individual and the collective which forms the sanctioned norm of ritual practice in societies" (Thomassen 1999: 65). Jonathan Z. Smith (1995 [reprint 2004]), on the other hand, sees "little merit in continuing the use of the substantive term 'magic' in second-order, theoretical academic discourse. We have better and more precise scholarly taxa for each of the phenomena commonly denoted by 'magic' which, among other benefits, create more useful categories for comparison" (Smith 2004: 218). Yet, given the cross-culturally widespread use of "magic" as a first-order classifier, Smith also realizes that "the name will not easily be rectified" and that abstention "will not settle 'magic'" (219), and Smith himself, despite his own objections, engages the category in various other essays (see, e.g., Smith 2004: 333).

Turning away from the study of ancient religions, in a quite entertaining book filled with examples based on fieldwork in Varanasi (India), Ariel Glucklich argues that there is a specific "magical" experience and thinking of which he identifies several preconditions or components (Glucklich 1997: 112). Basically, he claims that "the experience of magical events rests first and foremost on the sensory perception that all elements of the world are interrelated [...] in a tapestry of natural interactions" (22). In sociology, it seems that the category is mainly taken for granted (see, for example, the massive but uncritical work by O'Keefe [1982]). More recently, Rodney Stark, in an almost anachronistic fashion, still advocates, or seeks to re-establish, distinctions between "magic", "religion" and "science", respectively. He defines "magic" as follows: "Magic refers to all efforts to manipulate supernatural forces to gain rewards (or avoid costs) without reference to a God or Gods or to general explanations of existence" (Stark 2001: 111). In contrast, scholars of the study of Western Esotericism, in particular, have opted for abandoning "magic" as a second-order category in the last years (Pasi 2008; Hanegraaff 2012; Stuckrad forthcoming) and advocated the historicization of the concept: "The term 'magic' is an important object of historical research, but definitely unsuitable as an etic instrument for doing research" (Hanegraaff 2012: 168). In a similar vein, in his contribution to the present volume, Randall Styers finds that "little may be gained by the effort to define magic as a stable object of study; but magic offers a rich occasion for historical and cultural analysis" (see Chapter 25). In fact, all five of the following texts in one way or another reflect on that crisis of validity regarding the category.

While historians continue to be interested in exploring the fate of "magic" in different periods, during the last decades, psychologists have also suggested novel explanations of phenomena classified as "magic". Leonard Zusne and Warren H. Jones, in their *Anomalistic Psychology* (1982; 2nd ed. 1989) assign "magic" to the class of anomalistic phenomena – that is, "behavior and experience that have been explained in paranormal, supernatural, occult, in short, magical terms" (Zusne and Jones 1989: 2). "Magical" thinking, Zusne and Jones argue, "is wholly or partly at the root of any explanation of behavioural and experiential phenomena that violate some law of nature" (13). Roots of "magic", in their analysis, include "the absence of information about the physical causes of the events that surround us" (31) and reification and self-awareness as two strategies to compensate for this. Cognitively, moreover, we are told, both children and people from primal societies lack notions of causality. As indicated by the title of his book *Believing in Magic: The Psychology of Superstitions* (1997), when writing about "magic" Stuart A. Vyse has in mind "superstition" or superstitious behaviour that is found in social context such as sports, examinations and gambling, or paranormal beliefs including astrology. In his final analysis, Vyse finds, among other things, that superstition is only moderately related to personality, that it is not a form of psychopathology, is not limited to traditional cultures or people of low intelligence, but that it mainly springs from accidental conditioning (i.e., repeating apparently successful actions), the basic human motivation to control and that it helps to pass time while waiting in high-tension moments of life (Vyse 1997). Cognitive and evolutionary psychologists have also become interested in "magic". Here, "magic" refers to the tricks performed by stage magicians and the "science of magic" amounts to the systematic study of the apparent persuasiveness of the stage magician's performance, including their abilities to control attention, distort perception and influence choices (Kuhn et al. 2008). Others lump superstitious, "magical" and paranormal beliefs in one main category characterized by "category mistakes where the core attributes of mental, physical, and biological entities and processes are confused with each other" (Lindeman and Aarnio 2007: 734). In the experimental part of that study, beliefs in ghosts, religious beliefs, luck beliefs (e.g., that amulets bring luck) and astrology are treated as evidence for the category. It has also been suggested that "magical thinking could be considered an adaptive bias" (Markle 2010: 28): it may in the past have yielded higher fitness when dealing with threats that are or were "outside of the domain of knowledge available to the individual dealing with the threat" (26); but such claims thus far cannot be tested empirically. Markle distinguishes active from passive "magical" thinking, where the former involves actions by individuals (e.g., praying or putting up talismans), while the latter does not (think of the belief that a place is haunted by spirits).

# 21

# SUSAN GREENWOOD

"Magical Consciousness: A Legitimate Form of Knowledge"

Susan Greenwood is a British anthropologist. She is the author of a series of publications on "magic" including *Magic, Witchcraft and the Otherworld: An Anthropology* (2000), *The Nature of Magic: An Anthropology of Consciousness* (2005) and *The Anthropology of Magic* (2009). Contrary to the anthropologists appearing elsewhere in this book, Susan Greenwood writes also as a practitioner: "When I first started my doctoral research in the 1990s, I made the decision to study magic from the inside, as a practitioner of magic as well as an anthropologist. I wanted to discover what could be learned through direct experience. Over the years, I have explored various approaches to magic with Western magical practitioners, and I have participated in many witchcraft rituals, trained as a high magician, and worked with shamans" (Greenwood 2009: 1). In her case, the border between researcher and researched breaks down (she is not an outsider to an insider); instead, she wants to build bridges between practitioners and the academic discourse. Key notions for her understanding of magic are participation (which she adopts from Lévy-Bruhl), emotional relationships, subjectivity, analogy and mythological imaginations – elements that appear anathematic to the self-understanding of anthropology as a "rational" science. In her contribution to this volume, Greenwood proposes the concept of "magical consciousness" as an ancient, "intrinsic" and imaginal "mode of mind" and a "holistic engagement with material and non-material realities". She explores several theoretical avenues that could lend support to that experience-based claim.

## MAGICAL CONSCIOUSNESS: A LEGITIMATE FORM OF KNOWLEDGE

An old photograph shows a seven-year-old child standing on a beach, her bare toes wriggling in the sand and her fingers stiff with excitement.[1] I recall the moment well for this

---

1. Parts of this chapter have been adapted from my theoretical study of magic *The Anthropology of Magic* (2009) and also from my chapter "Toward an epistemology of imaginal reality: Fieldwork with the dragon", in Espirito Santo and Llera Blanes 2012.

is a photograph of me. The thrill of arriving at the seaside after a long car journey from London to the south coast of England is still fresh in my memory after many years. Once on the beach, I was fascinated with the rock pools with their dark purple frond-waving anemones, scuttling crabs and small, darting, semi-transparent shrimps. I felt that I was entering other worlds within these pools of otherness. My awareness expanded and I imagined that I became a sea dragon. Of course, I did not materially transform into a reptilian fire-breathing water monster; but later as an anthropologist studying British practitioners of magic[2] I revisited such childhood memories of the dragon as part of my fieldwork. In fact, early on in my research I had come to the conclusion that I would have to go beyond more usual methodological conventions and include myself as an informant in order to explore the depths of magic as a mode of consciousness.[3] In this sense, the anthropologist had to turn native.[4] My experience of magic, indeed, did make me a native;[5] but I propose that we are all natives of this type of thought – in a multiplicity of ways and to different degrees.

In order to further examine the experience of magic, I developed the concept of *magical consciousness* to refer to an imaginal aspect of awareness that can potentially be experienced by anyone, to varying extents. Having many historical and cross-cultural shapes and forms, magical consciousness can be expressed in a myriad of situations and contexts – ranging from the serendipity of childhood imaginative play to the more developed instrumental practice of witch doctors, medicine healers, spirit mediums and shamans, amongst many others. Magical consciousness is a specific and intrinsic mode of mind, one that might go back to humanity's earliest beginnings.[6] However, many social scientific theories have implicit assumptions about the inferiority of magic as a mode of thought when compared to science, or they explain magic solely in terms of its social or psychological effects. In this chapter, I focus on the imaginal experience of magic and offer an integrative conceptual model for understanding magical consciousness as a legitimate source of knowledge.

## MAGIC AND THE IMAGINATION

My approach to examining the experience of magic starts with the premise that magical consciousness is a type of imaginative associative thinking different from more abstract, analytical modes of thought. Magic has been actively explored by social scientists in the

---

2. I started my fieldwork on British practitioners of magic, focusing on issues of identity, gender and morality, in the 1990s and my PhD was published as *Magic, Witchcraft and the Otherworld* (2000), later followed by more research on magicians' attitudes to nature published as *The Nature of Magic* (2005).
3. At the time it was a big step to take, but I deemed it necessary to address the somewhat problematic concept of magic in the social sciences.
4. See, in particular, Kovach 2009.
5. Patric V. Giesler, a reviewer of *Magic, Witchcraft and the Otherworld* for the *American Ethnologist* 2002: 208, wrote that I gave a "native's account" and that this contributed a "unique twist" to experiential ethnography.
6. Lewis-Williams 2004: 45–47.

past as offering explanation for beliefs (Frazer and Tylor); in opposition to the social cohesion of religion (Durkheim and Mauss); as a cathartic release of emotional tension in the absence of reason and practical knowledge (Malinowski); forming a logically coherent set of beliefs and practices (Evans-Pritchard); and more recently magic has been seen as an analytical counterpoint to modernity's rational progress (Meyer and Pels).[7] Notwithstanding, as my earlier childhood example of the sea dragon shows, the imagination is intrinsic to the conception of magic as a mode of thought. Magic has been defined by some contemporary Western practitioners as a "convenient word for a whole collection of techniques, all of which involve the mind" and includes emotion and the use of imaginative faculties, particularly the ability to visualize.[8] The first record of the English word *imagination* dates from the fourteenth century as a "faculty of the mind that forms and manipulates images". It comes initially from the Latin *imaginary* (to form a mental picture), and *imago* (image) and *imaginare* (to form an image of or represent something creatively).[9] *Imaginal* is a term coined, or at least appearing initially, in 1647 as relating to imagination, images or imagery.[10]

Returning to my opening example, as a child on the beach I imagined that I saw a sea dragon within the rock pools. As an anthropologist studying magic I remember the feeling of being a child at the seaside and having a magical experience, although I did not recognize it as such at the time. The memory of the dragon now encapsulates a feeling of encompassing wholeness; it is a symbol or metaphor of a state of being where anything can happen in the imagination. As children, perhaps we all use the imaginal mind in such ways, until we learn to grow out of it, keep quiet or give preference to other forms of cognition. But needless to say the imagination is not just the preserve of children, or those who refuse to grow up; it is a mytho-poetic terrain most obviously, but not exclusively, utilized by artists, poets and musicians.

Magical thinking is creative thinking that goes beyond the immediately apparent. If a wide perspective is taken, it is possible to investigate what lies beyond the horizon of the here and now by venturing into the imaginal mind. The imagination creates out of "nothing", as described by William Shakespeare in *A Midsummer Night's Dream* V. i:

> And as imagination bodies forth
> The forms of things unknown, the poet's pen
> Turns them to shapes, and gives to airy nothing
> A local habitation and a name.
> Such tricks hath strong imagination.[11]

---

7. See Greenwood 2009: 4–5; Meyer and Pels 2003: 1–3.
8. This is what Margot Adler (1986: 8) discovered from her research on American Pagans in *Drawing Down the Moon: Witches, Druids, Goddess-Worshippers, and Other Pagans in America Today*.
9. This definition comes from the Online Etymology Dictionary: http://www.etymonline.com/index.php?term=imagination, accessed 1 November 2011.
10. Defined in Merriam-Webster Dictionary, http://www.merriam-webster.com/dictionary/imaginal, accessed 1 November 2011.
11. Quoted in Nettle 2001: 3.

The imagination can trick the mind and turn perception inside out; it gives shape and place to what was nothing, creating the tangible from the intangible. Nevertheless, the imagination is an inherent aspect of human thinking and a source of creativity.[12] The imagination can combine and recombine an assortment of ideas in a creative manner described by neuroscientist Antonio Damasio as a "diversity generating mechanism":

> The first requirement here is the *strong generation of representational diversity.* What I mean by this is the ability to generate – to bring to your conscious mind – a variety of novel combinations of entities and parts of entities as images. These "images" are prompted by a stimulus that comes either from the world outside or from the inside world (one that you generate and recall) [...] Many of these representations have to be discarded because they are not relevant; but the images are there to choose from [...] The lay term "a very good imagination" really is an effective description of this diversity generating mechanism.[13]

"A very good imagination" can be a catalyst for synthesizing different types of knowledge. For Immanuel Kant the imagination was a faculty of consciousness, an element of all human apprehension. The imagination was a capacity involved in everything from the basic perception of objects to an engagement with an entirely immaterial knowledge. Trying to construct an overall picture of human knowing in his *Critique of Pure Reason* (1781) and *Critique of Judgment* (1790), Kant saw the imagination functioning to mediate between cognition and experience as different orientations towards the world. He thought that it was possible to work the material of experience from its diverse elements into something known. It was a function of the imagination to mediate between concepts and intuition, subject and object, thought and sensibility.[14] Kant's insight allowed for a synthetic formation of knowledge – a bringing together of diverse forms and appearances, as well as an ability to relate to them. Such a dynamic framing of the imagination had a clear and compelling articulation of how various essential elements of the imagination could relate dynamically one to one another, thus facilitating a much richer understanding of consciousness.

Kant's views raised in my mind the question of how could magical consciousness articulate within such a synthetic conception of knowledge? In order to address this question it is necessary to backtrack a little to consider methodological, theoretical and historical issues.

## A BRIDGE OF COMMUNICATION

An essential feature of my fieldwork has been to create a "bridge of communication" between practitioners of various forms of magic and academic discourse on magic in the belief that such a bridge could deepen knowledge of this complex subject and enrich our

---

12. *Ibid.*
13. Damasio 2001: 65.
14. Gibbons 1994: 1–2.

understanding. When I first started fieldwork with British magicians my aim was to create a bridge between the two very different worlds of scholarly critical analysis, on the one hand, and the magical panorama of my informants, on the other. I wanted to make one explicable to the other, and vice versa. Social scientists have described magic in various derogatory ways. For example, Edward Tylor in *Primitive Culture* (1871) saw magic as "the most pernicious delusion that ever vexed mankind". James Frazer thought that magic was a "pseudo-science"; it tried to do what science did, but failed because it was based on false premises. Sigmund Freud thought there was a parallel between primitive magical beliefs and neurotic and infantile delusions, and Émile Durkheim viewed magic as a negative and private activity opposed to public religion. By contrast to these earlier views, my aim was to open up a different dimension of scholarly examinations of magic. I wrote an encyclopaedia on magic and witchcraft, a book that attempted to make anthropological ideas on this subject more accessible for contemporary Western practitioners of magic, as well as for a general audience.[15] My bridging work continues in a forthcoming book on Magical Consciousness as an explication of the fundamental conceptual and experiential aspects of thinking magically, guided by the spirit of anthropology as a "sustained and disciplined inquiry into the conditions and potentials of human life".[16] In this work I found it possible to imagine an interactive space of magical consciousness where communication with imaginal entities might occur through my own research experience.

In order to fully understand what I was experiencing, I searched for theories that could help me to explain magical consciousness as an aspect of the imaginal mind in which meanings were felt rather than reasoned. But I had to apprehend the meanings first; this is why I started analysing my own childhood experiences of magic. In other words, I had to return to being a native. From this perspective it seemed that the dragon was speaking to me of another mode of being, one that was individual as well as connecting with what felt like a universal energy. At one and the same time, the dragon is specific to each life experience, as well as having significance to wider social, cultural and cosmological contexts.

The dragon appears in all sorts of places, cross-culturally and through time. In China the creature is called *lung*; Hawaii, *kelekona* or *moʻo*; Croatia and Serbia, *zmaj*; Finland, *lohikaarme*; Poland, *smok*; Turkey, *ejderha*; Hungary, *sarkany*; Japan, *tatsu*; Wales *draig*; Germany, *lindwurm*; Holland, *draak*; for the Maori of New Zealand, *tarakona*; the Lakota Sioux, *unhcegila*; and for the Cherokee Indians, *unktena*.[17] The word for dragon in Anglo-Saxon or Old English is *wyrm*, in Old High German it is *wurm*, whereas in Old Norse it is *ormr*. Frequently the meaning of the term *dragon* relates to serpents, worms and snakes and these creatures appear to be interchangeable with one another. A winged serpent, the dragon generally lives underground in a cave and it is seen to be symbolic of the elements earth, air, fire and water, as well as spirit.

Essentially an elemental force of nature, the dragon appears in different shapes and forms. The dragon is both a universal and a highly specific symbol, a condensation of

---

15. Greenwood [2001] 2011.
16. Ingold 2011: 3.
17. Jones 2000: 2–3.

varied human experiences with the natural world. In Australasia rainbow serpents are often considered to be spirits protecting the land and appear frequently in creation myths. Likewise, the lizard-like *moʻo* of Hawaii are guardians of lakes and rivers, while the *Apep*, is an Egyptian serpent of darkness, thunderstorms, lightning and whirlwinds. A changeable being, the dragon is often portrayed with a horse's head and a snake's tail; alternatively, it has a camel's head, stag's horns, eyes of a demon, neck of a snake, belly of a clam, carp scales, eagle claws, soles of a tiger, and the ears of a cow.[18] Chameleon-like, the dragon seems to change from creature to creature, transmuting into many things.

Dragons are mythical beasts – they are the mainstay of many fantastic encounters in popular culture through the ages: in stories, legends, folktales, film, fiction and theatre. In Western cultures, dragons have come to be seen as evil, representing adversity, the senses and sexuality. Conversely, in Chinese traditions they represent the creativity and destruction of life. Chinese philosopher Hwai Nan Tsze, who died in 122 BCE, called the dragon the origin of all creatures. The dragon has been described as "the animating principle of every place – the *genius loci* of trees and rocks, of pools, rivers, mountains and seas, of bridges and buildings, of men, women and children".[19] The Chinese cultural understanding of dragons is more in tune with how I came to understand my experience of the dragon as a metaphor or symbol of an elemental feeling about nature, such as my childhood experience with the rock pools on the beach.

Having explored my own relationship with magical consciousness through the dragon, I started my anthropological examination with Lévy-Bruhl's notion of *participation*, a social psychological perception of the world based on a mystical mentality, "the emotional association between persons and things in contact with a non-ordinary spirit reality".[20] This definition seemed to address the emotion and imagination of my childhood dragon encounter. Everyone's experience of the dragon is varied: the creature's very mutability (its ability to change and shift its very being) lends itself to many interpretations. My intuitive feelings were that the dragon was about changing perception from everyday common sense to participatory magical consciousness. An example of my own participatory experience that I recall was an occasion when a friend and I were talking about magic as we walked by a flowing stream close to her cottage in the Brecon Beacons, one of the sources of the River Taff in Wales. As we reached a few trees by the side of the stream, I stopped to look at the beautiful reflection that the tree branches and the sky made in the water – at that moment the depths of the water, with its little rushing eddies over the stones of the river bed, combined with the sun and the white clouds in the blue summer sky. All formed part of a pattern of participation – the sky was mirrored in the water and they intermingled in my imagination. My friend threw a stick into the stream for her dog to fetch and instantly the pattern broke into a myriad of shimmering fragments. Ripples formed from the point where the stick hit the water and gradually spread out, forming another pattern, until the waters regained their own momentum and the reflections of the

---

18. de Visser 2008 [1913]: 70.
19. Huxley 1989: 5–6.
20. Cited in Tambiah 1990: 91.

clouds reappeared in the river. Watching the movement of the ripples on water, I realized that seemingly ordinary moments like these could take me into magical consciousness through participation with the tree, sky, water, river bed, sun, the ripples, my friend, the dog, the stick and all the feelings and connections with this myriad of kaleidoscopic imaginal associations in time.

I can sum up this experience as the dragon; it was similar to the feeling that I had as a child looking into the rock pool on the beach when I felt my awareness expanding many years ago. First I had the participatory experience of being connected to the moment in time when my friend threw the stick for her dog, or the recollection of a child looking into the rock pool watching the sea anemones on the beach; and then that feeling was associated with an awareness of the dragon, almost as a form of shorthand for a multiplicity of feelings, most of which seemed inexpressible through words. I came to understand magical consciousness as a faculty of human awareness that could connect with spirit through the imagination. This occurred primarily through emotion and intuition, and then secondarily through symbols and metaphor as a condensation of relevant meanings and associations. Such participatory associations between the individual and an inspirited cosmos can also be understood psychologically though Jung's notion of synchronicity whereby relationships are based on causally unrelated events of spirit coming together in a meaningful way.[21] The notion of synchronicity does not challenge anthropological analysis or causality, but reveals the different *modus operandi* of magical consciousness.

## A WIDENING ORIENTATION

If magical consciousness is a human faculty understood anthropologically and psychologically, it also seemed that the perspective of human physiology might offer an illuminating biological insight. In physiological terms, magical consciousness, as a participatory awareness, equates with the workings of the right hemisphere of the human brain. The right hemisphere has a wide take on the world, compared to the narrow categorizing focus of the left hemisphere. Both hemispheres are involved with all the brain's functions, such as emotion, reasoning, visual imagery and mathematical thinking, but they have different orientations.[22] This process has come to be seen as more flexible than earlier formulations,[23] where the left and right hemispheres were seen to function more independently of one another. The right hemisphere is dominant in shape-shifting – for example, when a shamanic practitioner "becomes" her spirit guide in her imagination. Practitioners of magic – whether shamans, spirit mediums, medicine people, witch doctors or Western druids – develop the right hemisphere as a mode of consciousness for the instrumental practice

---

21. Jung 1960: 417–519.
22. McGilchrist 2011: 1068–1069; see McGilchrist 2009. See also "Jill Bolte Taylor's Stroke of Insight", TED talk, http://www.ted.com/talks/jill_bolte_taylor_s_powerful_stroke_of_insight.html, posted March 2008, accessed 21 August 2011.
23. Ornstein 1977.

of magic to effect change. The two orientations arising from the two hemispheres function interchangeably, and with experience the move from one to the other can become fluid.[24]

Recently, I was walking along the beach, near the same beach where I experienced the sea dragon in a rock pool as a small child, and I was drawn to a strangely shaped stone that looked like a dragon's head. The stone took my attention. I picked it up, looked at it, and then put it back without further reference. Sitting down to look at the sea, my hand rested on the beach and my fingers touched a stone. Lifting it up, I saw to my surprise that I had picked up the same stone. This time I noticed that there was a segmented pattern that threaded around one half of the dragon's head, covering one eye and reaching around half of the pebble. Perhaps it was a fossilized prehistoric sea creature – a sea dragon. Yet again, I put it back among the millions of other stones in that particular area of beach and admired the lapping of the waves as they glinted in the sun. Eventually, as I got up to leave, something drew me back again to the dragon stone. Taking it up yet again, I examined its shape and looked at its two halves. I realised that the stone seemed to represent different orientations of the two hemispheres of the brain in my imagination: one of the wide, participatory dragon of magical consciousness, understood primarily through the brain's right hemisphere; and the other the more focused and analytical thinking of the left hemisphere. As I turned the stone in my hand, I found that I could move between the two dimensions in my awareness. I was struck by the thought that if I could learn to utilize this fluidity of thinking more generally, then it might lead me to other dimensions of experience that went beyond my everyday thinking.

One conclusion from the above experience is that my childhood relationship with the dragon can be seen as communication with an imaginal spirit entity. This raised the anthropological dilemma of a belief in spirits – they might exist in the imagination, but not in reality. I found that developing the concept of magical consciousness could overcome the difficulty:

> When a person is "in" that part of their awareness [magical consciousness] it makes no difference whatsoever if they believe in spirits, or if spirit communications are labelled as psychological – if they are explained as a part of their own internal thought processes – or whether they think the entities with which they are communicating are independent of them and have a being of their own. Whilst participating in a magical aspect of consciousness the question of belief is irrelevant: "belief" is not a necessary condition to communicate with an inspirited world.[25]

Questions of belief or the reality or non-reality of spirits, while interesting in principle, can be a straitjacket for an alternative perception afforded by communication with non-material entities. The issue is one of a different perception afforded by magical consciousness. Western cultural history has made an examination of magical experience rather problematic, and it is necessary to consider some historical implications that have impeded such an approach.

---

24. Greenwood 2009: 139–41.
25. *Ibid.*: 140.

## THE SPLIT BETWEEN SPIRIT AND MATTER

As we have seen, magical consciousness has a holistic engagement with material and non-material realities; but historically the splitting of spirit and matter, and the corresponding separation between mind and body, has largely precluded further exegesis of a part of human experience. In general scientific terms, we tend to see consciousness as a product of the brain; but magical consciousness is concerned with a widening rather than a narrow orientation. Historically, since Descartes associated mind with individual human reasoning, mind has been located in the brain. Descartes claimed that the human body (as opposed to the human mind), acted from mechanical instinct like animals. Putting an emphasis on reason as the basis of analytic knowledge, he argued that truth was derived from rational reflection rather than from the untrustworthy senses. By contrast, the body was material and part of the mechanistic universe; it had no soul and no consciousness, being under the control of its emotions and external stimuli. A soul without a body would have consciousness, but only of innate ideas lacking sensory impressions of the world.[26] Descartes's philosophy was highly influential and it was forged out of his attempts to understand the world upon certainties of geometrical reasoning. Descartes's work contributed to the mathematization of the world picture, and his mechanical philosophy marked a definite break with the past and set the seal upon how science would come to be seen.[27]

Descartes's legacy was the separation of spirit (mind) from matter, and this notion has had an abiding influence on Western culture – it is thought, rather than experience of the senses, that is valued. The valuing of reason over experience has hampered an understanding of the experience of magic. The Cartesian legacy has shaped Western notions of science; its rationalism is still evident in anthropological thinking today. Magic is now contrasted with the Western style of thought that firmly locates knowledge of the world in science. In the seventeenth century, during what has come to be termed the Scientific Revolution, the practical experimental aspects of magic were absorbed into science, while spiritual features of magic were denounced as irrational. The shift from a magical view, in which there was no division between spirit and matter, to the rational pursuit of science largely instigated by the adoption of a Cartesian worldview entailed the material and immaterial aspects of natural philosophy becoming separated. Prior to the rise of the Cartesian perspective, the prevailing natural philosophy had been a complete system that incorporated spirit and matter – with disciplinary traditions ranging from astronomy, mechanics, anatomy, medicine, metaphysics, pharmacology, cartography, mining and metallurgy to optics, music and physiology, amongst others – that aimed to describe the entire system of the world.[28]

The scientific worldview developed partly out of a wedding of a rationalizing natural philosophy and the pragmatic and empirical tradition of sympathetic magic. Natural philosophy, as defined by Galilei Galileo (b. 1564; d. 1642), an Italian physicist, astronomer

---

26. Morris 1991: 6–14.
27. Henry 1997: 4.
28. *Ibid.*: 43–44, 172.

and philosopher, Auguste Comte (b. 1798; d. 1857), a French philosopher, and the English naturalist Charles Darwin (b. 1809; d. 1882), concerned a pursuit of objective knowledge of phenomena.[29] Magic, on the other hand, was chiefly concerned with exploiting the sympathies and antipathies between corresponding things. Based on an assumption that certain things had hidden or occult powers to affect other things, sympathetic magic was dependent upon a profound knowledge of how to use these powers to achieve a desired outcome. A reforming rationalizing natural philosophy denounced magic and at the same time took what was useful. Francis Bacon was one of the first natural philosophers to advocate the experimental method as the most reliable way of acquiring knowledge of the natural world. Rationalist and speculative natural philosophy and experimental natural magic had once been completely separate traditions; but Bacon advocated the use of the experimental method of the magician in a reformed natural philosophy. The supposedly good ideas in magic were incorporated within the reformed natural knowledge, while the "bad" ideas were used to denounce magic as "a sink of false and ludicrous beliefs".[30]

Yet, magical traditions played an important part in the major shift from scholastic natural philosophy to the new more practically useful empirical natural philosophy of the Scientific Revolution. As historian John Henry notes: "The history of magic since the eighteenth century has been the history of what was left of that tradition after major elements of natural magic had been absorbed into natural philosophy."[31] Natural magic disappeared from the Western conception of magic due to its most fundamental aspects having been co-opted. This eventually had a major impact upon how magic is now conventionally viewed in academia. During this period the course was set for the advancement of causal logic over magical thinking, and these ideas reached their full expression during the eighteenth-century Enlightenment, a time when occult phenomena were no longer significant as a form of explanation and were deemed mere superstition, a relic of a dark and primitive past. As the term suggests, during the period an attempt was made to shed greater light on the conduct of human affairs: the perceived dark mysteries of traditional attitudes in religion and political life were pushed back, and in their place a new outlook grew up, informed by reason and the power of scientific research and discovery.[32] God was seen as having created the world as a perfect rational machine. Humans could become part of rationality through the knowledge of the self-perfection of God's design; if God's laws of nature were rational, then it was through reason that people could discover them. The global effort of the Enlightenment was to explain other religions as false, and the beliefs of other societies were seen as primitive, backward and unenlightened.

In some respects, these attitudes still linger and they are reflected in a general distrust of the experience of magic. A focus of my work has been on reconciling the historical split that has reduced magic to only its material effects. For social scientists to fully address the question of "what is magic?", it is necessary to go beyond the rationalizing tendency of

---

29. Faivre 1989: 24.
30. Henry 2002: 5, 64, 79.
31. Henry 1997: 42.
32. Ibid.: 19–20.

some perspectives. It is vital that we do not limit our understanding of magic to observable material or cultural manifestations – such as, for example, the effect that beliefs in magic have on psychological and social life. Including an experiential perspective allows the possibility for a non-material imaginal dimension to be considered as part of a wider discussion of magic, and this helps to heal the historical split between spirit and matter.

## A TOTAL FIELD OF RELATIONS

Returning to the issue of magical consciousness, I sought a more inclusive approach for the examination of imaginal experience. As we have seen, social scientific views of individual consciousness tend to be limited in their scope to brain activity; but if the concept of "mind" is extended to body–mind, it overcomes the Cartesian division between body and mind. Further, if body–mind is defined as the personal aspects of individual process, and "consciousness" as an intrinsic quality of the wider universe of which individual body–mind is but one part, then body–mind and consciousness are linked. If consciousness is more broadly defined as wider than the individual human body–mind, then that body–mind might be shared with other beings. If we understand these other beings as spirits that have a different order of existence than the material dimension of reality, or are invisible but nonetheless real dimensions of material reality, then it is possible to take the view that these beings also have body–mind when they "inhabit" a physical being.

If we entertain the proposition that during an experience of magical consciousness spirits share a degree of corporeal materiality and possess mind, then the minds of entities – in whatever form – and ours can meet in a wider consciousness.[33] This was a view common before Descartes, and one that the eighteenth-century poet and artist William Blake tried to re-invoke. The view that all of life is infused with spirit, soul and consciousness was common in the ancient world prior to the dawning development of the rationalizing scientific worldview of Blake's time. Aristotle (384–322 BCE), for example, thought the soul was equivalent to psyche – it was the "principle of life" that animates. It is only relatively lately that psychology has developed as a discipline to study psyche in the human head, for originally psyche was considered much more widely as inherent in all things. Blake, for example, envisioned a world in which every creature was an inspired person living within the total freedom of its Imagination.[34]

Taking a similarly synthetic view, Gregory Bateson, in his characteristically bold way, saw such an interactive space in nature. He argued that the body, the mind and the whole ecosystem was linked within a meta-pattern or a "dance of interacting parts (only secondarily pegged down by physical limits)".[35] Bateson, a holistic thinker, saw the mind as being a part of nature. In *Mind and Nature: A Necessary Unity* (1985), he tried to understand an integrated world and sought to find a language of relationship with which to communicate.

---

33. Bateson 2000: 467; see also Greenwood 2005: 97.
34. Raine 1991: 11–12.
35. Bateson 1985: 22.

Thinking that logic was not suitable for the description of biological patterns, he turned to metaphor as the language of nature. Seeking an "ecological epistemology" in *Angel's Fear* (1987) and "A sacred unity" (1991), he tried to build a bridge of communication between all branches of the world of experience – intellectual, emotional, observational, theoretical, verbal and wordless.[36] Bateson was interested in cybernetics, the science of communication in machines and living beings. He looked at the nature of mental processes and the relationship of communication between thought and the material world in terms of interconnection and interdependence of ecosystems.

My work on contemporary Western pagans' notions of nature has been shaped by Bateson's theory of consciousness and its challenge to the Enlightenment's separation of mind from nature.[37] Tim Ingold also takes his cue from Bateson when he discusses a worldview envisaged from within a "total field of relations whose unfolding is tantamount to the process of life itself".[38] Both Bateson and Ingold see the mind as immanent in the whole system of the organism–environment,[39] and continuing in this vein, my aim is to try to analyse mind, as "body–mind", through a process of interconnection with nature and the inspirited imagination of magical consciousness as a legitimate source of knowledge.

## A LEGITIMATE SOURCE OF KNOWLEDGE

Using my childhood experience with the sea dragon may seem a far stretch to some who might still be concerned with the subjective encroaching into theoretical and methodological social scientific discourse. But it is a highly pertinent example as my aim is to show how magical consciousness is an intrinsic human experience. Magic is at the heart of anthropology in terms of the issues it raises in relation to people's lived realities and the meaning of science. However, for any change of anthropological understanding to occur, magical consciousness needs to be recognized as a universal mode of perception. Although there have been academic approaches, such as phenomenology, that seek to ameliorate the problem, the separation of spirit from matter has left a world that is largely de-spirited, and this has corresponded with the development of science as a rationalistic pursuit that largely renders invisible magical consciousness.

In order to examine magical consciousness, I sought a broader and more inclusive scientific framework, one that not only could include an in-depth analysis of the process of magical experience, but also allow for a fresh and experientially based exploration of the reality of spirits. Essentially, what was required was a model that would recombine the disparate elements of knowledge, thus overcoming the historical fragmentation that had started during the seventeenth-century Scientific Revolution. To this end, I employed Geoffrey Samuel's *multimodal framework*, a descriptive model that features the metaphor

---

36. Bateson 1991: 231–32. Cited in Harries-Jones 2002: 3–9, 15.
37. Greenwood 2005.
38. Ingold 2001: 13–19.
39. Greenwood 2005: 9–10, 89–97, 116, 136–38, 166, 197.

of a web as an integrated conceptual space for all knowledges, including magical, each bringing a nuanced and enriching perspective.[40] Space prevents an explication here; but I have discussed the use of this framework more fully elsewhere.[41] Within the integrative approach put forward by Samuel, I sought to articulate the concept of multiple conceptions of reality. I adopted and developed Gregory Bateson's two pivotal notions of *ideation* and *abduction* to further explore magical consciousness. Ideation is a concept for constructing mental patterns, the term coming from "ideate", to imagine and conceive ideas in the mind. Abduction, on the other hand, is the intuitive process of reasoning through metaphors, of recognizing patterns in dreams, parable, allegory, poetry, even the whole of science and the whole of religion.[42] In this way we can see knowledge as patterns of understanding, and as patterns for understanding in complex global situations where many varieties of magical, religious, political, developmental and institutional ideologies come into play.

Applying the above notions of multiple conceptions of reality to the subject of spirits, it is possible to see how a rationalistic orientation, in which spirits do not exist, can be examined *alongside* a magical consciousness orientation with its inspired worldview. The purpose is to consider how we might understand and apply these different perspectives in a new way. The analytical focus and the magical focus in this framework are presented as two patterns of knowledge that need not be seen as mutually exclusive systems of understanding separated by belief or non-belief in spirits.

| Ideation | Abduction |
|---|---|
|  | **Analytical orientation:** |
|  | • I stand outside myself observing child's imagination. |
|  | • Spirits do not exist except as believed in individual psychology. |
|  | • Theorization and categorization. |
|  | • Domain of left-brain hemisphere. |
| "Becoming a sea dragon" | **Magical consciousness:** |
|  | • Domain of right-brain hemisphere. |
|  | • Spirits exist. |
|  | • Consciousness and imagination is wider than the individual. |
|  | • Expansive sense of energy. |
|  | • I become sea dragon. |

The table in this chapter shows how magical consciousness can become one aspect of multiple orderings of reality and thus have a place as a legitimate form of knowledge within a synthetic view of science. It demonstrates how we can hold both perspectives if we shift

---

40. Samuel 1990.
41. See Greenwood 2009: Chapter 9.
42. Bateson 1985: 153.

between the analytical mode and the focus that acknowledges our native experience. We do not necessarily have to choose one or the other. It is possible to accommodate both aspects and then apply whichever is the most appropriate at any given point in time, or for any specific situation. Thus, a rationalistic orientation, in which spirits do not exist, can be examined alongside a magical orientation with its inspirited worldview. The purpose is to consider how we might understand and apply these different approaches in a new manner. This model might help to explain how people can come to hold together and at the same time what might appear to be conflicting beliefs in both "science" and "magic".

## CONCLUSION

Magical consciousness is experienced in varying ways and to different degrees; it is shaped and developed cross-culturally through varying philosophies, worldviews, life-worlds and cosmologies. The lived experience of magic is formalized into a variety of expressions, but underlying all the diversity is the common human propensity to think magically – to participate in an imaginal consciousness. Magic is as personal as it is universal. Magic is deep rooted in the human mind, and experiences such as my encounter with the sea dragon are just one example of how the imagination comes to shape magical consciousness. What is required is a corresponding attitude towards the study of magic, one that breaches the historical divide between magic and science, enabling magic to be viewed within an integrative conception of science. The model that I am proposing explains how magical consciousness, as one aspect of human experience, is neither rendered invisible, nor does it threaten canons of reason, rationality and analysis. The use of this model not only validates an important area of study that cannot otherwise be readily examined, but it also helps to explain how changing, diverse and contradictory beliefs can be held at the same time in increasingly complex global contexts.

## ACKNOWLEDGEMENTS

My thanks go to Brian Bates for reading earlier drafts of this chapter and for offering critical comment and support. I am particularly grateful for the opportunity to present two keynote lectures on magical consciousness that helped to develop my thinking. The first was to the Danish Ethnographic Society/Anthropologist Society Annual Meeting, University of Copenhagen, Denmark in November 2007; and the second to "Rethinking Shamanism: Perceptions of Body and Soul in Multidimensional Environments" NORDIC Network for Amerindian Studies, Research Seminar, Kastrup, Denmark, on 27 May 2010. I would like to thank Lise Paulsen Galal and Maruska Mosegaard, and Hanne Veber, respectively. Appreciation is also due to Sophia Wellbeloved for the chance to present "Threads of the spider's web: New patterns for exploring magic and science" to the Legitimate Forms of Knowledge? Research Seminar for the Cambridge Centre for Western Esotericism at Girton College, Cambridge University on 14 May 2010.

# 22

# CHRISTOPHER I. LEHRICH

"Magic in Theoretical Practice"

Christopher I. Lehrich is an American historian of religions. In 2003, he published a monograph on Heinrich Cornelius Agrippa of Nettesheim (see Chapter 8); a book with the title *The Occult Mind: Magic in Theory and Practice* followed in 2007. In *The Occult Mind* he not only discusses the work of some selected early modern "magicians" (i.e., theoreticians of "magic"), but also some of the main interpretations of their work and interpretations of "magic" in general. Lehrich advocates the interdisciplinary study of (early modern) "magic" and engages wide-ranging (cross-cultural but also theoretical) comparisons. His theoretical agenda is mainly inspired by structuralism (Lévi-Strauss) and post-structuralism (Derrida). In his contribution to the present volume, Lehrich acknowledges the persistent need to define "magic" (which "is not 'out there' to find") and he provides his own definition, the form of which is inspired by Geertz's famous definition of "religion". Lehrich defends "magic" as a "generalizable" (but not as a universal) category. He also argues for its distinctiveness from both science (including the humanities) and religion and stands up for the value of comparison both for ethnographic and historical work (against suspicions of ethnocentrism and a naïve focus on emic terminology). Lehrich considers the denial of the category "an ethical problem" and points to the problems of implicitly believing that "our" discourses are fundamentally different from those of the people whom we study.

## MAGIC IN THEORETICAL PRACTICE

> **Magic, n.** An art of converting superstition into coin. There are other arts serving the same high purpose, but the discreet lexicographer does not name them.
> Ambrose Bierce, *The Devil's Dictionary*

### I

The present volume may appear to demonstrate that definitions never solve anything. Indeed, it seems remarkably unlikely that arguing about defining magic will ever come to a truly definitive end. But this is rarely a useful standard by which to evaluate scholarly discourse. What is more, the understandable frustration engendered by more than a century of inconclusive debate serves all too often as an excuse for jettisoning the project, which merely substitutes a *de facto* end for an intelligible one. And I shall later suggest that this substitution passes off mystification as rigour.

Looking back, the history of these definitions manifests itself, above all, in a remarkable flexibility of thought. One constantly finds scholars reaching out beyond the normative boundaries of fields and disciplines. It is as though magic, because nobody can ever quite pin it down, prompts the thinker to grasp at links and connections that go against the grain of scholarly practice. The study of magic has thus been interdisciplinary *avant la lettre*.

Yet, now that "interdisciplinary" has already begun to wane as an academic buzzword, replaced by such corporate-inspired variants as "linkages" and "synergies", this older suppleness of discourse has declined. In many ways the current mild rigidity reflects the past generation of scholarship in religious studies, which has so often tried to dislocate itself into other disciplines (anthropology, history, philosophy, area studies) in order to exorcize a demonized theology from our own. Pragmatically, it is true that study of magic is less respectable than in the past, largely because we have lost the claim to legitimacy through distancing: time was, you could study magicians if you made clear that they were laughably wrong. And, though it may be unfashionable to mention this, the discomfort with study of magic arises from a new uncertainty, in that nobody imagined Frazer actually *practising* magic; but these days your new junior colleague might be a witch.

As a result of these factors, and others I shall not enumerate, study of magic spends a good deal of time trying to legitimate itself by academic "in-group" posturing. Instead of challenging other areas by being more-interdisciplinary-than-thou, as in the past, we repeatedly ape fashions in scholarly rigour already long in the tooth. It has been some time since "the problem of insider/outsider discourse" was a burning topic in the study of religion, so it is sadly unsurprising to find the question surfacing more recently in the study of magic, esotericism or occultism. Surely scholars in this field ought not to perform textual secret handshakes!

I have elsewhere argued that study of magic requires a generous interdisciplinarity, not only in surface approaches but in deeper theoretical engagement.[1] Unfortunately, interdisciplinary definitions are a tricky sort of thing.

II

If debating definitions achieves anything, it forces to consciousness layers of presupposition that underlie scholarly work. Serious scholarship is relentlessly self-critical and reflexive, and definitions are an especially powerful locus for such labours.

---

1. Lehrich 2008: 252–66.

The proposals in the present volume, however, reveal that a useful definition is more about scholarly positioning than about whatever we might usually wish to call data. After all, if every definition in this book were taken entirely on board, what would *not* fall under our gaze in the study of magic? At base, study of magic (as, indeed, of religion) is more a question of how we go about things than of the data examined.[2] A definition must therefore serve as a jumping-off point for critical reflection that at the same time affords a basis for debating particular data.

In what follows, then, I attempt a definition-sketch of this kind. In the interests of clarity, let me note that I take for granted that there is no difference in principle between Agrippa's and Mauss's definitions of magic. After all, if a useful definition of magic concerns approaches to people who perform magic in verbal, textual, gestural and any other media, what precisely distinguishes "them" from "us"? Is not a definition of magic an act thereof? Still, for clarity's sake, this definition ought to be couched in an academic jargon rather than another idiom.

Without further ado, then, and without undue apology to Clifford Geertz, magic is:

1. a generalizable category of symbolic behaviour and belief;
2. properly definable in relation to either or both of science and religion;
3. whose contours can be determined inductively;
4. from ethnographic data; and
5. from historical evidence.

## A generalizable category of symbolic behaviour and belief

The great difficulty of generalizable categories is that generalization requires means that can be evaluated rigorously. Methods for achieving this are always contested and in Western intellectual history tend to get caught up in philosophical arguments about scientific knowledge. Rather recently, it has become fashionable on this basis to discard the whole problem: only positivists and materialists make claims to scientific knowledge. But this is to ignore more fundamental difficulties.

Part of the rejection of generalizable definition arises from confusion between *general* and *universal*. It should by now be clear that *universal* definitions of magic are impossible, for somewhat the same reasons as are universal definitions of religion or science. Such categories are historically contingent and in our usage necessarily arise, in the first instance, from the political-intellectual history of early modern Europe. Magic, science and religion do not exist as objects "out there" that need only be recognized, but are rather constructed by us, for our purposes. But when rejection of *universal* definitions becomes a justification for discarding *generalizing* ones, we have no means by which to use any categories of this kind, for any purposes whatever. Comparison becomes, in principle, impossible – and by the same token, so does interpretation.[3]

---

2. At least in the study of religion, this is hardly a novel argument.
3. I set aside here the logical point that generalization is inevitable, which is not true of universalizing claims.

Consider Clifford Geertz's spirited attacks on Claude Lévi-Strauss about this issue. In his account, "Lévi-Strauss generalizes [Boas's] permutational view of thinking to savage thought in general."[4] For Geertz, this generalization is unacceptable: "even if there are not many 'true savages' out there any more, there are enough vividly peculiar human individuals around to make any doctrine of man which sees him as the bearer of changeless truths of reason – an 'original logic' proceeding from 'the structure of the mind' – seem merely quaint, an academic curiosity." After all, "however much it is set round with symbolic logic, matrix algebra, or structural linguistics, can we […] still believe in the sovereignty of the intellect?"[5] Lévi-Strauss's would-be scientific approach generalizes the particular details of particular individuals and groups by framing them within a purely intellectual context: "anthropology is [in this view] only apparently the study of customs, beliefs, or institutions. Fundamentally it is the study of thought."[6] For Geertz, then, "Lévi-Strauss has made for himself […] an infernal culture machine. It annuls history, reduces sentiment to a shadow of the intellect, and replaces the particular minds of particular savages in particular jungles with the Savage Mind immanent in us all."[7]

But recall Geertz's own moves to generalization. To take an especially famous example, Geertz, at the end of "Deep play: Notes on the Balinese cockfight", draws a comparison between cockfighting and *Macbeth* on the principle that, in either case, one has a theatrical spectacle through which one encounters, and thus has the opportunity imaginatively to grapple with, "life as the Balinese most deeply do not want it".[8] What precisely validates this comparison? Must we have impressionistic aesthetic generalization in place of a method that strives for rigour? If Lévi-Strauss does not fully succeed in constructing a scientific mode of comparative analysis, should we substitute an entirely subjective method and claim that this cleaves more faithfully to our sources – and is somehow "science"?[9]

A similar problem arises in early modern occult philosophies, as witness the famous acrid debate between Johannes Kepler and Robert Fludd.[10] Fludd attacked Kepler while defending William Harvey on the grounds that their scientific achievements validated the total Hermetic-Paracelsian system of Christian knowledge that Fludd understood himself to be (re)discovering; his objection to Kepler was that the latter denied this interpretation. Livid, Kepler insisted that his work was rigorously mathematical, a system of precise logical inferences, based on repeatable calculations, using the finest observational

---

4. Geertz 1973a: 353.
5. *Ibid.*, 359.
6. *Ibid.*, 352.
7. *Ibid.*, 355.
8. Geertz 1973b: 446. The remark is adapted from a comment by Northrop Frye on *King Lear*.
9. It is sometimes forgotten that Geertz described the study of culture as one that "asserts itself to be a science", and, against his contemporaries, said that "I, myself, am not timid about the matter at all." Indeed, he conceived of "thick description" as a move towards scientific understanding: "Thick description: Toward an interpretive theory of culture", in Geertz 1973b: 24.
10. On the Kepler–Fludd debate, see Pauli 1955: 147–240. On Kepler's thought, see especially Stephenson 1994. Frances Yates's brief account is principally remarkable for what it reveals about her peculiar vision of science, early modern and contemporary: Yates 1964: 403–7. For the connection of these issues to Newtonian gravitation, see Hutchison 1982: 233–53.

data available. To link such science with mystical speculations about Pythagorean tuning and alchemical imagery was simply ludicrous in Kepler's view because, at base, a project such as Fludd's required fabricating unwarranted and untestable correspondences between unrelated terms. And, indeed, much the same criticism had been levelled at astrology by Giovanni Pico della Mirandola more than a century earlier.[11]

As the physicist Wolfgang Pauli noted in his seminal essay, however, from an exterior perspective it is difficult to see precisely what distinction Kepler wished to draw here. After all, this great astronomer was deeply invested in Pythagorean integer progressions, spending years trying to make planetary orbits align in a system of nested regular polyhedra. Kepler's Third Law is remarkable not least because, unlike the First and Second, it predicts and describes nothing: it is simply an interesting mathematical relation.[12] And we should not permit Newton's analysis of universal gravitation to distract us from the fact that for Kepler, the laws revealed an *anima motrix*, acting at a distance, which links satellites to the bodies they orbit by means that one can only describe through effects and not mechanisms. As Kepler and Newton recognized, this makes the *anima motrix*, or Newtonian gravity, an *occult quality*. The only absolute difference between Kepler and Fludd – and it is an important one – is that Kepler rejected all theoretical justifications or explanations that he could not verify through mathematical analysis of empirical data.

A comparison of the Kepler–Fludd debate to that between Geertz and Lévi-Strauss, if fully drawn, would be extremely revealing, not least because of a certain instability in how one would go about it. For a start, who's who? One could see Geertz as the scientific Kepler, attacking Lévi-Strauss/Fludd for his grandiose pretensions in drawing together every possible form of knowledge into one supposedly self-consistent system. But one could also read Lévi-Strauss as Kepler, with Geertz/Fludd the one who constructs unverifiable correspondences and pretends that they are scientific because of an unsystematic (ab)use of a few isolated facts.

Once we recognize the peculiarity of Kepler as modern scientist, with his astrology, Pythagoreanism, and occult qualities, the whole comparison shifts yet again, becoming rather more revealing for our own methodological difficulties. One can read the Kepler–Fludd division as about the relationship of theory to evidence, with the moral of the story that one should always make theory submit to the absolute dominance of empirical data. But this lesson goes against the historical grain, making Kepler an empiricist of the Baconian stripe. More to the point, Newton was ultimately to demonstrate that strict empiricism of this kind produces bad science because one's data often does not show

---

11. A convenient if problematic account of Pico's critique may be found in Shumaker 1972: 16–27. For more reliable analysis, see the numerous works of Sheila J. Rabin on the subject, e.g., Rabin 2008: 152–78, and Rabin's references.
12. Kepler's First and Second Laws say that (1) planets move along elliptical paths with the sun at one of the two foci, such that (2) a line between a planet and a sun will sweep out equal areas in equal times throughout the orbit. The Third Law, however, says merely that the square of a planet's orbital period [T] is directly proportional to the cube of the mean distance [a] from the sun: i.e., $T^2 = k\,a^3$, where k is a constant, the same for all planets.

what it appears to show, and can only be properly evaluated by being positioned within a theoretical framework.

However we draw the comparison to Geertz and Lévi-Strauss, the currently popular scholarly division between generalization and particularism can only engender sterility. If Geertz rightly insists on scrupulous attention to particular data as it appears on the ground, to what he elsewhere calls "local knowledge", he does not provide a rigorous means of evaluating this data in relation to anything else, leaving particularism in much the same bind as prevented Bacon's empiricism from achieving the results he sought. Yet since categories such as magic and religion do not refer to independent objects, it is not clear whether a generalizing system like Lévi-Strauss's could ever serve the function that mathematics does for Newton, without which one would seem to fall back into Fludd's ever-expanding systems of correspondence.

### … properly definable in relation to either or both of science and religion

Of the many debates about this categorical intersection, that between Robin Horton and Stanley J. Tambiah has had a significant impact across the last generation, and illustrates several core principles of the reigning theoretical orthodoxy. Important dimensions of the questions asked, and the answers proposed, nevertheless reveal gaps that have not received satisfactory attention.

The gist of the debate was straightforward enough, though its intricacies were anything but. Horton (see Chapter 18) compared certain dimensions of African traditional thought and practice to Western science on the grounds that these various systems act as coherent, rational and theoretical modes for interpreting phenomena. This proposal importantly inverts the old Frazer-style comparison, in which magic is ill-conceived and erroneous science: for Frazer (see Chapter 12), the comparison of magic to science reveals the former's weakness and stupidity, whereas for Horton, the same comparison is effectively ennobling, showing that African traditional thought should be taken seriously as an on-going intellectual achievement.

Tambiah's reply challenges Horton on two levels. First, using Evans-Pritchard's famous work on the Azande (see Chapter 16) to exemplify detailed descriptive accounts of African traditional analogical thought and practice, Tambiah argues against the comparison to (Western) science on the grounds that, at a logical level, they operate differently. Second, shifting to a meta-analytical plane, Tambiah attacks the comparison itself: it is not a question of correcting an ill-constructed analogy, but rather that no positive ends are served by making the analogy at all.

Tambiah (see Chapter 19) concludes with a point that has had considerable force in the current rejection of "magic" as a useful, generalizable category:

> By simply naming rituals of non-Western societies as "magic" […] we cannot thereby attribute to the phenomena so named, by virtue of that naming, characteristics that may be peculiar to one's own contemporary civilization. It is only a short step from here to go on to measure these same ritual practices and ideas as

equivalent to, but of course misguided and falling short of, empirical science. It is not that such a perspective is wrong but that it may hide from view the positive, persuasive and creative, though "non-scientific", features of analogical thought and action expressed in magical rites. The dangers of excessive historical universalization should be kept in view.[13]

Here Tambiah makes an important distinction that has often gone unnoticed. To compare magic and science is not *intrinsically* invalid, but the analogy lends itself all too easily to a mode of ethnocentric evaluation that obscures other more interesting dimensions of magic.

In evaluating such a comparison, then, the crucial question is what positive results one achieves in understanding the data compared. What *theoretical* problem is addressed? In Tambiah's reading of Horton or Evans-Pritchard (and *a fortiori* Frazer or Tylor), the point of the comparison ultimately rests on the matter of empirical falsification, by which standard magical rituals fall considerably short of experimental science. Tambiah develops his ideas about illocutionary and perlocutionary speech-acts to shift this ground, in that one cannot appropriately evaluate illocutionary speech-acts in terms of falsification: the speech-act "I now pronounce you man and wife" does not submit to verification in these terms, but must be located contextually and evaluated persuasively. Since modern scientific experiment, by contrast, is not properly evaluated in contextual, persuasive terms, the comparison of magic to science misdirects analytical attention.

Rereading Horton from this perspective, one notes that he seems not to have recognized alternative implications of his own arguments. The first part of his long article on "African traditional thought and Western science" makes a double argument, whereas the second (see Chapter 18) narrows in such a way as to make Tambiah's criticisms devastating. A useful reopening of the "magic, science and religion" question might begin by investigating the omitted layer implicit in Horton's argument.

In the first portion of the paper, Horton refers to science in an unusually restrictive sense, under which the operative term for the comparison to "traditional African religious thinking" is *theory*. By so constricting science, Horton sets aside its practice and institutions, which allows him largely to sidestep the problem of empirical falsification. But this limitation actually widens the comparison: properly speaking, he aims to compare modes of *theoretical thought*, wherever it occurs, focusing in this instance on African-traditional and Western-natural-scientific examples. For instance, Horton illustrates his claim that "theory places things in a causal context wider than that provided by common sense" with the observation:

> To say of the traditional African thinker that he is interested in supernatural rather than natural causes makes little more sense […] than to say of the physicist that he is interested in nuclear rather than natural causes. In fact, both are making the

---

13. Tambiah 1973: 228–29.

same use of theory to transcend the limited vision of natural causes provided by common sense.[14]

Horton's point has wide-ranging application. If we hope to understand the systematic qualities of magical thought, certainly we cannot simply compare at an empirical level to experimental science. Shifting to the theoretical plane, however, resolves this problem by making the objects more properly comparable in their own terms, and furthermore makes the underlying analytical problem a matter of overcoming the strangeness of "a thoroughly unfamiliar idiom".[15]

When all this is granted (and Tambiah does grant it), a new question arises. If we wish to translate an "unfamiliar" theoretical system by means of another better known to us, why privilege the natural sciences? Given that most scholars interested in magic are not deeply knowledgeable about contemporary Western natural science, what makes us choose such science as especially relevant? To some degree, of course, we do so because of a persistent and insidious wish to derogate magic, the other's fallacious knowledge, before our obvious superiority. Tambiah's is among the more effective formulations of this criticism, and I think one cannot but agree that, however unwillingly and unwittingly, Horton, in the second part of his article, falls squarely into that old trap.

But can one be absolutely certain that Tambiah (and even more, those who have used him to argue against all such comparisons – indeed, against the term "magic" as intrinsically pejorative, a falsehood to which Tambiah does not here subscribe) does not in this denial obscure the subscription to a view that Horton had hoped precisely to demystify? Horton's argument would seem to lend itself more directly to a sideways motion: if Western natural science is a poor analogy, what of the Western human sciences?

The absolute refusal to compare theoretical modes is here authorized by a limitation of theory that we would not otherwise accept. Considering just how often contemporary scholars of magic in whatever discipline denounce the scientific pretensions of earlier theorists, it is remarkable to find the same scholars willing to sweep all Western modes of knowledge under the sanitizing carpet of science.

Conversely, Horton's arguments raise the troubling spectre of bi-directional comparison, of the kind Lévi-Strauss sometimes attempted, under which it is not so clear that Western theory would come out the winner. The defence here is an insistence that falsification *must* be the basis of any such comparison. Setting aside the question of whether Western human sciences do so well on this score themselves, it is again remarkable to find critics of reductive, ethnocentric comparisons happily reducing Western science in such a way as to mystify the politics and ideologies of its practice and institutions.

In short, Tambiah's critique should prompt a rethinking of the problems attendant upon comparisons between and among magic, science and religion. Too often, however, it has served to authorize mystifying rejection of a threatening categorical question.

---

14. Horton 1993: 202.
15. *Ibid.*: 200.

## … whose contours can be discerned inductively

Randall Styers (see also Chapter 25) has powerfully demonstrated that definitions of magic have commonly worked to stabilize ideologically motivated claims about religion and science. In short, magic has operated negatively as a contrasting other against which to construct truth. Perhaps the most remarkable point about his compelling argument is that it took so long to get made so clearly – which also goes some way toward demonstrating just how badly theorists want magic to serve as a shadowy proof-text for religion and science.

In fact, the historical moment in which "religion" and "science" were born already contained this pattern. Michel de Certeau's scintillating account of the possessions in 1630s Loudun reveals ways in which elite intellectuals struggled to formulate and stabilize knowledge through their interpretations of the abnormality represented by possession. Certeau labels this process a "teratology of truth":

> If medicine in this period is a philosophical locus, it is because sickness at this time has an essential relationship to truth. The learned who pass judgment on the possession seek not so much to extract the natural from evil and the authentic from deception as to recognize nature (or supernature) in its deformed state, and truth that has become monstrous or erroneous. A bold intent, to be sure; it risks turning into its opposite, for it leads them to ask whether nature is not fundamentally ailing, or whether truth is not an illusion that does not know it. Skepticism creeps in everywhere.[16]

Ultimately, the physicians and exorcists become complicit in a reduction by which the afflicted nuns become *quadrupedia*:

> The physicians seem to forget that they are supposed to give care, it is so important to them to diagnose, and they are so much in demand to "render an opinion". The exorcists give priority to the demonstration the possessed allow them to carry out, rather than to their deliverance. The learned seek to designate what is true more than to eliminate evil. Identification wins out over therapy. The means of healing become the means of knowing.[17]

The same dynamic has often controlled the scholarly study of magic. Tambiah's already-noted remarks on Horton reveal that the question in studying magic is just what positive understanding might be achieved. The teratological discourses of Loudun add a crucial dimension: understanding *of what*? Are we studying magic in order to understand magical data, or to clarify or stabilize our knowledge of something else?

---

16. de Certeau 2000: 123.
17. *Ibid.*

Much of the ethnocentric exoticism of early theorists can be, as Styers shows, read as an effect of their positioning magic as the absolute outside, the radical other of all legitimate thought. This also explains the common theoretical disregard for basic principles of definition, what Jonathan Z. Smith calls the "[repeal of] the law of the excluded middle".[18] For Styers, the history of theoretical interpretations of magic thus reveals a discourse that mystifies itself, a situation in which Western conceptions of knowledge and power have sought to shore themselves up at the expense of that which they claimed to study. But is there no positive here, nothing of value that we might now draw from this history?

The Loudun possessions afford some new possibilities. Most straightforwardly, we ought to avoid complicity in the ways in which the possessions constituted an aberration that shaped the experts' teratology. The experts' tactics aimed "to have the body send back, as if by a mirror, the image of a theoretical knowledge", to achieve which end it was necessary to exclude that which made those bodies *people*. To make the possessed evidentiary for the nascent boundaries of elite knowledge, doctors and exorcists alike treated their bodies as experimental animals, their speech as that of the demonic other.[19] For us to turn away, to reject the whole question of what such people might have wished to *say*, is to accept the dehumanizing classification of the experts. One might recall here Carlo Ginzburg's work on the *benandanti*: to dismiss the matter, on the grounds, for example, that the data is insufficient as well as so grossly biased that effective reconstruction is impossible, is to leave these people where we last saw them – in the hands of the Inquisition.[20] A parallel conclusion can be drawn from Styers's discussion of modern theories about magic. Analysing magic as problematically other, as aberrant (whether because bizarre and superstitious or else a mere categorical imposition by colonialist scholars) serves principally to stabilize our discourses of knowledge – which is to say, always, of *power*. The violence and virulence of such classifications thus makes the currently popular rejection of "magic" as category an ethical problem.

A more interesting possibility, perhaps more fruitful, would follow the tortuous logic of theorists – the doctor at Loudun, the African traditional thinker, the modern interpreter of magic – in their processes of situating particular data in general theoretical frameworks. If Styers and Certeau show examples of such a procedure, they indirectly reveal a vast range of examples to be analysed comparatively. And what is more, by this means one could use "magic" as the other precisely by examining how others have othered it, making "magic" an unusually powerful (because unusually overt) instance of a common trope of power discourses.[21]

---

18. Smith 2004: 215.
19. de Certeau 2000. See also de Certeau 1988: 244–68. In the previous chapter ("Ethno-graphy", pp209–43), Certeau demonstrates the intricate ways in which Jean de Léry's account of the Tupi (1578) already used the figure of the other to frame Western discourses of knowledge, both religious and scientific.
20. See Ginzburg 1983, and especially the "Introduction" to Ginzburg 1989: 1–30.
21. An extraordinary pioneering example of such an interpretation links *mana*, magic and "the heterogeneous": Bataille 1979: 64–87, especially 68–70.

### ... from ethnographic data and ...

For too long it was presumed that ethnographic data must be privileged because it was among "savages" that one found magic, more civilized peoples having largely put such nonsense behind them. The traditional defence of this gesture, once the pseudo-evolutionism of Tylor and Frazer (see Chapters 11 and 12) had begun to recede, was Durkheim's reference to the methodological desirability of simplicity.[22] If the case is simple, he reasoned, it will be easier to see general principles, in much the same way as for Freud or James a psychological extreme makes apparent what is normally occult.

But first of all, magic is never simple for the same reason as culture is never simple. One can say that a given society has more or less complex technologies according to some definable rubric; but there is no warrant for presuming that technological complexity tracks any other sort.[23] As Mircea Eliade noted: "an evolution in the religious phenomenon, from 'simple to complex', [...] is only an undemonstrable hypothesis".[24] More importantly, a methodology making specific facts maximally apparent presumes that there are general magical facts or principles "out there" to find. But as we have seen, there is no reason to think this, and every reason not to.

At issue is the utility of scholarship outside one's narrowly determined academic bailiwick. Since Alan Macfarlane and others first used anthropological theory for help in explaining early modern witchcraft,[25] it has become *de rigeur* for historians of certain stripes to make reference to anthropology in one way or another. Since Stephen Greenblatt and others first drew powerfully on cultural history for understanding literary products, historians and literary critics have had more productive conversations than in the past. But this entails a crucial inverse reflection in that while we gain more "tools" when we reach far afield methodologically, we also take on the histories of those tools. "Magic" is not "out there" to find, but neither, by the same token, can the tendencies or habits of the many relevant academic disciplines be taken as given.

For example, "everyone knows" that magic carries pejorative weight and has constantly underwritten trivializing "others" from within a wide range of Western discourses of power. To speak of magic generally, then, is to perpetuate colonialist categories and assumptions. To speak of magic at all, one must speak of a specific local discourse in which the term – or anyway something that can legitimately be translated thus – is active.

But by this logic, "magic" cannot be spoken of outside the West. How can we translate a term in a non-Western language as "magic" without imposing that category through translation? As already indicated, the extension of this category in the West to touch on such categories as "science" and "religion" entails that their deployment elsewhere

---

22. On Durkheim's "reasons of method" in reference to simplicity, see Durkheim 1995: 3–8.
23. Lévi-Strauss's work should also raise the question of whether myth and magic do not themselves constitute sophisticated technologies at a level far advanced from our own; see particularly *La pensée sauvage*, 1962; the unsigned English translation as *The Savage Mind* is too textually problematic for serious work.
24. Eliade 1970: 12; cf. the translation in *Patterns in Comparative Religion*, trans. Rosemary Sheed 1959: xiv.
25. Macfarlane 1970.

continues the gesture. To speak of "magic, science or religion" in Melanesia is always an act of colonialism.

While there is important truth in this now obvious claim, it has tended to obscure the fact that such colonizing acts cannot be sanitized by repression. To impose "magic" on the Other is not simply destructive because it is properly speaking an attempt at translation – which is to say, always, a *comparison*. Comparison is principally valuable in so far as it subjects both terms to destabilizing critique. Relating "their" categories to "ours" should make us see the ways in which our own categories are unstable. In so far as we claim that such relation is impossible, that nothing of "theirs" could ever be comparable to "our" magic, we thereby claim that our categories are known and theirs forever occult.

A more general dimension of the problem is signalled in modern scholarly discourse, in that mystifying language style we call "jargon", by the constant abuse of the distinction emic/etic, under which *emic* means "from an insider viewpoint" and *etic*, "from an outsider perspective". There is little value in this: one could say "insider" instead of "emic" and nothing much changes. So why do we do it? Is it just showing off, indicating that one is an acad/emic insider, "one of the boys"? Or is it, rather, that this misused distinction acts to mystify the threatening distinction originally aimed at?

Originally, emic and etic extended from the linguistic distinction phonemic and phonetic, linked by André Martinet as "double articulation". Here the word "dog" divides into meaningful phonemes /dɑg/ (doggerel, dogma)[26] and then phonetically into the meaningless [d] [ɑ] [g]. By extension, elements of any symbolic discourse – ritual, myth, conversation, gesture – break into a meaningful *emic* level and subsequently into a purely statistical *etic* one. Much of the original anthropological debate about the utility of this distinction focused on what precisely would constitute the etic, with the general conclusion that the primary worth of statistical etic analysis is how it can, by contrast, provide access into layers of emic meaning. For example, if native understanding of kinship practice contradicts objectively verifiable statistical evidence, this clarifies what elements of native understanding are naturalized symbolic claims.[27]

One problem with magic, then, is that there is in this case no etic, nor can there ever be. In order to label something "magical", one must already participate in a system of meaning-ascription, native or outsider. The same could be said of myth and religion. But where magic differs, it seems, is that practices traditionally labelled thus often make empirically falsifiable claims, which seems to ensure the possibility of etic analysis. Unfortunately, this possibility, when it occurs, only complicates rather than simplifies matters.[28] If certain practices generate falsifiable claims, the problem becomes to identify the means by which such claims are manufactured – how meaningless facts about the natural world become invested with human meaning such that they can be employed in articulate symbolic

---

26. Those sceptical as to the meaningful status of /dɑg/ might try imagining describing a miserly African-American as "niggardly".
27. For a lucid critique of this distinction, see Lévi-Strauss 1985: especially 115–20.
28. It should also be noted that some, most notably Lévi-Strauss, have argued that exactly the same natural limitations bind myth and, to some extent, ritual, making the problem here described of far broader application. See Lehrich 2011: 305–25.

discourse. It has sometimes been claimed that religion is distinctive in making conceptual claims absolutely free of empirical limitation.[29] If this is accepted as a useful definitional criterion, it makes religion rather easier to deal with than magic because metaphysical imagination unfettered by natural law does not need an originary explanation, only one of continuation: the issue is why people believe it, not how they formulated it in the abstract. But when meaningful symbolic statements are composed of natural phenomena, as with much material traditionally labelled "magical", we must explain how statements operate and in what total conceptual system, in addition to why they continue to serve what functions we discern.

As I have argued elsewhere,[30] the core difficulty of purely emic data, as yet unresolved, is that one must situate it within an analytical framework. Even particularist representation does not escape: by narrating emic data one generates further emic data, thereby suppressing the voices of those studied.[31] If, on the other hand, we attempt a more rigorous schematization, the nature of the data interferes. Lévi-Strauss attempted (unsuccessfully, in my judgement) to formulate such a science of meaning, especially in the four-volume *Mythologiques*; but too little of his work has been thought through seriously within the study of magic or religion. And all too often, the dismissal of structuralism rests on a purely illogical claim: Lévi-Strauss attempted science, which we don't believe in, so we continue to impose our meanings over those we study because we have no tools with which to evaluate the divide.

## … from historical evidence.

On the whole, historians have been loose with a good deal of theoretical discourse about magic, which they make up for – as some see it, anyway – by their precision when it comes to local knowledge. In essence, it has become usual to decry generalization as imposition of anachronistic categories and to favour emphasis on "their" categories. A good example appears at the beginning of an important textbook on the history of medieval magic:

> This book will approach magic as a kind of crossroads where different pathways in medieval culture converge. First of all it is a point of intersection between religion and science. Demonic magic invokes evil spirits and rests upon a network of religious beliefs and practices, while natural magic exploits "occult" power within nature and is essentially a branch of medieval science. Yet demonic magic and

---

29. Notably by Rappaport 1999.
30. Lehrich 2011.
31. Michel de Certeau (1988) makes a similar argument in rich, sophisticated terms at several points in *The Writing of History*; see, for example, his discussion of historiography and the discourse of (seeking) origins: "This discourse in its basic definition is *speech* articulated over what else *took place*; its own beginning is one which presupposes a *lost* object; its function is one of being, among human beings, the representation of a primitive scene that is effaces but is still an organizing force. Discourse is incessantly articulated over the death that it presupposes, but that the very practice of history constantly contradicts" (47, emphasis original). Certeau here, as so often, also reminds us that the presupposition of death entails the historian's complicity in it.

natural magic are not always as distinct in fact as they seem in principle. Even when magic is clearly nondemonic it sometimes mingles elements of religion and science.[32]

Theoretically speaking, the intent here is clear: we cannot speak of "magic" as though it were something found universally, but must rather understand it as it manifests within a specific historical domain. Many scholars refer to Michel Foucault in this context, pointing out that, as with sexuality or madness, such categories as "magic" cannot be treated as givens but rather have a history that must be unpacked genealogically. And certainly, without some gesture of this kind, one tends to fall into imposing modern categories on historical data, thereby not only obscuring history but also treating our categories as obvious, true ahistorical realities.

Unfortunately, such gestures all too often get used to discard trans-historical work. Comparisons and generalizations are rejected because they are, in principle, ahistorical. This move deconstructs itself.

For one thing, the quotation above makes a series of generalizations without explanation. Why is it necessary to be historically particular with magic but not religion or science? To say that magic "is a point of intersection between religion and science" presumes that we can, at least in principle, distinguish between religion and science; yet both are recent categories with complex ideological histories. The historian's attempt at rigorous local specificity returns to the issues raised by Styers: analysis of "magic" acts to stabilize "religion" and "science", by contrast.

Another, more serious problem underlies this. For Foucault, the value of recognizing the discursive, constructed nature of a category is to demystify its utility, in reference to not only the past but also our own historical situation. When we accept that sexuality is not given, that "sexuality" in any context always mobilizes a system of ideological constructs, we must grant that the operations of discourses of sexuality today are themselves ideological. Studying the history of sexuality not only interprets how "they" acted, thought or felt, but also *necessarily* works to expose (or conceal) how and why "we" do so.

Just so, any study of magic in history must undertake to expose, at least by differentiation if not by genealogy, uses of "magic" as ideological weapons in contemporary discourses. Legitimate historical study of magic is thus necessarily comparative and generalizing (and *never* universalizing): it always concerns systems of relations between how "they" used it and how "we" do. But with magic, this necessary entailment is commonly rejected, precisely by reference to a Foucaultian insistence on historical construction and specificity.

Commonly allied with this historicist defence mechanism, acting as a supplement in Derrida's sense, are references to what is "current" or "cutting-edge" in anthropology or another allied discipline, as against old-fashioned or dated references to most thinkers in the present volume. To claim superiority on a chronological basis assumes a

---

32. Kieckhefer 1989: 1.

model of progress against which again Foucault would have protested. It also positions "serious scholarship" in opposition to the ideas of those we study: their voices and ideas do not "count" except as data, domesticated products of our objectification. This is usually defended as its reverse: particularism or historicism are used to claim that we take lost or suppressed voices seriously, when in fact by representing "them" we replace their voices with our own. Such a process may perhaps be inevitable; but intellectual imperialism should not be claimed as a weapon of political freedom. Nor, *a fortiori*, should one claim that conquest is necessarily progress. These historicisms use Foucault apotropaically to ward off the curse of anachronism. By denying comparative generalization, the historian defends modern discourse against the past. One notes here the tendency to treat modern theoretical discourse, like that composed by Foucault, as fundamentally different from the discourses we study historically, thereby denying the historical nature of our categories. Ultimately, the refusal of trans-historical comparison on historical grounds amounts to a claim that the historian's gaze is uniquely privileged – what in a different context Nietzsche called "the myth of the immaculate perception".[33]

Foucault was not entirely free from these difficulties, as Derrida noted in reference to the problem of madness: "The attempt to write the history of the decision, division, difference runs the risk of construing the division as an event or a structure subsequent to the unity of an original presence, thereby confirming metaphysics in its fundamental operation."[34] Certainly, there is a risk here – converted into certainty when the division is reified as a difference by a decision to treat "their" discourse as radically other than "ours". The problems of writing a history of what modernity construes as unreason, whether madness or magic, cannot be avoided by nullification.

III

At the outset, I suggested that discarding definition as a project amounts to passing off mystification as rigour. The problem may conveniently be bracketed by Lévi-Strauss and Derrida.

Current refusals to define magic commonly rest on an ethical claim. If we define magic and thereby impose analytical judgement on those we study, we cannot but perpetuate imperialist gestures. By this reasoning, "our attempts to put different societies, including our own, into perspective, are said to be no more than a shamefaced way of admitting its superiority over all the others". But "behind the reasoning of these specious critics", Lévi-Strauss writes, "there is nothing but a bad pun: they try to pass off the mystification (in which they themselves indulge) as the reverse of mysticism (of which they wrongly accuse us)".[35]

---

33. I take Nietzsche's remark (from *Also Sprach Zarathustra*), in the first instance, from Smith 1988: 736.
34. Derrida 1978a: 40.
35. Lévi-Strauss 1992: 385.

Lévi-Strauss makes his point clear in a remarkable passage that deserves full citation:

> If we judge the achievements of other social groups in relation to the kind of objectives we set ourselves, we have at times to acknowledge their superiority; but in so doing we acquire the right to judge them, and hence to condemn all their other objectives which do not coincide with those we approve of [...] To re-establish an objective approach, we must abstain from making judgments of this kind. We must accept the fact that each society has made a certain choice, within the range of existing human possibilities, and that the various choices cannot be compared with each other: they are all equally valid. But in this case a new problem arises: while in the first instance we were in danger of falling into obscurantism, in the form of a blind refusal of everything foreign to us, we now run the risk of accepting a kind of eclecticism which would prevent us denouncing any feature of a given culture – not even cruelty, injustice and poverty, against which the very society suffering these ills may be protesting.[36]

Thus, the refusal to compare, to generalize, to see historical phenomena as instances of anything at all entails that scholarship can legitimately take no ethical position whatever in reference to the achievements or horrors of any society, even our own.

Derrida brilliantly inverts these arguments, extending rather than undermining Lévi-Strauss's (self-)criticisms:

> If one calls *bricolage* the necessity of borrowing one's concepts from the text of a heritage which is more or less coherent or ruined, it must be said that every discourse is *bricoleur*. The engineer, whom Lévi-Strauss opposes to the *bricoleur*, should be the one to construct the totality of his language, syntax, and lexicon. In this sense the engineer is a myth. A subject who supposedly would construct it "out of nothing", "out of whole cloth", would be the creator of the verb, the verb itself. The notion of the engineer who supposedly breaks with all forms of *bricolage* is therefore a theological idea; and since Lévi-Strauss tells us elsewhere that *bricolage* is mythopoetic, the odds are that the engineer is a myth produced by the *bricoleur*.[37]

The danger of using native categories, discerned historically or ethnographically, is that they deceive the scholar into thinking that his own position is effectively distanced from the data. To whatever extent this might be true, the material so reconstructed would by this token be properly etic: it would *lack meaning*. In so far as it is meaningful, the meaning proposed supplants and suppresses the native categories themselves.

One great virtue of Lévi-Strauss was his insistence on using categories disengaged from their positions, like gears removed from a clock. These categories are thus signs that have *had a use*, and carry their history with them, but are at the same time put *to a new use*. Of

---

36. Lévi-Strauss 1992: 385–86.
37. Derrida 1978b: 285.

course, as Derrida points out, this makes of his approach a mode of *bricolage*. But Derrida also notes that an opposed extreme, in which the would-be *ingénieur* attempts a position outside the data from which to construct new categories, leads to sterility if successful and is, in any case, literally unthinkable.

It has too often been thought that a definition of magic must be a stable centre from which to interpret data. But the absolute centring demanded entails a metaphysics in which uncertainty must always be deferred, such that definitions have acted principally to supplement ideological knowledge at the expense of those defined, as the contradictory comparisons to Western science reveal. A proper definition can therefore no longer pretend to universality or its opposite, but must seek a general position within the circle of deferral.

Derrida's formulation deserves careful consideration:

> For my part, although these two interpretations must acknowledge and accentuate their difference and define their irreducibility, I do not believe that today there is any question of *choosing* – in the first place because here we are in a region (let us say, provisionally, a region of historicity) where the category of choice seems particularly trivial; and in the second, because we must first try to conceive of the common ground, and the *differance* of this irreducible difference.[38]

Derrida's argument points in useful directions. We must recognize common ground underlying discourses about magic. To suppose an absolute distinction between our discourses and those we study is already to imagine a universal magic. This commonalty needs genealogical investigation, but also theoretical consideration of "the *differance* of this irreducible difference".

In the end – or *not*. For it is essential not to stop. To conclude discussion as though one had by concluding concluded, come to conclusions. If we conclude that there are no conclusions, then by concluding we mystify uncertainty and pretend for it a basis in certainty and even that scholarly rigour usually called "historical". What I have proposed is nothing but a continuation, not a shift. To continue, not on a new basis, which would, in turn, only occlude, only replace our discourse by displacing it.[39]

Yet, if therefore it seems as though one ought to re-imagine magic such that everything would act without centre, in playful circles of experimental engagement, I at once applaud the move and deplore it. Several recent works summon visions of scholarship in multiple media, mesmerizing hybrids that claim no definite (or defined) foundations, centres, certainties. This is, too, how many contemporary magicians present their work: unstable and destabilizing, flickering and playful. But I agree with Derrida: it is not a matter of choosing.

---

38. Derrida 1978b: 293. Note that Bass renders the French *différance* in italics with French orthography, which to my eye not only undermines Derrida's inverted pun but also hypostatizes the neologism.
39. This is precisely the failure evidenced by the proposed shift to "esotericism". By ending the old fights one simply precipitates oneself back into the new ones, and furthermore gives rise to a new paradigm of certainty.

Creative *brio* and stylistic play deserve celebration and attention for challenging norms and standards. But challenges and celebration only dislocate: the norm remains normative. To refuse the questions posed by the many traditions of definition, the spectres that haunt magic, is to accept uncertainty as truth.

We need definitions of magic. We always will. We are trapped by them, in a circle of our own drawing, drawn by everyone who has formulated the question. Submission is impossible: one cannot accept every definition except by denouncing all and proposing one's own, thereby continuing the evocation. Yet, to reject them is to pretend that they have no power, to deny others the dignity of engagement. So many quaint, exotic superstitions for our titillation. If it is not a matter of choosing, then to stop, to conclude defining, is to define conclusively. To choose.

# 23

# JESPER SØRENSEN

"Magic Reconsidered: Towards a Scientifically Valid Concept of Magic"

Jesper Sørensen is a Danish scholar of religion. His book *A Cognitive Theory of Magic* (2007a) tries to explain "magic" by drawing on the framework of cognitive sciences (in particular, cognitive linguistics and cognitive psychology). He analyses "magic" as a specific mode of ritual action and the parameters set by cognitive sciences are used to trace the mechanisms and processes at the origin of the permanent creation of magical agency. In his contribution to this volume, Sørensen defends the use of "magic" as a scholarly category once its "underlying traits" are identified and it is "fractioned into a number of empirically tractable problems". Sørensen argues that "magic" draws on ordinary conceptual mechanisms that appear to work in a special way given that they are embedded in ritualized behaviour that triggers specific cognitive processes. He holds that "magic" takes meaning out of actions and words in ritual ("de-symbolization") and outlines three tensions between "magic" and "religion" in terms of different attitudes to ritual interpretation, the status of ritual experts, and local context versus institutional codification.

## MAGIC RECONSIDERED: TOWARDS A SCIENTIFICALLY VALID CONCEPT OF MAGIC

Magic is among the many essentially contested concepts in the fields of anthropology and study of religion. Due to its dubious past as a polemical concept, considered inherently related to primitivism, or simply believed to be indistinguishable from religion, numerous scholars have called for its abandonment (e.g., Pocock 1972; Smith 1995). Still, the concept seems difficult to avoid and is widely used to refer to a particular range of, mostly ritual, practices (e.g., Taussig 1993). In the following I argue that essentially nothing is gained by abandoning the term and that we, in fact, risk losing sight of important features of ritual practice; that instead it should be recognized as a second-order synthetic concept encompassing a number of practices related for pragmatic reasons; and that redirecting attention to its basic cognitive constituents will help to solve old but fundamental questions of how ritual can be deemed pragmatically efficacious and how such representations relate to more institutionalized forms of religion.

PART IV: CONTEMPORARY VOICES

# A SHORT HISTORY OF MAGIC IN THE SOCIAL SCIENCES

If the concept of magic is likely to linger on in the study of religion, how should we proceed from here? We might start off with inductively trying to identify some of the underlying features most scholars seem to agree upon. In line with British philosopher W. B. Gallie's definition of essentially contested concepts (Gallie 1956), "magic" can be described as a contested concept with a prototypical core that most users, both inside and outside the scientific community, can identify. Thus, magic is generally conceived of as referring to a ritual practice aimed to produce a particular pragmatic and locally defined result by means of more or less opaque methods. Prototypical examples are attempts to harm an enemy by means of manipulating a doll or an image, attempts to attract rain by sprinkling water in the air, or the transfer of essential qualities from one person to another through contact.

There is little agreement, however, about to what extent this folk concept is a valuable scientific concept – that is, whether it in fact helps to delineate a range of human behaviour sufficiently distinct from the range of behaviour specified by other concepts. In short, the question boils down to whether "magic" is sufficiently distinct from both "religion" and "science" (Smith 2004). This question is pertinent, both because of the troubled past of "magic" – a past even more troubled than that of "religion" – and because the expansion of the range of phenomena subsumed under the concept has led to conceptual border disputes. From antiquity (Lloyd 1979) to early modern times (Thomas 1991), "magic" has been used to polemically segregate a number of practices, and its connection to disparaging terms such as superstition, heathenness, primitivism and childishness has only aggravated this discursive function. Despite its appearance as a technical concept, together with the advent of anthropology and the study of religion during the late nineteenth century, one could argue that "magic's" transformation from an emic to an etic concept (i.e., from a concept related to Western history of religion to a global designator) was not followed by a successful, simultaneous disengagement from the more polemical aspect inherent in the folk-concept. "Magic" simply retained too many parochial features to successfully make the necessary transformation into a synthetic, scientific concept. This is due to two distinct problems.

First, the use of "magic" in Protestant polemics against Catholic interpretations of Eucharist, *in casu* represented by the Catholic creed of *ex opera operato*, related it to representations of automatic ritual efficacy and, by extension, to non-Christian practices. Thus, from the very onset of anthropology and the study of religion, "magic" referred to representations of automatic instrumental efficacy of particular rituals (e.g., Frazer 1922); as the concept expanded to cover ritual practices of people gradually coming under European dominion, it was criticized as leading to misrepresentations of other people's rituals. Due to lack of knowledge of the cultural and/or doctrinal context of the rituals described, armchair anthropologists mistook foreign rituals as primitive attempts to manipulate the social and physical environment; furthermore, the very presence of such attempts indicated the childlike minds of the people in question.

Even if there is some truth to this critical picture, I think that the problem thus conceived has, in fact, been turned upside down. The primary problem is not the overestimation of representations of direct ritual efficacy among "the Other" (whether in present-day Congo or ancient Rome), but the radical *underestimation* of representations of such efficacy in the Protestant West. Rationalists, modernists and Protestant theologians had a common interest in relegating magic to the primitive Other, whether in the temporal past or in spatial distance, and thereby effectively concealing its everlasting presence within their own culture. This almost Freudian projection to the primitive Other of an illicit but still widespread conception of (Christian) rituals as able to influence or even determine contextually related pragmatic endeavours was taken over by early anthropology in its evolutionist version. Both Edward Tylor and James Frazer regarded magic as a stage of the past, a mode of manipulating the world found in primitive societies still living in this past, that, in due time, would be replaced by religion and science. This intimate association of magic to primitivism and Victorian social evolutionism is, indeed, deplorable, as intellectualist scholars, in fact, presented an otherwise promising first step toward the construction of a scientific model of magic based on a few universally present mental operations.

The underestimation of the importance of ritual efficacy in Western religious practice has affected us ever since. Reactions against the primitivism inherent in the evolutionist and intellectualist agenda of scholars such as Tylor and Frazer have led to the gradual marginalization of the concept of magic from scholarly discourse. The social turn in anthropology directed focus towards the social function of different practices, and less interest was given to underlying mental structures. For instance, Marcel Mauss and Henri Hubert understood magic as the illicit and non-altruistic appropriation of *mana*, the spiritual force present in sacred collective representations, for individual and generally anti-social purposes (Mauss 1972). In a slightly different vein, Émile Durkheim relegated magic to the realm of the private, specified as the pragmatically defined and economically regulated relation between an individual client and a professional (e.g., a healer), in contrast to the essentially social and collective nature of religious rituals confirming group solidarity and basic symbols (Durkheim 1995). Differences aside, in addition to arguing that religion, in fact, logically precedes magic, both approaches segregated magic into the marginal, the private and the morally dubious. Other aspects of the prevalent folk model of magic were thus accentuated: the non-institutional, illicit, individualist and, thus, most likely immoral aspects. Using such features as defining characteristics is problematic, however, as polemics against other people's rituals most often are based on allegations of anti-social behaviour. For instance, according to Origen, Celsus claimed that early Christians used incantations to attain special powers and were thereby acting against the social body of the Roman state in order to further their own egoistically informed goals (Origen, *Against Celsus*, Ch. IV). And this is by no means a solitary example. This points to the second problem: defining magic as an essentially anti-social behaviour effectively consigns magic at the emic level, where one man's religion is another man's magic. From one perspective, praying for a successful harvest in a church is a religious behaviour; from another perspective it is pure magic, and the categories of both religion and magic become instruments in local relations of power.

A natural consequence of this development has been to argue for the abandonment of the concept from scholarly discourse (Pocock 1972; Smith 2004). If magic is only a discursive instrument of oppression of a minority by a majority, it should be given up. Doing so, however, effectively reified the notion that Westerners were not subject to conceptions of immediate ritual efficacy, at the same time as it critically claimed that neither were the "primitive Other". Even if many later anthropologists still employed the concept to designate a particular range of human behaviour, the explanatory focus shifted away from how, why and when people interpret ritual actions as instrumental. Rather, the efficacious aspects of ritual were seen as a smokescreen potentially hindering the proper symbolic interpretation of the symbolic elements involved. As argued by anthropologist John Beattie, "although magic *is* magic because it is essentially expressive and symbolic, the people who use it think it is instrumental" (Beattie 1968: 212). The potential scandal of people performing allegedly instrumental actions deemed by the researcher as non-efficacious is avoided by relocating the practice in the expressive and symbolic sphere. Magic is, therefore, at one and the same time transformed from a question of explanation to that of interpretation, and from a universal question of mental processing to a question of an expression of local and particular symbolic systems.

One problem remained, however: the central phenomena described by the concept of magic persist despite scholars' attempts to re-describe particular rituals as symbolic and/or performative utterances. People still perform numerous ritual actions in conjunction with pragmatic endeavours and claim to do so based on beliefs in their particular and local effect. These performances, furthermore, share enough characteristic features to warrant a general explanation. For a number of reasons outlined below, recent advances in the cognitive sciences raise the hope that progress towards such an explanation is attainable, and in the remainder of this chapter I will present an outline of such explanation by means of a series of propositions. Each will be discussed only briefly, and I must refer to other works for a fuller discussion (Sørensen 2007a).

## ELEMENTARY TRAITS OF MAGICAL ACTIONS

Pointing to a number of elementary features of magic is based on two presumptions. First, by specifying underlying traits, magic is fractionated into a number of empirically tractable problems. Second, each trait is understood as an expression of general and universal aspects of human cognitive processing.

### Magic depends upon processes of conceptual integration

It is well known that Edward Tylor and James Frazer explained magic as a product of the improper use of two modes of reasoning (Tylor 1871; Frazer 1922). Inspired by empiricist philosophy, they argued that human reasoning is based on the experience of regularities in the environment leading to law-like representations, and that the misapplication of this mental process is at the core of magic. Pointing to two such mechanisms, similarity and contagion, Frazer argued that magic emerges as the result of a mistake or, more precisely, is a logically illicit overextension of otherwise ordinary cognitive processing (Frazer 1922:

49). About fifty years later in 1956, Roman Jakobson pointed out that, rather than being a mistake found only in magic, the processing described by Frazer is identical to that underlying the formation of metaphor and metonymy (Jakobson and Halle 2002), and that it therefore should be analysed as a more fundamental cognitive process. At the time of Jakobson, however, metaphor and metonymy were still mostly considered linguistic special cases – tropes reserved for poets and authors – that should be avoided in proper thinking (Johnson 1981).

Since the 1980s, this picture has changed considerably and today most cognitive scientists willingly include cognitive processes underlying the formation of metaphor, metonymy and, more broadly, analogy as very basic and indispensable to ordinary cognitive functioning (Lakoff and Johnson 1980; Gentner 1983; Lakoff 1990; Johnson 1992; Thagard 1996). Human reasoning depends upon the ability to understand one thing in terms of another or, more technically, to be able to map inferential potential between distinct experiential and ontological domains. This process can be broadly referred to as "conceptual integration" (Fauconnier 1994, 1997; Turner 1996; Fauconnier and Turner 2003). The rather obvious examples of this process, such as seeing a loved one as a rose or an enemy as a pig, should not hide more fundamental and less conspicuous examples. For instance, we tend to construct human groups as agents with essences or "personalities", intentions and proclivities. This, for good or for worse, enables us to understand the interaction between groups in terms of the relation and interaction between agents – that is, as based on such things as cooperation, trust, reciprocity, or mistrust, enmity, cheating and conflict. This tendency is so strong that even within the science of groups and their behaviour, sociology, the inclination to reify groups as intentional agents must be fought at every step of investigation (Jenkins 2008).

Another example is our ability to understand rather intangible things, such as time, in terms of more concrete aspects of experience, such as a movement through a physical landscape (e.g., "Christmas is approaching" and "We should put the past behind us"). In all these cases, however, no ontological commitment is necessary nor should any be presumed. I don't believe my enemy is "really" a pig and, *pace* Evans-Pritchard, Nuer does not mistake oxen for cucumbers (Evans-Pritchard 1956). Further, only some and not other inferences are transferred from one domain to another. This is important, as it emphasizes the strategic and heuristic function of conceptual integration: by mapping inferential potential from one domain to another, certain features are highlighted, whereas others are concealed.

In case of metonymic extension, one refers to or manipulates/interacts with a whole by means of a part. This makes it a common and indispensable referential device, as it enables us to refer to wholes not present by parts being present (e.g., a lock of hair of my loved one). Also in this case, however, we find less obvious usage. To extend the example above, individuals can be seen as metonymic extensions of a group – a mode of reasoning that is all too common in discriminatory behaviour. In a popular domain, possessions of famous persons, such as a dress worn by Princess Diana, have a special status and are sold in auctions for prizes many times their material value. As in the case of motivated similarity underlying metaphor, metonymies help to establish a connection between two conceptual spaces, from part to whole and from present to non-present. Both metaphor and metonymy thus allow "quick and dirty" inferences to be drawn, are part of both conscious and non-conscious processing, and play a fundamental role in the construction and extension of conceptual models built on basic-level categorization (Lakoff 1990).

But if these processes are so ordinary, how can we describe their particular employment in rituals? I suggest that conceptual integration has two distinct functions in magic. First, it enables the infusion of "magical agency" into the ritual by enabling a connection to a domain represented as powerful or "sacred". Magical agency refers to the element(s) present in the ritual that is indispensable for it to have efficacy. It need not be personal – it can be invested in an object, in a stipulated action sequence (including a linguistic formula), or even in a particular place or time. Of importance is that the ritual behaviour establishes a connection to some special or "sacred" entity that enables representations of efficacy. Second, conceptual integration is not only used to establish such agency. It is also an important factor in the construction of representations of concrete ritual efficacy.

We can analytically distinguish at least two basic methods specified by their pragmatic goal. Superficially, these might resemble Frazer's dichotomy of contagious and imitative magic. However, in contrast to Frazer, the distinction is not based upon the distinct methods of establishing an inferential mapping between two domains, but rather on the pragmatic effect attained by this connection – whether it produces a more or less permanent essential change or whether it manipulates schematic properties. Thus, in transformative magic (Sørensen 2007a), the basic purpose is to affect an essential change of some object or person, whether permanent or temporary. This is most usually done by means of behaviour in which essential qualities are transferred by means of contact, whether by ingestion, touching or merely looking. Experimental studies indicate that negative contagion (i.e., contamination) elicits a very basic inferential structure that is likely to have deep evolutionary roots. Avoiding contaminants has such obvious selective advantages that humans possibly have intuitive, automatic and unconscious processing of transfer of negative essences (Nemeroff and Rozin 2000). In the case of magical rituals, however, the essences are often regarded as desirable and it remains to be investigated if this should be explained as a reversal of the contamination avoidance affected by the ritual situation, or if cognitive processing of positive essence transfer is a distinct system potentially built on representations of food ingestion and/or emotional proximity.

In manipulative magic (Sørensen 2007a), the aim is to change schematic aspects of entities belonging to one domain by manipulating entities belonging to another domain. Numerous rituals around the globe have aims such as keeping pests out of fields, ensuring the love of a desired other, keeping rivals at bay, securing prosperous business deals, ensuring a safe journey, or even killing an enemy. Often such rituals involve manipulation of concrete objects, say dirt, linked to objects that are more difficult to manipulate, such as pests in the field (Malinowski 1937). As in the case of metaphor and metonymy used to express hard-to-grasp domains in terms of easier ones, magical ritual enables hard-to-manipulate domains such as pest control, safety on trip, luck in sexual endeavours and health, to be manipulated by means of proxies established through conceptual blending.

## Magic depends upon fundamental aspects of human ritualization

The description above points to a central question that any theory addressing "magic" must answer. Why is conceptual integration, at least sometimes, perceived to have causal efficacy – that is, to be able to influence particular aspects of the surrounding physical or social world? In short, why should magic not be regarded as merely a kind of symbolic behaviour? The short answer is *ritual*. Ritual actions are distinct from ordinary actions in a number of ways and the following argument is based on the assumption that the cognitive systems processing ordinary actions are also engaged in processing ritual actions, but that rituals contain distinctive features that alter this processing in a non-trivial way.

Ritual actions have, of course, been of central concern to both anthropology and the study of religion for more than a century (e.g., Gennep 1977; Turner 1995). But even if the peculiar features of ritual were noticed, until the late 1970s few scholars recognized that these "obvious aspects of ritual" were not (merely) expressive symbols that should be deciphered to unearth their inherent meaning (Sperber 1975; Rappaport 1979; Staal 1979). Arguing that ritualized behaviour *in itself* might have a causal role highlights the effect of surface properties of ritual actions on participant and observer alike. Identifying features such as redundancy, iteration and scriptedness and applying evolutionary theorizing, Rappaport, for instance, argued that ritual serves a basic function in human sociality by communicating adherence and acceptance of group authority solely by means of participation (Rappaport 1979, 1999). In a similar vein, more recent theorists have analysed rituals as a mode of costly signalling (Sosis and Alcorta 2003) or hard-to-fake signals (Bulbulia 2008), arguing that rituals function as an instrument of social cohesion furthering pro-social behaviour.

In contrast to such adaptationist models (i.e., models that explain cultural ritual as an adaptive result of cultural selection), Boyer and Liénard have recently opted for an epidemiological explanation of recurrent features of cultural rituals (Liénard and Boyer 2006; Boyer and Liénard 2006). Observing the similarities between symptoms of ritualistic actions performed by persons suffering from Obsessive Compulsive Disorder (OCD) and certain aspects of cultural rituals (Fiske and Haslam 1997), Boyer and Liénard hypothesize that successful cultural rituals employ actions that activate a Potential Hazard Precaution System. This cognitive system evolved to warn the organism of potential threats in the environment, such as contamination and intrusion; but, as is the case with all such systems, the system will activate if the input conditions are right, thus leading to a number of false positives. Cultural rituals, in short, parasitize cognitive systems evolved for other purposes and by doing so evoke strong motivation for performance. Without going into the details of their complex model, two features are of relevance in this context. First, Boyer and Liénard emphasize the role of "goal-demotion" in ritual behaviour and its effect on the cognitive system of the performer. Goal-demotion refers to the fact that rituals are causally opaque (i.e., the actions are not connected to their purported result), stipulated and often specified in detail, and the authors argue that this effectively overloads the working memory of the participants, as he or she has to pay attention to the minute detail of correct ritual performance. Second, Boyer and Liénard thereby connect an ultimate explanation of recurrent features of ritual (as an evolutionary by-product) with proximate explanation of *how* this information is processed by the human cognitive system.

Focusing on the proximate level of explanation, Nielbo and Sørensen have conducted a series of experiments investigating how goal-demotion affects online processing of observed actions. Building on the Event Segmentation Theory of Jeffrey Zacks (Zacks and Tversky 2001; Zacks et al. 2007), these studies show that subjects consistently parse observed non-functional actions on a finer level, a result that indicates that subjects find it harder to integrate sub-actions (e.g., lifting the kettle) into comprehensive action sequences guided by schematic representations (e.g., making coffee) when an action is goal-demoted (Nielbo and Sørensen 2011). This is in line with a conceptual model of ritual action according to which ritualized behaviour effects a disconnection of the dual system organizing ordinary action perception: a bottom-up process that constructs basic action gestalts based on perceptual features and mental simulation, and a top-down process of schematic expectations that integrates these basic action gestalts into larger, intentionally specified action sequences (Sørensen 2007b). Put differently, intuitive expectations and information from the senses are difficult to integrate automatically.

It is hypothesized that this disconnection of normal processing has a number of specific effects. First, one of the primary functions of our cognitive system is to predict future actions. Therefore goal-demotion is likely to result in a search for available perceptual cues that might help to construct a reliable global model of the action, and this has the interesting "side-effect" that greater attention is directed to details of the observed action. Thus, "weak causal cognition" focusing on perceptual cues such as contiguity and similarity (Kummer 1996) could be a secondary strategy in cases where actions cannot be predicted by strong causal schemas. Thus, ritual forces our cognitive systems towards using exactly those cues, contagion and similarity, designated by Frazer as fundamental to magic. Second, attention to perceptual detail is likely to impede memory encoding, as attentional resources are limited. This implies that interpretation of the "meaning" of ritual behaviour is likely to be a secondary process performed *after* and not during ritual performance and that this process is more dependent upon social negotiation than upon memory of the concrete ritual details (Xygalatos et al. forthcoming). Put together, this implies that ritual in itself will direct attention to the very aspects of associative learning argued to be central in magical actions (contagion and similarity), and that ascription of meaning to ritual is a secondary, cognitively slower and potentially collective process of rumination following ritual performance. Ritualization is thus likely to direct our cognitive system to the very features that underlie the construction of conceptual integration.

## Magic depends upon a process of de-symbolization

Based on the features mentioned above, all rituals can, in principle, elicit a magical interpretation in participant and observer alike. Some rituals, however, contain features that make magical interpretations more likely to appear. Prominent among these is the tendency to *de-symbolize* elements used in the ritual (Sørensen 2005a, 2007a). De-symbolization refers to the process by which conventional meaning is taken out of the actions and words employed in the ritual. Strictly speaking, this is part of the general process of ritualization described above; but as it forms such a prominent part in many prototypical magical rituals, it must be discussed separately.

The central claim is that we find a negative correlation between degree of interpretation of a ritual and representations of ritual efficacy. The more the elements of the ritual have been symbolically elaborated – that is, the more "meaningful" they are to participants – the less effective the ritual will be judged to be. The claim rests on two observations. First, worldwide exoticism goes hand in hand with representations of magical efficacy. Exoticism can be produced by spatial or temporal distance – that is, either by importing ritual features from outside or by using otherwise historically obsolete cultural forms. The first instance is witnessed by the widespread representations of neighbouring people as particularly versed in magic, and the second by the equally widespread tendency to employ old-fashioned or dead languages, strange grammatical forms, or even pure gibberish in rituals (Sørensen 2005a).

Second, the process of de-symbolization has particular cognitive effects as it redirects attention from the symbolic meaning of an utterance or action to its perceptible (iconic or indexical) features. Thus, if an utterance or action is perceived as meaningless, judgements of appropriateness can only be based on: (a) whether it is a correct iconic reproduction of the stipulated ritual act, and/or (b) whether it is performed by an authorized person. Further, de-symbolization allows the schematic properties of language to be foregrounded, leading to representations of investment of force (e.g., in iterations) and/or schematic redundancy. Together it is hypothesized that these two features of de-symbolization effectively direct attention towards perceptible features of the actions performed that will connect them to the immediate pragmatic context. It is further hypothesized that focusing on the symbolic content of a ritual will decrease representations of ritual efficacy, thus indicating a dynamic tension in religious traditions between interpretative strategies and ritual efficacy.

## Rituals are embedded in context-near event-frames

Humans represent actions in networks of interrelated event-frames that specify a relation between an action, its preconditions and its likely result. The purported effects as well as the point of departure of actions thus contextually specify actions, in general, and this is, of course, also the case in ritual actions. Even though we do find instances where a particular outcome is described as depending upon ritual performance alone, magical rituals are generally performed in conjunction with instrumental actions and both are regarded as necessary for a successful outcome. This observation stood behind Malinowski's rejection of the notion of pre-logical mentality (Lévy-Bruhl 1985). Malinowski observed that the Trobrianders combined instrumental actions, of which they exposed perfect rational mastery, with ritual actions in such endeavours as canoe building or farming, even if they never failed to distinguish the two modes of action. Neither would they ever only resort to magic in order to reach the desired result (Malinowski 1992). This raises two interconnected questions. First, how do rituals relate to locally constructed representations of events? Second, why are rituals performed in conjunction with non-ritual instrumental actions?

One of the effects of both ritualization and de-symbolization is the event-like character of the actions involved. Ritual actions are intentionally under-determined – that is, the action sequence performed is not specified by the intentions of the participants themselves (Humphrey and Laidlaw 1994). This should not be mistaken for the claim that participants are not motivated by intentions when performing a ritual. In many cases they are (at least by the intention to perform the ritual); but in contrast to most ordinary instrumental actions, the intention of individual performers has no or little effect on the concrete action sequence performed. This is important as it, ironically, enables rituals to function as the instrumental cause in numerous locally specified event-frames, and this contextual embedding is one of the defining features of magic. This is made possible both by recourse to stipulations defined by tradition ("when x occurs, do z"), and by the attention given to perceptual features that is a side-effect of ritualization. All actions contain numerous perceptual features (e.g., colour, form, weight) and it is highly likely that some of these would be able to relate the action performed to the locally specified purpose of the ritual. Ritual performance opens an "evocational field" (Sperber 1975) allowing participants to relate particular ritual features to instrumentally defined event-frames by means of perceptual cues, and ritualization thus enables rituals to be perceived as the instrumental cause in particular event-frames.

This purported causal effect can be directed towards producing a new state (prospective magic) or towards returning to a disrupted state (retrospective magic). In any case, it follows that the ritual is related to the preconditions through a diagnostic process (identifying the state of affairs) and to the represented outcome of the actions through a prognostic process (predicting a likely outcome). The ritual can thus be identified as the causal mechanisms allowing one to move from a precondition to a desired end-state. Embedding a ritual performance in a large event-frame, including numerous instrumental actions, further entails that counterfactual event-frames are potentially represented as a result of *not* performing the ritual. Even in cases where people do not have strong intuitions about the likely effect of a ritual, they often have strong representations about possible dire consequences of non-performance. This is likely to be an effect of the human proclivity to search for possible causes for undesirable events and outcomes, and one method is to link an unexpected outcome with failure to perform stipulated actions that, more often than not, are infused with cues of potential hazards eliciting feelings of anxiety (Boyer and Liénard 2007). So even though participants often have no representations of how a ritual works, the ritual performance is compelling as it is clearly stated that it *must* be performed.

There might, however, be an even stronger reason for linking ritual and instrumental behaviour. Already Malinowski pointed out that some actions are prone to be surrounded by rituals, whereas others are not. Thus, deep-sea fishing on the open sea is intimately connected to magical rituals, whereas lagoon fishing is not (Malinowski 1992). Malinowski explained this as an effect of the anxiety-reducing character of ritual performance when faced with uncertain and potentially dangerous endeavours – an effect that would enhance performance in itself. This explanation, however, is problematic for several reasons. In many cases, it seems as if ritual performance is more likely to provoke than reduce anxiety. Furthermore, it is unclear why some situations involving uncertainty should elicit a ritual response whereas others do not (Sørensen 2007c). A possible explanation concerning the later would be that it is not merely uncertainty but actions related to reproductive fitness that are likely to elicit a ritual response. Thus, only a certain range of actions involving uncertainty produces enough motivational force to elicit a ritual response.

However, if rituals cannot be explained as reducing anxiety, why are they often performed in conjunction with uncertain endeavours? Two hypotheses can be put forward. First, by performing a stipulated ritual action sequence that will always "succeed", the neurocognitive system produces a reward that affects subsequent judgements of success in adjacent risky endeavour in a positive direction. Thus, it is hypothesized that subjects will invest more in a risky endeavour if they have just engaged in a ritualized action sequence. If this is the case, ritual performance may effectively make you more optimistic about future actions whose result involves some degree of uncertainty. Such an explanation is supported by the observation that ritualized action sequences are often present in situations involving great uncertainty such as gambling and other (semi-)random situations, and that ritual behaviour seems to result in stronger belief in own luck and skills (Langer 1975; Wohl and Enzle 2002; Wood and Clapham 2005). Another compatible hypothesis would be that performance of a ritual in close proximity to a potentially risky and uncertain pragmatic endeavour may function as a social "insurance" policy by spreading responsibility to both the group (if any) performing the ritual, but also to the ritual procedure itself. The successful outcome of a pragmatic endeavour no longer depends solely upon the instrumental skills, luck and perseverance of the actor, but also upon correct ritual performance, the action of other ritual participants and, ultimately, upon potential superhuman agents evoked in the ritual. Thus, a series of possible *post hoc* rationalizations not involving the concrete instrumental action sequence becomes available in case of failure to reach the desired goal (Evans-Pritchard 1958 [1937]).

### Magic is a non-systemic and context-dependent interpretative strategy

One of the unfortunate misconceptions following the unsuccessful transformation of magic into a proper scientific model is the symmetric juxtaposition of magic and religion as competing and often mutually hostile systems of thought. This is unfortunate for two reasons. First, religion, like magic, is an impure category that appears recalcitrant to any clear definition (Boyer 1996). If both "religion" and "magic" are synthetic second-order concepts with the pragmatic function of delineating a particular range of phenomena, attempts to create clear boundaries are likely to be rather futile, and without such boundaries notions of conflict become misdirected. If causally relevant features used to explain the behaviour under investigation are found on the underlying levels of analysis, conflicts should be described in terms of these features. Second, juxtaposing magic and religion as competing *systems* of thought, whether as unfolding in an evolutionary sequence (e.g., Frazer 1922) or as co-present, alternative thought systems (e.g., Tambiah 1990), misdirects our attention towards an ultimately theologically informed focus on systemic properties of both. It is unfruitful to view magic as a system of thought, even if "religion" can be said to contain more or less formalized conceptual systems, at least in its theological and institutionalized versions (this aspect is likely to have been overrated; compare the theologizing tendency in both anthropology and the study of religion – see Boyer 1994). Rather, magic is better thought of as an *interpretative strategy* towards ritual actions utilized by individuals in particular situations, elicited by certain features of ritual actions and utilizing basic aspects of human categorization.

That being said, the often-noted hostility between religion and magic does point to a dynamic tension between different modes of ritual interpretation, doctrinal stabilization and institutionalization. In this context, three interrelated areas of tension should briefly be mentioned (Sørensen 2005b, 2007a). First, magical rituals or, more precisely, magical interpretations of ritual actions are specified by their instrumental relation to an immediate pragmatic context. Focus is on ritual efficacy, and the processes of de-symbolization and ritualization described above enable our cognitive system to relate perceptual features of the ritual actions (e.g., relations of similarity and contagion) to relevant elements in the immediate surroundings. In contrast to this focus on ritual efficacy, a "religious" interpretation of a ritual focuses on its alleged meaning – that is, its semantic relation to more or less systematized symbolic structures and systems of meaning and to the authority of institutional religious guilds. Rather than being specified by an instrumental relation to the immediate context, ritual elements are interpreted as symbolic signs in need of interpretation. Thus, understanding the Eucharist as a behavioural sign of commitment to a range of beliefs is quite different from understanding the same ritual as temporarily changing one's essence or as a cure from diseases and protection against evil. It should be emphasized, however, that both interpretations can coexist, even within the same individual, and that these interpretations are the result of distinct modes of cognitive processing rather than a deliberate, conscious choice.

Second, the two distinct interpretative strategies elicit different representations of ritual expertise and status. For a number of reasons, focus on ritual efficacy is likely to enhance the status of the agent performing the ritual. This can be due to direct charismatic authority (when magical agency is invested in the agent); but even when this is not the case the ritual agent will at least have authority due to knowledge of the correct ritual procedure and/or access to powerful objects. This authority is, however, rather unstable as it depends upon (a) the perceived efficacy of the ritual by participants, (b) the ability to rationalize away failure to achieve a purported result, and (c) the ability to compete with alternative rituals. In contrast, a "religious interpretation" of ritual with no special focus on ritual efficacy is not susceptible to falsification and is unlikely to be threatened by competing rituals. Therefore, the ritual agent also achieves a somewhat different status as a *representative* of a doctrinal tradition and more or less authoritative interpreter of ritual rather than as guarantee of ritual efficacy. Again, both positions might coexist, and representations of ritual efficacy are apparently hard to suppress. Ritual behaviour thus seems to activate a "charismatic proclivity" (Boyer 1994) according to which participants are likely to ascribe special qualities to ritual agents even if these are merely representatives of codified and perhaps even highly centralized ritual tradition (Sørensen 2005b).

This points to the third tension: that between the local use of rituals and its institutional codification. Rituals can be embedded in a local context and utilized as the instrumental cause in endeavours specified by this context, or they can be subsumed in a context-independent system of rituals defined by an abstract goal and related to a guild of religious experts and/or a more or less formalized doctrinal system. Whereas the first ensures the continuous relevance of the ritual due to its instrumental embedding in locally construed event-frames, the second is a necessary aspect of institutionalization and formation of religious guilds. Here the deeper tension, described above, between symbolic interpretation and representations of ritual efficacy becomes relevant. If it is true that we find a negative correlation between the degree of symbolic interpretation and the ascription of meaning to the ritual, on the one hand, and its perceived instrumental efficacy, on the other, this tension should have an important impact upon the historical development of religious traditions in terms of levels of centralized control, appropriation of local rituals and designation of illicit ritual practices. In short, every religious institution will face the problem that the codification, symbolic elaboration and doctrinal control needed to construct and expand the reach of the tradition at the same time seem to deplete the rituals of their perceived instrumental efficacy, effectively lowering the motivation to perform these in the first place (Sørensen 2005b). Thus, in contrast to the "tedium-effect" claimed by Whitehouse to undermine doctrinal ritual practice due to boredom (Whitehouse 2005), I suggest that this development results from a "triviality-effect" that undermines representations of ritual efficacy by means of symbolic over-determination. Focusing solely on the meaning of the ritual effectively undermines motivations for its performance – it renders ritual performance superfluous. Establishing a trade-off between local conceptions of ritual efficacy, on the one hand, and centralized control and doctrinal codification, on the other, can be solved in different manners, but must be addressed if institutionalization is to succeed.

## CONCLUSION

Having argued that "magic" is, in fact, an essentially contested concept, we are faced with a choice: do we need the concept to pragmatically delineate a range of human behaviours even if this delineating will remain contested? Is the concept useful or is it best abandoned? Above I have argued that we gain little or nothing by abandoning the concept and that being essentially contested is no reason to give up a concept. Just as we would not give up the concept of "art" even if little agreement can be found as to its proper definition, concepts in the study of religion should not be abandoned if they serve a pragmatic function. Abandoning the concept of "magic" will only reify the deplorable development whereby ritual efficacy has been exorcised from first the Western world and subsequently the rest of the world. Instead I propose to do the opposite. By creating proper scientific models of its underlying traits, magic can be appreciated as an aspect of human ritual behaviour *everywhere* in the world and not as a vestige of primitive mentality past or present.

That being said, magic should be considered a second-order concept that must undergo a transformation from emic to etic and from local to global. This transformation entails a shift of focus from the essentially fruitless questions of the relation between "magic" and "religion" (or "science", for that matter) to the underlying traits susceptible to explanatory investigations. Focusing on the cognitive processes elicited by ritualized behaviour appears to be a fruitful approach, as it allows us to explain a number of features by reference to universally found cognitive mechanisms. Further, this enables us to investigate particular processes as these unfold in dynamic tension within particular historical settings. Thus, the interaction of and tension between localized ritual performance and institutionalized religious traditions might shed light on patterns of historical development not explicable by social explanations alone (cf. Martin and Sørensen 2011).

# 24

# KIMBERLY B. STRATTON

"Magic Discourse in the Ancient World"

Kimberly B. Stratton is an American scholar of religions of antiquity. Her book *Naming the Witch: Magic, Ideology, and Stereotype in the Ancient World* (2007) reviews and advances the status quo of the study of "magic" in Athens, Rome, early Christianity and Rabbinic Judaism. The book navigates a third way between the denial of the category of "magic" and its uncritical reception; her analysis points to the contextual contingency of "magic" (its polyvalence and shiftiness in its various appearances in different places and periods) and its discursive continuity throughout the Mediterranean. Her book pays attention to emic terminology but also proposes an etic approach to "magic" as a form of social discourse (cast in Foucaultian terms). In her contribution to this volume, Stratton shows how the concept of "magic", once it was established in antiquity, became a powerful operator as a mode of social control and, at the same time, enabled people to engage in acts labelled as "magic". Stereotypical conceptions of magic can take different shapes in different groups and do not necessarily mirror the actions of actual people; but Stratton also finds a remarkable consistency of ritual practices referred to as "magic" across the Mediterranean world in Graeco-Roman times.

## MAGIC DISCOURSE IN THE ANCIENT WORLD

Magic as a category of human activity and scholarly enquiry has been subject to trenchant criticism during the past three decades. During the early 1980s, scholars raised methodological concerns about applying the term "magic" to aspects of the Greek Magical Papyri or to accepting at face value labels and accusations of magic in ancient literature.[1] The pendulum at that time swung from uncritically accepting the category "magic", as distinct from either "science" or "religion", to challenging the existence of magic as a discrete

---

1. Nock 1933: 183, first made this observation. Segal 1981 raised the question about labelling the Greek Magical Papyri "magic"; Remus 1982 and Garrett 1989: 4–5, emphasized the polemical use of magic terminology in early Christian writings.

analytical category and calling for a ban on use of this pejorative term in second-order scholarship.

In response to these criticisms, two main approaches to the study of practices traditionally labelled "magic" emerged. The first eschews the term magic altogether, asserting that magic never existed as a form of ritual practice; rather, it functioned only as a naming strategy, designed to malign opponents or entire groups of people with a pejorative label.[2] Instead of using the term "magic", these scholars employ emic terminology both to avoid the problems posed by using magic as a descriptive label and to achieve better precision when discussing a wide variety of ritual technologies, ranging from herbalism and wearing amulets to inscribing curses on lead tablets and burying them in a grave.[3] Scholars who choose this approach argue that magic is an unhelpful term to discuss these different practical methods since it is overly vague, imports disparaging associations not necessarily applicable in the ancient context (e.g., the wearing of amulets was widely accepted as legitimate medicine),[4] or falsely creates a dichotomy between the activity under consideration and another labelled "religion" or "science", thereby imposing category distinctions that reflect modern post-Enlightenment and post-Reformation thinking inappropriate for understanding the variety of ritual methods available in the ancient world.[5]

The second approach acknowledges difficulty with the term, but argues that to abandon magic as a heuristic category hobbles comparative second-order scholarship; instead, an important proponent of this approach advocates using a broad polythetic definition as a model to identify practices as magic when they exhibit a majority of the recognized characteristics.[6] A less sophisticated version of this position continues to use "magic" unproblematically as an analytical category, often relying on literary depictions or accusations of magic to reconstruct the "history" of magic without sufficient attention to the pejorative bias or polemical intentions of ancient texts.[7]

---

2. Phillips 1986: 2711; Gager 1992: 25; and Janowitz 2001: 2–3.
3. Gager 1992; Janowitz 2002; Eidinow 2007; and Trzcionka 2007 adopt this strategy. Otto (forthcoming) similarly advocates abandoning magic as an abstract category but, in an approach similar to mine, endorses use of the term when it is supported contextually and with due regard to the particular meaning the term carries in a given text.
4. Pliny, for example, cites numerous healing amulets as legitimate medicine (*Nat.* 28–9); the rabbis also sanction the use of amulets that have been proven to work (y. Shab. 6.9; b. Shab 67a). See also Veltri 1998, 2001.
5. Smith 1995: 13–16; Styers 2004: 9, 14.
6. Versnel 1991: 177–97. See also Hoffman 2002: 179–94; and Johnston 2003: 50–54, on the need for a heuristic model or etic terminology for comparative research. Other authors acknowledge the difficulties posed by using the category magic but do not reject use of the term altogether: Faraone and Obbink 1991: vi; Meyer and Smith 1994: 1; Graf 1997: 2; Meyer and Mirecki 1995: 2–3; Schäfer and Kippenberg 1997: xi; and Collins 2008: xi–xii. Thomassen 1999: 58, argues that not only is magic a useful category for second-order scholarship and one that existed in the ancient world, but a category of practice recognized by those engaged in it. In other words, some people knowingly pursued activities they and their society recognized as magic.
7. E.g., Dickie 2001, who actually falls between the two approaches; he does not engage in comparative second-order research, but strives to reconstruct a precise history of ancient magic and magicians based on careful attention to emic terminology. At the same time, he does not question the viability of magic as a

In this chapter I negotiate a theoretical path between these approaches; the stalemate arises, I argue, from defining magic as a particular set of objectively defined practices without recognizing the contextual nature of magic as a social construct. While the majority of human societies have some category of ritual practices designed to harness supernatural power that they regard as illegitimate, threatening, dangerous or anti-social – in opposition to practices they regard as legitimate – the way in which they conceive of these practices (or, in some cases, innate power) differs to such a degree that labelling them universally as magic or witchcraft misses the important differences between these cultural constructs and fails to illuminate the society or social practices under consideration.[8] I therefore concur strongly with the first approach discussed above, which advocates using emic terminology. Only emic terminology effectively captures the socially conferred meaning of a particular action. Lighting a candle, sacrificing an animal, burning some herbs do not in and of themselves constitute magic. It is society that defines when these activities count as magic and when they do not.[9] Often the label is facilely applied to external groups; thus Caribbeans, worshipping their saints in New York City, are widely considered to be practising magic or even Satanism rather than legitimate religion, reflecting their outsider status in the US. Christians praying to their crucified saviour in cities throughout the Roman Empire during the first three centuries CE were similarly regarded as practising a form of illegitimate and dangerous magic, justifying Rome's extraordinary effort to extirpate this subversive movement.[10] Consequently, any definition must fully take into account specific constructions of magic rather than adhere to a set of predefined objective criteria that will, in most cases, impose our own society's construction of magic without providing significant insight into the other culture, its beliefs and social practices.

The arguments for developing a heuristic model for second-order research, discussion and comparison are also compelling; using exclusively emic terminology narrows the conversation to one specific type of culture and activity, shutting down the opportunity to learn from comparison with analogous practices across cultures or historical periods.[11] I propose, therefore, that we define magic not according to a concrete set of practices, which are universally defined (even according to a broad polythetic model), but as culturally specific ideas about illegitimate and dangerous access to numinous power, whose local applications need to be considered on their own terms in order to understand the work they do in their respective societies. This approach avoids inappropriately imposing post-Enlightenment, post-Reformation categories and conceptions onto other cultures since attention to emic terminology and context reveals which practices are considered magic (or the equivalent) within that society and how those labels function ideologically. At the same time, such an approach enables the category magic to be applied comparatively when

---

  descriptive category and accepts the verisimilitude of his literary sources much too easily. See Frankfurter 2002; Johnston 2003: 53; and Stratton 2007: 83, for critique of this approach.
8. See Wilson 1951: 307–13, which demonstrates this point concisely.
9. Thomassen 1999: 57–58.
10. E.g., Origen, *Cels* 1.3 and, especially, 6. See also Wypustek 1997: 276–97, which is suggestive if speculative.
11. Smith 1995: 20; Versnel 1991: 177, 185.

the concept (or one that is analogous) is demonstrated to operate in that culture. In many cases, however, it will not. Matthew Dickie, for example, argues that applying the term magic to describe Egyptian beliefs in *Heka* (divine force) before the influence of Hellenism misrepresents the positive place of *Heka* within their religious system.[12]

The difference between this approach and Versnel's polythetic model[13] is that I emphasize the culturally specific nature of magic beliefs as well as the ideological work they do.[14] Claiming that someone meets secretly at night or coerces rather than supplicates the divine is an ideological act; it portrays that person or activity according to the stereotype of a magician, at least in Western societies, which is why Origen takes such pains to counter these charges by Celsus (1.3, 6–7, 9). Most ancient literature must be read with this in mind – "describing" a magical practice, even in imaginative literature, was a value-laden exercise that participated in constructing and maintaining social hierarchies, whether based on gender, culture/ethnicity, or political and economic rivalries. Furthermore, it is not sufficient merely to point out that magic was used to marginalize an individual or group, as many scholars have done.[15] In most cases, depictions of magic operated in larger debates over power, authority and how to run a proper society at moments of political and social change.[16] It did much more than marginalize opponents, although it certainly and effectively did this also.

## MAGIC AS A SOCIAL DISCOURSE

Magic is conceived differently in different ancient Mediterranean societies despite common features and shared mythologies. Where magic appears in ancient literary representations, clear patterns emerge along cultural lines, suggesting that specific influences, belief systems and social contexts shaped those portraits and the concerns they express. Increasingly, it became clear to me that these representations are literary tropes, which drew upon and re-inscribed powerful existing stereotypes in distinct social situations. In other words, ancient depictions of magic and magicians participated in dynamic social dramas of their time. As a social historian, discovering the underlying context and concerns that motivated these portraits is paramount for revealing the ideological work they did and, in many respects, continue to do as foundational texts for the Western concepts of "magic" and "witchcraft".

In response to the semantic debate over the term magic, therefore, I propose that magic is best understood as a discursive formation – a socially constructed body of knowledge that is enmeshed in and supports systems of power. What gets labelled magic is arbitrary and depends upon the society in question. Once the label is affixed, however, it enables

---

12. Dickie 2001: 22.
13. Versnel 1991: 186.
14. See Otto forthcoming for a similar approach.
15. Janowitz 2001: 1–3; Remus 1999: 148; Garrett 1989: 4–5; Gager 1992: 25, for some examples.
16. For examples and fuller discussion, see Stratton 2007.

certain practices to *become* magic by virtue of being regarded as such by members of the society. Magic becomes real by virtue of being conceived.

Especially relevant for understanding magic as a discursive formation is Michel Foucault's work revealing the agonistic character of discourses; they represent competing strategies of domination.[17] All knowledge is socially constructed and integrally bound up with power, especially to the degree that it is implicated in technologies which manipulate the body (medicine, corporal punishment, restraint, etc.).[18] There is no power relation, Foucault proposes, without the correlative field of knowledge, or any knowledge that does not presuppose and constitute power relations.[19] Furthermore, discourses have a history; they arise in particular contexts, responding to a complex interplay of social circumstances.[20] Consequently, discourses are never universal, but grounded in local dynamics and specific social conditions, serving specific needs.[21] This conception of discourse illuminates several features of ancient magic and provides a theoretical bridge between those who reject the use of magic as a descriptive term altogether and those who seek a comparative heuristic category.

Drawing on Foucault's conception of discourse, I propose that magic is a socially constructed object of knowledge that has a specific history and origin. Once it emerged in Western thought, magic acquired a social reality; it existed in both the minds and practices of people who believed in it. As accusations, fears, rumours, apotropaic measures for protection, or curses and binding spells, magic functioned in society, shaping behaviour and creating the possibility of a wide range of social actions. Like the discourses Foucault investigates, ancient magic was highly agonistic. Not merely as one weapon in an arsenal aimed at beating rivals in the competitive face-to-face society of ancient Greece, as Christopher Faraone has demonstrated,[22] but in that the very notion of magic – how it was conceived, depicted and deployed was heavily bound up with notions of power, and struggles for it, in the various societies where the discourse of magic operated.

The concept of magic, as understood in Western culture, can be traced to elite Greek writers in the fifth and fourth centuries, who actively sought to shape their society according to their own set of values and employed magic as a discourse of alterity towards this end.[23] Conveying ideas of Otherness and marginality most of the time,[24] it is not surprising that the idea of magic reflects not only the political and social concerns of these writers, but the xenophobia and misogyny that circulated among them and their compatriots at that time.[25] The association of magic with foolish (or conniving) women and foreign

---

17. Dreyfus and Rabinow 1983: 109.
18. See Foucault 1965, 1973, 1979, 1980a, 1980b.
19. Foucault 1979: 27.
20. Foucault 1972: 157; Dreyfus and Rabinow 1983: 77.
21. Foucault 1980b: 115; Foucault 1972: 224–25.
22. Faraone 1991: 3–32. See also Eidinow 2007: 4, who argues that curses were less a means of competition than of controlling risk.
23. Stratton 2007: 39–46; Graf 1997: 20–35; Versnel 1991: 188; Dickie 2001: 18–22.
24. See Otto forthcoming, who discusses cases where magic operates positively.
25. Versnel 1991: 182.

superstition, thus, does not originate with colonialist Europeans, but reflects an inherent aspect of the discourse present from its inception in ancient Greece. This is not to say that non-European cultures do not have similar discourses of alterity which resemble magic; but it is important to clarify that those discursive formations have their own history, social dynamics and local variations that are essential to comprehending them as cultural products.

Because of the agonistic nature of magic discourse, it is crucial to ask: who defines it? Which practices are labelled magic, and how was power negotiated through the application of this label? Discourse is not only knowledge; it is practice, which confers and regulates power through its application.[26] Once the concept of magic exists, it can operate as a form of social control through fear, rumour and accusation. It can also create the ability to *do* magic by enabling people to engage in activities labelled magic by that society. The specific activities may not differ in principle from those labelled religion (sacrifice, libation and invocation, for example, feature in both),[27] instigating the semantic debate discussed above; yet people in a society where the concept magic exists will be able to recognize one set of rituals as magic and another as religion – not only outsiders but, I suggest, those engaging in the "magic" practices themselves.[28] In some cases, those accused of practising magic contest the label, as early Christians did, arguing instead for the label "religion" (as scientology does today).[29] In other cases, people may consider their own actions to be magic, either reappraising that label positively or cultivating a counter-cultural stance. Modern Wicca, for example, reappropriates the term "witch" as feminist and empowering while deliberately rejecting mainstream monotheistic religions as oppressive and patriarchal;[30] Apuleius emphasized the original and positive connotations of magic as the pious art of the Magi in his own self-defence against the charge (*Apol.* 25–26), and magic appears as a self-applied label a few times in the Greek Magical Papyri (4.2289, 243, 2081), where it designates sacred arts for accessing esoteric knowledge and power.[31] In each of these cases, individuals deliberately challenge or reframe the dominant discourse of magic. The important point is that social historians should be aware of imposing their own conceptions of magic onto other cultures and strive to understand how the label operates in the society and context under consideration. It is only this emic approach that will illuminate how, when and why a particular practice or person is labelled magic in a specific context and what that reveals about larger social dynamics in the society being considered. Applying the label magic to practices that meet modern definitions of magic (i.e., contrasted with contemporary notions of science or religion) but are not regarded as magic by ancient observers obfuscates our understanding of what magic meant and how it operated (or did not operate) in that culture.[32]

---

26. Foucault 1972: 46.
27. See, for example, Smith 1995: 23–25; Johnston 2002: 344–57; and Johnston 2007: 140–41.
28. Thomassen 1999: 58; and Otto forthcoming both make this point.
29. Tertullian *Apol.* 1; Origen *Cels.* passim; www.religionfacts.com/scientology/index.htm.
30. Adler 1986: 5–6.
31. Otto forthcoming.
32. Dickie 2001: 22 makes this point well.

It is important to emphasize the difference between stereotypes of magic, which are complex, ambivalent and diachronic, accruing material like a snowball or avalanche with time and geographical distance, and the deployment of stereotypes in specific representations. Stereotypes are broadly construed reductionist conglomerates of images and ideas about a group or type of people.[33] They are amorphous and polyvalent, embracing competing and often contradictory associations that express widely held fears and fantasies about the Other.[34] Stereotypes of magic in ancient Greece, for example, encompassed ideas about women's herbal potions as well as male hucksters of binding spells. While distinct in principle, the two conceptions could play off and reinforce each other; Aristophanes, for example, combines a term associated with foreign magi (*manganeuousan*) to describe Circe's herbal potion (*pharmakeia*) (*Plutus* 310), strengthening the negative depiction of her as a nefarious woman, subverting male autonomy with magic potions, by reinforcing it with a term derived from *magos* to connote trickery or deceit.[35] The discourse of magic, I contend, constitutes this constellation of diverse and contrasting images that reinforce and reify each other.

Representations, in contrast, are local, synchronic and context dependent; they constitute *deployments* of specific aspects of larger stereotypes, drawing on a limited range of images or ideas in response to particular local situations. More importantly, representations naturalize particular stereotypes by giving them concrete expression, making them seem universal and "true".[36] For this reason, one can say that magic is often represented as a feminine practice, contributing to the construction of an enduring witch stereotype. But this observation alone does not explain why old women are depicted as sorceresses in Roman literature and younger women figure more prominently in Greek writings, nor does it preclude the possibility of depicting men as magicians, or drawing on other aspects of the stereotype for other purposes. It is important to keep in mind that even when only one aspect of a stereotype is deployed, the other latent aspects reinforce and colour it by association. By focusing on understanding magic as a discursive practice, the local nature of specific representations can be studied, while the broader configuration of magic as a stereotype can also be appreciated. In the following section, I consider some depictions of women and magic that illuminate the presence of a widely dispersed discourse of magic and how it was deployed in specific contexts. First, some thoughts on the connection between gender and magic.

Like magic, notions about sexual difference are socially constructed.[37] The concepts of male and female operate in binary opposition; one cannot be thought of without reference to the other. When focus is placed on the male, as it usually is in most societies, ideas about female act as a foil against which the concepts of "male" or "masculine" are constructed.

---

33. Bhabha 1994: 66.
34. Bhabha 1994: 81–82.
35. Dickie 2001: 34–35 demonstrates this point forcefully. See Collins 2008: 54 on the derivative relationship of *manganeuousan* from *magos*.
36. Hall 1997: 17, 24.
37. Scott 1988: 32; Ortner 1996: 21; Butler 1999: 10–13; and Gleason 1995: xxii.

This fact was meticulously demonstrated by Simone de Beauvoir in *Le deuxième Sexe*: "[Woman] is defined and differentiated with reference to man and not he with reference to her; she is the incidental, the inessential as opposed to the essential. He is the Subject, he is the Absolute – she is the Other."[38] Drawing on Existentialist philosophy, de Beauvoir argues that from the moment the idea of the Other emerges in the process of man's assertion of self as subject and free being, the Other poses a threat, a danger.[39]

More recently, feminist scholars have demonstrated the unequivocal relationship between gender and power; like all discourses – which are implicated in regimes of dominance – gender is also embedded in and supports systems of power.[40] Since the discourse of magic emerged principally (although not exclusively) as a discourse of alterity in ancient Greece and has continued to operate in that fashion throughout the history of Western thought, it comes as no surprise that ideas about gender and magic mutually support each other and are tightly enmeshed. This is not to suggest that gendered stereotypes of magic, which associate magic practices most often with women, are accurate or true. Rather, as Stuart Clark maintains, conceptions of magic are ideological creations that function independently of what people actually do and are enmeshed in larger debates and social conflicts.[41] The following examples briefly introduce this approach to reading magic as a discursive formation in ancient literature.

## DISCOURSE IN PRACTICE

Magic discourse emerged as a constellation of terms denoting ritual practices and practitioners in fifth century Greece.[42] Prior to the fifth century, these same terms operated independently, and often positively, as technical terms to denote practitioners of foreign cults (*magoi*, Heraclitus fr. 14.2),[43] the use of herbs to harm or heal (*pharmakeia*, *Il.* 4.21; *Od.* 1.261, 10.290–92 ), using songs or incantations to harm or heal (*epaeidō*, *Od.* 19.457, Pindar *Pyth.* 4.217), and as a vague term, often translated "sorcery" in later texts (*goēteia*), which derives from funerary lamentation (*goaō*, *Il.* 24.723.). By the end of the fifth century BCE, these terms intersected semantically with the writing of curses to bind someone (*katadeō*, Plato *Leg.* 933a–b), forming a semantic constellation that I identify with the emergence of magic discourse. This discursive formation included ritual practices (*katadesmoi, pharmakeia* and *epoidai*), as well as negative associations with foreign superstition, fraud and harmful rituals (*mageia, goēteia*). These terms could now be used interchangeably and not at all technically to designate illegitimate religion (Euripides *Bacch.* 233–238), poison or curse tablets (Euripides *Medea* 789; Plato *Leg.* 932e–933a), fraudulent rituals

---

38. de Beauvoir 1989: xxii.
39. de Beauvoir 1989: 79.
40. Scott 1988: 32.
41. Clark 1997: 25–26.
42. Stratton 2007: 26–30.
43. Diels and Kranz, 1951.

that fail to help people (Plato *Resp.* 364b–365a; Hippocrates *Morb. sacr.*), as well as the people who do these things. In the mid-fourth century, these same terms appear in forensic speeches as generic terms of abuse and denigration (Aeschines *Ctes.* 137 and Demosthenes *Cor.* 276; *Fals. leg.* 102, 109; 3 *Aphob.* 32), demonstrating that they could operate independently of their technical meanings to convey alterity, broadly construed.[44]

While the constellation of terms designating the concept of "magic" largely carried negative connotations and was identified with Otherness and marginal practices, it was not exclusively associated with women in antiquity. Rather, its earliest association seems to have been with itinerant male healers, provisioners of cathartic and apotropaic rituals, or foreign religious experts who were portrayed by the elite authors as quacks, charlatans and deceivers (Heraclitus fr. 14.2; Plato *Resp.* 364b–365a and Hippocrates. *Morb. sacr.* 6.354–360[45]). Thus, two terms that formed part of this nascent discourse of magic, *magos* and *goēs*, came to convey the general sense of deceive, manipulate or "bewitch" someone and operated in political invective to disparage an opponent's credibility.

Alongside this discursive formation, founded most likely on the very real activities of itinerant ritual specialists, perhaps hailing from Persia (source of the word *magos*), depictions of women practising herbal magic surface in Attic drama and forensic speeches. In these texts, women employ herbal magic (*pharmakeia*) in domestic disputes. In nearly every instance that associates magic terminology with women, they employ *pharmakeia* in response to unfavourable love triangles. Thus, Hermione accuses her husband's concubine, Andromache, of using *pharmakeia* to make her infertile and unattractive to her husband (*Andr.* 32, 159); a stepmother is accused of deliberately killing her husband with poison (*pharmakon*), which she claims to have intended as a love potion (Antiphon *In Novercam*). In another case, two men are accused of being illegitimate sons of a slave mistress, who seduced their father with *pharmaka* so he would leave his wife in favour of her (Isaeus 6.21). The two most famous examples derive from Attic tragedy: Medea uses *pharmakeia* to murder the princess of Corinth in revenge for stealing Medea's husband, Jason. In Sophocles' *Thrachiniae*, Heracles' wife, Deianeira, accidentally murders him with what she believes is a love potion after he returns home with a war bride to be his live-in concubine. In each of these cases, the form of magic attributed to women is *pharmakeia*, the use of herbs to concoct potions or poisons – the distinction between which was fatally fuzzy.[46]

It would be easy as a historian to assume that these portraits reveal the genuine activities of women who lacked other more direct ways to control their fates in a patriarchal world, where men's sexual liberty went unquestioned. Very likely there is some truth behind these representations;[47] but what is interesting to note is that men wielded the same sexual prerogatives across the ancient Mediterranean – yet, this particular *pattern* of representation does not appear elsewhere. Rather, different patterns emerge when the

---

44. For a fuller discussion of all these terms and examples, see Stratton 2007: 26–30; Graf 1997: 20–35; and Dickie 2001: 12–17.
45. Littré 1849.
46. Faraone 1999: 127–28.
47. See Ripat forthcoming.

literature of Rome, early Christianity and rabbinic Judaism are taken into consideration. The emergence of patterns and, more significantly, of differences between those patterns despite similar social structures and gender roles suggests that these portraits and forensic speeches are not simply mirrors of women's historic activities. Rather, they reflect other social dynamics that need to be considered to understand the ideological forces shaping these representations. Monica Wilson's important study, which links specific conceptions of "witchcraft" to social structure in two African societies,[48] encourages us to look for similar social factors underlying the divergent portrayals of magic in antiquity.

Roman literature, for example, seems to lack depictions of magic as a theme until the late Republic. This could reflect a dearth of literary sources; but most scholars agree that the concept of magic and interest in it as a literary topos arises from contact with Greek literature during the Hellenistic period.[49] An interest in magic, primarily women's magic, flourishes in the Augustan period and persists throughout the first two centuries. What is remarkable and patent from even a cursory reading of this literature is how much more nefarious it has become: women, usually old and dishevelled, dig in cemeteries to find body parts for use in their magic.[50] More significantly, women in Latin literature employ magic for the purposes of seduction; they are depicted as sexually insatiable, possessing a masculine lust (*masculae libidinis*, Horace *Epod.* 5.41), and engaging in the most depraved forms of magic, including murder and infanticide, to control men's sexual desire. This very idea, of course, represents a violent transgression of male sexual rights and proper gender roles as conceived not only by Romans, but all societies of the ancient Mediterranean. These "witches" (they represent the origin of later witch stereotypes in Western thought) also possess far more sinister and supernatural powers; they can reverse the flow of rivers (Tibullus 1.2.44), reanimate corpses (Lucan 6.750–830), summon the moon (Propertius 4.5.13) and turn into animals (Apuleius *Met.* 3.21). In other words, they constitute a very different sort of sorceress than the desperate housewives of Greek tragedy and Athenian courtroom dramas.

To further emphasize the stark difference in conceptions of women's magic across the ancient Mediterranean, Christian literature portrays women as the victims of men's predatory magic rather than sorceresses themselves – victims of seduction rather than seductresses (e.g., Irenaeus *Haer.* 7.4.1-6; Acts of Andrew;[51] Jerome *Vit. Hil.* 21.2735–2765). Does this suggest that only Christian women were objects of male desire and magical predation (despite hundreds of seduction spells attesting otherwise)? Or that Christian women did not engage magic to control their errant husbands as Athenian women did? Or that only Roman women lusted after strange men and employed any means necessary to compel them into bed? Rather, it appears that depictions of women attacked by magic operated in debates over religious authority and ascetic power among early Christians. In texts that advocate celibacy and individual access to the Holy Spirit, consecrated virgins

---

48. Wilson 1951.
49. Graf 1997: 37–39; Tupet 1976: 107, 223–24; Gordon 1999: 164–65; Dickie 2001: 127.
50. Stratton 2007: Chapter 3. See also Spaeth forthcoming.
51. MacDonald 1990: 244–47.

of the church successfully defend themselves from magical seduction. In texts that advocate church hierarchy and control over access to spiritual power, virgins fall prey to male magical seduction and require the intervention of ecclesial authorities to save them.[52]

Rabbinic literature is less clear cut in its pattern of representing women's magic. Both Jewish and gentile women are regarded as sources of dangerous magic. Unlike Greek and Roman literature, however, women's magic in rabbinic texts never seems to target any one in particular or is a motive attributed to it. Rather, like terrorists, women leave dangerous magic spells in public places to harm the unwary at random. One pattern that does seem to emerge is the use of food to convey magic; eating and drinking poses a particular source of danger according to the rabbis. For example, a Palestinian rabbi staying at an inn is served a drink with a spell cast on it by an anonymous waitress (b. Sanh. 67b). He recognizes the spell and immediately disarms it with a counter-spell that turns the waitress into a donkey. Another Palestinian rabbi warns that one should not pick up food left on the side of the road since women probably used it for magic (or put a spell on it; the meaning is unclear) (b. Eruvin 64b). The daughters of a prominent Babylonian rabbi are accused of using magic to stir a pot of boiling water with their bare hands; not coincidentally, they are also accused of adultery (b. Gittin 45a). An anonymous woman (*matronita*) attempts to put a spell on two travelling rabbis, but fails because they do not eat vegetables from a bunch tied by the gardener (b. Hullin 105b). These and other examples suggest that food was strongly associated with women's magic in the imagination of the rabbis.

In contrast with these divergent portraits of women's magic in literature, the material evidence for ritual practices widely regarded as magic in the ancient world (*katadesmoi/defixiones* in Latin) is surprisingly consistent across the ancient Mediterranean from the Western border in Roman Britain to the Eastern frontier in Syria, demonstrating startling consistency and continuity across that geographic expanse and over centuries. The Greek Magical Papyri, for example, discovered in Egypt and dating to as late as the fifth century CE, reveal a great degree of stability in their ritual technology compared to examples found almost 1000 years earlier in Greece and Italy. They both invoke chthonic powers to bind a specific person. The biggest difference lies in the increased complexity of later binding formulae; over the centuries they have accrued more names, words of power and symbols to increase their potency or cover all possible divine bases; but, in essence, they follow the same logic and format as the earliest examples from the fifth century BCE.[53] It seems that there was a universal *technē* that was known and shared among practitioners of these rituals, who I would conjecture, understood themselves to be practising magic.[54] Amulets also, whose categorization as magic was ambiguous and debated in the ancient world, reflect a similar consistency across time and cultures; the rabbis transmit recipes for amulets that are not unlike those discussed by the natural scientist, Pliny, who records recipes for amulets he regards as medicinally sound (*Nat.* 28) while disparaging others as the chicanery of the magi (*Nat.* 30). Rabbis permitted proven amulets to be worn on the

---

52. Stratton 2007: 138–39.
53. Gager 1992: 6–7; Ogden 1999: 6–10.
54. Otto forthcoming; Thomassen 1999: 58.

Sabbath, while banning the use of those associated with forbidden practices, known as the "way of the amorites" (y. Shab. 6.9; b Shab. 67a).

In all of these cases, from curses to amulets, the practice of magic, as understood and defined by the ancients, was amazingly consistent across the Mediterranean world throughout the long Graeco-Roman period. Significantly, despite this consistency in the material remains of magic, representations of magic from different times and places diverge in an extraordinary way from the material record: literature (except early Christian writings from the first two and a half centuries) overwhelmingly portrays women as practitioners of magic while material evidence for magic actually practised in antiquity points overwhelmingly to men as both purveyors of magic spells and clients. So, why do the literary depictions vary so widely across cultures yet not reflect the actual practice of magic as it was understood in antiquity?

Clearly, the literary depictions are not snapshots of historic reality; they are ideological portraits that have very little connection with what people actually did. They reflect concerns, conflicts and social dramas unfolding in the societies that produced them. By looking at those societies more closely, specifically at contemporary debates and contests over defining legitimate power, authority and social boundaries unfolding during the period in which the portraits were produced, I propose that we can identify ideological factors contributing to the shape of those depictions.[55] In other words, we can detect the discourse of magic in practice, operating in the negotiation of power and authority.

---

55. Examples of this kind of social rhetorical analysis can be found in Stratton 2007.

# 25

# RANDALL STYERS

"Magic and the Play of Power"

In his *Making Magic: Religion, Magic, and Science in the Modern World* (2004), Randall Styers turns the modern scholarly discourses on "magic" itself into the object of study. In addition to pointing to numerous theoretical contradictions, inconsistencies and tensions in the treatment of "magic", Styers reads these discourses as functional tools (or foils) of self-fashioning and exploring the limits of modernity and the modern subject – for example, by drawing boundaries around legitimate religion, desire, reason and science. Definitions of "magic" can never be true, but instead serve as symptoms for something else. "Magic has held great appeal to scholars because of its capacity both to re-inscribe and to subvert the self-representations of the modern world" (Styers 2004: 226). The theoreticians of "magic" are unmasked as the "magicians" of modernity. In his contribution to the present volume, Styers follows up on this agenda. He explains the recurrent attempt to define "magic" in spite of the grandiose failures of all earlier attempts as motivated by "something more than a desire for conceptual clarity". Styers holds that "the term is too amorphous and shape-shifting – and its deployment too polemical" to allow for "a definition of magic as some type of stable object of study". Yet, he goes on to highlight "a few of magic's most illuminating features" as sites or occasions of study. In the end, paradoxically, the modern denial of "magic" cannot hide that "potent forms of enchantment" surround us in modernity.

## MAGIC AND THE PLAY OF POWER

In his 1996 *Savage Systems: Colonialism and Comparative Religion in Southern Africa*, David Chidester emphatically asserts that "*religion* and *religions* are not objects but occasions for analysis". Rather than attempt to reify these terms or seek to contain them within firm conceptual boundaries, Chidester calls instead for an open definition of religion that would allow for "analyzing the fluid, mobile dynamics of the production of meaning and the contestation of power in situations of cultural contact".[1]

---

1. Chidester 1996: 260 (emphasis in original).

Chidester's claim here about the amorphous nature of "religion" derives from a set of interrelated scholarly trajectories in the study of religion. A number of important recent scholars have developed Wilfred Cantwell Smith's insights on the specifically Western (and Christian) origins of the modern notion of religion and have questioned the application of such a concept in distant cultural contexts.[2] In addition, Western scholars long debated how best to define "religion", and given the polymorphous nature of the notion, many have questioned the value of attempts to reify or stabilize the concept.[3] Chidester's own work on the fluctuating dynamics through which religion was or was not seen to exist among the indigenous peoples of southern Africa during the Dutch and British colonial conquests of the region also richly illuminates the ways in which the deployment of this term is deeply shaped by concerns with power and social control. Andrew Aghapour highlights the over-determined nature of the concept:

> "Religion" is a category employed to describe cultural phenomena, social groups, mental states, material practices, modes of action, texts, shared concepts, significant objects, individual beliefs, and a great deal more. The term "religion" does not point to a stable or universal thing-in-the-world; it is a discursive tool used to accomplish specific goals in varying circumstances.[4]

If religion is best understood not as an object of analysis but instead as an occasion for analysis, what more can possibly be said about magic? Since the nineteenth century, a large number of Western scholars from a range of academic disciplines have sought to formulate a plausible definition of magic. This effort has persisted among social scientists, philosophers, theologians and other social theorists. But after almost two centuries of concerted effort by a number of extremely influential thinkers, little consensus has emerged concerning the nature of magic. The competing proposals conflict with one another and often fall into astounding self-contradiction and inconsistency. The effort to find a stable trans-cultural definition seems doomed to failure, and in this light, as I have discussed elsewhere, it would seem that something more than a desire for conceptual clarity has driven these efforts to find a definition of magic.[5]

It is no coincidence that this modern preoccupation with defining magic emerged in the nineteenth century. As recent historical studies have detailed, the modern concept of science – a new mode of knowledge, practice and social institutions distinct from earlier forms of natural philosophy and natural history – took shape only in the nineteenth century.[6] Yet even as science has assumed such astounding social prominence and material

---

2. See Cantwell Smith 1963; Smith 1998; King 1999; and Masuzawa 2005.
3. For a classic recital of the difficulties in defining religion, see Leuba 1912: 339–61; and for a recent discussion of this issue, see Tweed 2006.
4. Aghapour 2011: 4.
5. See Styers 2004.
6. See, for example, the essays compiled in Thomas Dixon, Geoffrey Cantor and Stephen Pumphrey 2010, particularly Peter Harrison's "'Science' and 'religion': Constructing the boundaries": 23–49.

potency in the modern world, the basic notion of "science" has remained perplexingly unstable. David Lindberg has catalogued the disparate ways in which that particular term is used – to designate a systematic mode of human behaviour, a body of theoretical knowledge, a set of universal law-like propositions, a particular set of procedures, and so on.[7] Science is utterly central to the self-identify of modernity, but it is also disconcertingly illusive. And as this modern notion of science took shape, new concerns emerged concerning its relation to older systems of knowledge and social practice, particularly religious authority. Religion appeared to many enlightened moderns to be a primitive survival whose persistence in a new scientific age was deeply troubling. At the very least, with its distinctive emotional hold on the population, religion offered a challenge to social progress and the advance of reason.

It was in the context of these anxieties that a new preoccupation with magic emerged among Western social theorists. As this volume demonstrates, there is a long history in the West of stigmatizing and marginalizing magic, moving from the legal restrictions of the ancient world, through medieval attacks on witchcraft, on to the counter-polemics of the Reformation, and then through Enlightenment denunciation of superstition. And as new notions of religion and science took hold in the nineteenth century, magic itself assumed a new prominence and new contours. Modern theorists came to reconfigure magic as the simultaneous "bastard sister" of religion – materialistic, self-serving and impious – and "bastard sister" of science – immoderate, irrational and primitive.[8] As Alexander Le Roy stated it in 1922: "magic is the perversion of science as well as of religion".[9]

Yet this disreputable and perverted sibling proved to be remarkably serviceable. Magic could be invoked as a mediating buffer, insulating religion and science securely away from one another. And at the same time, debates over precise failings of magic offered modern social theorists a particularly apt site at which to articulate a broad range of social norms for proper comportment in the modern world, what exactly it might mean to be modern. Magic was configured as modernity's foil, and scholarly debates over magic provided a fertile site for articulating the norms for modern identity. As Peter Pels states it:

> [...] *the modern study of magic is largely a study of human subjectivity*. Whether they mark questions of how human beings make intellectual associations, of what they can and cannot perceive, of how they constitute their desire for the future of what makes the practices they engage in persuasive, or of whether and how they can be called rational or deluded, no present-day speculation about magic can escape the modern discursive boundary between the ideal, modern subject that makes true perceptions and practices a rational discipline and a magical subject that is set up in contrast as backward, immature, or dysfunctional.[10]

---

7. Lindberg 1992: 1–2.
8. Idowi 1973: 191, quoted by Gesch 1979: 137; and Frazer 1922: 50.
9. Le Roy 1922: 35.
10. Pels 2003: 31 (emphasis in original).

Magic has functioned as a prime polemical tool for the self-fashioning of modernity.

In the context of this long tradition of modern scholarly debate and in the context of the even lengthier history of the stigmatizing of magic, it appears that there is little value in attempting to formulate a definition of magic as some type of stable object of study. The term is too amorphous and shape shifting – and its deployment too polemical – ever to offer up any meaningful conceptual clarity, particularly in any type of trans-cultural or trans-historical fashion. After two centuries of this scholarly effort to clarify the nature of magic in order to define exactly what it might mean to be modern, it seems best to move beyond the effort to identify or pin down this elusive magical apparition. And perhaps then we might reconcile ourselves to the fact that we have never been modern: the effort to purify our conceptual categories, our modes of thought and our social institutions, to differentiate and stabilize our identities in this manner, was always a deceptive fantasy.[11]

So with this conclusion, what more might be said about magic? A great deal, in fact. David Chidester cautions again the attempt to formalize or reify religion as an object of study, but he also demonstrates what a fertile occasion religion offers for analysis. The same holds for magic: little might be gained by the effort to define magic as a stable object of study, but magic offers a rich occasion for historical and cultural analysis, a potent site for further "analyzing the fluid, mobile dynamics of the production of meaning and the contestation of power in situations of cultural contact".[12] Let me underscore just a few of magic's most illuminating features.

First, particularly in the modern world, the designation of any behaviour or practice as magic involves an effort to produce important cultural effects. The study of magic allows us to explore the cultural work being accomplished in the invocation of this label. In many contexts, the designation has served to stigmatize various practices, to label them as un-modern, disruptive or undesirable. Identifying a practice as magical often serves not merely to describe the marginality of a practice or its practitioners, but actually to produce that marginality.

At the same time, though, the term can also be used by various social agents to label their own practices, and in these situations those agents are often self-consciously positioning themselves as orthogonal to the dominant modes of social power. In such a context, magic can marshal the power of the margins, serving as a vehicle for critique of the social status quo or as a strategy for challenging various aspects of modern forms of disenchantment. Whether magic is a label attributed to someone else or a label appropriated as a self-description, these dynamics of identification are often deeply illuminating of central social dynamics. We have here a vivid example of the magical power of words.

The importance of the cultural effects at stake in the deployment of magic is demonstrated by the remarkable resourcefulness and creativity devoted to the legitimation of magic by its proponents in the modern world. Whether in working to give magic a patina of scientific method and empirical verification, or in positioning modern magical subcultures within venerable historical lineages, or in applying magical idioms to mediate and

---

11. See Latour 1993; and see also Latour 2010.
12. Chidester 1996: 260.

transform the possibilities for personal experience, modern practitioners of magic respond to the challenge of legitimacy with extraordinary energy and innovation.[13]

The value of magic as a site for cultural analysis becomes even more apparent when we turn to consider the specific forms of social power being wielded or contested in circumstances where the label is in issue. Flows of power are pervasive in modernity, but this power is often most effective when it is hidden from view, normalized by ideologies of propriety, consent and inevitability. Yet the rhetoric surrounding magic offers a provocative tool to name and contest these flows.

This theme of differential power operates in the scholarly theories of magic in a number of different registers. On an initial level, scholars have commonly attributed magic to those with limited access to legitimate forms of social power. Magic is configured as the refuge of primitives, women, children, the ignorant, the poor, the marginal. What we see in these theories is the claim that the socially marginal are prone to magic. But this claim itself often seems to serve as a potent form of theoretical counter-magic, a scholarly sleight of hand, masking the power of the social elites.

One of the constitutive modern explorations of the power differentials central to magic appears in Marcel Mauss's *Esquisse d'une théorie générale de la magic* (1902–1903), written in collaboration with Henri Hubert (see Chapter 13). As Mauss and Hubert explain:

> […] the magical value of persons or things results from the relative position they occupy within society or in relation to society. The two separate notions of magical virtue and social position coincide in so far as one depends on the other. Basically in magic it is always a matter of the respective values recognized by society. These values do not depend, in fact, on the intrinsic qualities of a thing or a person, but on the status or rank attributed to them by all-powerful public opinion, by its prejudices.[14]

Magic, then, according to Mauss and Hubert, depends upon a differential in social value. People and objects only possess magical value because of an underlying difference in their social valuation. But, Mauss and Hubert proceed to explain, it is not merely that an abstract difference in power leads the social group to ascribe magic; instead, it is that difference itself that constitutes the magic. They explain this concerning *mana*, their primary idiom for spiritual force or potency:

> It is not enough to say that the quality of *mana* is attributed to certain things because of the relative position they hold in society. We must add that the idea of *mana* is none other than the idea of these relative values and the idea of these differences in potential. Here we come face to face with the whole idea on which magic is founded, in fact with magic itself.[15]

---

13. See Hammer 2001.
14. Mauss 1972: 148.
15. *Ibid.*: 148–49.

Magic thus materializes, Mauss and Hubert assert, as this very difference in social potency or potential. Despite the ways in which Mauss and Hubert themselves might mystify the operations of *mana*,[16] their formulation places the constitutive nature of the differential in social power at the heart of magic. It signals the value of magic as a central occasion for the analysis of the play of social power.

And at a broader level, questions of power – the appropriate scope of individual desire, autonomy and action – have been central to modern Western debates concerning the nature of magic and its relation to religion and science. Scholars have condemned magic as the source of a host of contradictory social ills. Practitioners of magic are regularly portrayed as seeking to exert selfishly disruptive and anti-social agency, using magic to violate divine, natural and societal laws and the proper bounds of human humility. Or, in the alternative, magic is configured as a tool for mass deception and mystification, used by authoritarian and charismatic leaders to consolidate coercive and repressive power. Social cohesion would appear to require a rather precisely calibrated degree of autonomous agency: neither too much individualism, nor too much conformity. Magicians are accused alternately of anarchy or of authoritarianism but in either case they are seen as engaged in a socially disruptive exercise of untrammelled personal power.

Religion, by contrast, has been configured by the dominant voices in this scholarly tradition as the realm in which human agency remains responsibly chastened in the face of an inexorable divine, natural and social order. The proper objects of religion are not mundane or material, but instead purely transcendent and supra-empirical. Any concern with worldly power or efficacy is thus condemned as petty, selfish and magical. Particularly in the Protestant frame that has exerted such deep influence on so many modern Western scholars, religion is – or should be – a pious and ethereal business, unencumbered by concerns with worldly power.

This scholarly configuration of magic, and the idealized normative vision of religion that it produces, serves a number of complementary functions. On the one hand, it works to defang religion, to consign it to a private and spiritualized realm, to dampen its political or economic potency and align it with the social status quo. But in the same gesture, this cultural frame serves to mask the concrete forms of material power exercised by religious ideologies and agents. Religion maintains enormous social potency, but a rhetoric that frames religion as essentially ethereal, spiritual and transcendent serves to obfuscate that power.[17]

Throughout the modern scholarly literature on magic, we can find extraordinarily broad versions of this configuration of idealized religion. Repeatedly scholars assert that all possible concern with power – indeed, any mode of purposive human action – is fundamentally magical.[18] For example, in 1923 W. J. Perry explained the essence of magic in these terms: "By the aid of certain substances or objects, or by means of certain acts, men believe, in certain circumstances, that they can influence each other, and also

---

16. See Pocock 1972: 7, quoting Lévi-Strauss 1950: xlv.
17. See Fitzgerald 2000: 15, 20.
18. See Styers 2004: 219–23.

natural phenomena, for their own advantage."[19] In 1948, William Howells asserted that "magic, properly, means all the formulas for doing things which are beyond one's personal powers".[20] In his 1970 *Sociology of Religion*, Werner Stark stated that magic arises from the magician's desire "to insert himself into the natural nexus of cause and effect, to introduce his wish, his subjective whim, into the objective texture of events".[21] And in his 1995 text on the anthropology of religion, Morton Klass defined magic as the set of "techniques employed by those who believe that in specific circumstances persons, powers, beings, or even events are subject to control or coercion".[22]

In these extraordinary formulations, any sense that human agency can produce effects on other human beings or the natural world, that personal power can be augmented by material objects or ritualistic behaviours, that the human will plays a role in the cause–effect relationships of the material and social worlds – any such sense falls into magic. This sweeping definition of magic is widespread throughout modern social scientific literature, and its very familiarity can serve to occlude the rather astonishing underlying claim: the assertion that all purposive human endeavour is magical. Such a claim is surely incoherent (and likely inadvertent), since a vast portion of human activity is aimed at affecting human and natural phenomena, or expanding one's power, or inserting one's will into various chains of causality – almost no human activity would fall outside this definition of magic. But the prevalence of this claim in the scholarly literature provides an important clue to the cultural logic underlying the modern preoccupation with magic. Scholarly theorizing about magic has revolved around this question of the proper scope of personal agency, but at the same time it has been busily engaged in the task of disclaiming that fascination – projecting it onto a primitive magical mentality.[23]

Just as the theories of magic serve to legitimate a vision of religion as pious and otherworldly, so also a similar dynamic occurs in relation to science. While magic is commonly portrayed by theorists as arrogant, wilful and selfish, an idealized notion of science as humble and chastened is given shape. As W. C. Dampier put it in 1943, far from the folly and arrogance of magic, science is guided by "a slow, cautious and humble-minded search for truth".[24] A number of other scholars echo this claim. Ignoring the massive social prominence of scientists and scientific institutions and the enormous potency of modern technology to reorder the world, theorists assert instead that science is at its heart a humble and modest affair. Magic, instead, is the site of arrogant manipulation and striving.

As modernity's foil, magic thus serves as a repository for all the repressed anxieties and desires that lie within the modern and that the modern has sought to expel. Modernity has been preoccupied with the operations of power, but it has also been deeply invested in disclaiming that preoccupation, in concealing the constitutive coercion on which modern

---

19. Perry 1923: 8.
20. Howells 1948: 47–48.
21. Stark 1970: 240.
22. Klass 1995: 89.
23. For more on this theme, see Styers forthcoming.
24. Dampier 1943: 57, 376.

social structures are founded, in naturalizing a distinctive allocation of social authority and a specific restrictive mode of subjectivity. Particularly potent forms of magical enchantment are thus constitutive of modernity; as Peter Pels states it, we are surrounded by "enchantments that are produced by practices culturally specific to modern states, economies, and societies – practices labelled as representation, commodification, and discipline".[25] Exploring the surreptitious power undergirding the enchanted forms of modern representation, commodification and discipline – through the cultural analysis occasioned by the study of magic – we might recognize the deep and pervasive magical potency surrounding us. Modernity has depended upon the surreptitious – and magical – power it so denies, and the study of magic provides a vivid window onto the cultural logics upon which the modern world has been structured.

---

25. Pels 2003: 5 (emphasis in original).

# BIBLIOGRAPHY

Adler, M. 1986. *Drawing Down the Moon: Witches, Druids, Goddess-Worshippers, and Other Pagans in America Today*. Boston, MA: Beacon Press.
Aghapour, A. 2011. "Of Gods and Man: The Biocognitive Event in Religious Studies", MA thesis. Chapel Hill, NC: University of North Carolina.
Agrippa von Nettesheim, H.C. 1527. *De Incertitudine et Vanitate Scientiarum*. Cologne.
Agrippa von Nettesheim, H.C. 1533. *De Occulta Philosophia*. Cologne.
Allier. R. 1927. *Le non-civilisé et nous*. Paris: Payot.
Amiel, H.-F. 1890. *Amiel's Journal: The Journal in Time of Henri-Frederic Amiel*, trans. M. A. Ward. London.
Arbmann, E. 1931. "Seele und mana". *Archiv für Religionswissenschaft* 29: 293–394.
Arms, P. 2000. *Pokemon and Harry Potter: A Fatal Attraction – An Exposé of the Secret War against the Youth of America*. Oklahoma City, IL: Hearthstone Publishing.
Austin, J. L. 1962. *How to Do Things with Words*. Oxford: Clarendon Press.
Bacon, F. 1620. *Novum Organum Scientiarum*.
Barnes, B. 1973. "The Comparison of Belief Systems: Anomaly Versus Falsehood". In *Modes of Thought: Essays on Thinking in Western and Non-Western Societies*, R. Horton & R. Finnegan (eds), 182–99. London: Faber & Faber.
Bartlett, F. C. 1923. *Psychology and Primitive Culture*. Cambridge: Cambridge University Press.
Bastian, A. 1860. *Der Mensch in der Geschichte*, vol. III. Leipzig.
Bastian, Adolf. 1866. *Die Völker des oestlichen Asien*, vol. I. Leipzig.
Bataille, G. 1979. "The Psychological Structure of Fascism", trans. C. R. Lovitt. *New German Critique* 16 (winter): 64–87.
Bateson, G. 1985. *Mind and Nature: A Necessary Unity*. London: Fontana.
Bateson, G. 1991. "A Sacred Unity". In *Sacred Unity: Further Steps to an Ecology of Mind*, G. Bateson & R. E. Donaldson (eds), 231–32. New York: HarperCollins.
Bateson, G. 2000. *Steps to an Ecology of Mind*, Chicago, IL: University of Chicago Press.
Beattie, J. H. M. 1966. "Ritual and Social Change". *Man* 1: 60–74.
Beattie, J. 1968. *Other Cultures: Aims, Methods and Achievements in Social Anthropology*. New York: Macmillan.
Beattie, J. H. M. 1970. "On Understanding Ritual". In *Rationality*, B. R. Wilson (ed.), 240–68. Oxford: Oxford University Press.
Benavides, G. 2006. "Magic". In *The Blackwell Companion to the Study of Religion*, R. A. Segal (ed.), 295–308. Malden, MA: Blackwell Publishers.
Benedict, R. 1938. "Religion". In *General Anthropology*, F. Boas (ed.), 627–65. Boston, MA: D. C. Heath.
Berger, H. A. 1999. *A Community of Witches: Contemporary Neo-Paganism and Witchcraft in the United States*. Columbia, SC: University of South Carolina Press.
Berger, H. A. 2005. "Witchcraft and Neopaganism". In *Witchcraft and Magic: Contemporary North America*, H. Berger (ed.), 28–54. Philadelphia, PA: University of Pennsylvania Press.

Bertholet, A. 1927. "Das Wesen der Magie". *Nachrichten von der Gesellschaft der Wissenschaften zu Göttingen*: 62–85.
Beth, K. 1914. *Religion und Magie bei den Naturvölkern*. Leipzig: Teubner.
Bhabha, H. K. 1994. "The Other Question: Stereotype, Discrimination and the Discourse of Colonialism". In his *The Location of Culture*, 66–84. London: Routledge.
Bidney, D. 1953. *Theoretical Anthropology*. New York: Columbia University Press.
Biezais, H. 1978. "Von der Wesensidentität der Religion und Magie". *Acta Academiae Aboensis* 55: 5–31.
Binswanger, L. 1928. *Wandlungen in der Auffassung und Deutung des Traumes von den Griechen bis zur Gegenwart*. Berlin: Springer.
Blavatsky, H. P. 1986 (1892). *Theosophical Glossary*. New Delhi: Asian Publications Services.
Blavatsky, H. P. 2002 (1889). *The Key to Theosophy: Being a Clear Exposition, in the Form of Question and Answer of the Ethics, Science, and Philosophy, for the Study of which the Theosophical Society Has Been Founded*. Pasadena: Theosophical University Press.
Boas, F. 1911. *The Mind of Primitive Man*. New York: Macmillan.
Boyer, P. 1994. *The Naturalness of Religious Ideas: A Cognitive Theory of Religion*. Berkeley, CA: University of California Press.
Boyer, P. 1996. "Religion as an Impure Subject: A Note on Cognitive Order in Religious Representation in Response to Brian Malley". *Method & Theory in the Study of Religion* **8**(2): 201–13.
Boyer, P. & P. Liénard 2006. "Why Ritualized Behavior? Precaution Systems and Action Parsing in Developmental, Pathological and Cultural Rituals". *Behavioral and Brain Sciences* **29**(6): 595–613.
Brand, J. 1777. *Observations on Popular Antiquities*, vol. III. London.
Brinton, D. G. 1899 (1897). *Religions of Primitive Peoples*, 3rd edn. New York.
Bulbulia, J. 2008. "Meme Infection or Religious Niche Construction? An Adaptationist Alternative to the Cultural Maladaptationist Hypothesis". *Method & Theory in the Study of Religion* **20**(1): 67–107.
Burton, R. F. 1865. *Wit and Wisdom from West Africa*. London.
Bury, R. G. (ed.) 1926. *Plato: Laws. Books VII-XII. With an English Translation by R. G. Bury*. Cambridge, MA: Harvard University Press.
Butler, J. 1999. *Gender Trouble: Feminism and the Subversion of Identity*. New York: Routledge.
Cantwell Smith, W. 1963. *The Meaning and End of Religion: A New Approach to the Religious Traditions of Mankind*. New York: Macmillan.
Cassirer, E. 1925. *Philosophie der symbolischen Formen. Teil II: Das mythische Denken*. Berlin: Cassirer.
Chidester, D. 1996. *Savage Systems: Colonial and Comparative Religion in Southern Africa*. Charlottesville, VA: University of Virginia Press.
Clark, S. 1997. *Thinking with Demons: The Idea of Witchcraft in Early Modern Europe*. Oxford: Oxford University Press.
Clemen, C. 1921. "Wesen und Ursprung, der Magie". *Arch. f. Rel.-Psych.* II–III.
Codrington, R. H. 1880. "Notes on the Customs of Mota, Bank Islands". *Transactions and Proceedings of the Royal Society of Victoria* XVI: 119–43.
Codrington, R. H. 1891. *The Melanesians: Studies in Their Anthropology and Folklore*. Oxford: Clarendon Press.
Collins, D. 1798. *An Account of the English Colony in New South Wales*, vol. I. London.
Collins, D. 2008. *Magic in the Ancient Greek World*, Blackwell Ancient Religions. Malden, MA: Blackwell Publishers.
Coomaraswamy, A. K. 1939. "De la Mentalité Primitive". *Études Traditionelles* 44.
Crawley, A. E. 1902. *The Mystic Rose: A Study of Primitive Marriage and of Primitive Thought in Its Bearing on Marriage*. London: Macmillan.
Crawley, A. E. 1905. *The Tree of Life: A Study of Religion*. London: Hutchinson & Co.
Cunningham, G. 1999. *Religion and Magic: Approaches and Theories*. New York: New York University Press.
Dalton, E. T. 1868. "The 'Kols' of Chota-Nagpore". *Transactions of the Ethnological Society of London* 6: 1–41.
Damasio, A. R. 2001. "Some Notes on Brain, Imagination and Creativity". In *The Origins of Creativity*, K. H. Pfenninger & V. R. Shubik (eds). Oxford: Oxford University Press.
Dampier, W. C. 1943. *A History of Science and Its Relations with Philosophy and Religion*. Cambridge: Cambridge University Press.
Danzel, T. W. 1922. "Die psychologischen Grundlagen der Mythologie". *Archiv für Religionswissenschaft* 21.

# BIBLIOGRAPHY

Danzel, T. W. 1924. *Kultur und Religion des primitiven Menschen*. Stuttgart: Strecker and Schroeder.
de Beauvoir, S. 1989. *The Second Sex*, trans. and ed. H. M. Parshley. New York: Vintage Books.
de Certeau, M. 1988. "Discourse Disturbed: The Sorcerer's Speech", in *The Writing of History*, trans. T. Conley, 244–68. New York: Columbia University Press.
de Certeau, M. 2000. *The Possession at Loudun*, trans. M. B. Smith. Chicago, IL: University of Chicago Press.
de Martino, E. 1988 (1977 [1948]). *Primitive Magic: The Psychic Powers of Shamans and Sorcerers*. Bridport: Cardinal Books.
D'Orbigny, A. D. 1839. *L'Homme Américain*, vol. II. Paris.
de Visser, M. W. 2008 (1913). *The Dragon in China and Japan*. New York: Cosimo.
Derrida, J. 1978a. "*Cogito* and the history of madness". In *Writing and Difference*, trans. A. Bass. Chicago, IL: University of Chicago Press.
Derrida, J. 1978b. "Structure, Sign, and Play in the Discourse of the Human Sciences". In *Writing and Difference*, trans. A. Bass. Chicago, IL: University of Chicago Press.
Dickie, M. W. 2001. *Magic and Magicians in the Greco-Roman World*. London: Routledge.
Diels, H. & W. Kranz (eds) 1951. *Die Fragmente der Vorsokratiker*, 6th ed., vol. 1. Berlin: Weidmann.
Dixon, T., G. Cantor & S. Pumphrey (eds) 2010. *Science and Religion: New Historical Perspectives*. Cambridge: Cambridge University Press.
Douglas, M. 1966. *Purity and Danger: An Analysis of the Concepts of Pollution and Taboo*. London: Routledge.
Dreyfus, H. L. & P. Rabinow 1983. *Michel Foucault: Beyond Structuralism and Hermeneutics*, 2nd edn. Chicago, IL: University of Chicago Press.
Durkheim, É. 1912. *Les formes élementaires de la vie religieuse*. Paris: Alcan.
Durkheim, É. 1994 (1975 [1898]). "Concerning the Definition of Religious Phenomena". In *Durkheim on Religion: A Selection of Readings with Bibliographies*, W. S. F. Pickering (ed.), 74–99. Atlanta, GA: Scholars Press.
Durkheim, É. 1995 (1912). *Elementary Forms of Religious Life*, trans. K. Fields. New York: The Free Press.
Ehrenreich, P. 1910. *Die allgemeine Mythologie und ihre ethnologischen Grundlagen*. Leipzig: Hinrichs.
Eidinow, E. 2007. *Oracles, Curses, and Risk among the Ancient Greeks*. Oxford: Oxford University Press.
Eliade, M. 1959. *Patterns in Comparative Religion*, trans. R. Sheed. London: Sheed and Ward.
Eliade, M. 1970. *Traité d'histoire des religions*, 2nd. edn. Paris: Payot.
Eliade, M. 1978. *Occultism, Witchcraft, and Cultural Fashions: Essays in Comparative Religions*. Chicago, IL: University of Chicago Press.
Eliade, M. 1988. *A History of Religious Ideas*, vol. 3, trans. W. R. Trask. Chicago, IL: University of Chicago Press.
Elliot, W. 1868. "On Ancient Sepulchral Remains in Southern India, and Particularly of Those in the Nilagiri Mountains". In *Congress of Prehistoric Archaeology: Transactions of the Third Session*. London. 240–55.
Ellis, W. 1853. *Polynesian Researches During a Residence of Nearly Eight Years in the Society and Sandwich Islands*, vol I. London.
Engler, S. and M. Stausberg 2011. "Introductory Essay. Crisis and Creativity: Opportunities and Threats in the Global Study of Religion\s". *Religion* 41(2): 127–43.
Espirito Santo, D. and R. Llera Blanes (eds) 2012. *The Social Life of Entities: Spirits and the Agency of Intangibles*. Chicago, IL: University of Chicago Press.
Evans-Pritchard, E. E. 1934. "Lévy-Bruhl's Theory of Primitive Mentality". *Bulletin of the Faculty of Arts* 2: 1–36.
Evans-Pritchard, E. 1956. *Nuer Religion*. New York: Oxford University Press.
Evans-Pritchard, E. E. 1958 (1937). *Witchcraft, Oracles and Magic among the Azande*, with a Foreword by C. G. Seligman FRS. Oxford: Oxford University Press.
Evans-Pritchard, E. 1965. *Theories of Primitive Religion*. Oxford: Clarendon Press
Eyre, E. J. 1845. *Journals of Expeditions of Discovery into Central Australia and Overland from Adelaide to King George's Sound in the Years 1840–1, vol. II*. London.
Faivre, A. 1989. "Speculations About Nature". In *Hidden Truths: Magic, Alchemy, and the Occult*, L. E. Sullivan (ed.). New York: Macmillan.
Faraone, C. 1991. "The Agonistic Context of Early Greek Binding Spells". In *Magika Hiera: Ancient Greek Magic and Religion*, C. Faraone and D. Obbink (eds), 3–32. New York: Oxford University Press.
Faraone, C. 1999. *Ancient Greek Love Magic*. Cambridge, MA: Harvard University Press.
Faraone, C. and D. Obbink (eds) 1991. *Magika Hiera: Ancient Greek Magic and Religion*. New York: Oxford University Press.

Fauconnier, G. 1994. *Mental Spaces: Aspects of Meaning Construction in Natural Language*. Cambridge: Cambridge University Press.
Fauconnier, G. 1997. *Mappings in Thought and Language*. Cambridge: Cambridge University Press.
Fauconnier, G. and M. Turner 2003. *The Way We Think: Conceptual Blending and the Mind's Hidden Complexities*. New York: Basic Books.
Filliozat, J. 1964. *The Classical Doctrine in Indian Medicine: Its Origin and Greek Parallels*. Delhi: Munshiram Manoharlal Oriental Booksellers and Publishers.
Finnegan, R. 1969. "How To Do Things With Words: Performative Utterances Among the Limba of Sierra Leone". *Man* 4(4): 537–52.
Fiske, A. and N. Haslam 1997. "Is Obsessive–Compulsive Disorder a Pathology of the Human Disposition to Perform Socially Meaningful Rituals? Evidence of Similar Content". *Journal of Nervous and Mental Disease* **185**(4): 211–22.
Fitzgerald, T. 2000. *The Ideology of Religious Studies*. New York: Oxford University Press.
Foucault, M. 1965. *Madness and Civilization: A History of Insanity in the Age of Reason*, trans. R. Howard. New York: New York American Library.
Foucault, M. 1972. *The Archaeology of Knowledge and the Discourse on Language*, trans. A. M. Sheridan Smith. New York: Pantheon Books.
Foucault, M. 1973. *The Birth of the Clinic: An Archaeology of Medical Perception*, trans. A. M. Smith. New York: Random House.
Foucault, M. 1979. *Discipline and Punishment: The Birth of the Prison*, trans. A. Sheridan. New York: Random House.
Foucault, M. 1980a. "An Introduction". In *The History of Sexuality*, vol. I, trans. R. Hurley. New York: Random House.
Foucault, M. 1980b. *Power/Knowledge: Selected Writings and Other Interviews 1972–1977*, ed. C. Gordon, trans. C. Gordon, L. Marshal, J. Mepham & K. Soper. New York: Pantheon.
Frankfurter, D. 2002. "Review of *Magic and Magicians in the Greco-Roman World* by Matthew W. Dickie". *Bryn Mawr Classical Review (online)*, 26 February.
Frazer, J. G. 1900. *The Golden Bough: A Study in Magic and Religion*, 2nd. edn, 3 vols. London: Macmillan.
Frazer, J. G. 1905. *Lectures on the Early History of Kingship*. London: Macmillan.
Frazer, J. G. 1906–1915. *The Golden Bough: A Study in Magic and Religion*, 3rd edn, 12 vols. London: Macmillan.
Frazer, J. G. 1906. *The Golden Bough: A Study in Magic and Religion*, 3rd edn. Part I: *The Magic Art and the Evolution of Kings, Vol. I*. London: Macmillan.
Frazer, J. G. 1910. *Totemism and Exogamy: A Treatise on Certain Early Forms of Superstition and Society*, 4 vols. London: Macmillan.
Frazer, J. G. 1913. *The Belief in Immortality and the Worship of the Dead*, 3 vols. London: Macmillan.
Frazer, J. G. 1919. *Folk-Lore in the Old Testament: Studies in Comparative Religion and Law*, 3 vols. London: Macmillan.
Frazer, J. G. 1922. *The Golden Bough: A Study in Magic and Religion*, abridged edn. New York: Macmillan.
Freud, S. 2007. *The Standard Edition of the Complete Psychological Works of Sigmund Freud, vol. XIII*. London: Vintage.
Freud, S. 2010 [1913]. *Totem and Taboo: Some Points of Agreement between the Mental Lives of Savages and Neurotics*, trans. J. Strachey. London: International Psychoanalytic Association.
Gager, J. G. 1992. *Curse Tablets and Binding Spells from the Ancient World*. Oxford: Oxford University Press.
Gallie, W. B. 1956. "Essentially Contested Concepts". *Proceedings of the Aristotelian Society* 56: 167–98.
Gandavo, P. de M. 1837. *Histoire de la province de Sancta-Cruz*. Paris.
Gardner, J. 1858–1860. *Faiths of the World: An Account of All Religions and Religious Sects, Their Doctrines, Rites, Ceremonies, and Customs*. Edinburgh.
Garrett, S. 1989. *The Demise of the Devil: Magic and the Demonic in Luke's Writings*. Minneapolis, MN: Fortress Press.
Geertz, C. 1973a. "The Cerebral Savage: On the Work of Claude Lévi-Strauss". In his *The Interpretation of Cultures*. New York: Basic Books.
Geertz, C. 1973b. "Deep Play: Notes on the Balinese Cockfight". In his *The Interpretation of Cultures*. New York: Basic Books.

Geertz, C. 1973c. "Thick Description: Toward an Interpretive Theory of Culture". In his *The Interpretation of Cultures*. New York: Basic Books.
Gell, A. 1988. "Technology and Magic". *Anthropology Today* **4**(2): 6–9.
Gennep, A. van. 1909. *Les rites de passage*. Paris: Nourry.
Gennep, A. van 1977. *The Rites of Passage*. London: Routledge & Kegan Paul.
Gentner, D. 1983. "Structure-mapping: A Theoretical Framework for Analogy". *Cognitive Science* **7**(2): 155–70.
Gesch, P. F. 1979. "Magic as a Process of Social Discernment". In *Powers, Plumes and Piglets: Phenomena of Melanesian Religion*, N. C. Habel (ed.) Bedford Park, S. Australia: Australian Association for the Study of Religions.
Gibbons, S. L. 1994. *Kant's Theory of Imagination: Bridging Gaps in Judgement and Experience*. Oxford: Oxford University Press.
Giesler, P. V. 2002. "Review of *Magic, Witchcraft and the Otherworld*". *American Ethnologist* **29**(1) February: 208.
Ginzburg, C. 1983. *The Night Battles*, trans. J. and A. Tedeschi. Baltimore, MD: Johns Hopkins University Press.
Ginzburg, C. 1989. "Introduction". In *Ecstasies: Deciphering the Witches" Sabbath*, trans. J. and A. Tedeschi, 1–30. Baltimore, MD: Johns Hopkins University Press.
Gleason, M. W. 1995. *Making Men: Sophists and Self-Presentation in Ancient Rome*. Princeton, NJ: Princeton University Press.
Glucklich, A. 1997. *The End of Magic*. New York: Oxford University Press.
Goethe, J. W. von 1832. *Faust: der Tragödie, zweiter Teil*.
Goldenweiser, A. A. 1921. *Early Civilization: An Introduction to Anthropology*. London: Harrap.
Goode, W. J. 1949. "Magic and Religion: A Continuum". *Ethnos* 14: 172–82.
Goody, J. 1961. "Religion and Ritual: The Definitional Problem". *British Journal of Sociology* 12: 142–64.
Gordon, R. 1999. "Imagining Greek and Roman magic". In *Witchcraft and Magic in Europe: Ancient Greece and Rome*, B. Ankarloo and S. Clark (eds), 159–275. Philadelphia, PA: University of Pennsylvania Press.
Graebner, F. 1924. *Das Weltbild der Primitiven: Eine Untersuchung der Urformen weltanschaulichen Denkens bei Naturvölkern*. Munich: Reinhardt.
Graf, F. 1997. *Magic in the Ancient World*, trans. F. Philip. Cambridge, MA: Harvard University Press.
Greenwood, S. 2000. *Magic, Witchcraft and the Otherworld: An Anthropology*. Oxford: Berg.
Greenwood, S. 2005. *The Nature of Magic: An Anthropology of Consciousness*. Oxford: Berg.
Greenwood, S. 2009. *The Anthropology of Magic*. Oxford: Berg.
Greenwood, S. 2011 (2001). *The Encyclopedia of Magic and Witchcraft*. London: Lorenz.
Greenwood, S. 2012. "Toward an Epistemology of Imaginal Reality: Fieldwork with the Dragon". In *The Social Life of Entities: Spirits and the Agency of Intangibles*, D. Espirito Santo & R. Llera Blanes (eds). Chicago, IL: University of Chicago Press.
Gregory, W. 1851. *Letters to a Candid Inquirer, on Animal Magnetism*. Philadelphia, PA.
Grimm, J. 1835. *Deutsche Mythologie*. Göttingen.
Grote, G. 1849. *A History of Greece*, vol. III. New York.
Grout, L. 1860. *Zulu-Land: Or Life among the Zulu-Kafirs of Natal and Zulu-Land, South Africa*. London.
Hall, S. (ed.) 1997. *Representation: Cultural Representations and Signifying Practices*. London: Sage.
Hammer, O. 2001. *Claiming Knowledge: Strategies of Epistemology from Theosophy to the New Age*. Leiden: Brill.
Hammond, D. 1970. "Magic: A Problem in Semantics". *American Anthropologist* 72: 1349–56.
Hanegraaff, W. J. 1999. "Defining Religion in spite of History". In *The Pragmatics of Defining Religion: Contexts, Concepts and Contests*, J. Platvoet and A. L. Molendijk (eds), 337–78. Leiden: Brill.
Hanegraaff, W. 2012. *Esotericism and the Academy: Rejected Knowledge in Western Culture*. Cambridge: Cambridge University Press.
Hanusch, I. J. 1842. *Die Wissenschaft des Slawischen Mythus*. Lemberg.
Hardy, R. S. 1850. *Eastern Monachism*. London.
Harries-Jones, P. 2002. *A Recursive Vision: Ecological Understanding and Gregory Bateson*. Toronto: University of Toronto Press.
Harrison, J. E. 1912. *Themis: A Study of the Social Origins of Greek Religion*. Cambridge: Cambridge University Press.
Harrison, P. 2010. "'Science' and 'Religion': Constructing the Boundaries", in *Science and Religion: New Historical Perspectives*, T. Dixon, G. Cantor & S. Pumphrey (eds), 23–49. Cambridge: Cambridge University Press.

Harrison, S. (ed.) 2011. *Apuleius: Rhetorical Works*, trans. and annotated S. Harrison, J. Hilton & V. Hunink. Oxford: Oxford University Press.
Hastings, J. 1908–1921. *Encyclopedia of Religion and Ethics*. 12 vols. Edinburgh: Clark.
Hegel, G. & W. Friedrich 1995 (1987). *Lectures on the Philosophy of Religion. Vol. II: Determinate Religion*, trans. P. C. Hodgson. Berkeley, CA: University of California Press.
Heidegger, M. 1927. *Sein und Zeit*. Halle: Niemeyer.
Henry, J. 1997. *The Scientific Revolution and the Origins of Modern Science*. Basingstoke: Macmillan.
Henry, J. 2002. *Knowledge Is Power: How Magic, the Government and an Apocalyptic Vision Inspired Francis Bacon to Create Modern Science*. Cambridge: Icon Books.
Hidding, K. A. H. 1933. *Gebruiken en godsdienst der Soendaneezer*. Bandung: Drukkerij A. C. Nix.
Hobhouse, L. T. 1915 (1906). *Morals in Evolution: A Study in Comparative Ethics*, 2nd edn. London: Chapman & Hall.
Hoffman, C. A. 2002. "Fiat Magia", in *Magic and Ritual in the Ancient World*, P. Mirecki & M. Meyer (eds), 179–94. Leiden: Brill.
Horton, R. 1960. *The Gods as Guests: An Aspect of Kalabari Religious Life*. Lagos: Nigeria Magazine Special Publications.
Horton, R. 1967 "African Traditional Thought and Western Science. Part II". *Africa* 37: 155–87.
Horton, R. 1968. "Neo-Tylorianism: Sound Sense or Sinister Prejudice?". *Man* 3: 625–34.
Horton, R. 1993. *Patterns of Thought in Africa and the West: Essays on Magic, Religion, and Science*. Cambridge: Cambridge University Press.
Horton, R. & R. Finnegan (eds) 1973. *Modes of Thought: Essays on Thinking in Western and Non-Western Societies*. London: Faber & Faber.
Howells. W. 1948. *The Heathens: Primitive Man and His Religions*. Garden City, NY: Doubleday.
Howitt, A. W. 1904. *Native Tribes of South East Australia*. London: Macmillan.
Hubert, H. 1877. "Magia". In *Dictionnaire des antiquités Greques et Romaines*, C. Daremberg & E. Saglio (eds). Paris.
Hubert, H. & M. Mauss 1902–03. "Esquisse d'une theorie générale de la magie". *L'Année sociologique* 7: 1–146.
Hubert, H. & M. Mauss 1909. *Mélanges d'histoire des religions*. Paris: Alcan.
Humphrey, C. & J. Laidlaw 1994. *The Archetypal Actions of Ritual: A Theory of Ritual Illustrated by the Jain Rite of Worship*. Oxford: Oxford University Press.
Hunt, R. 1865. *Popular Romances of the West of England*, 2nd series. London.
Hutchison, K. 1982. "What Happened to Occult Qualities in the Scientific Revolution?". *Isis* 73(2), June: 233–53.
Huxley, F. 1989. *The Dragon: Nature of Spirit, Spirit of Nature*. London: Thames and Hudson.
Idowi, E. B. 1973. *African Traditional Religion*. London: SMC Press.
Ingold, T. 2001. *The Perception of the Environment: Essays in Livelihood, Dwelling and Skill*. London: Routledge.
Ingold, T. 2011. *Being Alive: Essays on Movement, Knowledge and Description*. London: Routledge.
Jakobson, R. & M. Halle. 1956. *Fundamentals of Language*. 'S-Gravenhage: Mouton.
Jakobson, R. & M. Halle. 2002. *Fundamentals of Language*, 2nd edn. Berlin: Mouton.
Janowitz, N. 2001. *Magic in the Roman World*. London: Routledge.
Janowitz, N. 2002. *Icons of Power: Ritual Practices in Late Antiquity*. University Park, PA: Pennsylvania State University Press.
Jarvie, I. C. & J. Agassi 1967. "The Problem of the Rationality of Magic". *British Journal of Anthropology* 18: 55–74.
Jarvie, I. C. & J. Agassi 1973. "Magic and Rationality Again". *British Journal of Sociology* 24: 236–45.
Jaspers, K. 1920 (1913). *Allgemeine Psychopathologie*. Berlin: Springer.
Jenkins, R. 2008. *Rethinking Ethnicity*, 2nd edn. Thousand Oaks, CA: Sage.
Johnson, M. 1981. *Philosophical Perspectives on Metaphor*. Minneapolis, MN: University of Minnesota Press.
Johnson, M. 1992. *The Body in the Mind: The Bodily Basis of Meaning, Imagination, and Reason*. Chicago, IL: University of Chicago Press.
Johnston, S. I. 2002. "Sacrifice in the Greek Magical Papyri". In *Magic and Ritual in the Ancient World*, P. Mirecki & M. Meyer (eds), 344–57. Leiden: Brill.
Johnston, S. I. 2003. "Describing the Undefinable: New Books on Magic and Old Problems of Definition". *History of Religions* 43(1): 50–54.

# BIBLIOGRAPHY

Johnston, S. I. 2007. "Magic". In *Ancient Religions*, S. I. Johnston (ed.), 139–52. Cambridge, MA: Belknap Press of Harvard University Press.

Jones, D. E. 2000. *An Instinct for Dragons*. New York: Routledge.

Jordan, D. R., H. Montgomery & E. Thomasson (eds) 1999. *The World of Ancient Magic*. Bergen: Norwegian Institute at Athens.

Jung, C. 1960. *The Structure and Dynamics of the Psyche (Collected Works of C. G. Jung, Volume 8)*. Princeton, NJ: Princeton University Press.

Kapferer, B. 1997. *The Feast of the Sorcerer: Practices of Consciousness and Power*. Chicago, IL: University of Chicago Press.

Kieckhefer. R. 1989. *Magic in the Middle Ages*. Cambridge: Cambridge University Press.

King, I. 1910. *The Development of Religion: A Study in Anthropology and Social Psychology*. New York: Macmillan.

King, R. 1999. *Orientalism and Religion: Postcolonial Theory, India and "The Mystic East"*. London: Routledge.

Kippenberg, H. G. & B. Luchesi (eds) 1987 (1978). *Magie: Die sozialwissenschaftliche Kontroverse über das Verstehen fremden Denkens*. Frankfurt am Main: Suhrkamp.

Klass, M. 1995. *Ordered Universes: Approaches to the Anthropology of Religion*. Boulder, CO: Westview.

Klemm, G. 1844. *Allgemeine Cultur-Geschichte*, vol. III. Leipzig.

Kluckhohn, C. 1953. "Universal Categories of Culture". In *Anthropology Today: An Encyclopedic Inventory*, S. Tax *et al.* (eds), 507–23. Chicago, IL: University of Chicago Press.

Kovach, M. 2009. *Indigenous Methodologies: Characteristics, Conversations, and Contexts*. Toronto: University of Toronto Press.

Kretschmer, E. 1922. *Medizinische Psychologie: Ein Leitfaden für Studium und Praxis*. Leipzig: Georg Thieme Verlag.

Kroeber, A. L. 1923. *Anthropology*. New York: Harcourt, Brace & Co.

Kuhn, G., A. A. Amlani & R. A. Rensink 2008. "Towards a Science of Magic". *Trends in Cognitive Sciences* 12: 349–54.

Kummer, H. 1996. "Causal Knowledge in Animals". In *Causal Cognition: A Multidisciplinary Debate*, D. Sperber, D. Premack & A. J. Premack (eds). Oxford: Clarendon Press.

Lakoff, G. 1990. *Women, Fire, and Dangerous Things: What Categories Reveal about the Mind*. Chicago, IL: University of Chicago Press.

Lakoff, G. & M. Johnson. 1980. *Metaphors We Live By*. Chicago, IL: University of Chicago Press.

Lang, A. 1898. *The Making of Religion*. London.

Lang, A. 1901. *Magic and Religion*. London.

Langer, E. J. 1975. "The Illusion of Control". *Journal of Personality and Social Psychology* 32(2): 311–28.

Latour, B. 1993. *We Have Never Been Modern*, trans. C. Porter. Cambridge, MA: Harvard University Press.

Latour, B. 2010. *On the Modern Cult of the Factish Gods*. Durham, NC: Duke University Press.

Le Roy, A. 1922. *The Religion of the Primitives*, trans. N. Thompson. New York: Macmillan.

Leach, E. R. 1958. "Magical Hair". *Journal of the Royal Anthropological Institute of Great Britain and Ireland* 88: 147–64.

Leach, E. 1964. "Magic". In *A Dictionary of the Social Sciences*, J. Gould & W. L. Kolb (eds). New York: The Free Press.

Leach, E. 1982. *Social Anthropology*. Glasgow: Fontana.

Leach, E. 1991. *Culture and Communication: The Logic by which Symbols are Connected. An Introduction to the Use of Structuralist Analysis in Social Anthropology*. Cambridge: Cambridge University Press.

Lee, D. D. 1949. "Being and Value in a Primitive Culture". *Journal of Philosophy* 46: 401–15.

Leeuw, G. van der 1928. *La structure de la mentalité primitive*. Strasbourg: Impr. Alsacienne.

Leeuw, G. van der 1986 (1953). *Religion in Essence and Manifestation*, trans. J. E. Turner. Princeton, NJ: Princeton University Press.

Lehrich, C. I. 2007. *The Occult Mind: Magic in Theory and Practice*. Ithaca, NY: Cornell University Press.

Lehrich, C. I. 2008. "Finding One's Place". In *Introducing Religion: Essays in Honor of Jonathan Z. Smith*, W. Braun & R. T. McCutcheon (eds), 252–66. London: Equinox.

Lehrich, C. I. 2011. "Overture and Finale: Lévi-Strauss, Music, and Religion". *Method and Theory in the Study of Religion* 23: 305–25.

Leuba, J. H. 1912. "Appendix: Definitions of Religion and Critical Comments". In *A Psychological Study of Religion: Its Origin, Function, and Future*, 339–61. New York: AMS Press.
Lévi-Strauss, C. 1950. "Introduction à l'œuvre Marcel Mauss". In *Sociologie et anthropologie*, M. Mauss (ed.). Paris: Presses Universitaires de France.
Lévi-Strauss, C. 1962. *La pensée sauvage*. Paris: Plon.
Lévi-Strauss, C. 1963. *Structural Anthropology*, trans C. Jacobson & B. Grundfest Schoepf. New York: Basic Books.
Lévi-Strauss, C. 1966. *The Savage Mind*. The Nature of Human Society Series. Chicago, IL: University of Chicago Press.
Lévi-Strauss, C. 1985. "Structuralism and Ecology". In *The View from Afar*, trans. J. Neugroschel & P. Hoss. New York: Basic Books.
Lévi-Strauss, C. 1992. *Tristes Tropiques*, trans. J. & D. Weightman. New York: Penguin.
Lévy-Bruhl, L. 1910. *Les Fonctions mentales dans les sociétés inférieures*. Paris: F. Alcan.
Lévy-Bruhl, L. 1923. *Primitive Mentality*. London: Allen & Unwin.
Lévy-Bruhl, L. 1926. *How Natives Think*. London: Allen & Unwin.
Lévy-Bruhl, L. 1929. "L'âme primitive", *Société française de philosophie* **29**(3).
Lévy-Bruhl, L. 1935. *Primitives and the Supernatural*. New York: Haskell House Publishers.
Lewis-Williams, D. 2004. *The Mind in the Cave*. London: Thames and Hudson.
Liénard, P. & P. Boyer 2006. "Whence Collective Rituals? A Cultural Selection Model of Ritualized Behavior". *American Anthropologist* **108**(4): 814–27.
Lindberg, D. C. 1992. *The Beginnings of Western Science: The European Scientific Tradition in Philosophical, Religion, and Institutional Context, 600 BC to AD 1450*. Chicago, IL: University of Chicago Press.
Lindeman, M. & K. Aarnio 2007. "Superstitious, Magical, and Paranormal Beliefs: An Integrative Model". *Journal of Research in Personality* 41: 731–44.
Lindworsky, J. 1926. "Die Primitiven und das kausale Denken". *Int. Woche für Religionsethnologie*, IV. Tagung.
Littré, É. 1849. *Œuvres Complètes d'Hippocrate*. Paris.
Lloyd, G. 1979. *Magic, Reason, and Experience: Studies in the Origin and Development of Greek Science*. Cambridge: Cambridge University Press.
Lowie, R. H. 1920. *Primitive Society*. New York: Boni and Liveright Language.
Lowie, R. H. 1997 (1925). *Primitive Religion*. New York: Oxford University Press.
Luhrmann, T. M. 1989. *Persuasions of the Witch's Craft*, Cambridge, MA: Harvard University Press.
Lukes, S. 1973. "On the Social Determination of Truth". In *Modes of Thought: Essays on Thinking in Western and Non-Western Societies*, R. Horton & R. Finnegan (eds), 230–49. London: Faber & Faber.
MacDonald, D. (ed.) 1990. *The Acts of Andrew and the Acts of Andrew and Matthias in the City of the Cannibals*. Atlanta, GA: Scholars Press.
Macfarlane, A. 1970. *Witchcraft in Tudor and Stuart England: A Regional and Comparative Study*. London: Routledge & Kegan Paul.
Macpherson, S. C. 1865. *Memorials of Service in India*. London.
Malinowski, B. 1915. "The Natives of Mailu". *Transactions of the Royal Society of South Australia* 39: 494–706.
Malinowski, B. 1916. "Baloma: Spirits of the Dead in the Trobriand Islands". *Journal of the Royal Anthropological Institute* 46: 354–430.
Malinowski, B. 1922. *Argonauts of the Western Pacific*. London: London School of Economics and Political Science.
Malinowski, B. 1923. "Psychology of Sex and the Foundations of Kinship in Primitive Society". *Psyche* 3: 98–128.
Malinowski, B. 1924. "Psychoanalysis and Anthropology". *Psyche* 4: 293–332.
Malinowski, B. 1925. "Complex and Myth in Mother-right". *Psyche* 5: 194-216.
Malinowski, B. 1935. *Coral Gardens and Their Magic: A Study of the Methods of Tilling the Soil and of Agricultural Rites in the Trobriand Islands*. London: Allen & Unwin. (Reprinted 1965, Bloomington, IN: Indiana University Press.)
Malinowski, B. 1937. *The Coral Gardens and Their Magic*. London: Allen & Unwin.
Malinowski, B. 1948. "Magic, Science and Religion". In *Magic, Science and Religion and other Essays*, with an Introduction by Robert Redfield, 1–71. New York: Kessinger Publishings.
Malinowski, B. 1992. *Magic, Science, and Religion, and Other Essays*. Prospect Heights, IL: Waveland Press.

Marett, R. R. 1909. *The Threshold of Religion*. London: Methuen.
Marett, R. R. 1932. *Faith, Hope and Charity in Primitive Religion*. Oxford: Clarendon Press.
Markle, D. T. 2010. "The Magic that Binds Us All: Magical Thinking and Inclusive Fitness". *Journal of Social, Evolutionary, and Cultural Psychology* 4: 18–33.
Martin, L. & J. Sørensen 2011. *Past Minds: Studies in Cognitive Historiography*. London: Equinox.
Masuzawa, T. 2005. *The Invention of World Religions*. Chicago, IL: University of Chicago Press.
Mauss, M. 1972. *A General Theory of Magic*, trans. R. Brain. London: Routledge & Kegan Paul.
Mayer-Gross, W. 1927. "Zur Frage der psychologischen Eigenart der sog. Naturvölker". *International Congress of Psychology, Proceedings and Papers* 8.
McGilchrist, I. 2009. *The Master and his Emissary: The Divided Brain and the Making of the Western World*. New Haven, CT: Yale.
McGilchrist, I. 2011. "Paying Attention to the Bipartite Brain". *The Lancet* **377**(9771), 26 March: 1068–9.
McLennan, J. F. 1886. *Studies in Ancient History*. London.
Meyer. B. & Pels, P. (eds) 2003. *Magic and Modernity: Interfaces of Revelation and Concealment*. Stanford, CA: Stanford University Press.
Meyer, M. & P. Mirecki (eds) 1995. *Ancient Magic and Ritual Power*. Leiden: Brill.
Meyer, M. & R. Smith (eds) 1994. *Ancient Christian Magic: Coptic Texts of Ritual Power*. San Francisco, CA: Harper Collins.
Moore, H. & T. Sanders 2001. *Magical Interpretations, Material Realities: Modernity, Witchcraft and the Occult in Postcolonial Africa*. London: Sage.
Morris, B. 1991. *Western Conceptions of the Individual*. Oxford: Berg.
Muir, J. 1860. *Original Sanskrit Texts on the Origin and History of the People of India, Their Religion and Institutions, Part II*. London.
Negrioli, A. 1900. *Dei Genii presso i Romani*. Bologna: Ditto Nicola Zanichelli.
Nemeroff, C. & P. Rozin 2000. "The Makings of the Magical Mind: The Nature and Function of Sympathetic Magical Thinking". In *Imagining the Impossible: Magical, Scientific, and Religious Thinking in Children*, K. Rosengren, C. N. Johnson & P. L. Harris (eds). Cambridge: Cambridge University Press.
Nettle, D. 2001. *Strong Imagination: Madness, Creativity and Human Nature*. Oxford: Oxford University Press.
Nielbo, K. L. & J. Sørensen 2011. "Spontaneous Processing of Functional and Nonfunctional Action Sequences". *Religion, Brain and Behavior* **1**(1): 18–30
Nietzsche, F. W. 1910. *Human, All Too Human I*. Edinburgh: Foulis Edition.
Nock, A. D. 1933. "Paul and the Magus". In *The Beginnings of Christianity, Part I*, F. J. Foakes Jackson & K. Lake (eds), 164–88. London: Macmillan.
Ogden, D. 1999. "Binding Spells: Curse Tablets and Voodoo Dolls in the Greek and Roman Worlds". In *Witchcraft and Magic in Europe: Ancient Greece and Rome*, B. Ankarloo & S. Clark (eds), 3–90. Philadelphia, PA: University of Pennsylvania Press.
Ogden, D. 2002. *Magic, Witchcraft, and Ghosts in the Greek and Roman Worlds: A Sourcebook*. Oxford: Oxford University Press.
O'Keefe, D. 1982 *Stolen Lightning: Social Theory of Magic*. Oxford: Martin Robertson.
Oldfield, A. 1865. "On the Aborigines of Australia". *Transactions of the Ethnological Society of London* 3: 215–98.
Ornstein, R. E. 1977. *The Psychology of Consciousness*. New York: Harcourt Brace Jovanovich.
Ortner, S. B. 1996. "Is Male to Female as Nature is to Culture?". In *Making Gender: The Politics and Erotics of Culture*, 21–42. Boston, MA: Beacon Press.
Otto, B.-C. 2011. *Magie: Rezeptions- und Diskursgeschichtliche Analysen von der Antike bis zur Neuzeit*. Berlin: De Gruyter.
Otto, B.-C. Forthcoming. "Towards Historicizing 'Magic' in Antiquity". *Numen*.
Otto, R. 1939 (1917). *The Idea of the Holy: An Inquiry into the Non-Rational Factor in the Idea of the Divine and Its Relation to the Rational*, trans. J. W. Harvey. London: Oxford University Press.
Otto, W. F. 1909. *Archiv für Religionswissenschaft* 12.
Otto, W. F. 1929. *Die Götter Griechlands: das Bild des Göttlichen im Spiegel des griechischen Geistes*. Bonn: Cohen.
Palmer, C. T., L. B. Steadman, C. Cassidy & C. Koe. 2010. "The Importance of Magic to Social Relationships". *Zygon* 45: 317–37.

Pasi, M. 2008. "Theses de magia". *Societas Magica Newsletter* 20: 1–8.
Pauli, W. 1955. "The Influence of Archetypal Ideas on the Scientific Theories of Kepler". In *The Interpretation of Nature and the Psyche*, C. G. Jung & W. Pauli (eds), trans. P. Silz, 147–240. London: Routledge & Kegan Paul.
Pearce, N. 1831. *The Life and Adventures of Nathaniel Pearce*, J. J. Halls (ed.), vol. I. London.
Peel, J. D. Y. 1969. "Understanding Alien Belief Systems". *British Journal of Sociology* 20: 69–84.
Pels, P. 2003. "Introduction: Magic and Modernity". In *Magic and Modernity: Interfaces of Revelation and Concealment*, B. Meyer & P. Pels (eds). Stanford, CA: Stanford University Press.
Perry, W. J. 1923. *The Origin of Magic and Religion*. London: Methuen.
Pettersson, O. 1957. "Magic – Religion: Some Marginal Notes to an Old Problem". *Ethnos* 22: 109–19.
Phillips, C. R. 1986. "The Sociology of Religious Knowledge in the Roman Empire to AD 284". In *Aufstieg und Niedergang der römischen Welt: Geschichte u. Kultur Roms im Spiegel der neueren Forschung, Teil 2 (Principat)*, Bd. 16 (Religion), Teilband 3, H. Temporini & W. Haase (eds), 2677–773. Berlin: De Gruyter.
Philsooph, H. 1971. "Primitive Magic and Mana". *Man* 6: 182–203.
Pocock, D. 1972. "Foreword". In *A General Theory of Magic*, M. Mauss, trans. R. Brain. London: Routledge & Kegan Paul.
Polack, J. S. 1838. *New Zealand: Being a Narrative of Travels and Adventures During a Residence in that Country between the Years 1831 and 1837, vol. I*. London.
Preisendanz, K. (ed.). 1928, 1931. *Papyri Graecae Magicae: die griechischen Zauberpapyri*. 2 vols. Leipzig: Teubner.
Preuss, K. T. 1904. *Der Ursprung der Religion und Kunst*. Braunschweig: Friedrich Viehweg.
Preuss, K. T. 1914. "Die geistige Kultur der Naturvölker". *Natur und Geisteswelt* 452.
Prinzhorn, H. 1923. *Bildnerei der Geisteskranken: Ein Beitrag zur Psychologie und Psychopathologie der Gestaltung*, 2. Auflage. Berlin: Springer.
Raabe, W. 1920. *Das Odfeld. Gutmanns Reisen [in Sämtliche Werke, 4]*. Berlin: Klemm.
Rabin, S. J. 2008. "Pico on Magic and Astrology". In *Pico della Mirandola: New Essays*, M. V. Dougherty (ed.), 152–78. Cambridge: Cambridge University Press.
Radcliffe-Brown, A. R. 1952. *Structure and Function in Primitive Society*. Glencoe, IL: The Free Press.
Raine, K. 1991. *Golgonooza: City of Imagination*. Ipswich: Golgonooza Press.
Rappaport, R. 1979. *Ecology, Meaning, and Religion*. Richmond, VA: North Atlantic Books.
Rappaport, R. 1999. *Ritual and Religion in the Making of Humanity*. Cambridge: Cambridge University Press.
Reinach, S. 1909. *Orpheus: Histoire Générale des Religions*. Paris: Picard. Published in English as *Orpheus: A History of Religions* (London: Heinemann, 1923).
Remus, H. 1982. "Does Terminology Distinguish Early Christian from Pagan Miracles?". *Journal of Biblical Literature* **101**(4): 531–51.
Remus, H. 1999. "'Magic,' Method, Madness". *Method and Theory in the Study of Religion* 11: 258–98.
Ripat, P. Forthcoming. "Cheating Women: Curse Tablets and Roman Wives". In *Daughters of Hecate: Women and Magic in the Ancient World*, K. Stratton & D. Kalleres (eds). New York: Oxford University Press.
Rühs, F. 1809. *Finland und seine Bewohner*. Leipzig.
Sabatier, A. 1997. *Esquisse d'une philosophic de la religion d'après la Psychologie et l'Histoire*. Paris: Fischbacher.
Saintyves, P. 1914. *La force magique: du mana des primitifs au dynamisme scientifique*. Paris: Nourry.
Samuel, G. 1990. *Mind, Body and Culture*. Cambridge: Cambridge University Press.
Schäfer, P. and H. G. Kippenberg (eds) 1997. *Envisioning Magic: A Princeton Seminar and Symposium*. Leiden: Brill.
Schmidt, W. 1912. *Der Ursprung der Gottesidee: eine historisch-kritische und positive Studie*. Münster: Aschendorff.
Scott, J. W. 1988. "Gender: A Useful Category of Historical Analysis". In her *Gender and the Politics of History*, 28–50. New York: Columbia University Press.
Searle, J. R. 1969. *Speech Acts: An Essay in the Philosophy of Language*. Cambridge: Cambridge University Press.
Segal, A. F. 1981. "Hellenistic Magic: Some Qquestions of Definition". In *Studies in Gnosticism and Hellenistic Religion*, R. Van den Broeke & M. J. Vermaseren (eds), 349–75. Leiden: Brill.
Seligman, C. G. 1910. *The Melanesians of British New Guinea*. Cambridge: Cambridge University Press.
Shanafelt, R. 2004. "Magic, Miracles and Marvels in Anthropology". *Ethnos* 69: 317–40.
Shortt, J. 1868. "A Contribution to the Ethnology of Jeypore". *Transactions of the Ethnological Society of London* 6: 264–81, 364.

Shortt, J. 1869. "An Account of the Hill Tribes of the Neilgherries". *Transactions of the Ethnological Society of London* 7: 230–90.
Shumaker, W. 1972. *The Occult Sciences in the Renaissance*. Berkeley, CA: University of California Press.
Smith, J. Z. 1988. "Narratives into Problems". *Journal of the American Academy of Religion* 56(4), winter: 736.
Smith, J. Z. 1995. "Trading Places". In *Ancient Magic and Ritual Power*, M. Marvin and P. Mirecki (eds), 13–27. Leiden: Brill.
Smith, J. Z. 1998. "Religion, Religions, Religious". In *Critical Terms for Religious Study*, M. C. Taylor (ed.). Chicago: University of Chicago Press.
Smith, J. Z. 2004. *Relating Religion: Essays in the Study of Religion*. Chicago, IL: University of Chicago Press.
Smith, W. R. 1889. *Lectures on the Religion of the Semites*. London.
Söderblom, N. 1916. *Das Werden des Gottesglaubens: Untersuchungen über die Anfänge der Religion*. Leipzig: Hinrichs.
Sørensen, J. 2005a. "The Problem of Magic – or How Gibberish Becomes Efficacious Action". *Recherches sémiotiques/Semiotic Inquiry* 25(1): 93–117.
Sørensen, J. 2005b. "Charisma, Tradition, and Ritual: A Cognitive Approach to Magical Agency". In *Mind and Religion: Psychological and Cognitive Foundations of Religiosity*, H. Whitehouse & R. McCauley (eds), 167–86. Walnut Creek, CA: AltaMira Press.
Sørensen, J. 2007a. *A Cognitive Theory of Magic*. Lanham, MD: Rowman & Littlefield.
Sørensen, J. 2007b. "Acts that Work: A Cognitive Approach to Ritual Agency". *Method & Theory in the Study of Religion* 19(3): 281.
Sørensen, J. 2007c. "Malinowski and Magical Ritual". In *Religion, Anthropology, and Cognitive Science*, H. Whitehouse and J. Laidlaw (eds), 81–104. Durham, NC: Carolina Academic Press.
Sosis, R. and C. Alcorta 2003. "Signaling, Solidarity, and the Sacred: The Evolution of Religious Behavior". *Evolutionary Anthropology: Issues, News, and Reviews* 12(6): 264–74.
Spaeth, B. S. Forthcoming "From Goddess to Hag: The Greek and the Roman Witch in Classical Literature". In *Daughters of Hecate: Women and Magic in the Ancient World*, K. Stratton & D. Kalleres (eds). New York: Oxford University Press.
Spencer, B. & F. J. Gillen 1889. *The Native Tribes of Central Australia*. London: Macmillan.
Spencer, B. & F. J. Gillen 1904. *Northern Tribes of Central Australia*. London: Macmillan.
Spencer, H. 1886. *Ecclesiastical Institutions*, Part VI of *The Principles of Sociology*, Chapter 16. New York: D. Appleton.
Sperber, D. 1975. *Rethinking Symbolism*. Cambridge: Cambridge University Press.
Spiegel, F. von (ed.) 1853. *Avesta: die heiligen Schriften der Parsen, vol. I.* Vienna.
Spranger, E. 1921 (1910). *Lebensformen: geisteswissenschaftliche Psychologie und Ethik der Persönlichkeit*. Halle: Niemeyer.
Spranger, E. 1924. *Psychologie des Jugendalters*. Leipzig: Quelle & Meyer.
St John, S. 1862. *Life in the Forests of Far East, vol. I.* London.
Staal, F. 1979. "The Meaninglessness of Ritual". *Numen* 26(1): 2–22.
Stanbridge, W. E. 1861. "Some Particulars of the General Characteristics, Astronomy, and Mythology of the Tribes in the Central Part of Victoria, Southern Australia". *Transactions of the Ethnological Society of London* 1: 286–304.
Stark, R. 2001. "Reconceptualizing Religion, Magic, and Science". *Review of Religious Research* 43: 101–20.
Stark, W. 1970. *The Sociology of Religion: A Study of Christendom*, 4 vol. New York: Fordham University Press.
Stausberg, M. 1998. *Faszination Zarathushtra. Zoroaster und die europäische Religionsgeschichte der Frühen Neuzeit*. Berlin: De Gruyter.
Stephenson, B. 1994. *Kepler's Physical Astronomy*. Princeton, NJ: Princeton University Press.
Storch, A. 1922. *Das archaisch-primitive Erleben und Denken der Schizophrenen*. Berlin: Springer.
Stratton, K. 2007. *Naming the Witch: Magic, Ideology, and Stereotype in the Ancient World*. New York: Columbia University Press.
Stroeken, K. 2010. *Moral Power: The Magic of Witchcraft*. New York: Berghahn.
Styers, R. 2004. *Making Magic: Religion, Magic, and Science in the Modern World*. New York: Oxford University Press.
Styers, R. Forthcoming. "Mana and Mystification". *WSQ: Women's Studies Quarterly*.

Tambiah, S. J. 1968. "The Magical Power of Words". *Man* 3: 175–208.
Tambiah, S. J. 1973. "Form and Meaning of Magical Acts: A Point of View". In *Modes of Thought. Essays on Thinking in Western and Non-Western Societies*, R. Horton & R. Finnegan (eds), 228–9. London: Faber & Faber.
Tambiah, S. 1990. *Magic, Science, Religion and the Scope of Rationality*. Cambridge: Cambridge University Press.
Tambiah, S. 2002. *Edmund Leach: An Anthropological Life*. Cambridge: Cambridge University Press.
Taussig, M. 1993. *Mimesis and Alterity: Particular History of the Senses*. New York: Routledge.
Taussig, M. 1997. *The Magic of the State*. London: Routledge.
Taussig, M. 1998. "Viscerality, Faith and Skepticism: Another Theory of Magic". In *Near Ruins: Cultural Theory at the End of the Century*, N. B. Dirks (ed.), 221–56. Minneapolis, MN: University of Minnesota Press. Reprinted in Meyer and Pels (eds) 2003, 272–306 and in Taussig, M. 2006, *Walter Benjamin's Grave*, 121–156. Chicago, IL: University of Chicago Press.
Thagard, P. 1996. *Mind: Introduction to Cognitive Science*. Cambridge: MIT Press.
Thomas, K. 1971. *Religion and the Decline of Magic: Studies in Popular Beliefs in Sixteenth and Seventeenth Century England*. London: Weidenfeld and Nicholson.
Thomas, K. 1991. *Religion and the Decline of Magic: Studies in Popular Beliefs in Sixteenth and Seventeenth Century England*. London: Penguin.
Thomassen, E. 1999. "Is Magic a Subclass of Ritual?". In *The World of Ancient Magic. Papers from the First International Samson Eitrem Seminar at the Norwegian Institute of Athens, 4–8 May 1997*, D. R. Jordan, H. Montgomery & E. Thomassen (eds), 55–66. Bergen: Norwegian Institute of Athens.
Thurnwald, R. 1912. *Forschungen auf den Solomo-Inseln und den Bismarck-Archipel*, 3 vols. Berlin: Reimer.
Thurnwald, R. 1921. *Die Gemeinde der Bánaro*. Stuttgart: Enke.
Thurnwald, R. 1927. "Die Lüge in der primitiven Kultur". In *Die Lüge in psychologischer, philosophischer, juristischer, pädagogischer, historischer, soziologischer, sprach- und literaturwissenschaftlicher und entwicklungsgeschichtlicher Betrachtung*, O. Lippmann & P. Plaut (eds), 396–410. Leipzig: Barth.
Thurnwald, R. 1928. *Bequemes Denken: Entwicklung und Gestaltung sozialer Gebilde bei Naturvölkern*. Paris: Nourry.
Thurnwald, R. 1929. "Zauber". In *Reallexikon der Vorgeschichte*, M. Ebert (ed.). Berlin: De Gruyter.
Tillich, P. 1929. *Religiöse Verwirklichung*. Berlin: Furche-Verlag.
Trzcionka, S. 2007. *Magic and the Supernatural in Fourth-Century Syria*. London: Routledge, Kindle Edition.
Tupet, A.-M. 1976. *La Magie dans la Poésie latine*. Paris: Les Belles Lettres.
Turner, M. 1996. *The Literary Mind*. Oxford: Oxford University Press.
Turner, V. 1995. *The Ritual Process: Structure and Anti-Structure*. New York: Aldine de Gruyter.
Tweed, T. A. 2006. *Crossing and Dwelling: A Theory of Religion*. Cambridge, MA: Harvard University Press.
Tylor, E. B. 1865. *Researches into the Early History of Mankind and the Development of Civilization*. London.
Tylor, E. B. 1871. *Primitive Culture: Researches into the Development of Mythology, Philosophy, Religion, Art, and Custom*. London: Routledge and Thoemmes Press.
Tylor, E. B. 1883. "Magic". In *Encyclopedia Britannica*, 9th edition, vol. 15: 199–206.
Tylor, E. B. 1903 (1871). *Primitive Culture: Researches into the Development of Mythology, Philosophy, Religion, Art, and Custom*, vol. 1. London: Routledge.
van Baal, J. 1963 "Magic as a Religious Phenomenon". *Higher Education and Research in the Netherlands* 7: 10–21.
Veltri, G. 1998. "The Rabbis and Pliny the Elder: Jewish and Greco-Roman Attitudes Toward Magic and Empirical Knowledge". *Poetics Today* **19**(1), spring: 63–89.
Veltri, G. 2001. "Der Magier im antiken Judentum: von empirisher Wissenschaft zur Theologie". In *Der Magus: seine Ursprünge und seine Geschichte in verschiedenen Kulturen*, A. Grafton & M. Idel, 147–67. Berlin: Akademie Verlag.
Versnel, H. S. 1991. "Some Reflections on the Relationship Magic–Religion". *Numen* **38**(2): 177–97.
Vierkandt, A. 1907. "Die Anfänge der Religion und Zauberei". In *Globus: Illustrierte Zeitschrift für Länder und Völkerkunde* 92.
von Stuckrad, K. Forthcoming. "Magic". In *The Blackwell Companion to the Study of Religion*, 2nd edn, R. A. Segal (ed.). Malden, MA: Blackwell Publishers.
von Wilamowitz-Möllendorf, U. 1931. *Der Glaube der Hellenen, Band 1*. Berlin: Weidmann.

# BIBLIOGRAPHY

Vyse, S. A. 1997. *Believing in Magic: The Psychology of Superstition*. Oxford: Oxford University Press.
Wax, M. & R. Wax. 1963. "The Notion of Magic". *Current Anthropology* 4: 495–518.
Weber, M. 1964. *The Sociology of Religion*, trans. E. Fischoff. Boston, MA: Beacon Press.
Werner, H. 1926. *Einführung in die Entwicklungspsychologie*. Leipzig.
Westermarck, E. 1905. *The Origin and Development of the Moral Ideas*. 2 vols. London: Macmillan.
Whitehouse, H. 2005. *Modes of Religiosity: A Cognitive Theory of Religious Transmission*. Walnut Creek, IN: AltaMira Press.
Wilson, B R. (ed.) 1970. *Rationality*. Oxford: Oxford University Press.
Wilson, J. L. 1856. *Western Africa: Its History, Condition and Prospects*. London.
Wilson, M. H. 1951. "Witch Beliefs and Social Structures". *American Journal of Sociology* 56: 307–13.
Winch, P. 1964. "Understanding a Primitive Society". *American Philosophical Quarterly* 1: 307–24.
Winkelman, M. 1982. "Magic: A Theoretical Reassessment". *Current Anthropology* 23: 37–65.
Wohl, M. J. A. & M. E. Enzle 2002. "The Deployment of Personal Luck: Sympathetic Magic and Illusory Control in Games of Pure Chance". *Personality and Social Psychology Bulletin* **28**(10): 1388.
Wood, W. S. & M. M. Clapham 2005. "Development of the Drake Beliefs about Chance Inventory". *Journal of Gambling Studies* **21**(4): 411–30.
Wundt, W. 1900. *Völkerpsychologie: eine Untersuchung der Entwicklungsgesetze von Sprache, Mythus und Sitte*. Leipzig.
Wuttke, A. 1860. *Der deutsche Volksaberglaube der Gegenwart*. Hamburg.
Wypustek, A. 1997. "Magic, Montanism, Perpetua, and the Severan Persecution". *Vigiliae Christianae* **51**(3), August: 276–97.
Xygalatas, D., U. Schjødt, J. Bulbulia, I. Konvalinka, E.-M. Jegindø, P. Reddish, A. W. Geertz & A. Roepstoff Forthcoming. "Emotional Regulation and Memory Repression in a Fire-walking Ritual", *Memory*.
Yate, W. 1835. *An Account of New Zealand and the Formation and Progress of the Church Missionary Society's Mission in the Northern Island*. London.
Yates, F. 1964. *Giordano Bruno and the Hermetic Tradition*. Chicago, IL: University of Chicago Press.
Zacks, J. M, & B. Tversky 2001. "Event Structure in Perception and Conception". *Psychological Bulletin* **127**(1): 3–21.
Zacks, J. M., N. K. Speer, K. M. Swallow, T. S. Braver & J. R. Reynolds. 2007. "Event Perception: A Mind-Brain Perspective". *Psychological Bulletin* **133**(2): 273–93.
Zeininger, K. 1929. *Magische Geisteshaltung im Kindesalter und ihre Bedeutung für die religiöse Entwicklung*. Leipzig: J. A. Barth.
Zusne, L. & W. H. Jones 1989. *Anomalistic Psychology: A Study of Magical Thinking*. Hillsdale, NJ: Lawrence Erlbaum.

# INDEX

Africa  172–7, 183–4, 194–5, 216, 217–18
Aghapour, Andrew  256
Agrippa of Nettesheim  17, 54–8
alterity  247–8, 250
amulets  36, 44, 49, 52–3, 253–4
analogy  72, 178, 179, 184, 216, 217, 233
animatism  126
animism  69, 72, 76–8, 126, 138
anthropological approaches  4, 13, 127–91
anti-magical rhetoric  18
    see also negative stereotypes; polemic approaches
Aquinas, Thomas  48–53
association of ideas  71–80, 83, 84, 88, 89, 119–20, 156
astrology  23, 24, 37–8, 44, 47, 54–5, 59, 61, 185, 196, 215
augury  40, 41, 44, 77
Augustine of Hippo  17, 33–40
Austin, John Langshaw  180, 181
autism  135–6, 138
Azande beliefs see Zande

Bateson, Gregory  207–9
beliefs  85, 97, 165–6, 168, 213–15
    see also representations
Benedict, Ruth  5, 126
bewitchment  118–19
Biezais, Harald  126
black magic  10, 61, 62, 64, 66, 158–60
Blavatsky, Helena Petrovna  12, 18, 64–6
body–mind  205, 207
Boyer, Pascal  235–6
brain physiology  203–4
bricolage  226, 227

Brown, Alfred Radcliffe  127
Byzantine *Suda*  17, 46–7

Cartesian perspectives  205, 207
catathymia  136, 140
causality  5, 143–55, 182–3, 184–5, 235, 236, 238
celestial world  54, 55, 56–7, 59, 61
ceremonial magic  54, 59, 61
Chidester, David  255–6, 258
Christianity  17, 33–8, 41–2, 70, 85, 230, 252–3
Chrysostom  52–53
civilization  68, 72–6, 80, 89, 90, 110, 185–6, 221
    see also primitive cultures
closed systems  173–5, 183–4
coercion  20, 97, 105, 261–2
cognitive processes  232-2
collectivity  97, 104, 105–7, 110, 111, 231
colonialism  6, 221, 222
communication  187–91, 200–203
conceptual integration  232–4, 235–6
confederate organizations  112–13
consciousness  9, 106, 120, 122, 127, 132, 134, 139–40, 194, 197–210
contagion  81, 82, 83, 84, 118–19, 123, 189, 232, 234, 236
contextual approaches  237–41, 243, 245–54
contiguity  83, 84, 88–9, 119, 188, 190, 236
continuum models  5, 81, 126, 195
counter-magic  166–7
cults  102, 112, 113, 116
cultural evolution  65, 72, 81
culture  65, 68, 72, 81, 173–5, 183, 187–91, 258–9
    see also primitive cultures

# INDEX

de Certeau, Michel  219
de Martino, Ernesto  127
de-symbolization  236–7
death  150, 153
demons
   generalization  223–4
   intercourse and agreement with  39–40
   magical influence  113–14
   operations of force  127
   pacts with  17, 33, 34, 48–9, 50–51
   power  127, 134
   religion  103
   work of  41, 48
Derrida, Jacques  226–7
Descartes, René  177, 205, 207
deviance theory  7–8, 23–4, 60
Diderot, Denis  18, 59–63
divination  33, 35, 38–9, 41, 43–5, 78
divine things  49, 59, 60, 86–7, 92
   *see also* sacred entities
Douglas, Mary  128
dragons  198, 199, 201–2, 204
dreams  139–40
Durkheim, Émile  5, 69, 97, 111–23, 126, 127, 201, 231

Eliade, Mircea  127
emic terminology  222, 223, 243, 244, 245
emotions  4, 23, 24, 28, 68, 106–7, 157, 158–60, 163–4, 167, 177
empirical approaches  143, 149–50, 187, 215–16, 217–18, 222–3
enchantment  29–30, 31–2, 43, 72–73, 255, 262
Enlightenment  5, 18, 59, 72, 206, 208, 245, 254, 257
esotericism  4, 7, 12, 64, 65, 195, 212, 227
ethics  85, 225–6
   *see also* morality
ethnocentrism  4, 6–7, 13, 178, 195, 218, 220
ethnography  72, 80, 129, 221–3
etic approaches  222, 243
etymology  3, 16, 19
European perspectives  73–4, 185–6
Evans-Pritchard, Edward E.  4, 128, 141–55, 173–4, 178, 183, 184–5
evolutionist/evolutionary approaches  65, 68, 69, 72, 81–2, 88–9, 94, 156, 220, 231
exoticism  220, 237
experience  122, 162–6, 167, 185–6, 195, 197, 198–210

faith  157, 60, 63, 66, 84, 85, 90, 91, 93, 94, 106, 122, 123, 128, 139, 154, 157, 165, 168, 169, 176, 177, 183
falsification of magic  91–3, 142, 194, 217–18, 222–3
Fludd, Robert  214, 215
fortune-telling  51–2
Foucault, Michel  224, 225, 247
fraudulent concepts  23, 24, 26, 64, 65, 78, 156
Frazer, James George  29, 68, 69, 81–96, 100, 119, 126, 127, 188–189, 201, 216, 232, 234
Freud, Sigmund  69, 201
functionalism  70, 108–9, 126, 156–71, 255

Geertz, Clifford  211, 214, 216
Gell, Alfred  194
gender  249–50, 251–2
generalization  17, 162, 213–15, 223–5, 226
Glucklich, Ariel  195
goal-demotion  235, 236
*goēteía/ goëtia*  22, 46, 64, 66, 250
Goode, William J.  5, 126
Goody, Jack  128
Greenwood, Susan  5, 197–210

haruspicy  43–4, 47
healing  11, 48, 49, 59, 62, 63, 64, 66, 71, 159, 219, 632
Hegel, Georg Wilhelm Friedrich  68, 127
Holy Spirit  87–8, 252
homeopathic magic  55, 82, 83, 84, 119, 188, 189
horoscopes  44
   *see also* astrology
Horton, Robin  4–5, 128, 172–7, 183–4, 216, 217–18
Hubert, Henri  97–110, 123, 231, 259–60
hydromancers  43

Idealism  176–7
ideation  209
identity  7–8, 257
idolatry  34, 36, 39, 43
illocutionary acts  178, 179–80, 181–3, 184, 217
imagination  60, 62–3, 91, 94, 198–210
imitative magic *see* homeopathic magic
incantations  31, 41, 43, 49, 50, 52, 53
India  73, 86, 87, 186
indicators of magic  9–10
indices  187, 189–90
individualism  105, 107, 108, 115, 116, 117, 126, 231, 260
institutionalization  240, 241, 242

278

# INDEX

intellect   89–90, 122, 152, 153, 176–7, 231
intellectualist approaches   54, 55, 126, 127
interdisciplinary approaches   211, 212
interpretative strategies   239–41
irrational/irrationality   18, 29–30, 31, 32, 107
irreducible difference   227
Isidore of Seville   41–5

Jakobson, Roman   232–3
Jones, Warren H.   196
Judaism   111, 243, 253–4

Kant, Immanuel   200
Kapferer, Bruce   194
Kepler, Johannes   214–15
Kluckhohn, Clyde   127
knowledge
  cognitive processing   232–42
  discursive formation   246–7
  empirical   149–50
  magical consciousness   197–210
  passing on   107
  primitive cultures   169
  systemization of   109
  technical efficiency   150–51
  see also science

language   175–7, 178–82, 188, 222, 233
Law of Contagion see contagion
Law of Similarity see similarity
Leach, Edmund R.   187–91
legitimacy   5, 212, 258–9
Lehrich, Christopher   5, 211–28
Lévi-Strauss, Claude   214, 216, 223, 226
Lévy-Bruhl, Lucien   69, 129, 130, 202
Lienard, Pierre   235–6
Lindberg, David   257
locutionary acts   178, 180, 181
love   28, 29, 31, 137, 138, 157, 158, 160, 163-7, 169, 233, 234, 251
Lowie, Robert   127

*mageia*   7, 16, 19, 28, 46
magic–science–religion triad   4–6, 126, 128, 156–71, 214–15, 216–18, 219
  see also religion; science
magicity   10–12
magico-religious continuum   69, 72
  see also continuum models
Malinowski, Bronislaw   5, 126, 128, 156–71, 237, 238–9

*mana*   106–7, 161–2, 231, 259–60
manipulative magic   10, 11, 234
Marett, Robert Ranulph   68, 69, 126
marginalization   7, 231, 258, 259
Mauss, Marcel   69, 97–110, 123, 231, 259–60
medicine   25, 99, 102, 153, 155, 186
megalomania   132–3, 135
metonymy   190, 233–4
military coups   190–91
mimetic magic   82, 112, 119–21, 126
  see also homeopathic magic
miracles   34–5, 65, 165
misfortune   4, 36, 141, 143–4, 145, 146, 150
modernity   10, 199, 255, 257–62
morality   85, 117, 121, 122
  see also ethics
mysticism   131, 139, 141, 142, 150
mythology   135, 138–9, 140, 160, 165, 166, 168, 202

natural magic   17–18, 54, 59, 60–61, 64, 66, 206
natural philosophy   56–8, 205–6
nature   86, 90–95, 109, 123, 160–61, 207–8, 218, 222–3
nature of magic   97–8, 104–10
necromancers   41, 43
negative interpretations   79, 111, 184, 234, 251
negative stereotypes   16–17, 23–4, 59
neoplatonism   17, 28

objective reality   136, 141, 143
obsessive desire   156–7, 163–4
open cultures   173, 175
Otto, Rudolf   126–7

participation   69, 129, 130–31, 132, 139, 202–3
passion   163, 164
Pels, Peter   257, 262
performative acts   5, 231
  see also illocutionary acts; perlocutionary acts
perlocutionary acts   178, 180, 181, 217
Persia   16, 19, 20, 21, 24–6, 25, 251
Pettersson, Olof   127–8
*pharmakeia*   16, 19, 21, 22, 46, 251
phenomenological approaches   2–3, 13, 126, 146, 147, 149
philosophy   54–8, 205–6
physiology   203–4
Plato   12, 16, 19–22
Pliny the Elder   17, 23–7
Plotinus   17, 28–32

# INDEX

polemic approaches  7, 18, 23–4, 33, 34, 229, 230, 258
  *see also* negative stereotypes
politics  59, 155, 188, 190–91, 213, 225, 246, 260
polythetic approaches  244, 246
positive interpretations  1, 64–8, 112, 164–5, 248
power
  gender  250
  invisible  92, 94, 105
  *mana*  161, 162
  megalomania  132–3, 135
  play of  255–62
  religion  129, 260
  socially constructed knowledge  247
  supernatural  131
  words  175, 177
practical elements  82, 85, 86, 93, 167, 250–54
prayer  28, 30–31, 69, 70
priests  33, 41, 65, 70, 74, 75, 86–8, 101, 114, 115
primitive cultures
  association of ideas  71–80
  causation and witchcraft  143–55
  dreams  139–40
  fallacy of magic  93
  knowledge  169
  magic association  231
  mentality  129, 130, 131, 132, 134, 135, 138, 188–9
  mythology  166
  tradition  169
primitive magic  157
productive magic  154
pseudo-science  68, 78, 156, 167, 201, 216
psychoanalytical concepts  69
psychological approaches  157, 196
punishment  16–17, 20, 22, 62–3, 117–18

Rabbinic literature  111, 243, 253–4
race  72–6
radicalization  17, 34
rationality  4–5, 70, 128, 142, 178, 184, 205, 206, 210
reality  135–6, 138, 139–40, 175, 176, 194, 208–9
reason  205, 206, 232, 233
regulative philosophy  56
relational approaches  7
religion
  amorphous nature of  255–6
  collectivity  105, 111
  competing systems of thought  239–41
  discursive formation  8, 248

elementary forms of  111–23
emotions  167–9
evolutionary processes  68, 81
functional identity  108
magic distinction  5–6, 195, 230
magic relationship  83–96, 126
phenomenology of  129–40
power  129, 260
social processes  69–70
sympathetic rites  100–101
  *see also* Christianity; magic–science–religion triad
representations  102, 103, 110, 234, 238, 240, 246, 249, 251–3
  *see also* beliefs
resemblance  88–9, 119
reversing an action  134–5
risky actions  239
rites/rituals
  attitudes  111
  behaviour  143
  coercive vs. submissive  97
  collectivity  105
  efficacy of  98, 99, 121, 122, 230, 231, 232, 237, 240, 241
  elementary traits  234, 235–9
  form and meaning  179–85
  initiation  116
  magic discourse  250, 253
  *mana*  161, 162
  primitive man  93
  rationality debate  128
  religious and magical contrast  100–102, 103, 240
  representations  104
  spells  158–60
  traditional practices  98–100

sacred entities  112, 113, 117, 118, 123, 234
  *see also* divine things
sacred words  52–3
sacrifice  101, 105
satanic forces  33
schizophrenia  132, 135
science
  African and Western contrast  173–7, 183–4
  Cartesian perspectives  205
  collective phenomenon  105
  evolution of  94–5
  functional identity  109–10
  illocutionary acts  179

magic contrast   82–3, 84–5, 86, 201
modern concepts of   256–7
valid concepts of magic   229–42
Zande belief   142
*see also* magic–science–religion triad; pseudo-science
sense-images   188, 189, 190
signals   189, 191
signs   51–2, 187–8
similarity   81, 82, 83, 84, 232, 236
Smith, Jonathan Z.   195, 220
social control, magic   243
sociological approaches   127, 157, 162–6
sorcery   3–4, 47, 62, 68, 73–4, 78, 80, 104, 141, 144, 153, 154, 190–91, 194, 250
Sørensen, Jesper   229–42
souls   28, 113, 116, 153, 205, 207
speech acts   5, 178–9, 180–82, 217
spells   68–9, 161, 162
spirits   46, 47, 104, 204, 205–7, 208–9
stereotypes   16–17, 23–4, 59, 243, 246, 249–52
Stratton, Kimberly B.   243–54
structuralism   11, 223
Styers, Randall   10–11, 24, 68, 196, 220, 255–62
supernatural magic   59, 60, 61–2, 66, 131, 134, 152
superstition   34, 36–7, 39–40, 48, 49–50, 62, 63, 72–6, 90, 196
survival   55, 72, 74, 76, 79, 257
symbolic interpretations   128, 188, 201–2, 213–15, 222–3, 231, 241
symbolic magic   72–6, 76–8, 79
*sympatheía*   28, 29
sympathetic magic   29, 81, 82–4, 90, 97, 100, 118–19, 123, 126–7, 205–6

Tambiah, Stanley J.   5, 128, 178–86, 216–17, 218
Taussig, Michael   194
technical strategies   99–100, 103, 150–51, 189, 194
technique   108–9, 126, 134, 168, 253
techno-magic   191
technology   108–9

teratology of truth   219, 220
theoretical alternatives   172–7
theoretical practice   82, 211–28
theosophical approaches   64–8
*theurgia*   64, 66
Thomassen, Einar   195
totemism   111, 119, 120–21
tradition   98–100, 160–61, 169, 185, 206
transformative magic   234
Tylor, Edward B.   5, 68, 71–80, 119, 201, 231, 232

van der Leeuw, Gerardus   13, 126, 127, 129–40
vengeance-magic   154, 155
Vernsel, Hendrik S.   195
Virgil   35, 41, 54, 56–7
virtue of magic   161–2
Vyse, Stuart   196

Wax, Murray and Rosalie   5–6, 126
Weber, Max   69–70, 126
Western perspectives
    African thought   172–7, 183–4
    esotericism   65
    ethnocentrism   4, 6–7, 13, 178, 195, 218, 220
    European experience   185–6
    natural magic   17–18
    power   221
    social reality   247
    *see also* magic–science–religion triad
Winch, Peter   128
Winkelman, Michael   5
witchcraft   3–4, 47, 71, 73–4, 78, 105–6, 128, 158, 166–7, 194–5, 197, 201, 246, 252
    *see also* Zande
women   251–3, 254
word pictures   159–60
words   11, 175–7, 178

Zande   4, 141–55, 173–4, 178, 183, 184–5
Zoroaster   19, 21, 24, 41, 42
Zusne, Leonard   196

Printed in Great Britain
by Amazon